LYNCHBURG, VIRGINIA
AND
NELSON COUNTY, VIRGINIA
WILLS, DEEDS AND MARRIAGES

1807-1831

By

THE REV. BAILEY FULTON DAVIS

Please direct all correspondence and orders to:

www.southernhistoricalpress.com
or
SOUTHERN HISTORICAL PRESS, Inc.
PO BOX 1267
375 West Broad Street
Greenville, SC   29601
southernhistoricalpress@gmail.com

ISBN #0-89308-289-9

Printed in the United States of America

CONTENTS

ABSTRACT OF WILL BOOK A - LYNCHBURG, VIRGINIA

The Corporation court system in Virginia is a bit hard for some to understand. Large cities have their own courts and are apart from counties in which they are located. Lynchburg actually is a part of Campbell and Bedford in a geographic sense, but has kept her own court records for citizens for many years. One can search in vain in Rustburg or Bedford for data and then find it in Lynchburg.

This will book has this notation in the front of it: All inventories, guardian accounts, executors and administrators' accounts and sales and C previous to 1 January 1824 are recorded in the several deed books previous to and up to that day.

1. CAROLINE MATILDA ROSE--debts to be paid; L40 divided to JOHN, ISAAC, DAVID and JOSHUA TINSLEY--L10 to each and amount received from them for my dower claim in a certain tract bought by them of my late husband. My son, HUGH ROSE, and heirs; son, GUSTAVUS A. ROSE, and heirs--named slaves. To LANDON and DR. GEORGE CABELL and GUSTAVUS A. ROSE as trustees of my daughter, EMILY COUPLAND, and heirs--if any. If none, then to revert to GUSTAVUS A. ROSE or heirs. EMILY gets my wearing clothes. Three trustees to administer. 16 May 1809; 5 June 1809. Witnesses: WILLIAM NORVELL, JONATHAN WIATT, WILLIAM OWENS.

2. JOHN MILLER--of Lynchburg; old and infirm. Wife, MARY, former widow of BENJAMIN JOHNSON--under direction of THOMAS WIATT and my daughter, SALLY WIATT--furniture and slaves. Amherst tract about two miles from Madison--about 350 acres--to children of THOMAS WIATT when of age. They are the children of SALLY WIATT, my daughter. Or if married before age. May sell. Children of ANSELM LYNCH by my daughter, SUKEY, deceased: CHARLES HENRY, MARY ANN, JONATHAN P., SARAH C. and SUSAN LYNCH as of age or married. To widow and children of my deceased son, ELIJAH MILLER; widow and children of my deceased son, JOHN; to HENRY MILLER for his family; son, PLEASANT M., and children of THOMAS WIATT--lot and housed in Lynchburg now occupied by me--one half to each. If they can't agree, then to be sold and divided. Executors of Lynchburg: THOMAS WIATT, PLEASANT M. MILLER, WILLIAM NORVELL. March --, 1812, Thursday, 5 November 1812. Witnesses: E. B. NORVELL, A. ROBERTSON, JAMES DUNNINGHAM, ANDREW JAMIESON. WIATT and MILLER qualified. Bondsmen: JONATHAN WIATT, EDWARD LYNCH. WILL NORVELL, Clerk.

4. SAMUEL IRVINE--of Lynchburg; my wife--dower; furniture; books; prints; pictures; musical instruments--at her will and disposal to my children--some promised or in possession. Executors: THOMAS WIATT, SAMUEL ROSE, JAMES PLEASANTS, JONATHAN M. GORDON. 5 July 1812 in fiftieth year of my age. Thursday, 8 April 1813. Produced by JAMES PLEASANTS, JR. and JONATHAN M. GORDON, two of executors. THOMAS S. MC CLELLAND and CHRISTOPHER ANTHONY testified as to handwriting.

5. JONATHAN NEEDHAM--of Lynchburg; bad health. Wife, ELIZABETH-- all save my slaves; my two children: FRANCES KIRBY and JANE when of age or married--slaves. If either dies before 21, then to her sister; if both die, then to my wife who is to administer. 3 June 1815; Friday, 5 July 1816. Witnesses: MILES CARY, BENJAMIN HAM, JAMES LATIMER.

6. JONATHAN SMITH--of Lynchburg; wife and children--to be
educated. Executors: friend, JONATHAN S. LEE, and my brother,
GEORGE S. SMITH. No date when written; probated 9 January 1818.
Witnesses: N. M. VAUGHAN, J. WATKINS, WILLIAM M. HOLMAN. Produced
by LEE.

7. ADDISON DAVIES--of Lynchburg. Low in health--to needy relatives
and nothing to those well provided; to sell house and lot in
this town; mountain tract in Bedford--Rich Mountain; interest in
father's estate in Campbell County--two-ninths. Wife, ELIZA ANN
DAVIES--if with issue; my brother, HOWEL DAVIES, if no issue; one
moiety to ROBERT L. COLEMAN and wife, MARY T.; if my mother desires,
they are to live with her and care for her. My mother--at her
death, money to my niece, LUCY HENRY LANDONIA COBBS; nephew, EMMET J.
MANSON; if NATHANIEL J. MANSON attends to business of my mother,
when asked--to pay niece COBBS when estate falls to his son or
child; if COBBS dies, then to oldest living child of EDMUND COBBS
by present wife, ELIZABETH. Refers to final termination of suits
of father's estate. Two slaves to be with my mother four years
and then to choose freedom; other slaves are to choose masters.
My brothers and sisters: MARY T. COLEMAN, MRS. MERIWETHER--she is
to have REES' Encyclopedia, if she will take it back; nephew,
ROBERT EMMET MANSON gets various books; my brother, HOWELL DAVIES.
My interest in store of LEWIS and DAVIES. Executors: friends,
JONATHAN J. CABELL, NATHANIEL J. MANSON, ROBERT L. COLEMAN and
guardian of my child--if my wife has one. COLEMAN is to manage
for my wife. 8 May 1817; Thursday, 5 June 1817. Witnesses: NAT
DODSON, HENRY L. DAVIES, JONATHAN C. REID.

11. DANIEL BROWN--of Lynchburg. Sick and weak--wife, POLLY and
my children; tract on Seneca Creek, about 670 acres, to be
sold and more convenient one bought. When oldest son is of age.
Have been merchant for years in firm, BROWN, LEFTWICH and Company--
formerly at Goose Creek; DANIEL BROWN and Company in Franklin County
and latterly BROWN, LEFTWICH and Company of Lynchburg; SAMUEL CLAYTOR
and Company on Goose Creek in Bedford--not settled among partners.
House and lot where I live is to be rented until oldest son is of
age and slaves are to be hired out. Five sons as of age: SAMUEL,
HENRY, DANIEL, AMMON and JAMES. My sister, ELIZABETH WALKER,
my brothers, HENRY and SAMUEL. My father-in-law, SAMUEL HANCOCK--
he and my brothers are to be executors. 12 April 1817; 10 July
1817. Witnesses: SAMUEL C. TYREE, WILL STEPTOE, HENRY BROWN, JR.
Produced by HENRY BROWN and HANCOCK and proved by TYREE and HENRY
BROWN, JR.

13. WILLIAM ROYALL--of Lynchburg. Executors: JOSEPH EDWIN
ROYALL, JAMES TOWNES ROYALL and THOMAS A. HOLCOMB. Wife,
JUDITH ARCHER ROYALL--slaves and life estate in house and ground
occupied by me. "This natural and exciting clause--5" prompts me
as father and Republican to make (as I trust it will all Americans
after me) equal division to my children: JONATHAN JAMES, BENJAMIN
FRANKLIN, MARY ELIZA, WILLIAM RICHARD, THOMAS EDWIN and JOSEPH
ARCHER ROYALL as of age or married. If wife is pregnant, children
to be educated well and virtuously, but avoid a school where
religion sways the teacher. 9 September 1816; 8 August 1817.
Produced by T. A. HOLCOMBE and JOSEPH E. ROYALL. Handwriting by
CHRISTOPHER ANTHONY and SAMUEL J. HARRISON.

15. JAMES GRAHAM--memo to ELIZA GRAHAM, now acquiring an education
at New London Female Academy--slave; two houses on Main Street
in Lynchburg. Joins MARY ROHR. Rented to C. SULLY and A. WINSTON
and C, cabinet-maker. Executor: good friend, JONATHAN MURRELL.
3 February 1819; Tuesday, 2 March 1819. Produced by JONATHAN
MURRELL. Handwriting by him, JAMES BENAGH and JAMES STEWART.

15. ENOCH ROBERTS--wife to raise GEORGE and ELIZABETH to lawful
age and to support MATILDA and ELIZABETH while single;
CHRISTOPHER to be placed to some mechanical trade. Executors:
WILLIAM DAVIS, JR., EDWARD LYNCH and RODERICK TALIAFERRO. 15 February
1819; 1 June 1819. Produced by DAVIS. Handwriting by SAMUEL GARLAND
and WILLIAM STEEN. Note: when I put this type of notation as to
handwriting it simply means that these persons attested as to it.

16. EDWARD TERRELL, Campbell County--wife gets old Mansion house
occupied by JOSEPH FLEMING and all land on that side of creek
from SCOTT's fence--RICHARD PERKINS' mill seat; furniture; cattle.
Daughter, JUDITH TERRELL, is to live with her mother while single
and to be supported. My children: LUCY COGGESHALL's children;
SARAH THURMON, EDWARD TERRELL, ELIZABETH LASLY, MARY SMITHSON,
JUDITH TERRELL and CHRISTOPHER TERRELL. JOHNSON TERRELL has taken
his portion and gone; EDWARD and CHRISTOPHER have had sums; ELIZABETH
LASLEY--per part on loan and at death to her children. Executors
may lay it out in western lands. Executors: ANSELM LYNCH, SR.,
WILLIAM DAVIS, JR., THOMAS HIGGINBOTHAM and GERARD E. JOHNSON.
11 March 1820; Wednesday, 2 August 1820. Witnesses: THOMAS
DILLARD, JONATHAN F. HAWKINS, DONNY C. MOORMAN. Produced by JOHNSON
and proved by DILLARD and MOORMAN.

17. JOHN LYNCH--of Lynchburg. Wife, MARY--house and lot where I
live--Numbers 129, 131 and 119 on Town plans; all benefits
from Lynchburg Mills, Liberty and Lynch Warehouse and toll of
Lynchburg Toll bridge; rent due from PETER DETTO; grocery rent from
place on Fishing Creek where ISHAM ROBERTS lives; also rent from
widow FEARS between turnpike and new road to TATE's land and
bordering on the town lands; rents on brick house built by my son,
CHRISTOPHER LYNCH, in part--torn here--lot #22; rents of lot #33
lying between Liberty Warehouse and Lynch Street on third alley.
Daughter, MATILDA ROBERTS--lot where she lives and bought from
SAMUEL K. JENNING; most of lot #60 and two unimproved lots on
opposite side of street--64 and 66; also one half acre between
Lynch Street and Blackwater--below and opposite where MICHAEL NIGAR
lives and where ENOCH ROBERTS built a stable; also tract on Fishing
Creek--200 acres. Lines: TATE, her sister, TELINDA DAVIS, old
road called Chestnut Oak stand, RICHARD PERKINS, JONATHAN and
NEWBY JOHNSON, WILLIAM DANIEL, ENOCH ROBERTS--bought of ACHILLES
MOORMAN--crossing Turnpike road to TATE; also one half acre lot--
#11--and deed made to her husband, ENOCH ROBERTS; four lots between
eighth and ninth street and fifth and seventh alleys--383, 384,
393, 394 and executed to her husband. Daughter, TELINDA DAVIS--
tract on Fishing Creek below and joining tract given to her sister,
MATILDA--200 acres--lines: TATE, her sister, Turnpike road, crossing
road from Lynchburg to former dividing (?) house of WILLIAM DAVIS,
JR., place where considerable sand has been got for building; lot
94 where she lives; lot 98 on other side of street and opposite 94;
also #9 where WILLIAM DAVIS, JR. built store (stone?) house and
deed made to him; part of lot 3 on Second Street where WILLIAM DAVIS,
JR. built a brick house and deed made; also -- feet whereon PETER
DETTO now occupies a grocery--part of 3; also lot where CHARLES
HOYLE's old stable stands between Lynch Street and Blackwater and
occupied by DAVID R. EDLEY as lumber yard and fronting on #17; also
four lots between C (?) and seventh streets and between seventh and
ninth alleys--221 and 223, 238, 239--to TELINDA DAVIS and children.
Son, EDWARD LYNCH--where he lives and deeded to him--including
grist mill, paper mill on fishing creek, lot 35 where THOMAS
HIGGINBOTHAM et al. live, lot whereon widow of HENRY L. DAVIES
lived for several years--between Lynch Street and Blackwater and
opposite 33--to EDWARD and children. Daughter, POLLY LIGGAT--tract
whereon NANNY JACKSON lives near Candler Mountain--200 acres.
Lines: ROLAND JONES' estate, ROBERT JOHNSON, SAMUEL IRVINE's estate--
residue to her mother, timber for repairs for life, lot where
WILLIAM PERROW lives and opposite Lynch warehouse--part of #3 and
deed made to her husband, ALEXANDER LIGGAT; also where they live--
#117, small part taken off for Courthouse offices--parts of 43 and
47 and in front of where POLLY andmyself now live. At death of my

wife, MARY--129, 131 and 119 to POLLY LIGGAT and children. Son,
WILLIAM B. LYNCH--two deeds made to him--1. Tract on West side of
Meeting House branch joining RICHARD CHILTON and EDMUND TATE. 2. East
side of Meeting house branch and joining #1 and includes houses
and lots where he lives; four lots between seventh and eighth
street and seventh and ninth alleys--410, 402, 411, 412; also lot
on second street--#96 and occupied by lawyer SMITH and deed made;
also $97; my half of Blackwater Mills and lands at death of his
mother--to WILLIAM B. and children. Son, MICAJAH LYNCH--tract on
both sides Rockcastle Creek where I formerly lived--600 acres;
deed made to him; lots on the hill between fifth and sixth street
and seventh and ninth alleys--217, 219, 236, 237 and deed made;
also -- feet on second street and on Water Street--part of #3 and
deed made to him; also four lots of one half acre each where
CHRISTOPHER LYNCH had brick yards between eighth and ninth street
and first and third alleys--305, 307, 325, 327--to MICAJAH and
children. To grandson, JOHN DAVIS--one half acre lot--$95, on second
street, excluding part owned by widow TOMPKINS and where she lives--
to JOHN DAVIS and children. Three great grandsons, WILLIAM POWELL
ROBERTS, GEORGE EDWARD ROBERTS and CHRISTOPHER ROBERTS--children of
SAMUEL ROBERTS--tract where -- DOWDY lives--70 or 80 acres. Lines:
WARD's road where WILLIAM JOHNSON's old meeting house path crosses
road, old Iron Works road on ridge which WILLIAM JOHNSON in latter
time used to go to meeting house; WILLIAM NORVELL, JOHNSON's old
meeting house path. Son, MICAJAH, to be guardian of the ROBERTS
children. Executors to sell Seneca Creek and Amherst County lands--
reserving that which borders on the river until it goes below
mouth of the branch below Horseford and then lot 65, formerly
owned by DAVID MOORE. Son, WILLIAM B., has my half of Blackwater
Mills and gets no part of Lynchburg Mills. Children are not to go
to court, but are to submit any suits contemplated--disputes--to
WILLIAM DAVIS, SR., WILLIAM DANIEL, THOMAS WIATT and CHISWELL
DABNEY. Executors: wife and sons, EDWARD, WILLIAM B., MICAJAH
and ANSELM LYNCH. 10 August 1820. Witnesses: WILLIAM DANIEL,
C. ANTHONY, JAMES STEWART, JAMES C. MOORMAN. Produced on Tuesday,
5 December 1820, by EDWARD LYNCH and proved by WILLIAM DANIEL and
CHRISTOPHER ANTHONY. Someone, perhaps clerk, WILLIAM W. NORVELL--
has this notation: "3020 words."

23. CHARLES LEWIS--of Lynchburg. Debt to Farmers' Bank of
     Virginia and securities as friends: MAJOR WILLIAM LEWIS
and DR. HOWEL DAVIES. Wife, SUSAN R. and heirs. Executor: friend,
HAWES N. COLEMAN. 31 December 1821; Friday, 8 March 1822. Witnesses:
JA. N. CARDOZA, SARAH and JAMES FRAZER.

        This next will prove that there is nothing new under the sun.
We hear a lot of talk about miscegnation, but this shows that it
is an old problem. One can consult my Amherst County works and
find more of it. I am not calling any names, but one Amherst deed
was made by a very prominent man wherein he freed his female slave
and her children by him. He gives them a name other than his own.
He was a colonel in the Revolutionary War and married into one of
the most prominent families in Amherst County. He was also a
county official.

24. NANCY COUSINS--Campbell County. To my servant, DANIEL, whom
     I have had children by and so solemnly and firmly emancipate
at my death--to have and to hold and to dispose of as he may think
proper--all of my remaining estate--to have care of my children
that may survive me. Executor: WILLIAM DAVIS. 12 February 1822;
Monday, 6 May 1822. Witnesses: WILLIAM BURD, VINCENT TABB, RICHARD
THURMON. Produced by DAVIS and proved by TABB and THURMON. I am
not of belief that this was a white man who was an indentured
servant for I find that items dealing with them give a last name.

25. POLLY PERKINS--of Lynchburg. Money in hands of JAMES W.
     DIBRELL; slave, CELIA, to be freed--furniture; brother,
GEORGE M. PERKINS--slave for his life and then to be freed.
Friend, JAMES W. DIBRELL--watch that I loaned him. Nephew,
BENJAMIN WALES PERKINS, son of brother, BENJAMIN PERKINS, when of
age. Niece, ELIZABETH PERKINS, daughter of WILLIAM PERKINS; nephew,
JAMES HARTWELL PERKINS, son of RICHARD PERKINS--clock to parents
until of age; sister, MELINDA MARTIN; sister, SUSANNAH DUNCAN.
GEORGE M. PERKINS to administrator--my beloved. 19 May 1822;
Monday, 7 October 1822. Witnesses: THOMAS WIATT, ARMISTEAD TRUSLOW,
CHARLES L. DIBRELL.

26. ABNER NASH--of Lynchburg. Wife, MATILDA--he married in
     Amherst on 11 July 1792, and was from Prince Edward County--
bride, MATILDA PENN, daughter of GABRIEL PENN--and my children are
to be educated--not provided for by me. Slaves and furniture to
be kept together for wife and children (younger ones)--when of age
or married. If any are bound out, not to lose interest on my
money. Executor may buy situation for family. Son, FRANCIS, to
have classical education, if a genius for learning; if not, then
to be put to some trade. Wife and son, ABNER, to administrator.
17 September 1822. My son, GABRIEL P. NASH, and my daughter,
PAMELIA P. JONES, are provided for. Probated, 5 May 1823. Handwriting by ELIJAH and TIMOTHY FLETCHER and THOMAS CREWS.

27. WILLIAM NORVELL--of Lynchburg. Wife, NANCY--mansion house--
     all that part of the square lying to southeast of line parallel
with alley of town and near my garden fence--next to lot occupied
by JONATHAN M. OTEY--well used by family. Eight slaves to wife--
three female and five males; all interest from Bank or bridge stocks.
Married and adult children have had advances--private ledger in my
desk. To WILLIAM W. NORVELL, JONATHAN M. and LUCY MINA OTEY,
JONATHAN M. and CAROLINE WARWICK; CHISWELL DABNEY married my oldest
daughter, now dead--my grandson, GEORGE WILLIAM DABNEY. My sons
and daughters: note that WILLIAM NORVELL married in Amherst to
NANCY or ANN WIATT, 13 July 1794--in one item he signed as JR. She
was daughter of JOHN WIATT. Children: JONATHAN EDMUNDSON, SAMUEL
GUSTAVUS, FAYETTE HENRY, GEORGE EDWARD NORVELL, MARTHA MARIA LOUISA
and FLORA ANN EMMELINE NORVELL, young daughters, as long as children
are with my wife--to have educations as did older ones. Sons may
have four years at college and pay half from their shares. Wife
and children have lived in good harmony with MISS JANE BENAGH and
are attached to her--to continue. Have had conversation with
CHISWELL DABNEY and he intends to give my grandson, GEORGE WILLIAM
DABNEY, a fair portion of his estate when of age. Negroes not
chosen by wife and children are to be sold. Wife may choose some
other house. It sometimes happens in families remarkable for prudent
habits that some one of children given evidence of his or her incapa-
bility to take care of and keep from waste-pray God that such is not
the case; if so, trustees are to be appointed--if wife refuses,
marries or dies, children are to be protected. May sell houses and
lots in town and Radcliff. Until sold, to allow CAPTAIN OTEY and
wife and WARWICK and wife to keep and occupy houses where they are.
I have charged CAPTAIN OTEY two or three hundred dollars--advanced
him when he and wife went to the Springs and other expenses for
LUCY MINA's health. Executors: wife, ANN, WILLIAM WARWICK,
Amherst County, son, WILLIAM W., late son-in-law, CHISWELL DABNEY,
sons-in-law, JONATHAN M. OTEY and JONATHAN M. WARWICK. Let
WILLIAM W. receive sums and half of executors sign checks--all are
guardians. 1 May 1822; 5 November 1823. Proved by JAMES BENAGH as
to handwriting.

36. GEORGE CABELL--Campbell County and Lynchburg. Wife and friend,
    THOMAS T. BOULDIN, Judge of General Court, to administer--
equal shares to my children; wife to live where I now live. Bedford
tract of 700 acres to children of DR. BENNET MOSELEY, deceased.
CABELL MOSELEY's share for education. 16 November 1823; Tuesday,
2 December 1823. Witnesses: WILLIAM DANIEL, C. ANTHONY, JONATHAN T. W.
READ. Produced by BOULDIN. Proved, 5 January 1824, by DANIEL.
SARAH CABELL qualified and so did BOULDIN. I do not want to be
dogmatic for I may have the wrong GEORGE CABELL in mind. However,
there was a GEORGE CABELL whom I believe to have been a doctor in
Lynchburg. Historians there have promoted a drive to restore his
home which is called Point of Honor. It stands close to the James
on Cabell street and the street has run down--several beautiful
homes are on it and another has been taken over by one historical
group. Point of Honor had several very run down houses near it
and most of these have now been demolished or moved. The grounds
are being landscaped and it is planned to make it a shrine and
tourist attraction. This may be the same man, but I am not making
an authoritative assertion that this is the one who owned Point of
Honor.

37. CURTIS HOLMES--of Botetourt but now of Lynchburg. Wife,
    SALLY, sisters, LUCY and BETSY HOLMES--all furniture left to
me by my father and one dollar ($1.00). Cemetery in Botetourt
wherein are two deceased children--to be enclosed with lime rock.
Brother, JOSHUA R. HOLMES and friend, ELISHA BETTS, to administrator
or DR. JONATHAN YALL, if BETTS refuses. 11 December 1823; 5 January
1824. Witnesses: WILLIAM M. RIVES, WILLIAM BAILEY, J. L. WATROUS.
JOSHUA R. HOLMES qualified on 2 February 1824.

38. PETER DETTO--inventory, 1821. $2288.69. JONATHAN VICTOR,
    P. MATTHEWS, W. L. BELL, JONATHAN HOLLINGS, 3 December 1823.
Signed by JAMES ROSE. Recorded 5 January 1824. WILLIAM W. NORVELL,
Clerk.

41. WILLIAM NORVELL--order to appraise, 5 November 1823, JAMES
    BENAGH, Deputy Clerk. THOMAS A. HOLCOMBE, JONATHAN EARLY,
HENRY DAVIS, JONATHAN WARWICK, J. THURMON; done, 13 January 1824,
in Lynchburg and Radcliff in Campbell County--twenty-six slaves;
tobacco in hands of ANDERSON; BLAIR and ANDERSON; to Liverpool to
MAURY LALTAM and Company; tobacco in hands of PERKINS. Signed by
SAMUEL NOWLIN--$10,323.50. Additional accounts on page 45; no
total.

46. JONATHAN LYNCH--estate account by EDWARD and ANSELM LYNCH
    from six month, 1820. Bedford and Campbell tickets; Wythe
courthouse--BOLES heirs versus KING and C; many names--non-LYNCH;
Amherst land surveyed by EDMUND MEREDITH; opinion of lawyer,
JONATHAN WICKHAM on will of JONATHAN LYNCH, SR.; CHRISTOPHER LYNCH
mentioned; old tavern bought from DR. MOORE; brick office on Main
Street. 4 October 1823. WILLIAM DAVIS, JAMES BULLOCK, JAMES
BENAGH. Recorded 6 October 1823.

52. GEORGE EDWARD ROBERTS--account by guardian, WILLIAM DAVIS, JR.:
    cash from estate of ENOCH ROBERTS--from eleventh month, 1822.
DAVID RODES, JAMES BENAGH, WILLIAM W. NORVELL. Recorded 3 May 1824.
Also account by DAVIS and guardian of ELIZABETH ROBERTS as for
GEORGE EDWARD ROBERTS and recorded on same date.

53. MARY SADLER, late JOHNSON--7 January 1822; inventory order
    to WILLIAM BURD, WILLIAM TARDY, JONATHAN VICTOR, EDWARD
DUFFELL. Done, 11 January 1822; small; no total--by BURD, DUFFELL
and TARDY. Recorded 4 May 1824.

54. January 7, 1822. Same men as above to take inventory of
    CHARLES Y. JOHNSON. SAMUEL BRADFORD, Sergeant and administrator;
no total. Recorded, Tuesday, 4 May 1824.

55. MARY SADLER, late JOHNSON--sale, 23 January 1822, SAMUEL
     BRANSFORD (note I erred in item above as to his name), Sergeant
and administrator. No total; many buyers; no family names.
Recorded 4 May 1824.

56. CHARLES Y. JOHNSON--data as above, but WILLIAM JOHNSON was
     a buyer; no total.

57. JAMES BROWN and spouse, MARGARET BURNIE, otherwise BROWN--
     21 March 1817 at Edinburg, Scotland, residing in Kincurdbright,
settle to prevent disputes--in favor of IRVING BROWN, commonly
called JONATHAN BROWN, acknowledged of our deceased son, JONATHAN
BROWN, sometimes GEORGE ROBERTSON, Lynchburg, Virginia, by JANET
CONE (?)--some of this is difficult to decipher--presently shopkeeper
to JAMES BAILIF, Hatter, in Dumfries--all lands etc. of ours. Our
one-fourth of property of deceased son, WILLIAM , late of Lynchburg,
Virginia in favor of IRVING BROWN (JONATHAN BROWN). We are given
to understand that our deceased son, JONATHAN, left natural daughter
in Lynchburg or somewhere in Virginia. Her name is not known, but
if found in three years, and she agrees to come and live in Scotland,
she will get one-fifth. If she is found, but won't come to live
with us, then L500 of L10,000 estate of WILLIAM BROWN. Our daughter,
MARY BROWN; daughter, JENE, wife of ROBERT MUCE in Netherthurl;
daughter, ISABELLA, spouse of AGNEW BLACK, deceased, living at
MILTON DOUGLAS. If I, JAMES BROWN, die before my spouse, then
JANET COWIE (?) is to have no part--daughters or children--JAMES
BROWN, farmer, in Ingliston of Arongray. WILLIAM MC DOWELL, Dyer
at Waulkmiles; BORWLAND of Kirkendbright; ROBERT GORDON, writer of
same place--they are to be executors. THOMAS THOMSON, Advocate.
Stamped by ROBERT GORDON at Kirkenbright, 21 February 1815. THOMAS
THORNTON is named as Advocate in 1817 at start of this long and
involved instrument. Witnesses: JAMES DYSON, weaver; WILLIAM
KERR, CARTWRIGHT, JAMES and MARGARETT BROWN. To ISABELLA BROWN,
sister of JAMES, and JANET BURNIE, spouse of the deceased--JONATHAN
CARSON, mariner, in K--bright; ISABEL EDGAR, Waulkinsler (?)--
annuities; twenty guineas to the Poor of the Parish of Twynholm
and to be increased to L50 by property received from estates of our
sons. Creditors when I left the farm of Deldam--recall name of
WILLIAM MC DOWELL as executor. Reference to this as a codicil,
23 December 1815. Witnesses: WILLIAM MC DOWEL, Surgeon in
Kircudbright, 12 January 1822--what is written on this and thirteen
pages before and subscribed on each page by sign of GEORGE ROBERTSON,
is the extract entitled "Settlement by JAMES BROWN and spouse,
21 February and 23 December 1815. Registered, 21 March 1817.
Affidavit of WILLIAM BARKLEY, --IRWLAND GORDON, Notary Public
before Chief Magistrate of Kircundbright, this day. WILLIAM B. J.
GORDON, Notary Public. Recorded in Lynchburg, Monday, 3 May 1824,
by SAMUEL GARLAND.

62. MRS. MARGARET BROWN--THOMAS THOMPSON, Advocate for her--MRS.
     MARGARET BURNIE, otherwise BROWN, and relict of JAMES BROWN,
late of Kircudbright--now at Netherwood; settlement by us of
21 February 1815, and codicil of 23 December 1815, and recorded
on 21 March, ----; reference to settlement of deceased son, WILLIAM,
Lynchburg, Virginia--by his will; so far not recovered by us--our
grandson, IRVING BROWN--commonly JONATHAN BROWN, acknowledged son
of our deceased son, JONATHAN BROWN, Lynchburg, by JANET CARRIE (?),
and then shopkeeper to JOSEPH BAILIFF, Hatter in Dumfries, and now
of Netherwood. JONATHAN (IRVING), JAMES BROWN, Ingliston, WILLIAM
MC DOWELL, WAULKMILER and ROBERT GORDON, writer of Kirkcudbright.
Our daughter, MARY, and at her death to any children--but still
single and advanced in years. THOMAS THOMPSON to be my procurator,
Netherwood, 24 May 1817. ROBERT GORDON, writer. ANDREW HENDERSON,
Showmaker, presently at Netherwood, WILLIAM LANNIE, farm servant
there. They were witnesses. Court of Sessions in Scotland--each
page signed by THOMAS PEAT, writer, 12 January 1822. Registered
24 April 1821. JAMES BURNIE, Provost Chief Magistrate of Kirkendbright.
Recorded in Lynchburg, 2 May 1824, by SAMUEL GARLAND.

67. JOSEPH ECHOLS--Lynchburg. Executor to sell, but may buy for
     my children or self--articles for favorite domestic servants.
If any child is born hereafter, to share with wife and others when
of age. Wife of administer and be guardian of minors, but, if
remarried, then DR. WILLIAM LAMBETH is to take over. No date;
probated Monday, 7 June 1824. Witnesses: RALPH SMITH, JR., DAVID
BRADFUTE. Produced by widow.

68. JONATHAN YORE--order to appraise, July Term, 1823, to WILLIAM
     TARDY; JONATHAN H. WARD; CHARLES LEWALLEN and JONATHAN R. D.
PAYNE. Total: $453.63. Recorded 3 August 1824.

70. JONATHAN BYARS--account by administrator, JONATHAN LYNCH,
     from 20 December 1819; nails sold etc.; liquors; name of
GEORGE BYARS by COLONEL W. BYARS; BYARS and SMITH; DAVIS and
BYARS: $10,770.61. DAVID R. EDLEY, AMMON HANCOCK, J. MALLORY.
Order of 7 March 1823, to THOMAS A. HOLCOMBE, EDLEY, HANCOCK,
et al. to examine accounts. Recorded 4 September 1824.

74. JAMES GARVIN--JONATHAN LYNCH, Lynchburg Sergeant administrator--
     from 20 December 1817; balance to his brothers and sisters:
$1131.05. JAMES NEWHALL, J. MALLORY, WILLIAM L. HALL, committee;
order of 5 November 1823.

75. CHARLES TODD--JONATHAN LYNCH as above; many books; shoemaker's
     tools: $135.55. NEWHALL, MALLORY and WILLIAM L. BELL on
order as above. Recorded 4 October 1824.

76. JANE GIBBS--JONATHAN LYNCH as above; from 16 March 1828.
     $104.67. Balance to heirs. Committee as above. Recorded
4 October 1824.

77. JOHN YORE--ELIZABETH YORE, executrix--for LOUISA's tuition
     to HENRY MORRIS; JAMES FRAZER for coffin--$22.00; carpenter's
tools: $395.17, 13 July 1824. DAVID HOFFMAN, JONATHAN HOLLINS,
WILLIAM TARDY, committee.

78. WILLIAM EDENFIELD--of Lynchburg. To WILLIAM ROUSE, son of
     LUCY ROUSE--lot on hill bought from JONATHAN LYNCH and HENRY
MEREDITH; also my religious books; to ELIZABETH ROUSE, third daughter
of LUCY ROUSE--36f to said lot--joins PENNELL; fifth street;
JONATHAN M. SETTLES' former lot. LUCY ROUSE may live in house
where she now lives; my sister, POLLEY GIBSTON (GIBSON), Kent
County, Delaware; if living, or to children; WILLIAM and ELIZABETH
ROUSE, when of age; if they die, to POLLEY GIBSON or heirs.
Executors: friends, THOMAS MOORMAN and DR. WILLIAM OWENS. Witnesses:
FRANCIS T. ROWAN, JONATHAN BOYD, JONATHAN ROBINSON. April 30, 1823;
codicil; no date--L100 instead of $500 to POLLY GIBSON. Witnesses:
ROBINSON and BOYD. Produced 1 November 1284, and proved by ROBINSON;
5 November 1824, by BOYD.

80. Account of Overseers of the Poor from 5 October 1822 until
     6 December 1824--nursing sick and maintaining orphans;
coffins; medical accounts; records for sundry free negroes from
Campbell County office in 1823; BETSY COOPER, pauper, removed.
JONATHAN T. MASON, Clerk. WILLIAM DAVIS, RICHARD TYREE, HOWELL
DAVIES, JONATHAN SCHOOLFIELD, committee; 6 December 1824. JAMES
BENAGH, Clerk.

81. CHARLES LEWIS--SUSAN R. LEWIS, executrix, 5 May 1823. GEORGE
     WHITLOCKE, RICHARD POLLARD, JONATHAN WILLS and JAMES BENAGH
to settle accounts from 2 February 1822--JAMES FRAZER for coffin--
$30.00; clothing for negroes--$15.89; horse hire to Nelson on estate
business; J. GARRETT's expenses to North Carolina on estate business.
J. BRANSFORD, present administrator, 19 March 1824. Inventory in
Spotsylvania--controversy in Fredericksburg--no details. Recorded
3 May 1824.

84. ROBERT PERRIN--May term, 1823. This name is hard to decipher,
but on page 114 it is plain--JAMES GILLIAM, EDWARD DUFFELL,
DAVID B. PATTERSON--JONATHAN VICTOR, recorded; small estate--books,
etc. Recorded 3 January 1825.

85. WESLEY PADGET--March term, 1824. Small estate, 30 March 1824.
THOMAS HUMPHREYS, A. F. BIGGERS, PLEASANT PARTIN.

86. January term, 1824. PETTER DETTO's estate, WILLIAM TARDY
administrator. WILLIAM DIGGES, NORBORNE M. TALIAFERRO,
PATRICK MATTHEWS, JONATHAN HOLLINS, WILLIAM L. BELL. From 7 September
1821. Sold to WILCOX--the oyster man; cash from estate of RODERICK
TALIAFERRO, MRS. DETTO, MRS. VENABLE for rent of house on Cocke
Street--long--several houses; grocery bill. Recorded 6 December 1824.

91. ENOCH ROBERTS--WILLIAM DAVIS, JR., administrator from sixth
month, 1819; JOHN HOCKADAY for coffin--$48.00; WILLIAM STEEN
on a settlement; material to close back yard occupied by A. R. NORTH;
to A. F. BIGGARS by consent of MATILDA ROBERTS the devisee in part
of his wife's legacy; ditto to SAMUEL, WILLIAM, CHRISTOPHER ROBERTS,
MARY ANN MAYS, GEORGE EDWARD ROBERTS--I am his guardian--ditto as
to ELIZABETH ROBERTS, December, 1824. CHRISTOPHER WINFREE, DANIEL
BROWN, AMMON HANCOCK. February 18, 1825; final, 8 March 1825.

95. RODERICK TALIAFERRO--by BENJAMIN TALIAFERRO, administrator,
from March, 1822--Nelson County suit; Amherst County suit.
A. LIGGATT, J. W. DIBRELL, D. R. EDLEY. 7 March 1825.

98. WILLIAM NORVELL--ANN NORVELL, WILLIAM WARWICK, WILLIAM W.
NORVELL, CHISWELL DABNEY, administrators, from tenth month,
1823. Amherst sales; JONATHAN LYNCH for writing deeds; house
occupied by MARY LYNCH, SR.; tracts sold in Lynchburg; JONATHAN
LYNCH and JAMES C. MOORMAN were partners in milling business; also
THOMAS WIATT--settlement and suit in Lynchburg District Court.
7 March 1825. JAMES BULLOCK, WILLIAM DAVIS, SAMUEL ANTHONY.

108. DANIEL BROWN--account by HENRY BROWN and SAMUEL HANCOCK;
from 19 December 1822--to MRS. POLLY BROWN, SAMUEL H., HENRY,
MARY BROWN; tuition for DANIEL and SAMUEL H. BROWN; HENRY, JR.--
tuition at Chapel Hill; ELIZABETH WALKER's support; HENRY BROWN, SR.
3 December 1824; DANIEL BROWN, S. H. DAVIS, WILLIAM DAVIS, JR.

111. CHARLES Y. JOHNSON's orphans--guardian account by JAMES
JONES, guardian, from 6 November 1822--MARTHA and MARY
JOHNSON; WILLIAM JOHNSON for lay-out for CHARLES--hat for THOMAS;
Irvinity (?); mending shoes; board for CHARLES: MARY and MARTHA,
CHARLES--board since 6 October 1823 till 6 December 1824. Irvinity
for board--hard to decipher. JAMES GILLIAM, SAMUEL LANCASTER,
A. LIGGATT. Guardian states that law allows so much and "poorly
paid at that."

114. ROBERT PERRIN--SAMUEL BRANSFORD's account. JAMES FRAZER for
burial--$21.21; 30 March 1825. CHARLES WINFREE, JONATHAN
WILLIAMS, PLEASANT PARTIN.

SAMUEL IRVINE--account by JONATHAN M. GORDON, acting executor
from 22 May 1817; decree of fifth Circuit Court in favor of
L. E. AMELONG and wife, SOPHIA, administrators of ALBERT S. CAMP
versus Heirs of SAMUEL IRVINE and executors. 7 February 1823;
JONATHAN R. D. PAYNE, THOMAS A. HOLCOMBE.

119. JAMES LEFTWICH--Lynchburg. Nephew, JAMES L. CLAYTOR and
heirs--house on Main or second occupied by LEFTWICH and
CLAYTOR; library, too, and $8,000.00. Nephew, SAMUEL CLAYTOR;
nephew, JONATHAN P. CLAYTOR and heirs; niece, SALLY POPE CLAYTOR,
if married--her three brothers just named. My brother, WILLIAM
LEFTWICH; nephew, WILEY STRATTON. JAMES L. BROWN, son of my deceased
partner, DANIEL BROWN, when 21. Children of deceased's sister,
CHARLOTTE CLAYTOR; children of brother, WILLIAM LEFTWICH; children
of sister, ELIZABETH STRATTON; children of sister, SUSANNAH THURMON--
if any die before marriage. AMELIA STRATTON, daughter of ELISABETH
STRATTON, has married CHARLES WHITELEY and has died; SUSANNA THURMON's
childrens' part in trust to SAMUEL CLAYTOR--when 21 or married.
Executors: nephew, SAMUEL CLAYTOR, and friend, CHISWELL DABNEY.
7 September 1822; 5 September 1825. Witnesses: JONATHAN SMITH, JR.,
JONATHAN W. BAGWELL, JONATHAN LEE, WILL OWENS.

121. MILDRED C. JOHNSON--guardian account by SAMUEL NOWLIN from
29 March 1825--to your husband, HENRY HANDLEY (or STANLEY?)
from commissioners of JONATHAN JOHNSON's estate. October term,
1825. SAMUEL LANCASTER, BENJAMIN VAWTER, WILLIAM TARDY.

122. Overseers of Poor--annual report, to 3 December 1825;
maintaining and supporting the poor, nursing the sick and
furnishing the poorhouse for Corporation with suitable bedding:
$221.69; burials--$25.00; rent of poorhouse--$25.00; medicine--
$12.18; services of overseers--$41.00. JONATHAN T. MASON, Clerk.
WILLIAM DAVIS, JONATHAN SCHOOLFIELD, CHRISTOPHER WINFREE, HOWELL
DAVIES. 3 December 1825.

122. CHRISTOPHER FLETCHER--inventory, 3 December 1825, by JONATHAN
HOLLINS, JONATHAN T. MASON, CHRISTOPHER FLETCHER; very small.
Order of September, 1825. Error: Last name is CHRISTOPHER WINFREE.

123. VINCENT S. BAILEY--inventory. 13 January 1825: $291.11 by
JOHN HANCOCK, HENRY M. DIDLAKE, JOSHUA R. HOLMES, S. DUIGUID.
6 February 1826.

125. WILLIAM NORVELL--account by administrators: ANN NORVELL,
WILLIAM WARWICK, WILLIAM W. NORVELL, CHISWELL DABNEY, JONATHAN M.
OTEY, JONATHAN M. WARWICK--from 15 November 1824. To widow for
family; WILLIAM W. NORVELL--one year as acting executor; JONATHAN (?) M.
ROBERTS--guardian of SAMUEL ROBERTS' children. MRS. M. ROBERTS
could be name for JONATHAN M.; repairs to white house on Main street
lot next to Franklin Hotel; in part of CAPTAIN WILLIAM IRVINE's
debt; slaves names and hires; DR. J. T. STEVENS for rent on white
house on main; JONATHAN HANCOCK--rent of brick kitchen near
Franklin Hotel. 6 March 1826. CHRISTOPHER WINFREE. WILLIAM W.
NORVELL, Clerk.

130. MICAJAH LYNCH--Campbell County. Friend, JONATHAN HOLLINS,
Lynchburg; brother, WILLIAM B. LYNCH--600 acres where I live
about four miles from Lynchburg in Campbell County; lots and houses
in Lynchburg occupied by JUDGE WILLIAM DAVIS; other property in
Lynchburg--Main or Second and Water Street where JONATHAN HOLLINS
keeps a grocery--from my father, JONATHAN LYNCH, deceased. Administrators: WILLIAM B. LYNCH, JONATHAN HOLLINS of Lynchburg, CHISWELL
DABNEY of Amherst County. 15 December 1825; 5 June 1826. Witnesses:
DANIEL BROWN, SAMUEL BRANSFORD, AMMON HANCOCK.

131. WILLIAM B. LYNCH--of Lynchburg. Wife, ANN JANE; several
houses; son, WILLIAM B., 276 acres in Campbell County near
Lynchburg--where the Dutch gardener has his vineyard; among lots
is one on Main opposite Presbyterian Church and joining it. Wife
to administer. 18 July 1825; Tuesday, 6 June 1826. Handwriting
by DANIEL BROWN, PETER DUDLEY, JONATHAN HOLLINS.

133. MARY FRENCH--of Lynchburg. Widowed sisters, ANN HENDRON and
     MARGARET RICHARDSON--child or children. Brother, MASON
FRENCH, loaned deceased brother-in-law, GEORGE RICHARDSON--Executor:
friend, JAMES BENAGH. 14 June 1826. 2 October 1826. Witnesses:
J. WILLS, D. RODES.

134. CHARLES Y. JOHNSON--account by SAMUEL BRANSFORD from January,
     1822--he is administrator de bonis non--shoes for WINDLOW
(slave) and his hire; JAMES JONES for childrens' bond. 3 February
1826. WILLIAM TARDY, SAMUEL LANCASTER, A. LIGGAT.

136. MARY SADLER--account by SAMUEL BRANSFORD, Lynchburg Sergeant
     from 8 January 1822--burial for MRS. POLLY SADLER--DUIGUID--
$25.00; notes in account and one before death of CHARLES Y. JOHNSON;
cart and hand hire removing house--hold and kitchen furniture from
the river to Main Street; Buckingham ticket. 3 February 1826.
Same men as for CHARLES Y. JOHNSON.

137. JAMES LEFTWICH--order to appraise estate to DAVID G. MURRELL,
     ARCH. ROBERTSON, JONATHAN THURMON, SMITHSON H. DAVIS, 5 September
1825; very long; merchant; accounts due--page 168--many are noted
as insolvent. LEFTWICH names in list--not as insolvents--WILLIAM,
JABEZ (doubtful), ALEXANDER, JONATHAN O., AUGUSTINE, WILLIAM C.,
BROWN LEFTWICH and Company, JESS JOEL. 8 June 1826--very long and
hundreds of names and I recognize many as being from Amherst
County (BFD).

174. CHARLES Y. JOHNSON's orphans--JAMES JONES, guardian--from
     6 December 1824: MARTHA, CHARLES, ARVINTY (spelled IRVINITY
in other data), THOMAS. 3 February 1826. WILLIAM TARDY, SAMUEL
LANCASTER, A. LIGGAT.

176. CAPTAIN JAMES LEFTWICH--inventory. 5 September 1825. Order
     to JONATHAN HADEN, NICHOLAS ROBINSON, LEWIS WINGFIELD, DAVID W.
QUARLES--Bedford County order. Executors: SAMUEL CLAYTOR and
C. DABNEY--$5095.62½.

177. JAMES P. BULLOCK--5 June 1826. Inventory of $254.13. SAMUEL
     NOWLIN, HARGROVE MITCHUM, HEZEKIAH JORDAN. 10 June 1826.

179. THOMAS HUMPHREYS--inventory. 4 July 1826--$150.80. AMMON
     HANCOCK, CHRISTOPHER WINFREE, JONATHAN HOLLINS.

181. JONATHAN BYARS--JONATHAN LYNCH, administrator. From 4 September
     1824--GEORGE BYARS for crying property; amount due from J.
BYARS; Treasurer of Lynchburg and Salem Turnpike Company: $3284.58.
J. MALLORY, JAMES NEWHALL, AMMON HANCOCK. 2 October 1826.

183. DANIEL BROWN--HENRY BROWN and SAMUEL HANCOCK, administrators.
     From February 1825; sent cash to HENRY BROWN at Chapel Hill;
HENRY BROWN, minor; MARY BROWN, HENRY BROWN of Rockbridge, HENRY, JR.--
at Chapel Hill; AMMON H. BROWN, deceased; to MARY BROWN--her part
of A. H. BROWN from father's estate; to SAMUEL H. BROWN; HENRY
BROWN, SR.--an executor. WILLIAM DAVIS, JR., T. A. HOLCOMB, DANIEL
BROWN. 6 February 1826.

185. JONATHAN LYNCH, SR.--EDWARD and ANSELM LYNCH, executors--very
     long; MOORMAN and LYNCH; MICAJAH and MARY LYNCH; rents on
many houses.

189. DAVID BIBB--ALEXANDER M. CLAYTOR, administratir, 5 June 1826.
     GARRET M. QUARLES and CHARLES Y. KIMBROUGH before PLEASANT
HACKETT, Louisa Justice of the Peace. 14 August 1826.

190. Overseers of Poor--3 December 1825 to 1 December 1826; burials.
     5 December 1826.

191. MICAJAH LYNCH--inventory. 3 July 1826; CHARLES L. DIBRELL,
     AMMON HANCOCK, DANIEL BROWN; 19 July 1862: $527.95; 5 February
1827.

193. WILLIAM B. LYNCH--inventory, Monday, 3 July 1826; Blackwater
      Mills and tracts--about sixty acres; dam washed away and
mills out of repair; $2500.00; SAMUEL LANCASTER; ALEXANDER TOMPKINS,
SAMUEL NOWLIN, 2 September 1826. Thursday, 8 June 1826--$2575.83.
JONATHAN R. D. PAYNE, THOMAS A. HOLCOMB, AMMON HANCOCK, MICAJAH
DAVIS, JR.--several small items sold. July, 1826.

197. JONATHAN LYNCH, SR.--division by will. August 1826. MICAJAH
      DAVIS, JR.--guardian of WILLIAM B. LYNCH, orphan of WILLIAM B.
LYNCH, deceased. Appointed, June court, 1824, and JONATHAN LYNCH,
JR., too, to account. Met at ALEXANDER LIGGAT's house 19 August
1826; DAVIS as administrator of MICAJAH LYNCH who was administrator
of WILLIAM B. LYNCH. Adult heirs--six lots previously laid off
for six heirs. Asked for lots to be drawn. Lot 1--EDWARD LYNCH;
Lot 2--MICAJAH DAVIS, JR. for WILLIAM B. LYNCH, deceased, and infant
son; Lot 3--TELINDA DAVIS; Lot 4--MATILDA ROBERTS; Lot 5--ALEXANDER
LIGGAT and wife, POLLY; Lot 6--heirs of MICAJAH LYNCH, deceased.
Errors in surveys on Mountain tract and Fishing Creek and adjusted
in lots, 8 December 1826. C. DABNEY, DANIEL BROWN, A. HANCOCK,
S. H. DAVIS. Long list of tracts herein.

210. MATILDA ROBERTS--accounts. 8 December 1826; report of
      9 December 1826.

211. FRANCIS P. HARRIS--This is a document with terrible spelling.
      I am inclined to think that he was contemplating suicide
from the gist of the data. No date--"This is to surtify that sense
the day that I was mared--I am simply putting down words as shown
with no attempt to correct them--I have never found any fault with
her--But the sit was that I am plas in Bisness and trubels of the
cases to put astopt surch Amusibel lif--this Articl is to show how
I wish my Bis to Be dispos of--I wish my wif to to cas to be sold
the pise of land on Jos. Branc and lot of ground--and that to be
lad out in chuling the children--But the hous and lot my wif is
to have durin her life with furniture--But to go to my dauter(s)
at her death"--he seems to call daughter, WILLIAM HARRIS--"WILLIAM
SUMPTER is not to have any hand in this Biss--Becas I Donot con Sider
him--The Last Will an Testment--Memo--all the dets is Holcmomb's and
Owens--you find recits in the bag of color. Monday, 5 March 1825.
GEORGE GREGORY, BENJAMIN VAWTER, WILLIAM SUMPTER as to handwriting.
Someone has put this in pencil on margin, but I did not check it
out--"WILLIE ANN ? See Deed Book L: 340--page 280 married
DAVID E. BOOK--Will Book B:488."

212. JOHN WIATT--wife, MINA; children: ANN NORVELL, JUDITH THOMAS,
      SAMUEL I. WIATT, CAROLINE M. WINSTON; children, too, of
deceased daughter, SUSAN CABELL; and deceased son, JONATHAN J.
WIATT--son, JONATHAN WIATT. Executors: wife, son, SAMUEL I.,
son-in-law, EDMUND WINSTON, grandson, WILLIAM W. NORVELL. 17 February
1827; 5 March 1827. Witnesses: G. A. ROSE, WILLIAM S. REID.

213. ENOCK ROBERTS--WILLIAM DAVIS, JR., executor; August 8, 1826;
      DANIEL BROWN, CHRISTOPHER WINFREE, AMMON HANCOCK, JONATHAN R. D.
PAYNE--accounts from second month, 18-- to 1825. To MATILDA
ROBERTS. 3 February 1827.

215. SAMUEL IRVINE--JONATHAN M. GORDON, executor, 5 March 1827.
      JONATHAN R. D. PAYNE, THOMAS A. HOLCOMBE.

216. DANIEL BROWN--HENRY BROWN, JR. and SAMUEL HANCOCK, administrators
      from 1826--legacies of SAMUEL H. BROWN, HENRY BROWN, JR.,
MARY BROWN, HENRY BROWN, minor--due estate in hands of HENRY BROWN,
SR. 5 February 1827; 5 March 1827.

218. JOSEPH ECHOLS--inventory, June, 1825; many slaves named and
     suits; total: $10,158.75. JONATHAN HANCOCK, GEORGE K.
LAMBETH, 5 June 1826. JAMES W. DIBRELL swore in Richmond before
A. PLEASANTS, JR., 26 June 1826, as to inventory. Debts due from
his books from June, 1824. PREEGRINE (?) ECHOLS, ECHOLS and NORTH,
JONATHAN, DAVID, and COLEMAN ECHOLS.

224. WILLIAM NORVELL--Executors: ANN NORVELL, WILLIAM WARWICK,
     WILLIAM W. NORVELL, CHISWELL DABNEY, JONATHAN M. OTEY,
JONATHAN M. WARWICK. From 6 December 1825--to MRS. NORVELL for
self andfamily; JONATHAN E. NORVELL; third clause of will--MRS.
ROBERTS--guardian of children of SAMUEL ROBERTS; rent of farm
near MRS. POWELL; WILLIAM W. NORVELL. Very long; CAPTAIN WILLIAM W. (?)
IRVINE's account: 25 January 1827--$20,540.98. Friday, 31 October
1826; order of 4 December 1826. JAMES BENAGH, JONATHAN WILLS,
DANIEL RODES, 2 April 1827.

230. DAVID DAWSON--inventory, 28 March 1827; small; no total;
     ROBERT BUTLER, JACOB FEAGLE, EDWARD LYNCH. Recorded Monday,
2 April 1827.

231. COLONEL JONATHAN WIATT--inventory; Monday, 5 March 1827,
     order; ELIJAH FLETCHER, JAMES WARNER (?), SAMUEL BRANSFORD,
GEORGE WHITLOCK--$4336.25. Receipt of MINA WIATT to WILLIAM W.
NORVELL, executor. Witness: SAMUEL G. NORVELL.

234. JOHN CURLE--order of 7 April 1827, for inventory: HENRY
     DUNNINGTON, HENRY M. DIDLAKE, ROBERT GANNAWAY; done, 13 April
1827--$188.85; recorded: 4 June 1827. Page 236 testimony of
EDWARD PRICE and JESSE L. PERRY--JONATHAN CURLE called them between
1 January 1826 and 1 March; asked to have verbal will recorded
within three days after death and then to divide--after debts paid--
to two children: SALLY HOCKADAY and his son, RICHARDSON CURLE--
house and lot adjoining one given previously to SALLY--lot bought
from PETER ELLIOTT. 31 March 1827; Saturday, 7 April 1827.
JONATHAN HOCKADAY and RICHARDSON CURLE produced verbal will with
testimony.

237. ABNER NASH--MATILDA NASH, executrix. COLIN BUCKER, DAVID G.
     MURRELL, JAMES NEWHALL, 3 March 1827. Tuition for FRANCIS,
Duiguid for funeral--$25.00; EDWIN C's hat in lifetime of ABNER;
Duiguid for EDWIN's funeral; trip to Prince Edward for sums due;
to ABNER O. and ELIZABETH NASH; ABNER O's support from 12 May 1823
to 10 March 1825, at which time he became of age; to ELIZABETH F.
and FRANCIS W. NASH; reference to will of ABNER; cash on hand at
time of his death. 16 March 1823. Recorded 3 April 1827.

240. FRANCIS GRAY--inventory order of 7 May 1827 to SAMUEL NOWLIN;
     JONATHAN THURMON; NATHAN B. THURMON; JAMES NEWHALL--$45.75;
recorded, Monday, 4 June 1827.

241. JOSEPH ECHOLS--account by ELIZA F. ECHOLS from 10 June 1824
     as executrix. Clothes for JOSEPH LACY; bond of JONATHAN
ECHOLS; P. ECHOLAS trip to Liberty; repairs at Franklin hotel;
HARRIET's tuition; $1.00 to get wagon out of river; REUBEN's
expenses to get ISAAC out of jail in Cumberland--probably a slave
item--jail and fees--$16.75; hats for ROBERT and EDMUND (WARD?);
tickets for MOSES ECHOLS' estate; Georgia money to be returned in
ninety days in Virginia money; hack hire for children to MR. ANTHONY;
$100 to A. R. NORTH to buy marble slab for JOSEPH ECHOLS--very long.
E. FLETCHER, PAUL JONES, RICHARD PERKINS. 7 April 1827.

261. RODERICK TALIAFERRO--BENJAMIN TALIAFERRO, administrator; order of
     2 October 1826; to report 4 December 1826; modified 5 March 1827;
more commissiners; done by ALEXANDER LIGGAT, DAVID R. EDLEY, ELIJAH
FLETCHER, 5 June 1827; Nelson County tickets. WILLIAM ORGAN (MORGAN),
surviving partner; Henrico suit; Campbell County tickets; SARAH
PRICE's claim versus estate; amount from MRS. SUSAN TALIAFERRO--
$2688.53.

265. JAMES LEFTWICH--SAMUEL CLAYTOR, administrator from 5 September
     1825; LEFTWICH and CLAYTOR; many warehouses; trip to Powhatan;
AUGUSTINE LEFTWICH's note; Episcopal Church subscription; scores of
accounts of WILLIAM C. LEFTWICH, ALEXANDER LEFTWICH--JAMES L. CLAYTOR,
partner, and heir; amounts for SALLY P. CLAYTOR, JONATHAN P.
CLAYTOR, JESSE LEFTWICH (account), THOMAS A. LEFTWICH, acutioneer,
account of WILLIAM LEFTWICH. $14,484.09. A. ROBERTSON, JONATHAN
THURMOND; 7 August 1827. Names of JOSEPH BOWLING, Franklin; WILLIAM
LEFTWICH, B. H.--sic; SAMUEL STEVENS, boatman; JABEZ LEFTWICK;
JONATHAN O. LEFTWICH; WILLIAM C. LEFTWICH; BEOWN LEFTWICH and
Company; legacy from MRS. (?) BECKLEY's estate; JESSE and JOEL
LEFTWICH. 6 August 1827.

281. GEORGE M. PERKINS--7 January 1827. He talked to RALPH H.
     MARTIN as to distribution--to ELIZABETH PERKINS; MARIA, a
slave; JONATHAN MARTIN PERKINS--three slaves; children of sister,
SALLY. Asked HENRY MARTIN three or four times to notice what he
said and not to forget; HENRY to get a slave--name of WILLIAM DAY--
can't be sure that this is slave or another heir. Witness:
J. C. CLARK. Recorded Monday, 1 October 1827.

281. GEORGE W. ROBERTS--sale by BRADFUTE and TOMPKINS, 5 January
     1826: $119.11. Recorded Monday, 5 December 1827. Page 282
inventory; merchandise held by SAMUEL LANCASTER: $152.15. A. LIGGATT,
PATRICK MATTHEWS, WILLIAM TARDY. Page 283--THOMAS W. ROBERTS as
administrator from January, 1826 to August, 1827.

284. WILLIAM BLACK--MAURICE H. GARLAND, administrator, 9 November
     1827; books; slave and horse given to MRS. SAMUEL GARLAND--
small: $61.95. JONATHAN T. MASON, H. D. MURRELL, GEORGE W. TURNER.
3 December 1827.

285. JOSEPH ECHOLS--MRS. ELIZA ECHOLS, administratrix, from
     19 October 1826; Baptist church subscription; MR. LUCAS--
$10.00; estate of MOSES ECHOLS; note of P. ECHOLS; E. F. ECHOLS--
probably widow above. ELIJAH FLETCHER, SAMUEL NOWLIN, MARTIN W.
DAVENPORT. 24 October 1827.

291. CHARLES Y. JOHNSON--infant heir of CHARLES Y. JOHNSON,
     deceased; JAMES JONES, guardian, from 7 March 1826; books;
clothes; amount from estate of THOMAS JOHNSON, deceased. WILLIAM
TARDY, JONATHAN BOYD, JONATHAN HOLLING. This is followed by other
accounts of JONES--page 292 for THOMAS JOHNSON, infant of CHARLES Y.
JOHNSON; reference to division of slaves of THOMAS JOHNSON,
deceased, in Amherst County. Page 293 account for MARY JOHNSON,
as above; page 294 account for MARTHA JOHNSON as above. Data is
same for each. Recorded 1 August 1827. MARTHA is called MARTHA ANN
JOHNSON.

296. ANDREW C. RANKIN--25 April 1828; Monday, 7 July 1829.
     Witnesses: G. L. LECKIE, M. W. COLE, R. S. WHITE, JR.
Niece, FRANCES CATHERINE JANE COLE RANKIN--daughter of THOMAS
RANKIN--40 acres in Jefferson County, Tennessee, inherited from
my father, RICHARD RANKIN. Executor: brother, THOMAS RANKIN.

297. GEORGE W. NORVELL--22 December 1827; Monday, 4 August 1828.
     FRANCIS L. MILLER and EDMOND B. NORVELL as to handwriting.
My brothers and sisters: MARTHA JANE CASKIE, ANN ELIZA NORVELL,
AMUNELA MELVINA WALKER, LORENZO NORVELL, REUBEN BUTLER NORVELL;
mercantile inventory to be taken of G. R. and L. NORVELL; father
to be supported. JONATHAN CASKIE and DAVID WALKER may ask for
security; they are to administer along with LORENZO NORVELL.

298. WILLIAM NORVELL--ANN NORVELL, administratrix, along with
     others previously named in other items--from 24 November 1826;
MRS. NORVELL for self and family; legacy of JONATHAN E. NORVELL.
Tuesday, 6 November 1827; order; done 14 December 1827--CHRISTOPHER
WINFREE.

302. JOSEPH D. LOGAN--division on order: six children: MARY
     LOUISA, JAMES WILLIAM, JOSEPH W. P., JONATHAN S. L., ELIZABETH
J. L., HARRIET L. B.--first two are by first wife; slaves. Rest
to other four, 7 January 1828. MICAJAH DAVIS, JR., A. ROBERTSON,
E. B. NORVELL, DANIEL RODES. Motion of LOUISA LOGAN, widow and
guardian of last four children and consent of GEORGE WOODSON
PAYNE, guardian of others. Report of 8 January 1828; final:
Thursday, 6 March 1827.

303. Overseers of Poor--to 1 December 1827. ANN MORRIS taken to
     Maryland--$25.00; expenses set forth--$542.99. WILLIAM DAVIS,
JONATHAN T. MASON, Clerk. Recorded 4 December 1827.

304. WILLIAM M. WALLACE--SUSAN WALLACE, administratrix--from
     13 November 1821. Note that his showmaker's certificate was
lot; Bedford tickets; also Pittsylvania--$858.47. JONATHAN VICTOR,
WILLIAM SUMPTER, JAMES BENAGH. Thursday, 8 November 1827.

307. GEORGE W. ROBERTS--order of June, 1828 to divide to THOMAS H.
     and to ROBERT L. PARKS and wife, CATHERINE (THOMAS H.
ROBERTS) as heirs; lower side of third street next to REVEREND MR.
COLE and ISRAEL SNEAD; Monday, 1 September 1828; SAMUEL BRANSFORD,
ROBERT H. GRAY, SAMUEL NOWLIN, PLEASANT LABBY.

308. GEORGE R. NORVELL--inventory on order of 4 August 1828--$230.02;
     personal; goods and slaves--$16,322.79½. THOMAS A. HOLCOMBE,
JACOB ANDERSON, EDMOND N. BROWN. 29 August 1828.

309. JONATHAN BYERS--JONATHAN LYNCH, administrator. 5 June 1827--
     AMMON HANCOCK, D. R. EDLEY, JAMES NEWHALL. Monday, 1 September
1828.

310. DAVID BIBB--inventory, 28 February 1827; slaves--$775.00;
     JONATHAN and WILLIAM ELLIS, DAVID THOMPSON--administrator:
ALEXANDER M. CLAYTOR--page 311 he is called BLACK and later called
BIBB. CHARLES Y. KIMBROUGH, G. N. QUARLES. October 1828.

311. JONATHAN CURLE--EDWARD PRICE and JESSE L. PERRY, administrators,
     from 10 April 1827--cash from R. CURLE. JONATHAN HANCOCK,
HENRY M. DIDLAKE.

312. Overseers of the Poor from December 1828--$90.82; JONATHAN T.
     MASON and WILLIAM DAVIS make report.

313. LOWRY GREGORY--wife, AMELIA; three children: MARY F.,
     JONATHAN W. and JESSE GREGORY. Administrator: father-in-
law, JESSE RICHARDSON. 18 November 1828; Monday, 1 December 1828.
Witnesses: ALFRED RICHARDSON, JOSEPH P. DAVIDSON, VARLAND RICHESON,
MOORE F. CARTER.

313. This seems to account of office by JAMES MARTIN, DANIEL
     OGLESBY, FREDERICK KABLER, 2 November 1826; another by
JONATHAN ORGAN, EDMOND HERNDON, THOMAS FOX, 23 October 1824.

314. EDWARD TERRELL--GERRARD E. JOHNSON, administrator, Friday,
     26 October 1822; also signed by DANIEL OGLESBY et al. above.
Monday, 5 May 1828.

316. LOWRY GREGORY--inventory: $1017.75. HEZEKIAH JORDAN, JACOB
     FRAZEL, DAVID HERNELSON.

317. JONATHAN CURLE--Administrators: EDWARD PRICE and JESSE L.
     PERRY: accounts: $159.43.

15

318. ELIZABETH STEWART--JAMES STEWART, administrator, from 1819.
      To GATHWRITHT for coffin and grave plank--$44.00; WINSTON and
DUIGUID for hearsehire--$5.00; STEWART and TALIAFERRO account;
coffin for negro boy, ROBERT--$2.00; subscription for church stove--
$2.00; to WILLIAM STEWART's administrator, PHILIP LONG, who was
administrator of HENRY STEWART; JONATHAN H. PLEASANTS for defending
EMILY on felony charge; support of old slave, LUCY, for one year
at $50.00; many slaves named and hires--EMILY among them. Campbell
County Court order. Total: $1009.95. Accounts and several
thought to be insolvent--committee of LUTHER SMITH, ANTHONY NORTH,
JAMES ENGLAND, 1 August 1828; recorded October Term, 1828.

319. FRANCIS GRAY--order to settle accounts by May Term, 1828,
      court--ROBERT H. GRAY, administrator--from 8 June 1828.
D. S. MURRELL, JONATHAN THURMON, 29 November 1828.

320. COLONEL JONATHAN WIATT--WILLIAM W. NORVELL, administrator--
      Monday, 2 February 1829--ELIJAH FLETCHER, JAMES FRAZIER for
funeral--$48.00; MRS. EPPES for shroud; H. DUNNINGTON, constable;
whipping slaves--$2.50. Total: $102.59. Dates of 14 February 1827
and 17 February 1829.

322. HENRY CARLTON--inventory--late firm of deceased-- and Company;
      slave boy, MOONE, about twelve; EBENEZER GARDONER, HARVEY S.
WILLS, GEORGE T. WILLIAMS--$2550.72, 5 March 1829.

323. MICHAEL HUGH--inventory of $69.81, 14 March 1829; JONATHAN
      HOLLINS, RICHARD TYREE, JONATHAN HALSEY.

324. WILLIAM NORVELL--ANN NORVELL et al., see previous items,
      several administrators--from 28 November 1827. MRS. NORVELL
for support of family; MATILDA ROBERTS as guardian of SAMUEL
ROBERTS' children--rent of tract on turnpike near MRS. POWELL;
legacy to JONATHAN E. NORVELL; JAMES FRAZIER for making coffin for
negro child--$2.50; insurance on White house on Second Street;
JO E. ROYALL--rent on house on Federal Hill for one year--$70.00;
several places rented--$20,137.83½. December Term, 1828. Recorded
Monday, 2 February 1827.

328. ENOCH ROBERTS--WILLIAM DAVIS, JR., administrator from 1827--
      $2808.44. AMMON HANCOCK, DANIEL BROWN. Recorded Wednesday,
4 March 1827.

329. JOSEPH ECHOLS--November Term, 1828--ELIZA F. ECHOLS, executrix
      and guardian of HARRIET, EDWARD, ROBERT and JONATHAN ECHOLS,
children of JOSEPH ECHOLS, deceased, from 1 October 1827. ECHOLS
and NORTH mentioned many times in very long account--A. R. NORTH.
EDWARD's tuition; preparation to New Haven to educate the children
there--$755.00; and then $8711.47. Recorded 7 April 1829. Then
accounts as guardian--336f. HARRIET got prayer book; silver comb.
Page 340 EDWARD's account; page 342. EDBERT JOSEPH ECHOLS; page 343
JONATHAN--SAMUEL J. WIATT and MARTIN W. DAVENPORT.

344. WILLIAM DAVIS--thirty-first day of eighth month, 1829;
      September Term, 1829. For support of my family. Wife, MARY,
children: HENRY, SUSANNA DAVIS, ELIZABETH DAVIS, LOUISA DAVIS,
DEBORAH O. DAVIS, daughter, MARY PERRICE (?), children of JONATHAN
DAVIS, deceased: WILLIAM, CHRISTOPHER, MARY JANE DAVIS. Administrators:
WILLIAM DAVIS, JR., PETER DUDLEY, MICAJAH DAVIS, JR. Witnesses:
JONATHAN M. OTEY, GEORGE D. DAVIS, ZACHFIELD WADE.

346. ROBERT A. WARD--AUGUSTUS LEFTWICH, administrator; Wednesday,
      5 August 1829. From June 1829. GEORGE W. TURNER, GEORGE T.
WILLIAMS, MAURICE H. GARLAND. 2 September 1829.

347. CHARLES Y. JOHNSON's infants--November term, 1828; JAMES
      JONES, guardian--JONATHAN HOLLING, WILLIAM TARDY, JONATHAN
BOYD, committee. Accounts of MARTHA A., MARY V., THOMAS, and
CHARLES Y. JOHNSON. Recorded February, 1829.

350.   RODERICK TALIAFERRO--BENJAMIN TALIAFERRO, administrator; trip
       to Campbell County; suits in Amherst and Campbell; MISS SALLY
PRICE in Henrico; amount from SUSANNAH (?) TALIAFERRO--difficult
estate to manage and 7½% allowed. $2436.37. ELIJAH FLETCHER,
committeeman.

353.   BENJAMIN VAWTER's widow, MILDRED, gets dower, May, 1830--ALBION
       MC DANIEL, DAVID Y. MURRELL, JAMES NEWHALL, October 18, 1830--a
number of houses--one near POE's tanyard and occupied by MRS. BURNETT
on fifth. Lots to widow; BRANSFORD VAWTER; SILAS VAWTER. Recorded
4 November 1830.

354.   WILLIAM NORVELL--November term, 1829; CHRISTOPHER WINFREE,
       commissioner, and same executors as elsewhere in this book--
very long; widow and family; SAMUEL G. NORVELL as heir; widow for
self and family; many houses and tracts; slave hires--$17,218.52½.

360.   HENRY CARLTON--WILLIAM H. HUBBARD, administrator. HENRY
       CARLTON and Company; trip to Richmond; MRS. ANTOINETTE E.
CARLTON bought furniture; HUBBARD was partner; long list of accounts
due. JOSHUE R. HOLMES, E. G. GARDNER, GEORGE T. WILLIAMS.

362.   JONATHAN LYNCH--SAMUEL BRANSFORD, administrator; January,
       1830. ROBERT MORRIS, SAMUEL MILLER--very long; many houses
rented--from 13 August 1825; MARY LYNCH's Corporation tax. Recorded
3 May 1830.

367.   WILLIAM PETERS--Franklin County. Wife, ELIZABETH; codicil--
       all to wife. 28 January 1796; codicil of 2 September 1821;
4 March 1830. Handwriting by CHISWELL DABNEY and JONATHAN SCHOOLFIELD.

368.   THOMAS G. FOWLER--inventory by DOLPHIN DREW, HENRY M. DIDLAKE,
       SMITHSON H. DAVIS, DAVID THOMPSON. Slaves, etc.; no total.
Recorded 4 November 1830.

369.   PHILIP ROHR--3 June 1828; 4 November 1830. Mother, MARY
       ROHR--house and lot on Main for life; then to sell and equal
parts to heirs of JACOB ROHR; trustee account to WILLIAM BURD for
my wife, SARAH ROHR--house and lot where I live--Number 276 (then
altered by someone to 296); at her death to PHILIP, ANN and WILLIAM
RORH--heirs of JACOB ROHR.

370.   EBENEZER FRANCIS GARDNER--inventory--COLIN BUCKERN, DAVID H.
       MURRELL, JAMES NEWHALL, HOWSON S. WHITE, SAMUEL NOWLING,
JONATHAN SMITH, 13 September 1830, at residence, by rooms, interesting
list; furniture, books, maple bedstead, refrigerator, shower bath
machine, several slaves--one a mulatto, BETSY. Recorded 3 January
1831.

376.   Overseers of Poor from 1 December 1828 to 1 December 1829--
       burials: $25.00; to commissioners--$55.00; clerk--$20,00;
JONATHAN T. MASON, Clerk. JONATHAN SCHOOLFIELD, Commissioner.
Then account for 1829--1830, December to December; burials at $36.00.

377.   E. F. GARDNER--JOSHUA R. HOLMES, administrator; sale,
       October, 1830; MRS. GARDNER and JAMES H. GARDNER were buyers;
she bought domestic carpet, etc.; private and public sales; many
buyers: $521.48¾. Recorded 7 February 1831.

382.   VINCENT BAILEY--MARTHA J. BAILEY, administratrix; Duiguid for
       funeral--$25.00; from 28 February 1826; small estate; JOSHUA R.
HOLMES, ROBERT H. GRAY, SAMUEL NOWLIN. Recorded February, 1831.

384.   SAMUEL H. BROWN qualified before JONATHAN R. D. PAYNE, Justice
       of the Peace, 20 December 1830, as captain of company of
riflemen--131 st Virginia Regiment.

384.   BENJAMIN VAWTER--inventory; May, 1830--done, 18 October 1830;
       $731.22. JAMES NEWHALL, ALBON MC DANIEL, D. G. MURRELL.
Recorded 7 February 1831.

387. MATILDA ROBERTS--of Lynchburg; 10 February 1829; 3 January
      1831. To CHRISTOPHER ANTHONY--one-sixth of estate from will
of deceased father, JONATHAN LYNCH; also what is due me on mother's
death--as trustee of my son, SAMUEL ROBERTS, wife, children and
future ones. Daughter, MARY ANN MAYSE and heirs. Son, CHRISTOPHER
ROBERTS; daughter, MATILDA BIGGARS, wife of ABRAM F. BIGGARS--
ANTHONY as trustee--her children. I bought interest from BIGGARS--
his wife's--in estate of my deceased husband, ENOCH ROBERTS--
reference to deed--in trust. Daughter, ELIZABETH ROBERTS and heirs.
Son, GEORGE E. ROBERTS and heirs. Executors: ANTHONY and CHRISTOPHER
ROBERTS. Witnesses: WILLIAM DAVIS, JR., EDWARD LYNCH, THOMAS H.
ROBERTS.

389. LOWRY GREGORY--JESSE RICHESON, administrator, 4 October 1830;
      shrouding clothes--$8.07; land sold in Pittsylvania. $241.23.
Recorded Monday, 7 February 1831. CHARLES L. BARRET, commissioner.

392. WILLIAM NORVELL--Monday, 1 November 1830; see previous items
      as to several administrators: $22,273.65½. FORTUNATUS
SYDNOR, commissioner. Recorded 8 January 1831.

397. ENOCH ROBERTS--WILLIAM DAVIS, JR., administrator; from 2 February
      1829; to GEORGE E. ROBERTS, MATILDA ROBERTS; many rentals:
$3186.00; JONATHAN R. D. PAYNE, AMMON HANCOCK. Recorded Wednesday,
7 March 1831.

399. JOSEPH ECHOLS--ELIZA F. ECHOLS, administratrix from 31 January
      1829; JONATHAN HOLLINS and MARTIN W. DAVENPORT; postage on
Church Advocate; family expenses to New Haven; very long; $3891.37.
Recorded Monday, 7 February 1831.

404. CHARLES Y. JOHNSON's infants--JAMES JONES, guardian, 7 February
      1831; JONATHAN HOLLINS, ALEXANDER LIGGAT, JONATHAN BOYD.
Reports from various dates in 1829 for wards: MARTHY ANN, THOMAS
and MARY JOHNSON. Recorded Monday, 7 February 1831.

407. HARRIET, EDWARD, ROBERT JOSEPH and JONATHAN ECHOLS--guardian
      account by ELIZA F. ECHOLS, 3 January 1831: JONATHAN HOLLINS
and MARTIN W. DAVENPORT. From 26 November 1828; trip from Richmond
to New Haven Fountain Tavern; very interesting data; learning to
paint and set paints; MRS. WHITE for tuition; singing and music
lessons; one book--CHARLES; tuition in French; tooth brush--75
cents; eating sometimes at MISS LINE's; tooth powder, candy crackers
and mug box; expenses at North River in 1830; MR. DWIGHT for
tuition--$76.34. 7 February 1831.

421. EBENEZER F. GARDNER--JOSHUA R. HOLMES, administratory, by
      DAVID G. MURRELL, from 16 October 1830; expenses to Pattonsburg;
to JAMES H. GARDNER--$546.94. Recorded Monday, 7 February 1831.

These follow the usual pattern of my marriage data. The names of females appear and the groomsmen follow and data is in latter items. It will be noted that some bear return data as well, but not all have this material in the register. Some items were found in back of Deed Book A and bonds in register.

NANCY B. ACRE--WILLIAM DINWIDDIE

REBECCA W. ACRE--WILLIAM D. WRIGHT

2. (Denotes page in register) 12 April 1808. BENJAMIN ADAM and HANNAH LONG, of age. Security: WILLIAM JACKSON.

HANNAH ADAMS--BENJAMIN WHITESIDES

17. 9 December 1819. ABSALOM AILSTOCK and POLLY MASON. LAWRENCE MASON was her father. Security: JAMES TURNER.

31. 4 December 1827. THOMAS ALDRIDGE and JENNET SCOTT. Security: ROBERT L. COLEMAN. 113 return on same day by WILLIAM S. REID.

15. 11 December 1818. JAMES S. ALLEN and ELIZABETH BYARD, daughter of JONATHAN BYARS (sic). Securities: JOSEPH BOYCE, S. JOHNSON. 110 return of December 17 by WILLIAM S. REID.

JUDITH (JUDAH) ANDERSON--LUKE STEWART

MARTHA J. ANDERSON--VINCENT BAILEY

13. 22 December 1817. ROBERT S. ANDREWS and ELLANA THOMPSON; daughter of DAVID THOMPSON--also security.

8. 8 December 1813. SAMUEL ANTHONY and MARY IRVINE, daughter of ANN F. IRVINE. Security: E. B. NORVELL.

9. 19 April 1815. BENJAMIN ARMSTRONG and PRISSY EVANS, of age; daughter of ANN EVANS. Securities: JONATHAN MATTHEW, JONATHAN MOORHEAD, POWEL HUFF.

SARAH ANN ARMSTRONG--HENRY NORRIS

21. 14 November 1822. HECTOR ATKISON and SARAH W. FRANKLIN, daughter of SUSANNAH FRANKLIN, also her guardian.

MARY ANN BABSON--JORDAN MERCHANT

ELIZA A. BAILEY--ROBERT ORR

MARY J. BAILEY--WILLIAM H. LYDICK

SARAH BAILEY--EDMUND PATE

23. 22 December 1823. VINCENT BAILEY and MARTHA J. ANDERSON. HENRY F. BEAUMONT was her guardian and security.

MARY B. BALDWIN--WILLIAM W. DONAGHE

SALLY HENRY BALLANGER--JAMES CHEWNING

SUSAN BALLANGER--MACE PENDLETON

MARY BALLARD--JONATHAN LEAK

EDA BARNETT--FRANK FREEMAN

28. 20 December 1826. WILLIAM BARNETT and MARTHA ANN A. BROWN,
     under 21; daughter of ARCHER BROWN. Security: LEWIS GREGORY,
SIMEON FLESHMAN. 112 return on same day by CALEB LEACH.

4. 29 December 1810. CHARLES BARTLETT, free mulatto, and NANCY
    JONES, indentured servant of THOMAS HUMPHREYS. Her mother
was AMY JONES. Security was JONATHAN GOWING or GOING.

SARAH H. BAUGH--CHARLES M. GILLIAM

ELIZABETH BEAUMONT--THOMAS FERGUSON

FRANCES BECKHAM--SAMUEL YOUNG

30. 23 June 1827. JESSE L. BECKHAM and BETSY KIDD; JONATHAN KIDD,
     guardian. Securities: JONATHAN KIDD and WILLIAM DIGGES.
Page 113 has return for her as BETSY HEATH on same day by JONATHAN
WEBB.

15. 15 July 1818. GEORGE BELL and SUSANNA DODD, of age.
     Securities: WILLIAM I. ISBELL and P. CREASY.

2. 12 May 1808. JONATHAN BELL and BETSY (ELIZABETH) O. NEAL.
    Consent of B. ESSEX. Securities: JONATHAN THURMON and
JONATHAN MASON.

27. 23 October 1826. WILLIAM A. BENNETT and ELIZA JANE MORTON.
     Securities: JONATHAN VICTOR, ELIZABETH BARNETT, WILLIAM
SUMPTER. 112 return on 2 November by CALEB LEACH.

MARTHA A. BERNARD--JOSHUA R. HOLMES

MARY P. BERNARD--JONATHAN HANCOCK

18. 22 September 1821. A. F. BIGGERS and MATILDA ROBERTS, of
     age. Securities: AMMON HANCOCK, THOMAS H. ROBERTS.

MARY BINGHAM--HENRY MEREDITH

31. 17 December 1827. WILLIAM BISHOP and LAVINIA R. SCHOOLFIELD,
     daughter of BENJAMIN SCHOOLFIELD. Security: DAVID H. BISHOP.
113 return on same day by WILLIAM S. REID.

25. 17 March 1825. WASHINGTON BLUNT and MARGARET THOMPSON.
     Security: DAVID THOMPSON. 112 MR--same (this means Marriage
return on same date)--WILLIAM S. REID.

20. 24 June 1822. ASA P. BOALEY and ELIZABETH FEARE, daughter of
     ANN FEARE. Security: NELSON HUGHES.

ANNE MARIAH BOBSON--CHARLES MSITH

LAVINIA BOBSON--THOMAS HENRY

24. 26 October 1824. PRESLEY BOLEY and ANN FEAR. Security:
     PARHAM A. BOLEY, LEWIS GREGORY. 112 marriage return on same
date; ELI BALL, Baptist Church, Henrico County. In most cases,
BALL styles himself as pastor of Lynchburg Baptist Church.

2. 4 February 1808. JONATHAN BOLLING and PATIENCE LAIN, of
    age. Security: STEPHEN FARMER.

MARY B. BOOKER--DOLPHIN DREW

MARY ANN BOTNER--JONATHAN W. STEVENS

27. 20 April 1826. JAMES BOYD and ANN MARIA ROHR; PHILIP ROHR,
     guardian and security. 112 marriage return on same date;
CALEB LEACH, JAMES C. BOYD here.

32. 19 February 1828. JONATHAN BOYD and HARRIET HENDERSON.
     Security: THOMAS JONES.

     ANN P. BRANSFORD--JONATHAN H. TYREE

     MARY F. BRENT--TIPTON B. HARRISON

     MARY ANN BRIDGLAND--RICHARD LIGGON

9.   13 April 1815. DAVID BRIGGS and SUSAN STARKES, of age.
     Security: CALEB TAIT, JR., ROBERT--illegible.

11. 30 September 1818. BENJAMIN BROWDER and POLLY HUBBARD, of
     age. Security: JONATHAN MEHAFFEY, GEORGE MACKEY (?).

     ANGELINIA M. BROWN--JONATHAN B. OTEY

14. 2 May 1818. ARCHER BROWN and MARY FLESHMAN. Security:
     ROBERT GANNAWAY, ALLEN S. FLESHMAN.

22. 18 November 1823. F. F. BROWN and HANNAH ANN MITCHELL.
     Wife: ROBERT MORRIS, father--so evidently she was a widow.
Security: JAMES L. CLAYTOR, WILL MITCHELL, JR. 111 marriage
return on same date: WILLIAM S. REID.

13. 7 October 1817. HENRY BROWN and ELIZA TWOPENCE. USLEY ELLIS
     was bride's mother. Security: EDMUND ELLIS.

20. 19 February 1822. HENRY BROWN, JR. and ELEANOR C. L. CARTER,
     daughter of CHARLES CARTER. Security: GEORGE TUCKER, D. S.
TUCKER. 111 marriage return on same date--WILLIAM S. REID.

     MARTHA ANN A. BROWN--WILLIAM BARNETT

     SARAH L. BROWN--SAMUEL J. WIATT

16. 22 December 1818. ORRAN W. BRUNSON and SUSANNAH BONDURANT.
     Security: ISRAEL SNEAD.

12. 10 May 1817. JAMES BULLOCK and ISABELLA HUMPHREYS, daughter
     of THOMAS HUMPHREYS. Security: JONATHAN WALKER, JONATHAN
CASKIE.

4.   19 July 1810. JONATHAN BULLOCK and LUCY NORVILL. Security:
     PETER DUDLEY.

     SUSANNAH BONDURANT--ORRAN W. BRUNSON

24. 3 November 1824. SAMUEL BURCH and MAHALA PURYEAR. Security:
     W. L. LAMBETH, JONATHAN S. LEE.

     AMANDA BURD--WILLIAM PATTERSON

     ANN BURD--JONATHAN G. SHELTON

     EVELINA BURD--RICHARD S. TILDEN

     MARY ANN BURFORD--GEORGE COCKRAN

32. 24 January 1828. JOSEPH BUTCHER and MARGARETT OLDHOUSAN(M).
     Security: JONATHAN IRVIN.

     ELIZABETH BYARD--JAMES S. ALLEN

     ABBY W. BYRD--PHILLIP W. JACKSON

     ANNA O. BYRD--JAMES L. WRIGHT

     ELIZABETH BYRD--ALEXANDER TOMPKINS

EVELYN BYRD--QUARLES TOMPKINS

14. 25 April 1818. PAYTON BYRD and POLLY WILSON, a woman of
     color. Security: RICHARD CHAPMAN, JONATHAN WILLS, THOMAS
BUNTING.

ELIZABETH A. CABELL--WILLIAM R. PRESTON

26. 6 December 1825. MAYO CABELL and MARY CORNELIA DANIEL.
     Security: WILLIAM DANIEL. 112 marriage return on December 8th;
groom is noted as being from Nelson County; WILLIAM S. REID.

PAULINA J. CABELL--WILLIAM DANIEL

31. 31 December 1827. WILLIAM LEWIS CABELL and ELIZA B. DANIEL.
     Security: WILLIAM DANIEL. 113 marriage return on same date;
WILLIAM S. REID.

30. 3 September 1827. CHALRES CALBOUN and MARGARET E. TODD,
     daughter of CHRISTOPHER TODD. Security: W. DIGGS. 113
marriage return on same date; WILLIAM S. REID.

 9. 18 October 1815. JONATHAN CALLAWAY and NANCY GRAHAM--21 last
     April. Security: JONATHAN RICHARDSON.

NANCY CALLAWAY--JONATHAN W. MAHONE

SALLY CAMM--BENJAMIN A. DONALD

ELEANOR CAMPBELL--MILBY COTTONHAM

MARY CAMM--WILLIAM L. SAUNDERS

30. 17 October 1827. HENRY CARLTON and ANTIONETTE E. NEWHALL,
     daughter of JAMES NEWHALL. Security: AMBROSE CARLTON, JAMES S.
KEANE. 114 marriage return on same date: F. G. SMITH.

MARY CARROLL--ROBERT WHITE

ELEANOR C. L. CARTER--HENRY BROWN, JR.

ELIZABETH H. CHANDLER--WILLIAM PHAUP

25. 16 December 1824. JAMES CHEWNING and SALLY HENRY BALLANGER.
     Security: SAMUEL L. DAVIS.

MAHALA CLARK--WILLIAM MORTON

20. 21 January 1822. SAMUEL CLAYTOR and ROSANNA ELIZA MURRELL,
     daughter of JONATHAN MURRELL. Security: JAMES L. CLAYTOR.
111 marriage return on same date:

ELIZABETH ANN CLOPTON--WILLIAM J. HALCOMBE

HARRIET M. COCKE--CHARLES REYNOLDS

MARTHA COCKE--SIMEON ROBINSON

 6. 15 February 1812. GEORGE COCKRAM and MARY ANN BURFORD,
     daughter of DANIEL BURFORD. Security: JONATHAN and JOSEPH
DAVIS.

MARTHA ANN CODIL--GEORGE SMITH

26. 21 April 1825. JOSEPH COHEN and ARDELLA D. KIDD. Security:
     WILLIAM KIDD, JAMES BENAGH. 112 marriage return 25 April;
ELI BALL, Lynchburg Baptist--ARDELIA O. here.

Deed Book A--30 November 1809. THOMAS COHEN and POLLY W.
HEATH by SAMUEL (?) JENNINGS. Page 3 of register: same
date--WILLIAM HEATH as father of bride. Security: GEORGE W. RONALD.
109 marriage return same date; SAMUEL K. JENNINGS.

28. 5 December 1826. JOSIAH COLE and MRS. SUSANNA WALLACE.
Security: JONATHAN VICTOR. 112 marriage return December 7th;
CALEB LEACH.

25. 22 December 1824. ROBERT W. COLLINS and MAHALA FOWLER,
daughter of JANE FOWLER. Security: JONATHAN S. OGLESBY,
JOSEPH H. DUIGUID.

ELIZABETH COMPTON--LEWIS GREEN

2. 7 June 1807. ARCHIBALD COOPER and JUDITH DAVIS. Security:
DANIEL JACKSON, PLEASANT COSBY.

9. 15 April 1815. ARCHIBALD COOPER and MARY WRIGHT, of age.
Security: GEORGE COCKRAN, B. SCHOOLFIELD.

12. 7 March 1817. MILBY COTTONHAM and ELEANOR CAMPBELL; here
guardian was MRS. MARGARET CAMPBELL. Security: ANTHONY NORTH.

CATHERINE CRUMPTON--CHARLES PERROW

ELIZABETH R. CURLE--JESSE L. PERRY

SALLY A. CURLE--JONATHAN HOCKADAY

109. 1 January 1814. CHISWELL DABNEY and MARTHA ANN NORVEL

18. 4 October 1821. JONATHAN B. DABNEY and ELIZABETH L. TOWLES,
daughter of OLIVER TOWLES, JR. Security: JONATHAN F. WIATT.
111 marriage return on same date; WILLIAM S. REID.

POLLY DABNEY--MOSES MAYO

13. 16 December 1817. ALEXANDER S. DANDRIDGE and SALLY L. DUFFELL,
daughter of JAMES DUFFELL. Security: JONATHAN R. D. PAYNE.

20. 6 June 1822. LANDON DANGERFIELD and CATHERINE STONERER
(STONER). Security: JACOB MAJORS, WILLIAM MERCHANT, MARY
ANN STONER.

ELIZA B. DANIEL--WILLIAM LEWIS CABELL

MARY CORNELIA DANIEL--MAYO CABELL

27. 31 January 1826. WILLIAM DANIEL and PAULINA J. CABELL.
Security: MAYO and SARAH CABELL. 112 marriage return on
same date: F. G. SMITH.

BETSY DAVIDSON--JONATHAN S. LAINE

26. 21 July 1825. JONATHAN DAVIDSON and ANNA TALBOT. Security:
JESSE DAVIS. 113 marriage return on same date: JONATHAN WEBB.

15. 22 July 1818. HOWL DAVIES and HARRIET T. GODFREY. Security:
JAMES BENAGH. 110 marriage return on same date; WILLIAM S.
REID--HARRIET J. here.

21. 30 September 1822. HOWELL DAVIES and ABBY W. JACKSON.
Security: ALEXANDER TOMPKINS. 111 marriage return on same
date: WILLIAM S. REID.

CHARITY DAVIS--JOEL VANDEL

6. 20 February 1812. JONATHAN DAVIS and ANNE JENNINGS. Security:
JAMES WARWICK, JONATHAN FOWLER, CHRISTOPHER FOWLER.

JUDITH DAVIS--ARCHIBALD COOPER

MARY MATILDA DAVIS--HOBSON JOHNS

NANCY DAVIS--PETER DUDLEY

POLLY DAVIS--CORNELIUS PIERCE. I should point out that I
recognize many Amherst names in these items. I imagine that
folk living in southern end of Amherst found it better to go across
the river to "Town," as Amherst people usually call Lynchburg. The
roads were bad and it was a good distance to Amherst Courthouse.
CORNELIUS PIERCE shows in data in Amherst.

DELILAH P. DAWSON--LORENZO D. LAIN

15. 10 August 1818. JAMES DEANE and POLLY WHITESIDE, daughter of
BENJAMIN WHITESIDE--also security.

MARY B. DEANE--ROBERT GANNAWAY

MARY DETTO--WILLIAM TARDY

32. 28 May 1828. THOMAS W. DEVAM and CATHERINE M. GILLIAM,
daughter of C. GILLIAM. Security: ARCHIBALD LEWIS.

22. 13 May 1823. CHARLES L. DIBRELL and MARY JANE LAMBETH,
daughter of M. LAMBETH. Security: JOSEPH ECHOLS, ABRAM R.
NORTH. 111 marriage return on same date: WILLIAM S. REID. The
DIBRELL family also shows in Amherst and some of them went to Wayne
County, Kentucky. A CHARLES DIBRELL took up land there sometime
after 1800, but I can't say that it is the same man in this bond.
One is referred to the fine history of Wayne County, Kentucky, by
AUGUSTA PHILLIPS JOHNSON--1939. I am in possession of this volume
on a county in my native state of Kentucky.

FRANCES W. DIBRELL--WILLIAM W. HENDRICK

10. 18 January 1816. JAMES WATSON DIBBREL and LETITIA PERKINS,
her guardian was RICHARD PERKINS. Security: WILLIAM B.
LYNCH, D. SAUNDERS, JR., BOOKER SHELTON.

MARTHA R. DIBRELL--EZEKIEL B. GILBERT

27. 12 January 1826. WILLIAM W. DICKERSON and SARAH LIGGON.
Security: LEWIS GREGORY, SAMUEL SCHOOLFIELD.

21. 10 December 1822. THOMAS DILLARD and MARY H. PATTESON.
Security: DAVID R. EDLEY, J. J. SALMONS.

17. 2 May 1820. WILLIAM DINWIDDIE and NANCY B. ACRE, daughter
of DAVID ACRE. Security: WILLIAM STEEN.

SUSANNA DODD--GEORGE BELL

LUCINDY F. DOIL (DOYLE)--JAMES C. FISHBACK

19. 8 October 1821. WILLIAM W. DOUGLAS--error DONAGHE and
MARY B. BALDWIN, daughter of CORNELIUS BALDWIN of Frederick
County. Security: WILLIAM DANIEL, JONATHAN G. AFFLICK, ROBERT
MILLER (?).

23. 31 March 1824. BENJAMIN A. DONALD and SALLY CAMM, daughter
of ELIZABETH CAMM. Secruity: HOWSON S. WHITE, ROBERT CAMM.
111 marriage return on same date; WILLIAM S. REID; noted that groom
is of Bedford Cpunty.

MARY ANN DONALD--JAMES HOLMES

CATHERIN DOYLE--MICAJAH WATERFIELD

ELIZABETH A. DOYLE--LINDSEY SHOEMAKER

LUCINDY F. DOYLE (DOIL)--JAMES C. FISHBACK

23. 2 February 1824. DOLPHIN DREW and MARY B. BOOKER, daughter
of PETER E. BOOKER. Security: JAMES H. DUIGUID.

8. 12 January 1814. PETER DUDLEY and NANCY DAVIS. Security:
WILLIAM HARRISON, WILLIAM B. LYNCH.

CAROLINE DUFFEL--JONATHAN HALSEY

DEBORAH W. DUFFEL--ISAAC GREGORY

MATILDA DUFFELL--BENJAMIN WILKS

SALLY L. DUFFELL--ALEXANDER S. DANDRIDGE

17. 27 December 1820. HENRY DUNNINGTON and MARY E. P. LENTZ.
Security: MILES CARY. 111 marriage return on same date:
JONATHAN S. LEE.

29. 8 January 1827. JAMES H. DUIGUID and SALLY W. SNEAD,
daughter of EVAN SNEAD. Security: THOMAS G. and JONATHAN
FOWLER.

29. 8 January 1827. THOMAS J. DUVAL and ELIZABETH STEVENS,
JAMES L. (?) STEVENS was her guardian. Security: SETH
HALSEY. 113 marriage return on 17 January 1827 by WILLIAM S. REID.

ELIZABETH M. EARL--JONATHAN FARNSWORTH

MARY ANN EARL--GEORGE GREGORY

33. 11 September 1828. DAVID R. EDLEY and MISSOURI MORRISS,
daughter of DABNEY MORRISS. Security: JONATHAN WILLS.
114 marriage return 16 September; F. G. SMITH.

23. 10 April 1823. PETER ELLIOTT and MARY GODFREY. Security:
EDWARD BROWN.

ANN MARIA ELLIS--CHARLES YOUNG

11. 30 December 1818. EDMUND ELLIS and USLEY TUPPENCE. Security:
JAMES TUPPENCE, PETER BOWLES.

MARY ENGLAND--ALEXANDER SWAN

ELIZA ESSEX--MADAD LYMAN

27. 24 June 1826. JONATHAN EVANS and JUDY JENKINS. Security:
TARLTON JAMES.

PRISSY EVANS--BENJAMIN ARMSTRONG

24. 22 June 1824. JONATHAN FARNSWORTH and ELIZABETH M. EARL.
Security: JONATHAN VICTOR, GEORGE N. GREGORY.

ANN FEAR--PRESLEY BOLEY

ELIZABETH FEARE--AAS P. BOALEY

BITHA FIELDS--LAMMER MERCHANT

NANCY FINCH--WILLIAM HOWARD

21. 22 August 1822. MILES FINNEY and PEGGY GUINEA. Security:
CHESLEY YOUNG, WILLIAM MERCHANT.

Deed Book A, 15 December 1818. Some data shows 1811.
JAMES C. FISHBACK and LUCINDY F. DOIL--by F. KABLER. 5
14 December 1811 and DAVID DOYLE was father and security; 109
marriage return on December 15th by KABLER--1811.

MARY FLESHMAN--ARCHER BROWN

REBECCA FOE--THOMAS WILKINS

MARY FORE--ROBERT MARTIN

ELIZA FOWLER--WILLIAM ROBINSON

MAHALA FOWLER--ROBERT W. COLLINS

SARAH S. FOWLER--FREDERICK HICKEY

SARAH W. FRANKLIN--HECTOR ATKINSON

14. 24 March 1818. WILLIAM C. FRANKLIN and LUCY MAYS. Security:
NIMROD DONALD, WILLIAM FEATHERSTONE.

2. 8 October 1808. FRANK FREEMAN and EDE BARNETT, of age.
Security: FRANK FREEMAN, WILLIAM JOHNSON.

10. 8 December 1815. ROBERT FRENCH and ELIZABETH MARTIN, of
age. Security: DAVID CAMPBELL, WILL W. NORVELL.

20. 9 May 1822. THOMAS FERGUSON and ELIZABETH BEAUMONT.
Security: CHARLES W. BEAUMONT, HENRY F. BEAUMONT. 111 marriage
return on same date; WILLIAM S. REID.

29. 21 March 1827. GEORGE W. GAINES and ELIZA NORVELL. Security:
MITCHELL V. WATTS. 113 marriage return on 22 March; EDWARD
CANNON.

MARTHA F. GAINES (GOING)--WILLIAM KENDALL LEE

9. 27 September 1815. ROBERT GANNAWAY and MARY B. DEANE.
Security: JESSE L. PETTY.

16. 2 June 1819. WARREN GANNAWAY and ELIZABETH SNEAD, daughter
of WILLIAM SNEAD. Security: JESSE L. PERRY.

Deed Book A, 4 December 1805. JONATHAN GARRETT and ANN
WHITTENTON--signed by WILLIAM P. MARTIN. 1 Same dates--both
of age. Security: WILLIAM P. MARTIN, ROBERT C. SCOTT. 109 marriage
return on same date; WILLIAM P. MARTIN.

6. 19 May 1812. GEORGE GATEWOOD and BETSY TUPPENCE. ELIZABETH
DOUGLAS makes aff. that GEORGE is a free man of age. Security:
CHARLES BARTLETT, JONATHAN JOHNSON.

SARAH GEORGE--WILLIAM W. WILLIAMS

30. 28 June 1827. JAMES M. GILLIAM and MARGARET LILLY. Security:
ARCHIBALD LEWIS.

28. 2 November 1826. EZEKIEL B. GILBERT and MARTHA R. DIBRELL
of age. Security: ARCHIBALD HATCHER, CHARLES L. DIBRELL.
If memory serves me correctly, EZEKIEL B. GILBERT was a doctor in
Amherst, but I won't guarantee it from memory.

CATHERINE M. GILLIAM--THOMAS W. DEVAM

33. 30 June 1828. CHARLES M. GILLIAM and SARAH H. BAUGH, of
age. Security: GEORGE L. JOHNSON.

HARRIET J. (T) GODFREY--HOWEL DAVIES

MARY GODFREY--PETER ELLIOTT

MARTHA F. GOING or GAINES--WILLIAM KENDALL LEE

PAULINA GOING--LUKE VALENTINE

JANE GOSS--WILLIAM KIRBY

SALLY GOSS--WILLIAM JOHNSON

16. 17 August 1819. HENRY R. GOULDEN and LUCINDA ANN ROHR; her
guardian was WILLIAM STEEN and security. 110 marriage return
by WILLIAM S. REID and groom is GOULDER here; same date.

ELLENDER GRAHAM--JONATHAN RICHARDSON

32. 5 March 1828. FONTAINE GRAHAM and MARTHA JAMES WATSON.
Security: ARCH. HATCHER. 114 marriage return on same
date; WILLIAM S. REID.

NANCY GRAHAM--JONATHAN CALLAWAY

NANCY GRALEY--THOMAS H. LUCAS

14. 11 May 1818. WILLIAM GRAVES and LEATHY STARKES, of age.
Security: BENJAMIN BROWDER.

21. 17 December 1822. ROBERT H. GRAY and JANE JORDAN, daughter
of J. JORDAN. Security: GEORGE W. ROBERTS.

24. 14 July 1824. GEORGE GREGORY and MARY ANN EARL. Security:
JONATHAN VICTOR, WILLIAM SUMPTER.

8. 30 March 1814. ISAAC GREGORY and DEBORAH W. DUFFEL, daughter
of JAMES DUFFEL. Security: E. B. NORVELL.

29. 10 May 1827. LEWIS GREEN and ELIZABETH COMPTON, daughter
of SARAH COMPTON. Security: DANIEL B. PERROW.

ELIZABETH J. GRIFFIN--HARRY (HARVY) MITCHELL

RHODA GRIFFITH--ISHAM SCRUGGS

ELIZABETH GRIFFY (AY)--HENRY WRIGHT

POLLY GRIFFEY--EDWIN D. MEREDITH

SUSANNA GRIFFY--SOLOMON MORGAN

PEGGY GUINEA--MILES FINNEY

MILLY GUTHREY--BENJAMIN VAWTER

MARY ELIZABETH GWATKINS--JOSEPH E. ROYALL   (These are reversed)

ANN M. GWATHMY--WILLIAM MORGAN

28. 24 October 1826. LEVIN B. HAGERMAN and FRANCES THOMPSON,
daughter of DAVID THOMPSON. Security: ANDREW B. THOMPSON.
111 marriage return on same date; WILLIAM S. REID.

16. 10 February 1819. WILLIAM J. HALCOMBE and ELIZA ANN CLOPTON,
grand-daughter of JAMES WARWICK. Security: JAMES L. ROYALL,
JAMES BENAGH. 110 marriage return on same date; WILLIAM S. REID;
groom of Powhatan County.

21. 18 July 1822. HENRY HALL and CATHERINE W. TOMPKINS.
Security: JONATHAN H. PATTERSON, L. D. TOMPKINS.

SALLY HALLEY--JAMES ROBERTS

ELIZA H. HALSEY--CHRISTOPHER MC IVER

21.   30 July 1822. JONATHAN HALSEY and CAROLINE DUFFEL, daughter
      of EDWARD DUFFEL. Security: JONATHAN HOLLINS.

REBECCA HAMAN--GEORGE WALKER

21.   24 September 1822. JONATHAN HANCOCK and MARY P. BERNARD,
      daughter of MARTHA BERNARD. Security: JOSHUA R. HOLMES,
V. J. BAILEY.

ELIZABETH C. HARDWICK--ROBERT WATKINS

MARY E. HARDWICH--WILLIS B. HOPE

12.   15 April 1817. FRANCIS P. HARRIS and REBECCA ANN SUMPTER,
      of age. Security: WILLIAM and MARTHA SUMPTER. This explains
remarks of HARRIS in his will--see Book A. I have indicated that
I think that HARRIS took his own life from tenor of the will.

26.   24 June 1825. WILLIAM D. HARRIS and AREANNA B. JEFFREYS,
      daughter of PERMELIA JEFFREYS. Security: JOSEPH JEFFREYS,
ELIZABETH TOWNSLEY.

ANN MARIA HARRISON--WILLIAM WIATT NORVELL

MARTHA ANN NICHOLAS HARRISON--JAMES PENN

MARTHA J. HARRISON--ROBERT ROBINSON

18.   28 June 1821. TIPTON B. HARRISON and MARY F. BRENT, of age.
      Security: JONATHAN F. WIATT, MARY WOODROW. 111 marriage
return on same date; WILLIAM S. REID.

3.   17 July 1809. JOSEPH V. HARNICK and NANCY JOHNSON, daughter
      of CHARLES JOHNSON. Security: JONATHAN Y. JOHNSON, WILLIAM
COX.

LUZEA HASKINS--WILLIAM OLIVER

31.   29 December 1827. GILBERT HAYTH and ELIZABETH RUCKER,
      daughter of REUBEN RUCKER. Security: ISAAC M. and JANE E.
RUCKER.

8.   11 August 1814. JONATHAN HAYTH and SUSAN NICHOLS. Security:
      JOSEPH NICHOLS.

15.   24 June 1818. THOMAS HAYTH and MARY RAMSEY, of age. Security:
      SAMUEL P. RAMSEY.

BETSY HEATH (or KIDD, see bond and return)--JESSE L. BECKHAM

PATSY B. HEATH--THOMAS STEPHENS

POLLY W. HEATH--THOMAS COHEN

HARRIET HENDERSON--JONATHAN BOYD

33.   1 May 1828. WILLIAM W. HENDRICK, Buckingham County, and
      FRANCES W. DIBRELL. Security: ARCH. HATCHER.

18.   27 June 1821. THOMAS HENRY and LAVINIA BOBSON, daughter of
      LUCY BOBSON. Security: JAMES BOBSON.

24.   18 October 1824. FREDERICK HICKEY and SARAH S. FOWLER,
      daughter of JANE FOWLER. Security: JONATHAN S. OGLESBY,
WILLIAM C. ROBERTSON.

PEGGY HIGGINS--CHARLES T. (L) SNEAD

4. 19 January 1811. CALEB HILL and BETSY MATTHEWS, daughter of LUCY MATTHEWS. Security: JACK MATTHEWS.

PEGGY HILL--WILLIAM JACKSON

27. 20 March 1826. ANDREW M. HINCHIE and EMELINE VASS, formerly of Bath County. Security: JAMES IRVINE.

9. 12 January 1815. JAMES M. HITE and CAROLINE MATILDA IRVINE, daughter of ANN F. IRVINE who shows as her guardian; parent inferred. Security: CORNELIUS BALDWIN, JR.

12. 9 July 1817. JONATHAN HOCKADAY and SALLY A. CURLE, daughter of JONATHAN CURLE. Security: SAMUEL C. TYREE, R. TYREE.

27. 23 September 1826. ARTHUR HOLCOMBE and ADDELINE SCOTT--free woman of color; daughter of JOSEPH SCOTT. Security: PEYTON BURD, D. RODES, GEORGE H. WINDEMEYER.

Deed Book A. JACOB HOLLAY and CHARLOTTE MC GEORGE, November 25, 1806; WILLIAM P. MARTIN. 1. 19 November 1806. Security: LAWRENCE MC GEORGE, father of bride, JONATHAN WHITTENTON, GREGORY BROXSOM. 109 marriage return on 25th by WILLIAM P. MARTIN.

SALLY HOLLAY--JAMES ROBERTS

19. 28 November 1821. JAMES HOLMES and MARY ANN DONALD, daughter of JONATHAN O. (D) DONNELL (sic). Security: COLEN M. PERRY, B. FOWENS. 111 marriage return on same date: WILLIAM S. REID, DONALD here.

23. 18 February 1824. JOSHUA R. HOLMES and MARTHA A. BERNARD, daughter of MARTHA BERNARD. Security: DAVID R. EDLEY, ELIZABETH BERNARD. 112 marriage return on same date: ELI BALL, Lynchburg Baptist Church. Just below is return by BALL wherein he styles himself of Henrico County. SEMPLE does not mention BALL in his work on Virginia Baptists, but RYLAND has a number of items on a man by this name. He states in one place that he came from New England in 1823 so it may be another man. MAURICE GRISSOM, pastor of First Baptist Church, Lynchburg, is now in a revival with us--April, 1969, and I shall ask him what he knows of BALL.

33. 8 July 1828. WILLIS B. HOPE and MARY E. HARDWICK, daughter of J. V. HARDWICK. Security: JONATHAN W. DOREAN, JONATHAN GILLASPIE. 114 marriage return on same date: WILLIAM S. REID.

2. 19 June 1807. WILLIAM HOWARD and NANCY FINNCH. SW: JONATHAN FINCH. Error: bride is FINCH.

POLLY HUBBARD--BENJAMIN BROWDER

ELEANOR W. HUDGINS--JAMES SIMPSON

12. 10 April 1817. DAVID HUDSON and CAROLINE MATILDA LANE. Security: WYATT HYNES.

7. 2 April 1813. NELSON HUGHES and POLLY (MARY) OWENS. Security: GEORGE MITCHELL, EDMOND WHITNEY.

7. 15 July 1813. JONATHAN HUGHEY and PEGGY WAGGONER. Security: MARTIN WAGGONER.

ANN JANE HUMPHREYS--WILLIAM B. LYNCH

ISABELLA HUMPHREYS--JAMES BUXLLOCK (BULLOCK)

ANN ELIZA IRVINE--JONATHAN N. PLEASANTS

CAROLINE MATILDA IRVINE--JAMES M. HITE

FRANCES M. IRVINE--DR. JONATHAN H. PATTESON

MARY IRVINE--SAMUEL ANTHONY

ELIZABETH B. IVESON--SAMUEL NOWLIN

9. 8 November 1815. PHILIP W. JACKSON and ABBY W. BYRD, daughter
    of ANN BYRD. Security: ALEXANDER TOMPKINS, RICHARD B. WILLIAMS.
Note: ANNA for mother.

5. 24 December 1811. WILLIAM JACKSON and PEGGY HILL, of age;
    daughter of WYONY (?) HILL. Security: JONATHAN ANDERSON,
DANIEL JACKSON.

AREANNA B. JEFFREYS--WILLIAM D. HARRIS

JUDY JENKINS--JONATHAN EVANS

ANNE JENNINGS--JONATHAN DAVIS

26. 13 June 1825. BENJAMIN JENNINGS and ANN ELIZA WRIGHT.
     Security: HENRY WRIGHT.

25. 23 February 1825. HOBSON JOHNS and MARY MATILDA DAVIS,
     daughter of HENRY DAVIS. Security: PAUL JONES. 112 marriage
return 25 February: WILLIAM S. REID.

13. 27 November 1817. JONATHAN F. JOHNS (t) on and POLLY NICHOLS,
     daughter of JOSEPH NICHOLS, also security.

29. 7 June 1829. LILBOURN H. JOHNSON and FRANCES JORDAN. Security:
     HEZEKIAH JORDAN. 113 marriage return on same date: WILLIAM S.
REID.

MAHALA A. JOHNSON--AMBROSE PAGE

MARY JOHNSON--WILLIS SADLER

MILDRED JOHNSON--HENRY STANDLEY

NANCY JOHNSON--JOSEPH V. HARNICK

28. 6 February 1827. RICHARD JOHNSON and NANCY MERCHANT. Security:
     WILLIAM MERCHANT, RICHARD ELLIS. 113 marriage return 9 February:
JONATHAN WEBB.

4. 20 March 1810. WILLIAM JOHNSON and MARY ANN MC COY, of age.
    Security: WILLIAM HEATH.

14. 15 January 1818. WILLIAM JOHNSON and SALLY GOSS, of age,
     daughter of DICEY GOSS. Security: JOSEPH COHEN.

10. 18 April 1816. WILLIAM F. JOHNSON and SALLY MEAD, of age.
     Security: PETER DETTO, EDWARD PRICE.

16. 29 April 1818. EDWARD JONES and ELIZABETH NEEDHAM. Security:
     MILES CAREY, MARY E. P. LETNZ. 110 marriage return on same
date: WILLIAM S. REID.

LUCY JONES--NORBORN M. TALIAFERRO

NANCY JONES--CHARLES BARTLETT

32. 22 January 1828. PAUL JONES and MARY W. WALTON. Security:
     WILLIAM BAILEY, L. B. HOLMES. 114 marriage return on same
date: WILLIAM S. REID.

FRANCES JORDAN--LILBOURN H. JOHNSON

JANE JORDAN--ROBERT H. GRAY

ARDELLIA D. KIDD--JOSEPH COHEN

BETSY KIDD (or HEATH)--JESSE L. BECKHAM

7. 13 January 1813. JONATHAN KIDD and NANCY OLIVER. Security:
    RICHARD OLIVER, GEORGE CLAPSSADDLE.

24. 24 June 1824. WILLIAM KIRBY and JANE GOSS, daughter of DICEY
    GOSS. Security: MATTHEW LEE (SEE?), WILLIAM JOHNSON

19. 7 November 1821. JAMES V. KNIGHT and JOANNA SOWERS; ward of
    PLEASANT PARTIN and security.

29. 28 March 1827. JAMES V. KNIGHT and MAHALA MORTON. Security:
    PLEASANT PARTIN. 114 marriate return 29th March: CALEB LEACH.

19. 18 December 1821. JONATHAN LABBY and HARRIET WILSON, of age.
    Security: PLEASANT PARTIN.

30. 1 October 1827. PHILO LACY and MARY ANN REES. Security:
    JONATHAN REES.

29. 4 April 1827. LORENZO D. LAIN and DELILAH P. DAWSON. Security:
    JACOB DAWSON.

MARTHA LAIN--GEORGE THOMAS

PATIENCE LAIN--JONATHAN BOLLING

29. 3 April 1827. JONATHAN S. LAINE and BETSY DAVIDSON, daughter
    of JACOB DAVIDSON. Security: LORENZO D. LAINE. Note variations
in spelling of LAIN--LAINE is groom's name here.

    Deed Book A. 1 December 1812. JONATHAN F. LAMB and SUSANNA
    TAYLOR; return of 2 January 1812 (sic) by L. K. JENNINGS.
6. 2 January 1812 bond and she was daughter of RICHARDSON TAYLOR.
Security: WILLIAM OWENS, WILLIAM SUMPTER. 109 marriage return on
same day: SAMUEL K. JENNINGS.

MARY JANE LAMBETH--CHARLES L. DIBRELL

22. 3 December 1823. SAMUEL LANCASTER and ANN L. LYNCH, daughter
    of J. LYNCH. Security: CHARLES H. LYNCH. 111 marriage
return on same date: WILLIAM S. REID

CAROLINE MATILDA LANE--DAVID HUDSON

30. 17 November 1827. JONATHAN LEAK and MARY BALLARD. Security:
    ALBON MC DANIEL.

18. 28 March 1821. GRIFFIN L. LECKIE and EMILY S. STEEN, daughter
    of WILLIAM STEEN. Security: JONATHAN T. MASON, JONATHAN W.
SCHOLFIELD. 111 marriage return March 20 (sic): JONATHAN EARLY.

27. 27 June 1826. JONATHAN LECKIE and JANE THOMPSON. Security:
    DAVID THOMPSON. 111 marriage return on same date: WILLIAM S.
REID.

BETSY LEE--JOSEPH SEAY

15. 19 December 1818. WILLIAM KENDALL LEE and MARTHA F. GAINES
    or GOING. Security: SAMUEL NOWLIN. 110 marriage return on
December 23rd: JONATHAN S. LEE--GAINES here. LEE was a Baptist
minister.

28. 3 November 1826. THOMAS LEFTWICH and MARIA WARWICK, daughter
    of WILLIAM WARWICK. Security: HENRY C. WARD.

31

MARY E. P. LENTZ--HENRY DUNNINGTON

NANCY LESTER--ABSALOM SHANKLIN

27. 30 May 1826. JAMES LEVINGSTON and JANE WILLIAMS, daughter of
DANIEL WILLIAMS. Security: HOWARD S. SCHENCK. 111 marriage
return on same date: ELI BALL, Baptist Church of Henrico.

SARAH LEVISTON--FREDERICK WENEDEL

AGNESS H. LEWALLEN--SAMUEL LOVE

ELIZABETH B. LEWALLEN--EDWARD B. WELLS

MARY E. LEWALLEN--ROBERT NICAR

SALLY M. LEWELLIN--MITCHELL V. WATTS

16. 12 May 1819. ALEXANDER LIGGAT and MARY LYNCH. Security:
HENRY CLARK. 110 marriage return on same date: WILLIAM S.
REID.

32. 25 March 1828. RICHARD LIGGON and MARY ANN BRIDGLAND.
Security: ALEXANDER BRIDGLAND.

SARAH LIGGON--WILLIAM W. DICKERSON

MARGARET LILLY--JAMES M. GILLIAM

ANNE C. LIVINGSTON--NICHOLAS P. MOORE

HANNAH LONG--BEN ADAMS

21. 29 October 1822. SAMUEL LOVE and AGNESS H. LEWALLEN,
daughter of CHARLES LEWALLEN; also security.

17. 23 December 1820. THOMAS H. LUCAS and NANCY GRALEY. Security:
HENRY WRIGHT.

29. 10 April 1827. WINSTON H. LUCAS and MARTHA J. SMITH. Security:
SAMUEL BURCH. 113 marriage return on same date: J. L. LEE.

31. 6 December 1827. WILLIAM H. LYDICK and MARY J. BAILEY.
Security: JAMES BAILEY.

33. 25 November 1828. MADAD LYMAN and ELIZA ESSEX, daughter of
B. ESSEX. Security: WILLIAM J. HURSEY. 114 marriage return:
WILLIAM S. REID.

MARY LYNCH--ALEXANDER LIGGAT (out of place)

ANN L. LYNCH--SAMUEL LANCASTER

MATILDA LYNCH--CHARLES A. WATKINS; error: groom is CHARLES A.
WITHERS

10. 14 March 1816. WILLIAM B. LYNCH and ANN JANE HUMPHREYS, daughter
of THOMAS HUMPHRYS. Security: JOSEPH BOYCE, NETHERLAND TAIT.

20. 14 June 1822. JONATHAN W. MAHONE and NANCY CALLAWAY, daughter
of DUDLEY CALLAWAY. Security: DANIEL MAHONE, AMOS THACKER.

MARY MALLORY--EDWARD PRICE

MARY L. MARSHALL--DAVID REES

ELIZABETH MARTIN--ROBERT FRENCH

15. 18 November 1818. ROBERT MARTIN and MARY FORE, of age.
Se 'rity: JAMES BAILEY, SARAH G. ANDERSON.

32

Deed Book A. 24 July 1811. DAVID F. MASON and SEDNEY
SCHOOLFIELD; return 3 October 1818 by JONATHAN M. WEAVER (?).
5. 2 October 1811. SIDNEY here; daughter of B. SCHOOLFIELD.
Security: ROBERT THURMON. 109 marriage return JONATHAN WEAVER,
3 October.

17. 15 February 1820. JONATHAN T. MASON and NANCY T. SCHOOLFIELD,
    daughter of BENJAMIN SCHOOLFIELD. Security: JONATHAN W.
SCHOOLFIELD, BENJAMIN SCHOOLFIELD, JR.

POLLY MASON--ABSALOM AILSTOCK

BETSY MATTHEWS--CALEB HILL

NANCY MAY--FOUNTANE TANKERSLEY

NANCY MAYFIELD--SAMUEL SMALLBRIDGE

Deed Book A. 24 July 1811. MOSES MAYO and POLLY DABNEY;
return on same date by JONATHAN M. WEAVER (?). 5. 23 July
1811. Security: JAMES JAMES. 109 marriage return by JONATHAN
WEAVER on 24th July.

LUCY MAYS--WILLIAM C. FRANKLIN

MARY ANN MC COY--WILLIAM JOHNSON

12. 14 June 1817. ALEXANDER MC DANIEL and NANCY WALLACE, of age.
    Security: WILLIAM SUMPTER, R. A. HARRIS.

CLEOPATRA ALBERTINE MC DANIEL--ABNER WHITTON

CHARLOTTE MC GEORGE--JACOB HOLLAY

MARGARETE MC GEORGE--JONATHAN P. SWINEY

33. 12 November 1828. CHRISTOPHER MC IVER and ELIZA H. HALSEY,
    daughter of WILL A. HALSEY. Security: SETH and JONATHAN
HALSEY. 114 marriage return on same date: ROBERT RYLAND.

MARGARET MC KENZIE--JAMES S. MEDLEY

FANNY MC KINNEY--ALLEN WADE

SALLY MEAD--WILLIAM F. JOHNSON

10. 8 May 1816. JAMES S. (?) MEDLEY and MARGARET MC KINZIE, of
    age. Security: WILLIAM SUMPTER, HUGH BECKHAM.

ANN MEGANN--FLEMING MERRET

26. 20 August 1825. JORDAN MERCHANT and MARY ANN BOBSON. Security:
    ISRAEL BOBSON. 113 marriage return on 24 August: JONATHAN
WEBB.

33. 31 December 1828. LAMMER MERCHANT and BITHAX FIELD. Security:
    LEWIS ELLIS.

NANCY MERCHANT--RICHARD JOHNSON

1. 7 January 1807. EDWIN D. MEREDITH and POLLEY GRIFFEY, of
   age. Security: JAMES GILLIAM, JOSEPH MC CARTY.

13. 23 July 1817. HENRY MEREDITH and MARY BINGHAM. Security:
    GEORGE K. LAMBETH.

16. 13 March 1819. FLEMING MERRET and ANN MEGANN, daughter of
    NANCY MAGANN "father (sic). Security: JONATHAN BURRUS and
E ? M ?

33

7. 5 December 1812. LEWIS MERRIT and ELIZABETH NICHOLS. Security:
    JOSEPH NICHOLS.

22. 25 November 1823. FRANCIS S. MILLER and MARIA M. PERRY,
     daughter of COLLIN M. PERRY. Security: GEORGE T. WILLIAMS,
JONATHAN S. BROWN. 111 marriage return on same date: WILLIAM S.
REID.

12. 12 May 1817. GEORGE W. MITCHELL and SARAH T. VENABLE, daughter
     of A. B. VANABLE. Security: WILLIAM DIGGES, JR.

HANNAH ANN MITCHELL--F. F. BROWN

33. 22 July 1828. HARRY MITCHELL and ELIZABETH H. GRIFFIN; EDMOND
     PATE was her guardian and security. 114 marriage return on
same date; WILLIAM S. REID--HARVY here.

6. 16 April 1812. NICHOLAS P. MOORE and ANN C. LIVINGSTON.
    Security: CALEB TAIT.

10. 8 June 1816. SOLOMON MORGAN and SUSANNA GRIFFY, of age.
     Security: JOSEPH COHEN, BENJAMIN BROWDER.

25. 1 April 1825. WILLIAM MORGAN and ANN M. GWATHMY. Security:
     SAMUEL HANNAH, S. NOWLIN.

MARY H. MOORMAN--ROBERT PATTERSON

15. 30 November 1818. ARCHIBALD MORRIS and MARY JANE TWOPENCE,
     daughter of USLEY ELLIS. Security: EDWARD ELLIS, PETER
POINDEXTER.

MISSOURI MORRIS--DAVID R. EDLEY

ELIZA JANE MORTON--WILLIAM A. BENNETT

MAHALA MORTON--JAMES V. KNIGHT

11. 11 December 1818. WILLIAM MORTON and MAHALA CLARKE, of age.
     Security: PLEASANT PARTIN, MARY PARTIN. 110 marriage return
of 12 December: THOMAS MOORE.

ELIZABETH NEEDHAM--EDWARD JONES

ANTIONETTE E. NEWHALL--HENRY CARLTON

ANN NICAR--JONATHAN PHILLIPS

25. 23 March 1825. ROBERT NICAR and MARY E. LEWALLEN. Security:
     LEWIS GREGORY.

ELIZABETH NICHOLS--LEWIS MERRIT

25. 8 December 1824. JOSEPH NICHOLS and POLLY RAMSEY. Security:
     JONATHAN F. JOHNSON. 111 marriage return on same date:
JONATHAN WEBB.

POLLY NICHOLS--JONATHAN F. JOHNSON (JOHNSTON)

SUSAN NICHOLS--JONATHAN HAYTH

8. 29 December 1814. HENRY NORRIS and SARAH ANN ARMSTRONG, of
    age. Security: PETER NAPPER, JONATHAN WOODSON, JAMES ARMSTRONG.
110 marriage return on same date: SAMUEL K. JENNINGS.

AMANDA M. NORVELL--DAVID WALKER

ELIZA NORVELL--GEORGE W. GAINES

MARTHA ANN NORVEL--CHISWELL DABNEY

SUSANNAH CAROLINE NORVELL--JONATHAN M. WARWICK

110. 9 December 1818. WILLIAM WIATT NORVELL and ANN MARIA HARRISON.
Return by WILLIAM S. REID.

LUCY NORVIL--JONATHAN BULLOCK

13. 17 October 1817. SAMUEL NOWLIN and ELIZABETH B. IVESON.
Security: RICHARD GAINES.

MARGARET OLDHOUSEN--JOSEPH BUTCHER

MATILDA OLIVER--ARCH C. SNEED

NANCY OLIVER--JONATHAN KIDD

26. 13 May 1825. WILLIAM OLIVER and LUZEA HASKINS. Security:
ISAAC H. BUTTERWORTH. 113 marriage return on same date:
JONATHAN WEBB.

BETSY O'NEAL--JONATHAN BELL

23. 28 April 1824. ROBERT ORR and ELIZABETH A. BAILEY, daughter
of PARKER BAILEY. Security: WILLIAM M. BROWN, JAMES BAILEY.

12. 26 March 1817. JONATHAN B. OTEY and ANGELINA M. BROWN,
daughter of REED (?) BROWN. Security: JONATHAN M. OTEY.

POLLY (MARY) OWENS--NELSON HUGHES

20. 23 February 1822. WESLEY PADGET and SOPHIA POWELL. Security:
G. A. EDWARDS, WILLIAM H. TABB.

23. 10 February 1824. AMBROSE PAGE and MAHALA A. JOHNSON, JOSEPH
LEE, guardian and security for bride. Security: WILLIAM H. L.
TABB, GEORGE H. WEIDEMEYER.

11. 28 December 1818. JONATHAN PALMER--free man of color who came
from London with RICHARD CHILTON, JR. and SUCKY TWOPENCE, of
age and a free woman. Security: JAMES TWOPENCE, GEORGE GATEWOOD.

22. 1 January 1823. EDMUND PATE and SARAH BAILEY. Security:
DAVID SAUNDERS, JR., JONATHAN BAILEY. 111 marriage return
on same date: WILLIAM S. REID; groom of Botetourt County.

11. 18 November 1818. ROBERT PATTERSON and MARY H. MOORMAN,
daughter of HENRY MOORMAN. Security: HENRY F. MOORMAN,
ELIZABETH CLARK. 110 marriage return on 19 November; THOMAS MOORE.

6. 14 May 1812. SOLOMON PATTERSON and SALLY SCOTT, of age.
Security: CHARLES SCOTT.

24. 22 June 1824. WILLIAM PATTERSON and AMANDA BURD. Security:
ROBERT KYLE, RICHARD S. TILDEN, ROBERT KYLE, JR.

26. 29 December 1825. DR. JONATHAN H. PATTESON and FRANCES M.
IRVINE, daughter of ANN F. IRVINE. Security: LANDON CABELL,
SAMUEL R. IRVINE.

MARY H. PATTESON--THOMAS DILLARD

26. 12 April 1825. MACE PENDLETON and SUSAN BALLANGER. Security:
GEORGE MAGUIRE. 113 marriage return on same date: POINDEXTER P.
SMITH.

15. 4 November 1818. JAMES PENN and MARTHA ANN NICHOLAS HARRISON,
daughter of NICHOLAS HARRISON. Security: WILLIAM J. MORRIS.
110 marriage return on same date: WILLIAM S. REID.

8. 13 July 1814. GEORGE PERCIVAL and REBECCA WALLACE, of age.
Security: TOWSON TRUSLOW, SARAH WALLACE.

Deed Book A. 12 June 1813. JONATHAN PERCIVAL and MARGARET
WALLACE; return of 11 June 1813 by SAMUEL K. JENNINGS.
7. 11 June 1813 bond--she was of age. Security: WILLIAM SUMPTER,
TOWNSON TRUSLOW. 109 marriage return on 11 July by JENNINGS.

LETITIA PERKINS--JAMES WATSON DIBBRELL

SALLY M. PERKINS--WILLIAM W. PERKINS

5. 11 March 1811. WILLIAM W. PERKINS and SALLY M. PERKINS;
her guardian was RICHARD PERKINS. Security: BENJAMIN PERKINS.

23. 12 June 1824. CHARLES PERROW and CATHERINE CRUMPTON, daughter
of WILLIAM CRUMPTON; also security.

31. 24 November 1827. JESSE L. PERRY and ELIZABETH R. CURLE,
daughter of R. CURLE. Security: GEORGE P. PEERY.

MARIA M. PERRY--FRANCIS S. MILLER

16. 15 February 1819. WILLIAM PHAUP and ELIZABETH H. CHANDLER;
SAM CHANDLER was her father. Security: RICHARD W. CHANDLER,
JAMES HOPKINS. 110 marriage return on same date: WILLIAM S. REID.

12. 17 February 1817. JONATHAN PHILLIPS and ANN NICAR, daughter
of MICHAEL NICAR. Security: THOMAS MITCHELL, JR.

8. 28 July 1814. CORNELIUS PIERCE and POLLY DAVIS. Security:
WILLIAM HARRISON, NANCY DUDLEY.

14. 30 March 1818. JONATHAN H. PLEASANTS and ANN E. IRVINE,
daughter of ANN F. IRVINE. Security: JORDAN ANTHONY.
110 marriage return on same date: ANN ELIZA here; WILLIAM S. REID.

10. 23 December 1815. JONATHAN R. PLUNKET and SALLY TIMBERLAKE.
Security: GEORGE PERCIVAL, JUDITH SCHOLFIELD.

7. 27 August 1812. JONATHAN POE and NANCY TOMPKINS, of age.
Security: JOSEPH BOYCE.

ELIZA ANN PORTER--DANIEL WALKER

SOPHIA POWELL--WESLEY PADGET

30. 17 September 1827. MOSES H. PRESTON and ELIZABETH D. TYREE,
daughter of RICHARD TYREE. Security: JORDAN ANTHONY, S. G.
NORVELL. 113 marriage return on same date: WILLIAM S. REID.

17. 21 December 1819. WILLIAM PRESTON and ELIZABETH A. CABELL.
Security: LANDON CABELL. 110 marriage return on same date:
WILLIAM S. REID.

9. 17 February 1815. BENJAMIN PRICE and AGNES SCOTT. Security:
SOLOMON PATTERSON.

11. 17 October 1818. EDWARD PRICE and MARY MALLORY, of age.
Security: OSWALD BROKEMAN. 110 marriage return on October 7;
16 (sic): THOMAS MOORE.

MAHALA PURYEAR--SAMUEL BURCH

MARY RAMSEY--THOMAS HAYTH

POLLY RANSEY--JOSEPH NICHOLS

ELIZABETH REA--HANCOCK LEE TENNELL

20. 25 June 1822. DAVID REES and MARY L. MARSHALL. Security:
HARGROVE MITCHUM.

MARY ANN REES--PHILO LACY

25. 28 March 1825. CHARLES REYNOLDS and HARRIETT M. COCKE;
D. G. MURRELL was her guardian. Security: HARDIN D. MURRELL.
113 marriage return on 12 April: FREDERICK KABLER.

5. 24 October 1811. JONATHAN RICHARDSON and ELLENDER GRAHAM.
Security: JONATHAN BOLLING, WILLIAM COX, ELIZABETH BRIEN.

MARY ANN RICHARDSON--GEORGE W. WALKER

32. 2 February 1828. JONATHAN RICHERSON and SUSAN RUCKER, daughter
of REUBEN RUCKER. Security: GILBERT HAYTH, JOSHUA RUCKER,
ISAAC M. RUCKER.

ADALINE E. RISQUE--GILES WARD

MARTHA H. RIVES--ANDERSON M. WADDLE

Deed Book A. Return of 13 January 1810; JAMES ROBERTS and
SALLY HALLAY; WILLIAM P. MARTIN and then date of 3 January 1809.
3. 28 December 1808. JAMES HALLEY, father. Security: JACOB OGLESBY,
JAMES MARTIN. 109 marriage return 3 January 1809, by WILLIAM P.
MARTIN. This one is a mixed one.

MATILDA ROBERTS--A. F. BIGGERS

25. 19 January 1825. ROBERT ROBINSON and MARTHA J. HARRISON;
SAMUEL J. HARRISON, father. Security: WILLIAM W. NORVELL.
112 marriage return on same date: WILLIAM S. REID.

14. 9 June 1818. WILLIAM ROBINSON and ELIZA FOWLER. Security:
JOHN FOWLER; also security as well as witness.

7. 9 September 1813. SIMEON ROBINSON and MARTHA COCKE, of age.
Security: OWEN WILLIAMS.

ANN MARIA ROHR--JAMES BOYD

LUCINDA ANN ROHR and HENRY R. GOULDEN(ER)

20. 1 May 1822. JAMES ROSE and ELIZABETH PRICE TALIAFERRO,
daughter of S. TALIAFERRO. Security: WILLIAM H. MORGAN,
S. L. TALIAFERRO.

ELIZA ROYAL--FORTUNATUS SYDNOR

19. 19 December 1821. JOSEPH E. ROYALL and MARY ELIZABETH
GWATKINS, daughter of EDWARD GWATKINS. Security: JAMES
BENAGH, SAMUEL H. BROWN, WILSON H. OTEY. 111 marriage return on
same date: WILLIAM S. REID.

ELIZABETH RUCKER--GILBERT HAYTH

SUSAN RUCKER--JONATHAN RICHERSON

18. 28 May 1821. WILLIS SADLER and MARY JOHNSON. Security:
THOMAS J. COUCH. 110 marriage return on same date: WILLIAM S.
REID.

20. 3 April 1822. WILLIAM L. SAUNDERS and MARY CAMM, daughter of
ELIZABETH CAMM. Security: HOWSON WHITE. 111 marriage return
on same date: WILLIAM S. REID.

23. 1 April 1824. CORNELIUS SCHANCK and MARY WILLIAMS. Security:
SAMUEL NOWLIN. 111 marriage return on same date: ELI BALL,
Lynchburg Baptist Church.

LAVINIA R. SCHOOLFIELD--WILLIAM BISHOP

NANCY T. SCHOOLFIELD--JONATHAN T. MASON

SIDNEY SCHOOLFIELD--DAVID F. MASON

ADELINE SCOTT--ARTHUR HOLCOMBE

AGNES SCOTT--BENJAMIN PRICE

3. 8 December 1808. CHARLES SCOTT and LUCY THOMAS; JONATHAN
    LYNCH stated that she was daughter of a woman emancipated by
him and eighteen years old. Security: WILLIAM JOHNSON, MILLY GUTTRY.

JENNET SCOTT--THOMAS ALDRIDGE

SALLY SCOTT--SOLOMON PATTERSON

22. 20 August 1823. ISHAM SCRUGGS and RHODA GRIFFITH. Security:
    HENRY WRIGHT, THOMAS B. MEHONE. 111 marriage return on same
date: WILLIAM S. REID.

10. 25 November 1815. JOSEPH SEAY and BETSY LEE, daughter of
    POLLY (?) LEE and also guardian. Security: JAMES OLIVER,
GEORGE LEE.

3. 19 August 1809. ABSALOM SHANKLIN and NANCY LESTER, of age.
    Security: GEORGE COCKRAN, JAMES ADAMS.

32. 2 January 1828. JONATHAN G. SHELTON and ANN BURD, daughter
    of W. BURD. Security: B. W. HEWSON, WILLIAM THURMON. 114
marriage return 3 January: JONATHAN WEBB.

8. 2 June 1814. LINDSEY SHOEMAKER and ELIZABETH A. DOYLE, of
    age. Security: JONATHAN PRYOR, MICAJAH WATERFIELD.
109 marriage return on same date: WILLIAM S. REID--SHUMAKER here.

ELIZABETH SIMPSON--JONATHAN THURMON

32. 20 February 1828. JAMES SIMPSON and ELEANOR W. HUDGIN--21
    years of age. Security: JONTHAN THURMON.

24. 18 August 1824. SAMUEL SMALLBRIDGE and NANCY MAYFIELD.
    Security: JONATHAN MEHONE.

29. 19 April 1827. CHARLES SMITH and ANNE MARIAH BOBSON; LUCY
    BOBSON was grandmother. Security: JOSEPH GREEN. 113 marriage
return on same date: JONATHAN WEBB.

32. 3 January 1828. GEORGE SMITH and MARTHA ANN CODIL, of age.
    Security: JONATHAN IRVINE, LEE FEARS. 114 marriage return
on same date: JONATNAN WEBB.

18. 1 June 1821. JOHN H. SMITH and MARY M. SOWERS; PLEASANT PARTIN
    was her guardian and security. Security: JONATHAN WILLS.
111 marriage return on same date: WILLIAM S. REID.

MARTHA J. SMITH--WINSTON H. LUCAS

11. 30 July 1818. CHARLES T. (L) SNEAD and PEGGY HIGGINS; MARGARET
    HIGGINS, mother and guardian. Security: GIDEON SHAW, JOSHUA
BRIGHT.

ELIZABETH SNEAD--WARREN GANNAWAY

SALLY W. SNEAD--JAMES H. DUIGUID

30. 19 June 1827. ARCH C. SNEED and MATILDA OLIVER; ELIZABETH OLIVER
    was mother and guardian. Security: THOMAS BROWRIER (?):
NANCY A. CALDWELL. 113 marriage return on same date: JONATHAN WEBB.

JOANNA SOWERS--JAMES V. KNIGHT

30. 3 September 1827. JONATHAN A. SOWERS and EMELINE STOUT.
     Security: PLEASANT PARTIN. 114 marriage return on 20 September:
CALEB LEACH.

     MARY M. SOWERS--JONATHAN H. SMITH

26. 20 April 1825. HENRY STANDLEY and MILDRED JOHNSON; SAMUEL
     NOWLIN, guardian of bride. Security: GEORGE HUNT. 112 marriage
return on same date: ELI BALL.

     JUDITH STANTON--SAMUEL TYRE

     NANCY STARKE--CALEB TAIT

     LEATHY STARKES--WILLIAM GRAVES

     SUSANNA STARKES--DAVID BRIGGS

     EMILY S. STEEN--GRIFFIN L. LECKIE

8.   21 September 1814. THOMAS STEPHENS and PATSY B. HEATH;
     WILLIAM HEATH was her father. Security: THOMAS PARRACK.

     ELIZABETH STEVENS--THOMAS J. DUVAL

12. 24 April 1817. JONATHAN W. STEVANS and MARY ANN BOTNER, of
     age; JOSEPH BOTNER swore as to her age. Security: DAVID
CAMPBELL.

15. 27 August 1818. LUKE STEWART and JUDITH (JUDAH) ANDERSON--
     free woman of color. Security: ISAIAH ANDERSON, THOMAS
BUNTING.

     CATHERINE STONER--LANDON DANGERFIELD

     EMELINE STOUT--JONATHAN A. SOWERS

     REBECCA ANN SUMPTER--FRANCIS P. HARRIS

     Deed Book A. 7 December 1810. WILLIAM SUMPTER and MARTHA
     WALLACE; then a return of 1 November by ALEXANDER SALE.
4.   31 October 1810. Security: TOWNSEN TRUSLOW, SARAH WALLACE.

     Deed Book A. 2 December 1805. ALEXANDER SWAN and MARY ENGLAND
     by WILLIAM P. MARTIN. 1. October 28, 1805. Security: WILLIAM P.
MARTIN, WILLIAM BROWN. 109 marriage return on December 10 by MARTIN.

1.   1 March 1806. JONATHAN P. SWINEY, Bedford County, and MARGARET
     MC GEORGE. Security: STARK WHITTINGTON, JONATHAN WHITTENTON.

13. 13 November 1817. FORTUNATUS SYDNOR and ELIZA ROYAL; L(?) A.
     HOLCOMBE was her guardian. Security: WILLIAM W. NORVELL.

6.   14 February 1812. CALEB TAIT and NANCY STARKE. Security:
     ROBERT HUBBARD, THOMAS STEWART.

     ANNA TALBOT--JONATHAN DAVIDSON

     ELIZABETH PRICE TALIAFERRO--JAMES ROSE

22. 29 October 1823. NORBONE M. TALIAFERRO and LUCY JONES;
     WILLIAM R. CHAPLIN (?) was her guardian. Security: DANIEL
RODES, PAUL JONES.

14. 9 May 1818. FOUNTAINE TANKERSLEY and NANCY MAY, daughter of
     JOSEPH MAY. Security: VINCENT PARSONS.

Deed Book A. WILLIAM TARDY and ELIZABETH WALLACE, 20 March 1806 by WILLIAM P. MARTIN. 1. both of age, 15 March 1806. Security: WILLIAM WALLACE. 109 marriage return same as deed book by MARTIN.

4. 28 November 1810. WILLIAM TARDY and MARY DETTO, daughter of PETER DETTO; also security.

SUSANNA TAYLOR--JONATHAN F. LAMB

2. 23 March 1808, HANCOCK LEE TENNELL and ELIZABETH REA, of age. Security: THOMAS MICKS (?): LANCELOT REA.

4. 15 February 1810. GEORGE THOMAS and MARTHA LAIN, of age. Security: JONATHAN BOLLING.

LUCY THOMAS--CHARLES SCOTT

ELLANA THOMPSON--ROBERT S. ANDERSON

FRANCES THOMPSON--LEVIN B. HAGERMAN

JANE THOMPSON--JONATHAN LECKIE

MARGARET THOMPSON--WASHINGTON BLUNT

2. -- October 1808. JONATHAN THURMON and BETSY (ELIZABETH) SIMPSON. Security: BENJAMIN ESSEX.

12. 1 January 1817. RICHARD S. TILDEN and EVELINA BURD; consent of WILLIAM BURD. Security: JONATHAN VICTOR.

SALLY TIMBERLAKE--JONATHAN R. PLUNKET

MARGARET E. TODD--CHARLES CALBOUN

9. 3 August 1815. ALEXANDER TOMPKINS and ELIZABETH BYRD. Security: DAVIDSON BRADFUTE, ANNA BYRD.

CATHERINE W. TOMPKINS and HENRY HALL

NANCY TOMPKINS--JONATHAN POE

25. 8 February 1825. QUARLES TOMPKINS and EVELYN BYRD. Security: ALEXANDER TOMPKINS, DAVIDSON BRADFUTE.

SUSANNA S. TOMPKINS--JONATHAN WILLIAMS

4. 11 September 1810. TOWNSON TRUSLOW and SUSANNAH WALLACE. Security: WILLIAM SUMPTER, SAREY WALLACE.

BETSY TUPPENCE--GEORGE GATEWOOD

USLEY TUPPENCE--EDMOND ELLIS

ELIZABETH TWOPENCE--HENRY BROWN

MARY JANE TWOPENCE--ARCHIBALD MORRIS

SUCKEY TWOPENCE--JONATNAN PALMER

ELIZABETH D. TYREE--MOSES H. PRESTON

33. 13 October 1828. JONATHAN H. TYREE and ANN P. BRANSFORD, daughter of SAMUEL BRANSFORD. Security: SAMUEL G. NORVELL, GEORGE L. WILLIAMS.

Deed Book A. 13 July 1811. SAMUEL TYREE and JUDITH STANTON
by SAMUEL JENNINGS. 5. 12 July 1811 bond. Security:
JAMES JAMES, JONATHAN HUGHEY. 109 marriage return on same date by
JENNINGS.

1. 11 April 1807. LUKE VALENTINE and PAULINA GOING; AMY GOING
was her mother. Security: HENRY MOSS, AMY GOING, EDMOND TATE.

5. 2 September 1811. JOEL VANDEL and CHARITY DAVIS. Security:
JOSEPH and JONATHAN DAVIS.

EMELINE VASS--ANDREW M. HINCHIE

4. 7 January 1811. BENJAMIN VAWTER and MILLEY CUTREY. Security:
JOSEPH NEEDHAM, MILLY WADE.

SARAH T. VENABLE--GEORGE W. MITCHELL

2. 28 November 1807. ALLEN WADE and FANNY MC KINNEY, of age.
Security: JAMES GILLIAM.

14. 7 May 1818. ANDERSON M. WADDLE and MARTHA H. RIVES, daughter
of NATHANIEL RIVES. Security: DAVID SAUNDERS. 110 marriage
return on same date: WILLIAM S. REID.

PEGGY WAGGONER--JOHN HUGHEY

26. 28 June 1825. DANIEL WALKER and ELIZA ANN PORTER. Security:
JONATHAN H. PORTER. 113 marriage return on same date:
JONATHAN WEBB.

28. 11 December 1826. DAVID WALKER and AMANDA M. NORVELL, daughter
of REUBEN NORVELL. Security: JONATHAN W. WALKER, GEORGE R.
NORVELL. 111 marriage return on same date: WILLIAM S. REID.

Deed Book A. GEORGE WALKER and REBECCA HAMAN, 25 February
1806, by WILLIAM P. MARTIN. 1. HAMER here; bond of 22 February.
Security: ISAAC PIDGEON. 109 marriage return by MARTIN as in
deed book.

25. 30 December 1824. GEORGE W. WALKER and MARY ANN RICHARDSON;
MARIA F. BROWN was her mother and guardian. Security:
WALTER H. MIDDLETON, THOMAS J. DUVAL.

ELIZAGETH WALLACE--WILLIAM TARDY

MARGARET WALLACE--JONATHAN PERCIVAL

MARTHA WALLACE--WILLIAM SUMPTER

MANCY WALLACE--ALEXANDER MC DANIEL

REBECCA WALLACE--GEORGE PERCIVAL

MRS. SUSANNAH WALLACE--JOSIAH COLE

SUSANNAH WALLACE--TOWNSON TRUSLOW

MARY W. WALTON--PAUL JONES

17. 7 November 1820. GILES WARD and ADELINE E. RISQUE. Security:
WILLIAM M. RIVES. 110 marriage return on same date: WILLIAM S.
REID.

18. 26 February 1821. JONATHAN M. WARWICK and SUSANNAH CAROLINE
NORVELL. Security: SAMUEL STEVENS. 110 marriage return on
same date: WILLIAM S. REID.

MARIA WARWICK--THOMAS LEFTWICH

POLLY (MARY) WARWICK--CHRISTOPHER WINFREE

Deed Book A. 1 December 1812. MICAJAH WATERFIELD and CATHERINE
DOYLE; return of 15 November by SAMUEL K. JENNINGS. 7. Bond
of 14 November 1812. Security: WILLIAM DOYLE; 109 marriage return
as in deed by JENNINGS.

19. 15 November 1821. ROBERT WATKINS and ELIZABETH C. HARDWICK,
of age. Security: ROBERT MARTYN, SOPHIA SUMPTER.

MARTHA JAMES WATSON--FONTAINE GRAHAM

31. 20 November 1827. MITCHELL V. WATTS and SALLY M. LEWELLIN,
daughter of MARY LEWELLEN. Security: JONATHAN LEWELLIN,
JONATHAN IRVINE.

28. 24 November 1826. EDWARD B. WELLS and ELIZABETH B. LEWALLEN.
Security: JONATHAN LEWALLEN. 113 marriage return on same
date: EDWARD CANNON.

7. 4 September 1813. FREDERICK WENEDEL and SARAH LEVISTON.
Security: ALLEN HUGHEY, ISAAC BUTTERWORTH.

24. 6 November 1824. JAMES WHEATLEY, JR. and MILDRED L. WILLIAMS;
FIELDING L. WILLIAMS was her guardian. Security: JONATHAN
JONES. 111 marriage return on 9 November: WILLIAM S. REID.

13. 23 October 1817q ROBERT WHITE and MARY CARROLL, daughter of
ETHELDRED CARROLL and security; JAMES BENAGH was also a
security.

POLLY WHITESIDES--JAMES DEANE

6. 29 February 1812. BENJAMIN WHITESIDES and HANAH ADAMS.
Security: JONATHAN CLARKSON.

Deed Book A. 5 March 1813. ABNER WHITTEN and CLEOPATRA
MC DANIEL. Then 4 March by SAMUEL K. JENNINGS. 7. 2 March
1813. CLEOPATRA ALBERTINE MC DANIEL, daughter of GEORGE MC DANIEL.
Security: JONATHAN TOMPKINS. 109 groom of Bedford--4 March by
JENNINGS.

ANN WHITTENTON--JONATHAN GARRETT

27. 2 September 1826. SAMUEL J. WIATT and SARAH L. BROWN.
Security: CHARLES BROWN. 111 marriage return on same date:
F. G. SMITH.

18. 3 May 1821. THOMAS WILKINS and REBECCA FOE. Security:
JOSEPH V. (?) HARDWICK.

31. 17 December 1827. BENJAMIN WILKS and MATILDA DUFFEL, daughter
of JAMES DUFFEL. Security: JONATHAN HALSEY, H. L. DUFFEL.
113 marriage return on same date by R. RYLAND.

JANE WILLIAMS--JAMES LEVINGSTON

22. 19 September 1823. JEHU WILLIAMS and SUSANNA S. TOMPKINS,
daughter of MARY TOMPKINS. Security: JOHN H. PATTESON, HENRY
HILL.

MARY WILLIAMS--CORNELIUS SCHANCK

MILDRED L. WILLIAMS--JAMES WHEATLEY, JR.

14. 20 January 1818. WILLIAM W. WILLIAMS and SARAH GEORGE, of
age. Security: DAVID CAMPBELL.

HARRIET WILSON--JONATHAN LABBY

POLLY WILSON--PAYTON BYRD

3. 24 November 1808. CHRISTOPHER WINFREE and POLLY (MARY) WARWICK,
    daughter of W. WARWICK. Security: REUBEN NORVELL.

33. 23 December 1828. CHARLES A. WITHERS and MATILDA LYNCH,
     daughter of EDWARD LYNCH. Security: GRIEF B. TATE, MICAJAH L.
LYNCH. 114 marriage return on same date: F. G. SMITH.

ANN ELIZA WRIGHT--BENJAMIN JENNINGS

17. 30 May 1820. HENRY WRIGHT and ELIZABETH GRIFFY(AY). Security:
     JAMES GOLDEN.

18. 27 January 1821. JAMES L. WRIGHT and ANN O. BYRD; ANNE BYRD
     was her mother. Security: JONATHAN O. LEFTWICK, DAVIDSON
BRADFUTE. 110 marriage return on same date: WILLIAM S. REID.

MARY WRIGHT--ARCHIBALD COOPER

17. 4 September 1820. WILLIAM D. WRIGHT and REBECCA W. ACRE,
     daughter of DAVID ACRE. Security: NATHAN SCHOOLFIELD.

16. 20 January 1819. CHARLES YOUNG and ANN MARIA ELLIS. Security:
     ROBERT FRENCH, R. C. JOHNSON, O. H. BRUNSON.

22. 18 December 1823. SAMUEL YOUNG and FRANCES BECKHAM, daughter
     of MARY ANN BECKHAM--also guardian. Security: HARDIN D.
MURRELL. 111 marriage return on same date: WILLIAM S. REID.

ABSTRACT OF DEED BOOK A OF LYNCHBURG CORPORATION

June, 1805 to February, 1813

The streets have been changed since this book was used by
Lynchburg Corporation Court. There is an old map in Book I and
Third Street is now Church Street.

1. 12 April 1805. BENJAMIN PERKINS to GEORGE MC DANIEL, Bedford
County...$1.00 one-fourth acre lot northwest half--#46; where
JOSEPH NEEDHAM recently built two story frame house on Third Street.
Witnesses: WILL NORVELL, THOMAS S. MC CLELLALD, SETH WARD;
acknowledged, 4 June 1805.

1. 8 April 1805. CALEB TAIT to present wife, ANNE--previous to
    marriage, agreed that her property to be bestowed on her, not
put in legal form...$1.00 paid by THOMAS POLLARD, Hanover County.
Seven named slaves--ANNE's before marriage. She may dispose of them
by will; if not, then for use of GEORGE WHITLOCK, FANNY RICHARDSON,
FANNY BACON CLARK. In lieu of dower, but one-eighth to her for
life or widowhood. Witnesses: THOMAS WIATT, THOMAS W. COCKE,
NETHERLAND TAIT. Proved, 14 July 1805.

3. 18 January 1801. THOMAS STEWART to brother, JAMES STEWART...
    power of attorney as to estate of deceased father, HENRY
STEWART, Caroline County. Witnesses: W. WARWICK, THOMS MOORMAN,
JONATHAN D. CARTER, JONATHAN J. WIATT. Acknowledged, 25 May 1805.
Witnesses: NELSON DAVENPORT, HENRY RIVES, RODERICK TALIAFERRO.
NELSON DAVENPORT may be WILSON DAVENPORT.

3. 25 May 1805. ELIZABETH STEWART to brother, JAMES STEWART...
    power as above. Father, HENRY, CAROLINE. Witnesses as for
1805 above, but add THOMAS STEWART.

4. 18 June 1805. JONATHAN LYNCH and wife, MARY...in some deeds
    he is called SR.--to mayor and Lynchburg and inhabitants
generally--ground to erect courthouse and jail buildings; $1.00--
margin: to clerk of Council, 27 August 1856--lot on hill adjoining
Lynchburg--southwest of street on hill--sixty feet wide; opposite
Water Street; 50 feet towards LYNCH's present dwelling; 100 feet on
street and eight poles back. To leave street open on both sides--
alley at least twenty feet wide--if not used, to revert to heirs.
Proved, 1 July 1805. I do not know enough about old courthouses
to make a dogmatic statement. The old courthouse used before present
one is just across the street from new one on Court Street. It is
white and has tower and clock. It faces steep hill with steps on
Monument terrace to Church Street. It is really down hill all of the
way to the James and bridge over into Amherst County. There are
other streets below Church as one goes down to the James--Main,
Commerce, and then one along river where old depot used to be. One
goes on to bridge from Commerce Street. Let it be remembered that
the town is called the hilly city and this is not idle talk.

5. 1 July 1805. SAMUEL SCHOOLFIELD and wife, JUDITH, to JONATHAN
    THURMOND...L226 part of lot 13 on Second Street. Lines:
DR. JAMES GRAHAM, WILLIAM WARWICK. Witnesses: JOHN SCHOOLFIELD,
RICHARD THURMOND, BENJAMIN SCHOOLFIELD.

5. 13 July 1805. JONATHAN LYNCH and wife, MARY, to STERLING
    CLAIBORNE...L100 half acre lot; opposite #88 of THOMAS W.
COCKE. Witnesses: WILLIAM DAVIS, JR., CHRISTOPHER LYNCH, ACHILLES
DOUGLAS, SAMUEL WIATT.

6.   6 April 1805. CALEB TAIT and wife NANCY, to WADDY TATE...lot
     bought by JESSE TAIT, deceased--#53 for L51-10 and no deed was
made. JESSE devised by will to son, WADDY TATE--note difference in
spelling. Lines: third and alley; #55; 49; third street. Witnesses:
WILLIAM EDENFIELD, WILLIAM OWENS, CHARLES HOYLE, JR. Acknowledged,
2 September 1805.

8.   28 August 1805. WILLIAM WALLACE to THOMAS W. COCKE to secure
     GEORGE K. LAMBETH...$1.00; lot of 72½ feet--half acre; part of
#8 2; northwest junction of third street and seventh alley; #83.
Witnesses: JONATHAN HORSLEY, THOMAS B. KING, JONATHAN MILLER.

9.   25 June 1805. RICHMOND C. TYREE to STEPHEN FARMER...$90
     one-eighth acre; #78. Lines: southwest by BARKSDALE SNIDER;
part of #78; TYREE; fifth alley. Witnesses: THOMAS W. COCKE,
BARKSDALE SNIDER, JONATHAN HORSLEY.

10. 25 April 1805. BARKSDALE SNIDER to THOMAS WIATT, JOSIAH LEAKE
     and WILLIAM WARWICK to secure WILLIAM BROWN and Company,
Lynchburg...half of half acre lot where I live; other half is
RICHMOND TYREE's. Witnesses: ARCH. ROBERTSON, GEORGE POWELL,
ARCH. MAYS.

12. 6 July 1805. JONATHAN LYNCH and wife, MARY...Lynchburg trustees:
     CALEB TAIT, EDWARD LYNCH, WILLIAM DAVIS, SAMUEL J. HARRISON,
RODERICK TALIAFERRO, WILL NORVELL, THOMAS WIATT to ELIAS FISHER--
lot #72. Lines: fourth street and sixth alley; 70 and 60. Witnesses:
GEORGE ROBERTS, BENJAMIN A. WINTON, DANIEL BURGESS. Six shillings.

12. 6 July 1805. JONATHAN LYNCH et al. as above to GEORGE ROBERTS...
     six shillings; #67. Lines: third street, fifth alley, #'s
39 and 65--half acre. Witnesses: WINTON and BURGESS as above,
ELIAS FISHER.

13. 6 July 1805. JONATHAN LYNCH et al. as above to DANIEL BURGESS...
     six shillings, #77. Lines: third street, fifth alley, 78
and 82. Witnesses: GEORGE ROBERTS, WINTON, FISHER.

14. 27 August 1805. JONATHAN LYNCH et al. as above to WILLIAM
     FOWLER, SAMUEL SCHOOLFIELD and CULWELL WILLIAMSON...six
shillings; lot 84. Lines: second street, seventh alley, half acre.
Witnesses: WILLIAM EDENFIELD, WILLIAM JOHNSON, THOMAS W. COCKE.

14. 9 July 1805. JONATHAN LYNCH and wife, MARY, to PETER DETTO...
     $300; half acre lot near southwest junction of fourth street
and seventh alley--will leave public street--sixty feet wide.
Witnesses: GEORGE ROBERTS, EDWARD LYNCH, ELIAS FISHER, ASA PLUMMER (?).

16. 4 May 1805. FRANCIS HOLLEY, SR., Bedford County, to JAMES
     MARTIN and WILLIAM FOWLER for benefit of grandchild, SALLY
HOLLEY, daughter of JAMES HOLLY...love and $1.00; slave, GEORGE,
about 20--when SALLY is 21 or married. Witnesses: CHARLES JOHNSON,
JONATHAN FOWLER, CULLY WILLIAMSON.

17. 7 October 1805. THOMAS and MILLY JOHNSTON--signed JOHNSON...
     power of attorney to son, CHARLES JOHNSTON--as to business in
getting our share of estate of CHARLES YARBROUGH, deceased, --- County,
South Carolina. MILLEY is sister of CHARLES YARBROUGH and an heir.

18. 4 February 1808. JOSEPH NEEDHAM and wife, MARY, Campbell
     County, to BENJAMIN PERKINS...$700; lot #---. Witnesses:
STITH MAYNARD, EDWARD LYNCH, THOMAS ROBINSON, WILL NORVELL. Memo:
on third street and joins SAMUEL IRVINE and JUDAH HUSSEY. Same
witnesses.

19. 24 September 1805. JONATHAN LYNCH, SR. and wife, MARY, to
     JONATHAN HUBBARD...L 112-10 three-fourths of one-half acre
adjoining Lynchburg. Lines: northeast side of Lynch Street,
opposite MARTIN's warehouse; lot 81; near junction of second alley
and Lynch Street--towards Spring warehouse. Witnesses: THOMAS W.
COCKE, JONATHAN HORSLEY, ALEXANDER BRIDGLAND.

19. (two such pages and someone has put in pencil "One half")
     1 August 1801. STERLING and BULLER CLAIBORNE, Dinwiddie
County, to SAMUEL IRVINE...STERLING, with approval of father,
BULLER, binds himself to IRVINE until 20; will be fifteen in October
of 1805--seems to be date of 20th birthday. To learn art and mystery
of merchant. L 20 for first year; L 30 for second year; L 40 for
third year; L 50 for fourth and last year. Witness: JONATHAN
ROBINSON.

20. 7 October 1805. JONATHAN LYNCH and wife, MARY, and Lynchburg
     trustees to JAMES MALLORY...L120 half acre lot; #114. South-
west by Lynch Street; T. WIATT, JONATHAN LYNCH, eighth alley. See
12 for trustees.

21. 7 October 1805. JONATHAN LYNCH, SR. and wife, MARY, and
     trustees above to WILLIAM WALLACE...six shillings; $82.
Lines: third street; seventh alley; $83; 77; half acre. Reference
to page 98. It will be seen that this is dower relinquished.

22. 8 October 1805. THOMAS JOHNSON and wife, MILDRED, to BENJAMIN
     JOHNSON, Bedford County...$100; half of half acre lot--northwest
end; $45. Lines: third street, first alley, JONATHAN LYNCH,
JONATHAN POINTER. MILLICENT is correct name for wife.

22. 8 October 1805. BENJAMIN JOHNSON and wife, MARY, Bedford;
     THOMAS JOHNSON and wife, MILLICENT, to JONATHAN POINTER...$200;
other half of #45. Lines: third street, BENJAMIN JOHNSON, JONATHAN
LYNCH, ROLAND JONES.

23. 7 August 1805. WILLIAM TIMBERLAKE and wife, MOURNING; JONATHAN
     TIMBERLAKE and wife, MARY; CHARLES JOHNSON and wife, MARY, and
ELIZABETH TIMBERLAKE, widow and relict of PHILLIP TIMBERLAKE, Campbell
County, to ROLAND JONES...$750--WILLIAM and wife get $150; JONATHAN
and wife--$200; CHARLES and wife, $200; ELIZABETH, $200--lot on Main
Street--northwest. Lines: JONATHAN WARD, SR., former lot of WILLIAM
DAVIS fronts it--#12. Witnesses: THOMAS S. MC CLELLAND, SAMUEL
IRVINE, JONATHAN ROBINSON, THOMAS W. COCKE, J. LYNCH, JR., GABL.
JONES. Memo: as heirs of CHRISTOPHER JOHNSON, deceased, and
representing claims of BENJAMIN, NICHOLAS, THOMAS, DAVID and SAMUEL
JOHNSON, heirs of CHRISTOPHER JOHNSON. It is probable that other
heirs have departed this life, but had received sums in land or other
property--should they "or either of them" set up claims, JONES will
represent claims of grantors.

25. -- 1805. WILLIAM TIMBERLAKE and wife, MOURNING; ELIZABETH
     TIMBERLAKE, widow of PHILLIP TIMBERLAKE; JONATHAN TIMBERLAKE
and wife, MARY; CHARLES JOHNSON and wife, MARY, Campbell County, to
THOMAS HUMPHREYS, also as grantors for BENJAMIN, NICHOLAS, THOMAS,
DAVID and SAMUEL JOHNSON whose rights they bought for L150...one-
fourth acre; one equal moiety of #34. Original conveyed to ACHILLES
DOUGLAS and by him sold and conveyed to CHRISTOPHER JOHNSON. It
joins where HUMPHREY now lives. Some of children of CHRISTOPHER
JOHNSON received large sums--in life and some have died; some are
either minors or not living in Virginia. Acknowledged in part on
4 November 1805, and 2 December 1805.

27. 24 October 1805. Order to Campbell Justices of the Peace:
     GEORGE D. WINTON and RODERICK TALIAFERRO...JOSEPH NEEDHAM and
wife, MARY, 4 February 1805, to BENJAMIN PERKINS--joins SAMUEL IRVINE
and JUDAH HUSSEY on third street. Done, 15 November 1805.

28.   2 December 1805.   CHARLES HOYLE, SR. to JUNIOR for benefit of
      MARY BROWN, daughter of SR. and wife of JONATHAN BROWN...blank
sum; two slaves--formerly those of JONATHAN BROWN.

28.   2 December 1805.   GEORGE and SALLEY SULLIVAN to STITH MEAD,
      SAMUEL K. JENNINGS, WILLIAM HEATH, WILLIAM P. MARTIN, GEORGE
SULLIVAN, THOMAS WIATT, JONATHAN SCHOOLFIELD, WILLIAM BLAKE and
JAMES FOX...L52; lot #--. Lines: JONATHAN STEWART on southeast,
WILLIAM WARWICK on southwest, GEORGE SULLIVAN on northwest, third
street on east--52 foot front to build Methodist Episcopal Church.
Ministers to nominate all vacancies; must have been members of church
for one year and at least 21 years of age--nine trustees.

30.   26 October 1805.   DANIEL JACKSON to CHARLES Y. JOHNSON...
      DANIEL JACKSON is of age, but apprentices self as 1 above for
two years--$12 and suit at end of term; to live with CHARLES Y.
JOHNSON. Witnesses: S. WIATT, C. WARWICK.

31.   14 October 1805.   WILLIAM WALLACE to THOMAS W. COCKE to secure
      GEORGE K. LAMBETH...$1.00; part of #82--northwest junction of
third street and seventh alley; #83. Witnesses: JONATHAN DAVIS,
JR., CALEB TAIT, minor (?), JONATHAN HORSLEY.

33.   3 June 1805.   ALEXANDER STUART and wife, MARY, Richmond, to
      WILLIAM WARWICK...$1.00; half of #15, now occupied by WILLIAM
WARWICK and bought from ALEXANDER STUART; ALEXANDER STUART bought
from THOMAS WIATT. Witnesses: JAMES MOZELEY, JAMES STUART, SAMUEL
IRVINE.

34.   1 February 1806.   WILLIAM EDENFIELD to STEPHEN FARMER...
      consideration: title bond by HENRY MEREDITH, 28 January 1806,
and one-third of lot adjacent Lynchburg lines: southwest corner of
WASHINGTON LAMBETH, JONATHAN LYNCH--one-eighth acre. Lines: corner
of fifth alley and street on the hill running to DR. CABELL, fourth
street, $83, Farmer--one-fourth of #78 and that part on the street
on the hill. Witnesses: WILLIAM BAGBY, JONATHAN W. HORSLEY, WILLIAM
OWENS.

35.   5 November 1801.   CALEB TATE to WILLIAM HEATH...$150 per year;
      quarterly payments; lease of house and lot--one-fourth acre
occupied by JOSEPH DAKINGS. Lines: MAJOR WILLIAM WARWICK, TALIAFERRO
and STEWART; second street and alley--ten years from 12 January next;
accidents of fire excepted--can give notice at end of five years--
fire; ware (sic); acts of God excepted; may foreclose if eighteen
months behind; may not lease to persons of bad fame which would make
place a pest; must first consult TATE; HEATH to pay taxes. Witnesses:
LAW. MC GEORGE, JONATHAN J. CABELL.

36.   22 October 1805.   RICHMOND TYREE to WILLIAM EDENFIELD...$100
      one-eighth acre. Lines: corner of fifth alley and street on
the hill running by DR. CABELL; fourth street; #83; Farmer; fifth
alley; 78--one-fourth of it. Witnesses: WILL NORVELL, WILLIAM DAVIS,
WILLIAM OWENS.

37.   27 February 1806.   JACOB ROHR to CALEB TAIT...L 24--three due
      SAMUEL IRVINE--$1.00; stock; furniture; to advertize in
Gazette of Lynchburg. Witnesses: JAMES BENAGH, ROBERT ADAMS, THOMAS C.
GLAYTON, WILLIAM LYNCH.

38.   6 September 1805.   WILSON DAVENPORT to GEORGE D. WINSTON to
      secure SAMUEL IRVINE...$1.00; three named slaves. Witnesses:
BENAGH and CLAYTOR as above.

39. 1 October 1805. ZACH. TALIAFERRO, one of partners of TALIAFERRO,
     STEWART and Company, to JAMES STEWART and RODERICK TALIAFERRO,
other partners...six shillings--one third of lot whereon is store
house and other houses now occupied by firm; bought by all from
WILLIAM NORVELL; JONATHAN WIATT and THOMAS WIATT--"say one-fourth
of one-half acre" or one-eighth acres; #13. Lines: second or main
in front, CALEB TAIT, WILLIAM WARWICK, SAMUEL SCHOOLFIELD. Witnesses:
THOMAS STEWART, RICHARD THURMON, HUMPHREY STEWART, JR., ARCHIBALD
STEEN.

40. 13 September 1805. JAMES GILLIAM to JAMES MOSEBY to secure
     HODGSON, NICHOLSON and Company...$1.00; lot #38. Lines:
second street at corner, fourth alley, $40--formerly that of JONATHAN
WARD--bought by firm; to advertize in a Lynchburg paper edited nearest
GILLIAM's residence. Witnesses: THOMAS S. MC CLELLAND, THOMAS
NELLE, JONATHAN H. TRENT. Schedule of payments below; paid in full.

42. 19 February 1806. OWEN OWENS to JAMES H. BAIRD, Petersburg,
     Dinwiddie County...11 September 1792, MICHAEL ROHR and wife,
MARY, made deed to ISHAM H. BAIRD--all of Lynchburg; #29. Suit for
payments brought versus ISHAM H. BAIRD and OWEN OWENS became his
bail and judgement versus OWEN OWENS and he paid. 26 January 1797,
OWEN OWENS sued to recover and recovered lot on 20 February 1797--
forty shillings per year; will be paid by 27 May 1810. JAMES H.
BAIRD buys remainder for L 6-19-1; #29. Junction of second street
and third alley. Witnesses: WILSON DAVENPORT, STERLING CLAIBORNE,
WILLIAM PRESLEY, Clerk. Memo: BAIRD gives power of attorney to
DR. THOMAS HUMPHREYS, Lynchburg, 19 February 1806. Witnesses:
CLAIBORNE and DAVENPORT and JAMES MILLER.

44. 7 March 1806. JONATHAN LYNCH and wife, MARY, to Mayor of
     Lynchburg...margin: to COL. FORSBURG, 9 January 1871--$1.00;
to accomodate citizens for burying ground--half acre "on an hill on
west side Main road from upper end of Lynchburg toward New London"--
near fork of road from EDMUND TATES's mill and southwest of ANDREW
SMILEY's tanyard--may use for cemetery or build house of worship
for public; reversion clause. Witnesses: SAMUEL IRVINE, JAMES
BENAGH, THOMAS CLAYTOR.

45. 5 May 1806. JONATHAN LYNCH and wife, MARY, to ELISHA PERKINS,
     Bedford County...$500; #113. Lines: northeast side of Lynch
Street, RODERICK TALIAFERRO, #112, eighth alley. Witnesses: THOMAS W.
COCKE, JA TOMPKINS, EDWARD LYNCH, ELIAS FISHER.

46. 2 June 1806. JONATHAN LYNCH, SR. and wife, MARY, to THOMAS W.
     COCKE...$120 half acre. Lines: northwest corner of THOMAS W.
COCKE's lot, #88, JAMES GRAHAM, $87, street to be left open.

48. 7 February 1805. JONATHAN LYNCH, SR. and wife, MARY, to
     WILLIAM EDENFIELD, Campbell County...L65; half acre lot
adjoining Lynchburg. Lines: southwest corner of WASHINGTON LAMBETH,
HENRY MEREDITH.

49. 2 June 1806. JONATHAN LYNCH, SR. and wife, MARY, to HENRY
     MEREDITH...$300 half acre adjoining Lynchburg. Lines:
southwest corner of WASHINGTON LAMBETH, WILLIAM EDENFIELD.

50. 5 May 1806. JONATHAN LYNCH and wife, MARY, to JAMES TOMPKINS...
     $1.00; lot adjacent Lynchburg; southwest side of fourth street--
half acre. Witnesses: THOMAS W. COCKE, EDWARD LYNCH, ELIAS FISHER.
Memo: JAMES TOMPKINS will not disturb enclosure or graves on lot or
stones--shall be left for natural decay to obliterate; buys for lease
money. Witnesses: as above.

51. 2 June 1806. JONATHAN LYNCH, SR. and wife, MARY, to JONATHAN
     LYNCH, JR...$1.00; half acre lot; northwest of #62; one-fourth
acre. Lines: Lynch street, GEORGE K. LAMBETH, CULWELL WILLIAMSON,
JOHNSON.

52. 2 June 1806. JONATHAN LYNCH, SR. and wife, MARY, to JAMES
     STUART...six shillings; #56. Lines: fourth alley, fourth
street, #52, 54-half acre.

52. 27 June 1806. ASA MOORE to JONATHAN SCHOOLFIELD...$60. Corner
     of third street and third alley. Lines: ASA PLUMMER, JAMES
GRAHAM, THOMAS WIATT, JONATHAN MURRELL--half of #39. Bought from
Lynchburg trustees. Witnesses: BENJAMIN SCHOOLFIELD, JONATHAN
THURMONA, DAVID F. MASON.

53. 21 June 1806. ISHAM H. BAIRD and wife, CLARICY, Williamson
     County, Tennessee, to JONATHAN MURRELL...L104-10. 880 square
feet, part of #29. Lines: second street and third alley. Witnesses:
RODERICK TALIAFERRO, WILLIAM DAVIS, SAMUEL SCHOOLFIELD, SAM FISHER.

54. 23 January 1806. HENRY RIVES to DAVID CRAWFORD to secure
     CALEB TAIT...balance due on a negro; $1.00; slave, SQUIRE.
Witnesses: JONAH LEAKE, ROBERT MORRIS, NETHERLAND TAIT.

55. 2 August 1806. SAMUEL IRVINE to CHARLES HOYLE...lease--three
     story brick house--Indian Queen tavern; #19; another lot with
stable and garden--occupied by CHARLES HOYLE and on opposite side of
Lynch Street from house and lot of CALLAWAY and STEPTOE--occupied
by HENRY DAVIS--with sign, bell, porch--from 1 December 1802 for
ten years at $400 per year. Witnesses: THOMAS B. CLAYTOR, I. J.
MILES, CHRISTOPHER LYNCH, JONATHAN ROBINSON.

57. 6 Ocotber 1806. Inventory of JOSIAH LEAKE...$235.48. WILLIAM
     BROWN, THOMAS HIGGINBOTHAM, S. J. HARRISON.

58. 19 March 1806. WALTER IRVINE and wife, ANN, Buckingham, to
     STITH MEAD, Campbell County...$1200; part of #28 on Main.
Witnesses: WILLIAM HEATH, JAMES BENAGH, THOMAS CLAYTOR, CHRISTOPHER
ADAMS. W. CAMRON and BOAZ FORD, Lynchburg Justices of the Peace--
order thus reads, but then as Buckingham Justices of the Peace by
WILLIAM NORVELL, Clerk, Lynchburg.

59. 5 October 1805. JAMES FOX and wife, SARAH, to JONATHAN LYNCH...
     $1.00. Lines: #'s 33, 35, 61, 63, part of #35. Witnesses:
THOMAS WIATT, WILLIAM DAVIS, ISAAC PIDGEON, EDWARD LYNCH.

60. 5 October 1805. JONATHAN LYNCH and wife, MARY, to JAMES FOX,
     Campbell County...$1.00 part of #35. Lines: second street,
35, 63. Witnesses: as above--minus DAVIS.

61. 7 February 1806. MEREDITH LAMBETH and RODERICK TALIAFERRO
     as to JONATHAN LYNCH and wife, MARY, to WILLIAM EDENFIELD.

62. 30 April 1805. JOSEPH JACKSON and WILLIAM TEMPLE, attorneys
     in fact for HODGSON and THOMPSON to JAMES GILLIAM...JOSEPH
JACKSON in consideration of sum received from HODGSON, NICHOLSON,
ROTHON, THOMPSON and TEMPLE and $1.00; lot 38. Lines: 40--formerly
JONATHAN WARD's. Witnesses: SAMUEL ANTHONY, JAMES MOZELEY, MICAJAH
DAVIS, JR.

63. 6 January 1807. Inventory of EWELL FARMER...L34-2-3. THOMAS W.
     COCKE, ASA PLUMMER, DANIEL BURGESS.

64. 2 February 1807. WILLIAM WORD or WORD to CHARLES MORE...power
     of attorney, CHARLES MORE of Richmond.

64. -- 1806. SAMUEL SCHOOLFIELD and wife, JUDITH; WILLIAM FOWLER
     and wife, JANE; CULWELL WILLIAMSON to ALEXANDER BRIDGLAND,
Campbell County...$100; lot 84. Lines: second street and seventh
alley.

66. -- October 1806. JONATHAN LYNCH and wife, MARY, to THOMAS S.
     MC CLELLAND...L100. Lines: first alley, street on the hill
(fourth), #47, 45--part of 47.

67. -- September 1806. STEPHEN FARMER and wife, POLLEY, to
JONATHAN HUBBARD...$100 lot 78. Witnesses: EDWARD LYNCH,
SAMUEL MARTIN, JONATHAN FOWLER.

67. 14 January 1802? JONATHAN SCHOOLFIELD and wife, SARAH, to
BENJAMIN SCHOOLFIELD...L118-16; no. 29. Lines: JONATHAN
MURRELL, second street, JESSE TATE. Passage may be renewed.
Witnesses: ENOCH SCHOOLFIELD, MORRISON BRYANT, JONATHAN THURMON.

68. 2 March 1807. BENJAMIN JOHNSON and wife, MARY, Bedford, to
SAMUEL and ELIZABETH FISHER (formerly JOHNSON, and their daughter)...love and $1.00; no. 45--one half--third street and first
alley.

69. 1 September 1806. ISAAC PIGEON to WILLIAM NORVELL...L400--
junction of third street and fourth alley. Bought from ANDREW
DONALD and originally bought by JONATHAN WARD--#40; mansion thereon
and outhouses. Witnesses: SETH WARD, GEORGE K. LAMBETH, JONATHAN
MALLORY.

70. 3 February 1807. HENRY H. MEREDITH and wife, POLLY, to
BENJAMIN SCHOLFIELD...$150. Lines: WASHINGTON LAMBETH,
sixth alley, a street, on the hill. Witnesses: CHARLES HOYLE,
GEORGE ROBERTS, FRANCIS ODEN.

71. -- December 1806. GEORGE CABELL and wife, SARAH...GEORGE is
one of children of PAULINE CABELL, deceased, late wife of JONATHAN
CABELL and one of daughters of SAMUEL JORDAN, deceased, Buckingham,
to WILLIAM H. CABELL, Amherst County--L45--interest in estate of
tracts of SAMUEL JORDAN in Buckingham--may be lessened by CAROLINE
MATILDA ROSE, one of JORDAN's daughters--Henry County lands conveyed
to her by her father as an advance. Witnesses: F. and HECTOR
CABELL, JAMES THOMAS, THOMAS S. MC CLELLAND, THOMAS HIGGINBOTHAM,
REUBEN MICHELL.

73f. 18 December 1806. SUSANNA WIATT...suit pending in Culpepper--
instituted by THOMAS WIATT in lifetime and SUSANNA in own right--
versus GABRIEL JONES concerning certain slaves--five names; SUSANNA
claims as hers. Love for grandson, SAMUEL WIATT. Power of attorney
as to my interest. Suit makes me doubt efficacy of conveyance to
him and, if invalid, then is deed of gift or will. SAMUEL is to be
her executor. Witnesses: THOMAS WIATT, GEORGE WHITLOCK, WILLIAM P.
CLIABORNE.

74. 1 June 1807. JONATHAN LYNCH and wife, MARY, to CULWELL
WILLIAMSON...$1.00; #64, second street. Lines: GEORGE K.
LAMBETH. Witnesses: GEORGE ROBERTS, CHRISTOPHER LYNCH.

76. 5 February 1807. HENRY MEREDITH and wife, --, to WILLIAM
EDENFIELD...$100--one-third of one-half acre whereon HENRY
MEREDITH lives. Lines: JONATHAN LYNCH, WASHINGTON LAMBETH.
Witnesses: JAMES DUNNINGTON, GEORGE GARRANT, WILLIAM OWENS.

77. 16 June 1807. ARCHIBALD STEENE to BENJAMIN SCHOOLFIELD to
secure THOMAS HIGGINBOTHAM and Company, Lynchburg...dealings
at their store; to secure WILLIAM STEENE on open account; $1.00;
house on lot of CALEB TATE (TAIT). Lines: silver smith shop of
GEORGE SULLIVAN and occupied by ARCHIBALD STEENE; to advertise in
Lynchburg Star or Richmond papers, if Star is not in existence. Deed
of Trust and not meeting. Witnesses: JONATHAN LONDON, RICHARD
THURMOND, JOSEPH NEEDHAM, REUBEN MITCHELL.

77. 1 December 1806. JONATHAN LYNCH, SR. and wife, MARY, to
BENJAMIN SCHOOLFIELD...$250 lot on the hill. Lines: GABRIEL
JONES, sixth alley, street laid off by JONATHAN LYNCH, SR.--60 feet
wide parallel to Lynchburg streets, WILLIAM BROWN. Witnesses:
JONATHAN SCHOOLFIELD, JONATHAN THURMOND, WILLIAM STEEN.

79. 23 September 1807. BARDSDALE SNIDER and wife, SALLY, to
     WILLIAM HEATH, SR...$500; #78. Lines: fifth alley, BURGESS
WINSTON, HUBBARD, one half of lat where BARKSDALE SNIDER built and
lately resided. Witnesses: WILLIAM JOHNSON, WILLIAM BURD, ANDREW S.
SMILEY.

80. 4 July 1807. ALEXANDER BRIDGLAND and wife, HARRIET SUSANNA,
     to BENJAMIN COFFMAN, Botetourt County...$600; $84. Lines:
second street and seventh alley. Witnesses: THOMAS W. COCKE,
S. J. HARRISON, WILLIAM HARRISON.

81. 31 October 1807. WILLIAM NORVELL and wife, NANCY, to JAMES
     GILLIAM...L420; lot at junction of third street and fourth
alley. Bought from ISAAC PIDGEON, #40, one-half acre. Witnesses:
JONATHAN LONDON, E. B. NORVELL, HUMPHREY STEWART.

82. 31 October 1807. JAMES GILLIAM to THOMAS WIATT and THOMAS
     HIGGINBOTHAM to secure WILLIAM NORVELL...$1.00; #40. Witnesses:
as above.

83. 29 September 1805. EDWARD SANDERSON, Amherst County, to THOMAS
     MC CLELLAND, trusty friend...power of attorney to advertise
and sell at CH of Franklin County--tract near CH in Franklin--230
acres. Witnesses: THOMAS HIGGINBOTHAM, GEORGE CABELL.

84. 5 October 1807. STERLING CLAIBORNE to SAMUEL IRVINE...L64-15-3
     to comply with decree of Corporation Court of Chancery--all
rights by deed from JOHN LYNCH, SR.; lot; west side fourth street;
opposite 88 of THOMAS U. COCKE. Witnesses: WILLIAM NORVELL, WILLIAM P.
CLAIBOREN, OWEN OWENS, SAMUEL WIATT.

85. 14 August 1807. JONATHAN HUBBARD to THOMAS W. COCKE to secure
     JONATHAN FOWLER, JR., Campbell County...$1.00; #78 where
JONATHAN HUBBARD lives and bought from STEPHEN FARMER. Witnesses:
B. A. WINSTON, WILLIAM STEEN, JONATHAN DAVIS, JR.

86. 1 February 1808. JAMES GRAHAM to MATTHEW HARVEY, Botetourt...
     $100.00; two lots in town of Florence--Botetourt County; one-
fourth acre each; Main street; #'s 42 and 43.

87. 30 January 1808. JAMES NEWELL, Wythe County, to WILLIAM
     NORVELL...power of attorney to sell #19 occupied by DAVIS
MAYNARD and Company; seven-eighths. Witnesses: STITH MAYNARD,
WILLIAM DAVIS, JONATHAN H. HARVEY.

87. 29 January 1808. THOMAS W. COCKE, trustee of JONATHAN HUBBARD,
     to JONATHAN FOWLER...reference to Deed of Trust, 14 August 1807;
sold--L66; #78; where JONATHAN HUBBARD lives. Bought from STEPHEN
FARMER. Witnesses: CHARLES Y. JOHSNON, JONATHAN Y. JOHNSON, BENJAMIN
CORNELL.

89. 1 July 1807. Order of Hustings, June, 1807...inventory of
     JAMES TOMPKINS, deceased--that part in Pittsylvania County--
L 37-13-3. ABRAM PARRISH, JONATHAN HODGES, JAMES HART. Page 90
another inventory of 16 June 1807--L169-2 by THOMAS HIGGINBOTHAM,
GEORGE SULLIVAN, JONATHAN WIATT. Page 99. Account by JONATHAN
LYNCH and THOMAS WIATT, administrators; amount to EDWARD TOMPKINS;
trip to Pittsylvania; JONATHAN DAVIS for crying sale; funeral
L7-10--L 78-11 accounts due--page 92--EDMOND TOMPKINS, Concord
Society, Campbell--denied; New Glasgow Society; Amherst tickets;
EDWARD TOMINS, et al.; long list, 7 March 1808. WILL NORVELL,
JAMES MALLORY, JAMES STEWART. Note: TOMPKINS and not TOMPINS.

94. 4 April 1808. ROBERT G. JENNINGS to CHRISTOPHER WINFREY,
     Manchester...power of attorney to sell Chesterfield land--
195 acres bought from THOMAS WHITWORTH and wife, JANE; SAMUEL BRANCH
and wife, WINIFRED JOICE (?); CLEMENTS H. JENNINGS and wife, SARAH.

95. 26 December 1807. WILLIAM BARTEE to JONATHAN LYNCH, JR. to
     secure WILLIAM NORVELL...$1.00; slave boy, DAVE, about 16; to
advertise at some tavern door in Lynchburg. Witnesses: WILL ROSE,
JONATHAN H. TRENT.

96. 4 April 1808. GEORGE SULLIVAN and wife, SALLEY, to ENOCH
     SULLIVAN, Richmond...L400; lot in Lynchburg--#50. Lines:
third street, second alley, vacant lot of MAJOR WILLIAM WARWICK,
Methodist meeting house, part of where GEORGE SULLIVAN lives, 52
feet in front taken off for meeting house. Witnesses: WILLIAM HEATH,
WILLIAM THURMOND, JAMES CURLE.

96. 7 March 1808. Order of Campbell County Court...have examined
     account of HUBBARD FARMER, administrator of EWELL FARMER;
many names; STEVEN FARMER. L60-15-5.

98. 30 January 1806. Order to MEREDITH LAMBETH and JONATHAN
     SCHOOLFIELD...JONATHAN LYNCH and wife, MARY, 7 October 1805,
to WILLIAM WALLACE; #82; done, 16 May 1808.

99. 6 June 1808. JONATHAN LYNCH and wife, MARY, and Lynchburg
     trustees, to RICHARD TYREE...L95; #104; third street; sixth
alley; one-half acre. Trustees: JONATHAN LYNCH, JR., WILLIAM DAVIS,
M. LAMBETH, EDWARD LYNCH, RODERICK TALIAFERRO, WILL NORVELL.
Witnesses: SAMUEL WIATT, JONATHAN RICHARDSON, EDWARD PRICE, ETHERALD
CARROLL.

100. 6 June 1808. JONATHAN LYNCH et al. as above to JONATHAN
     LYNCH, JR...$1.00; #85; second street; seventh alley; 86;
JONATHAN LYNCH, SR. Witnesses: JONATHAN RICHARDSON, EDWARD PRICE,
ETHERALD CARROLL.

101. 6 June 1808. JONATHAN LYNCH, SR. et al. as above to WILLIAM
     STEENE...$200 second street; fifth alley; #63. West of stone
chimney of house occupied by STEENE. Witnesses: PRICE, RICHARDSON,
CARROLL.

102. 6 June 1808. JONATHAN LYNCH et al. as above to ARCHIBALD
     ALEXANDER...blank sum; new part of town; #74; corner of
second street and fifth alley. Witnesses: as above.

103. 6 June 1808. WILLIAM WALLACE and wife, ELIZABETH, to ARCHY
     COOPER...blank sum. West side third street, part of #82.
Lines: corner of house occupied by ARCHY COOPER.

104. 29 July 1808. CHRISTOPHER TERRELL by HENRY BURRUS, attorney
     in fact...CHRISTOPHER TERRELL's slaves in Caroline have sued
in county court for freedom; descendants of negro girl, MOLLY--
bought by JOEL PARRIS, Spotsylvania, from THOMAS WIATT, now deceased.
BURRUS of Caroline clears MRS. SUSANNA WIATT, widow of THOMAS, from
all damages, if negroes obtain freedom.

104. 25 June 1808. JONATHAN LYNCH and wife, MARY, to JEDIAH HUSSEY,
     North Caroline...L65; #42; third and Water streets. Lines:
SAMUEL IRVINE, GEORGE MC DANIEL. Witnesses: W. WARWICK, WILLIAM
DAVIS, JONATHAN JOHNSON.

105. Date not shown. CALEB TAIT, WILLIAM DAVIS, RODERICK TALIAFERRO,
     THOMAS WIATT, MEREDITH LAMBETH, WILLIAM NORVELL to THOMAS S.
MC CLELLAND...$1.00; #49; third street. Lines: DR. WADDY TATE,
DR. GEORGE CABELL (bought from COLONEL JONATHAN CALLAWAY); first
alley--where THOMAS S. MC CLELLAND's office stands. Witnesses:
BENJAMIN PERKINS, WILLIAM RADFORD, JAMES MALLORY. In 1808--see below.

106. 5 September 1808. THOMAS MC CLELLAND and wife, PAGGY, M.
     (signed MARGARET M.) to THOMAS WIATT...$1.00; lot above--where
THOMAS WIATT has built brick stable.

107. 30 July 1808. JONATHAN HUBBARD to WILLIAM NORVELL...L75;
     Lynch street--opposite MARTIN's warehouse--three-fourths acre.
Lines: second alley, Spring WH, towards river. Witnesses: JONATHAN
LONDON, ISAAC DAVIS, JONATHAN PERKINS.

107. 30 July 1808. JONATHAN HUBBARD to WILLIAM NORVELL...L75;
     Lynch street--opposite MARTIN's warehouse, three-fourths
acres. Lines: second alley, Spring WH, towards river. Witnesses:
JONATHAN LONDON, ISAAC DAVIS, JONATHAN PERKINS.

108. 14 July 1808. JAMES NEWELL, Wythe County, to WILLIAM RADFORD...
     power of attorney to sell lot with frame house thereon; #19.
Lines: Main street, LINSAY COLEMAN. Witnesses: A. ROBERTSON,
MATTHEW DUNNINGTON, WILLIAM OWENS.

108. 23 July 1808. JAMES NEWELL by WILLIAM RADFORD, attorney in
     fact, to WILLIAM MORGAN...$1.00; one-fourth acre; other part
belongs to estate of CHARLES RUSTON, deceased; #19. Witnesses:
F. BRADFORD, A. ROBERTSON, THOMAS MOORMAN.

109. 23 July 1808. WILLIAM MORGAN, 1; JAMES NEWELL, Wythe County, 2;
     WILLIAM RADFORD, 2; JONATHAN ROBINSON, 3...WILLIAM MORGAN owes
JAMES NEWELL and WILLIAM RADFORD for bonds; $1.00; lot above.
Witnesses: as above.

111. 30 November 1803. BENJAMIN A. WINSTON to THOMAS W. COCKE to
     secure ROWLAND JONES, bondsman, to SAMUEL IRVINE...$1.00; #83
where BENJAMIN A. WATSON is building a brick house. Lines: seventh
alley, fourth street, JONATHAN HUBBARD, WILLIAM HEATH, WILLIAM
WALLACE. Witnesses: PETER E. BOOKER, DAVID FOWLER, SETH W. LIGGON;
released, 17 January 1810.

113. Reference to NEWELL to MORGAN, page 108f...paid and released
     by RADFORD. Witnesses: F. BRADFORD.

113. 3 October 1808. JONATHAN LYNCH and wife, MARY, to WILLIAM
     NORVELL...$200. Lines: opposite MARTIN's WH, Lynch Street,
second alley, JONATHAN HUBBARD.

114. 13 February 1808. DAVID MOORE to THOMAS W. COCKE to secure
     JONATHAN MOORE, Botetourt County...$1.00; one-fourth acre.
Lines: the street, MRS. MARY ROHR--#65 where DAVID MOORE hath
built a large brick house. Witnesses: S. J. HARRISON, WILLIAM
BARTEL, ROWLAND JONES.

115. 14 September 1808. SETH WARD to WILLIAM DAVIS and THOMAS W.
     COCKE to secure THOMAS WIATT...$1.00; two lots: #38 whereon
is WARD's tavern; #49 whereon stands tavern stable. Bought from
THOMAS WIATT this day.

117. 14 September 1808. THOMAS WIATT and wife, SARAH, to SETH
     WARD...L1500. Lines: third street, third alley--where WARD's
Tavern stands; #31; nearly opposite tavern; also lot nearly opposite
tavern; part of 49; bought from THOMAS S. MC CLELLAND and stable
thereon.

118. 3 September 1808. JONATHAN LYNCH and wife, MARY, to WASH
     LAMBETH...six shillings. Lines: BENJAMIN SCHOOLFIELD, THOMAS
HIGGINBOTHAM, HENRY H. MEREDITH, GABRIEL JONES, fourth street--half
acre. Witnesses: WILLIAM DAVIS, THOMAS W. COCKE, S. J. HARRISON,
JONATHAN BURGESS.

119. 13 September 1808. WASHINGTON LAMBETH to THOMAS W. COCKE,
     RODERICK TALIAFERRO to secure HENRY DAVIS and Company, HIGGINBOTHAM
BROWN and Company, THOMAS HIGGINBOTHAM and Company, DAVIS MAYNARD and
Company...$1.00; half acre. Lines: northeast fourth--street running
on the hill, fifth alley, BENJAMIN SCHOOLFIELD, THOMAS HIGGINBOTHAM
and Company, HENRY MEREDITH. Witnesses: JONATHAN LONDON, HUMPHREY
STEWART, WILLIAM B. LYNCH.

121. -- September 1808. ROWLAND JONES and wife, NANCY, to
JONATHAN CABELL, JR...$1200. Lot bought from heirs of
CHRISTOPHER JOHNSON, deceased, 7 August 1805--second street; #12
on original plot. Lines: JONATHAN WARD, SAMUEL IRVINE. Witnesses:
THOMAS S. MC CLELLAND, STITH MAYNARD, G. A. ROSE. Memo: understood
that heirs of one BOWCOCK (BOCOCK) claim undivided one-eleventh and
have not relinquished claim; title does not extend to their part.
14 September 1808; witnesses: as above.

122. 5 December 1808. WILLIAM WALLACE and wife, ELIZABETH, to
ARCHIBALD COOPER...$1.00; #82. Lines: third street, grantee,
DANIEL BURGESS, WINSTON, BENJAMIN WINSTON, COOPER. To WILLIAM
WALLACE, 6 June 1808.

123. 17 October 1808. JONATHAN TIMBERLAKD, Campbell County,
attorney in fact for SAMUEL CRAIG and wife, FANNY, formerly
JOHNSON; JAMES KIMBERLING and wife, NANCY, formerly JOHNSON;
ANSELM LYNCH JOHNSON, all of Mason County, Virginia...heirs of
AGNES JOHNSON, wife of BENJAMIN JOHNSON, deceased, formerly of
Campbell County--AGNES was daughter of CHRISTOPHER JOHNSON, deceased,
Campbell County--power of attorney of 28 June 1805, attested by
WILLIAM OWENS, Justice of the Peace of Mason County and WILLIAM
STULL (?), Clerk of county, recorded in Campbell, 9 September 1805,
by ROBERT ALEXANDER, Clerk--to THOMAS HUMPHREYS $40; #34. Lines:
Lynch Street, grantee--bought from ACHILES DOYLE; 36; 62. Originally
by Lynchburg trustees to ACHILLES DOUGLAS--note error just before
where I put DOYLE. Sold by DOUGLAS to CHRISTOPHER JOHNSON,
deceased. Witnesses: CHARLES HOYLE, JONATHAN DAVIS, JR., ROWLAND
JONES, HENRY GEORGE.

126. 17 April 1806. THOMAS W. COCKE to SAMUEL IRVINE to secure
ROWLAND JONES...$1.00; lot where THOMAS W. COCKE lives:
#88--half acre. Lines: fourth street, seventh alley, DR. JAMES
GRAHAM--87. Advertise in Lynchburg Gazette and hand bills.
Witnesses: ROBT. MORRIS, JONATHAN DAVIS, JR., JONATHAN W. HORSLEY.
Memo: 4 March 1807. Acknowledged by both. Witnesses: WALKER
SANDERS, A. STEEN, WILLIAM PRESLEY CLAIBORNE, ROBERT M. ROSE.
Memo: 20 April 1808. Acknowledged by both. Witnesses: WILLIAM
FOWLER, JAMES DUNNINGTON, ROBERT M. ROSE.

129. 4 November 1808. JAMES ROBERTS to JACOB DABNEY, free mulatto...
JACOB is in jail on execution by Corp. of Lynchburg by JONATHAN C.
LYNCH L3-6-4; no way to pay; owes JAMES ROBERTS $750--save personal
labor. JAMES ROBERTS will pay and DABNEY binds self as servant for
one year. Will be paid $50 at end of time. Subjoins emancipation
evidence. Witnesses: THOMAS W. COCKE, THOMAS STEWART, PETER TOEL.
Memo: 4 October 1808--DABNEY is light of complexion, about 5 feet
8 inches; about 26 years old. Born free. Certificate filed in
Lynchburg from Bedford Clerk. Registered in Lynchburg, October, 1806.

130. 22 May 1808. JAMES MOSELEY to THOMAS W. COCKE to secure
various creditors...$1.00; all estate--books, papers, etc.;
bed and furniture. WILLIAM GALT had received assignment of JONATHAN M.
GORDON's bond on houses and lot. Witnesses: JONATHAN DABNEY,
SAMUEL JORDAN, HENRY GEORGE, CLEMENT TOWNSEND.

132. 17 October 1808. JONATHAN TIMBERLAKE, attorney for SAMUEL
CRAIG and wife, FANNY, formerly JOHNSON--see 123 for all
grantors--to ROWLAND JONES...$60 #12; one-half acre. Lines:
JONATHAN WARD, SR.--#4; SAMUEL IRVINE--#10; second alley; second
street. Witnesses: CHARLES HOYLE, JONATHAN DAVIS, JR., HENRY
GEORGE, THOMAS HUMPHREY.

135. 6 February 1809. JONATHAN LYNCH and wife, MARY, to MORRIS
and DUNNINGTON, merchants...six shillings. Lines: west side
fourth street, WILLIAM BROWN, BENJAMIN SCHOOLFIELD, fifth alley.
Sold to GABRIEL JONES, Bedford County.

136. 5 January 1808. ARCHIBALD ALEXANDER, Amherst County, to
      PHILIP ROHR...$150; #74. Lines: JONATHAN CABELL, second
street, JONATHAN LYNCH. Witnesses: NATHAN THURMOND, WILLIAM
STEENE, WILLIAM P. CORNELL.

137. 28 December 1808. ARCHIBALD ALEXANDER to JONATHAN CABELL...
      L90. Lines: Main street or second street, fifth alley--half
of lot bought from JONATHAN LYNCH, SR. Witnesses: CHRISTOPHER
LYNCH, RICHARD H. RAMSEY, RICHARD B. GAINES.

137. 4 March 1809. JONATHAN LYNCH and wife, MARY, to JONATHAN J.
      CABELL...$200 #74 on fifth alley. Witnesses: JAMES BENAGH,
WILLIAM DAVIS, ASA PLUMMER.

138. 3 April 1809. PHILIP ROHR and wife, SALLEY, to PETER DETTO...
      $170 one-fourth of one-half acre. Lines: southwest side of
fourth street, Water Street, remainder of lot where goal stands--
opposite 44 on fourth street.

140. 16 May 1809. CAROLINE MATILDA ROSE to JONATHAN, ISAAC, DAVID
      and JOSHUA TINSLEY...amount received from them for dower
claims on tract bought by them from my husbands--sons, HUGH and
GUSTAVUS A. ROSE--to LANDON and DR. GEORGE CABELL jointly and
GUSTAVUS A. ROSE; named slaves--for my daughter, EMILY COUPLAND,
and TINSLEYS are to be trustees. Witnesses: WILLIAM NORVELL,
WILLIAM OWENS, JONATHAN WIATT.

141. 24 April 1809. WILLIAM WALLACE and wife, ELIZABETH, to
      JOSEPH NEEDHAM...$1000.00. Lines: 82, third street and
seventh alley, 83. Part of a lot. Witnesses: THOMAS W. COCKE,
WILLIAM TARDY, WILLIAM D. MASON, WILLIAM SUMPTER.

142. 6 July 1808. JONATHAN J. CABELL...I have this day bought all
      rights of WILLIAM FORRILL to 548 acres on Beaver Creek,
Campbell County, as heir of FERRILL, the Elder--by court decree;
only his rights. Witnesses: WILLIAM HARRISON, THOMAS S. MC CLELLAND,
JONATHAN DAVIS, JR.

142. 14 April 1809. JONATHAN POINTER and wife, POLLY, to JAMES
      WADE, New London...L230; part of #45. Lines: third street,
BENJAMIN JOHNSON, JONATHAN LYNCH, ROWLAND JONES. Witnesses:
SAMUEL FISHER, WILLIAM BURD, SAMUEL K. JENNINGS.

143. 24 April 1809. JOSEPH NEEDHAM to THOMAS W. COCKE and THOMAS
      WIATT to secure WILLIAM WALLACE...$1.00. Part of #82; on
third street. Bought from WILLIAM WALLACE and wife, ELIZABETH,
24 April 1809. Witnesses: WILLIAM TARDY, WILLIAM D. MASON, WILLIAM
SUMPTER; dower relinquished to JONATHAN J. HARRISON and JONATHAN
SCHOOLFIELD by ELIZABETH WALLACE, 7 August 1809.

147. 28 July 1809. ELIZABETH WALLACE, wife of WILLIAM, relinquished
      dower on deed of 6 June 1809, to ARCHY COOPER...part of 82,
to M. LAMBETH and JAMES STEWART, Justices of the Peace.

148. 14 April 1809. ARCHIBALD ALEXANDER and wife, FRANCES,
      Amherst County, to JONATHAN POINTER...$1.00; one-fourth of
one-half acres--northwest one-fourth of #74--now in hands of PETER E.
BOOKER, tenant. Lines: second street. Witnesses: WILLIAM BURD,
JAMES WADE, SAMUEL FISHER.

149. 7 August 1809. WILLIAM WALLACE and wife, ELIZABETH, to
      THOMAS BURGESS...$1.00; west side third street; part of 82.
Lines: JOSEPH NEEDHAM, ARCHY COOPER, BENJAMIN A. WINSTON. Page
150 ELIZABETH relinquished dower to JONATHAN LYNCH, JR. and
SAMUEL J. HARRISON, -- August 1809.

151. -- August 1809. ELIZABETH WALLACE, wife of WILLIAM, relinquished
      dower to deed to ARCHIBALD COOPER, 28 July 1809...MEREDITH
LAMBETH and JAMES STEWART, Justices of the Peace.

152. 24 March 1809. WILLIAM NORVELL and wife, NANCY, on 31 October
1807, to JAMES GILLIAM...She relinquished dower to JONATHAN
LYNCH, JR. and JAMES MALLORY.

153. 1 September 1809. JONATHAN LYNCH, SR. and wife, MARY, to
WILLIAM NORVELL...$220--lot previously sold to WILLIAM
NORVELL; lot bought by WILLIAN NORVELL from JONATHAN HUBBARD;
second alley. Witnesses: THOMAS W. COCKE, EDWARD B. NORVELL.

154. 4 September 1809. JONATHAN LYNCH and wife, MARY, and
Lynchburg trustees to ROBERT MORRIS...$500; #79; half in
town; seventh alley and second street; one acre.

155. 24 August 1809. WILLIAM WALLCEE, presently of Lynchburg...
power of attorney to WILLIAM NORVELL--business in Amherst,
Campbell, Bedford. Witnesses: ETHELBREAD CARREL, JONATHAN S.
JOHNSON, CRISTOPHER WINFREEE. List of bonds due from JOSEPH
NEEDHAM, JAMES WADE, WILLIAM BURD, THOMAS WIATT, PHILLIP ROHR,
WILLIAM DAVIS, WILLIAM SNEAD, ELIJAH JOHNSON; WILLIAM WALCEE owes
JONATHAN ROBERTS, BEDFORD, JOSEPH NEEDHAM, DANIEL HOFFMAN, ISAAC
PIDGEON, JONATHAN BURGESS, JOSEPH BURGESS, JAMES GILLIAM, CHRISTOPHER
CLARKE.

156. 7 June 1809. WILLIAM R. COUPLAND to SAMUEL WIATT...$1.00;
slave, PATRICK--to secure GUSTAVUS A. ROSE on bond to BROOKS
BAKER. Witnesses: SAMUEL IRVINE, GEORGE W. RONALD.

157. 2 October 1809. JONATHAN LYNCH and wife, MARY, to son,
CHARLES C. LYNCH...love and $1.00; #30 on second street and
fourth alley.

158. 2 October 1809. JONATHAN LYNCH and wife, MARY, to son-in-law,
ENOCH ROBERTS, Campbell County...love and $1.00; #11; second
street and first alley; residue of lot.

159. 2 October 1809. JONATHAN LYNCH and wife, MARY, to son,
JONATHAN C. LYNCH...love and $1.00; southeast end of #3;
second street and Water Street.

160. 2 October 1809. JONATHAN LYNCH and wife, MARY, to son,
EDWARD LYNCH...love and $1.00; southeast part of #35; second
street and third alley.

161. 2 October 1809. JONATHAN LYNCH and wife, MARY, to son,
CHRISTOPHER LYNCH...love and $1.00; #22; second street and
second alley.

162. 2 October 1809. JONATHAN LYNCH and wife, MARY, to son-in-law,
WILLIAM DAVIS, JR...love and $1.00; #9; Lynch street and
first alley.

163. 2 October 1809. JONATHAN LYNCH and wife, MARY, to WILLIAM
JOHNSON...$200; lot opposite junction of Lynch Street and
fourth alley.

164. 7 August 1809. THOMAS W. COCKE to WILLIAM WALLACE...release
of Deed of Trust; reference to page 31f.

164. 31 October 1809. JONATHAN WIATT to daughter, JUSITH THOMAS
and children begotten by husband, NORBORNE THOMAS...to trustees
WILLIAM NORVELL, GEORGE CABELL, JR. and SAMUEL WIATT--sixteen named
slaves. NORBORNE THOMAS is to pay $1.00 per year for hires and at
death to JUDITH and heirs--when oldest child is 21 or a daughter
marries.

165. 4 December 1809. SAMUEL SCHOOLFIELD and wife, JUDITH, to
BENJAMIN ESSEX...$1000.00; part of #13 on second or Main Street.
Lines: TALIAFERRO, STEWART, MAJOR WILLIAM WARWICK, JONATHAN THURMON.

166. 27 November 1809. JONATHAN POINTER and wife, MARY, to PETER DOTTO...$120 part of #74 on second street and fifth alley. Witnesses: JONATHAN ROBINSON, THOMAS HIGGINBOTHAM, JONATHAN LONDON, RICHARD THURMON, JR.

167. 26 November 1809. THOMAS WIATT to SETH WARD...receipt in full for bonds from 1808. Witness: CORBIN WARWICK.

167. 16 December 1809. SAMUEL WIATT to WILLIAM R. COUPLAND... release--has tendered other property.

167. 14 June 1809. CHARLES JOHNSTON to THOMAS HIGGINBOTHAM, WILLIAM NORVELL and JONATHAN MURRELL to secure WILLIAM BROWN and Company...$1.00; #60 where he lives; furniture. Witnesses: ARCHELAUS MAYS, WILLIAM BLACK, JONATHAN HORSLEY, A. ROBERTSON.

169. 4 May 1809. SAMUEL HUBBARD to JAMES MALLORY to secure JONATHAN LYNCH, JR. and WILLIAM THURMOND...$1.00; slave, BETTY--about twenty-four. Witnesses: JONATHAN ROBINSON, WILL NORVELL, GEORGE CORKRAM.

170. 17 January 1810. BENJAMIN A. WINSTON to SAMUEL PANNILL... $1000.00 #83; fourth street and seventh alley. Lines: 77 and 82. Witnesses: THOMAS W. COCKE, THOMAS HUMPHREYS, GEORGE GARNETT, CHARLES HOYLE.

172. 12 January 1810. JONATHAN POINTER and wife, MARY, to JONATHAN J. CABELL...$60.00 #74. Lines: grantee, ROBERT MORRIS, 79. Witnesses: MAN C. SPENCER, ARCH. D. WRIGHT, RICHARD H. RAMSEY.

174. 13 October 1809. Order to JONATHAN LYNCH and wife, MARY... deed of 4 March 1809 to JONATHAN J. CABELL; lot above--#74. Done by JONATHAN LYNCH, JR. and JAMES STEWART on 19 December 1809.

175. 12 January 1810. ROBERT MORRIS and wife, SARAH, to JONATHAN J. CABELL...$110; two lots. Lines: JOHN POINTER; 79; second street; grantee. Witnesses: as for page 172.

176. 31 January 1810. Commissioners: JONATHAN WIATT, THOMAS W. COCKE, JAMES BENAGH under decree of SAMUEL IRVINE versus WILLIAM B. BROWN and wife, ELIZABETH, and WILLIAM S. REID...house and lot of WILSON DAVENPORT, deceased. $1375 paid by WILLIAM S. REID; #93; Main and eighth alley. Witnesses: TEMPLE GWATHMEY, WILLIAM HARRISON, JAMES DUNNINGTON.

177. 12 August 1809. BENJAMIN A. WINSTON to THOMAS W. COCKE... ARCHIBALD ALEXANDER of Amherst and GEORGE D. WISNTON, Campbell County, 17 August 1808, became his bondsman to secure HIGGINBOTHAM BROWN and Company--COCKE, Sergeant of Lynchburg--at Market House, 16 September 1808; also to secure RIVES HIGGINBOTHAM and Company. BENJAMIN A. WINSTON defaulted--$1.00; slave, CHARLOTTE--from WILLIAM ARMISTEAD, Amherst County. Witnesses: WILLIAM W. MORGAN, JAMES GILLIAM, JACOB OGLESBY.

180. 12 March 1810. JAMES STEPTOE, SR., Bedford, and GEORGE CALLEWAY, to JONATHAN LYNCH, SR...$1.00; #33; north side Lynch Street; Liberty WH; third alley. Witnesses: SAMUEL J. WIATT, JAMES BENAGH, WILLIAM RADFORD.

181. 20 March 1810. Lynchburg trustees: WILLIAM DAVIS, CALEB TAIT, THOMAS WIATT, JONATHAN LYNCH, JR., MEREDITH LAMBETH, SAMUEL J. HARRISON, WILLIAM NORVELL to JONATHAN MILLER...order from RO. MC COY in favor of EDWARD TERRELL and from EDWARD TERRELL in favor of MILLER; $1.00; #25. Lines: Lynch Street; 17; third alley.

182. 5 February 1810. BENJAMIN, JONATHAN and RICHARD PERKINS to Lynchburg Justices of the Peace, MEREDITH LAMBETH, JAMES STEWART, JONATHAN SCHOOLFIELD, WILLIAM MORGAN for BENJAMIN PERKINS as administrator of THOMAS PERKINS.

183. 14 March 1810. CHARLES JOHNSON, 1; THOMAS HIGGINBOTHAM,
      partner of late mercantile firm of THOMAS HIGGINBOTHAM and
Company, 2; to JONATHAN MURRELL and ARCHIBALD ROBERTSON, 3...CHARLES
JOHNSON owes THOMAS HIGGINBOTHAM; $1.00; #60. Lines: fourth or
Hill street; fourth alley; 58 and 77--where CHARLES JOHNSON lives.
Reference to Deed of Trust to JONATHAN MURRELL and ARCHIBALD
ROBERTSON to secure WILLIAM BROWN and Company. Witnesses: J. WRIGHT,
WILLIAM J. CABELL, S. J. HARRISON.

184. 13 October 1809. Order to Campbell County Justices of the
      Peace THOMAS HUMPHREYS, THOMAS W. COEKE, SAMUEL SCOTT...
ROWLAND JONES and wife, NANCY, September, 1808, to JONATHAN CABELL,
JR.--#12. Done by first two, 11 December 1809.

185. 8 March 1810. CALEB TAIT, 1; JONATHAN CABELL and THOMAS
      HIGGINBOTHAM, 2; CHARLES CLAY, Bedford, 3...$1000 due
CHARLES CLAY; $1.00; brick house occupied by JONATHAN CABELL--well
divides it from part occupied by WIATT and RHOR. Witnesses:
JONATHAN NETHERLAND, NATHANIEL S. STRANGE, CHARLES R. COBBS,
JONATHAN TOMPKINS.

187. 19 February 1810. JONATHAN WARD to JONATHAN LYNCH...$4000;
      #4; Water and second street. Witnesses: ANSELM LYNCH,
CHARLES L. TERRELL, ROBERT ADAMS, H. TERRELL, HENRY WARD, EDWARD
LYNCH, THOMAS STEWART, CHARLES C. LYNCH.

188. 28 November 1809. ROBERT MORRIS and wife, SARAH, to JONATHAN
      POINTER...$220; two lots on second street; #79 joins JONATHAN J.
CABELL; #74. Witnesses: CALEB TAIT, MATTHEW DUNNINGTON, JAMES
DUNNINGTON.

189. 29 May 1810. SAMUEL SCOTT and wife, ANN, to WILLIAM DAVIS...
      $600 #8. Lines: JAMES HOLLEY, Water Street; #6; WILLIAM
DAVIS; WH; #16. Witnesses: CHRISTOPHER WINFREE, MICAJAH T.
WILLIAMS, JONATHAN M. GORDON.

190. 29 May 1810. SAMUEL SCOTT and wife, ANN, to ISAAC PIDGEON,
      EDWARD LYNCH, JESSE WILLIAMS...$3400; #6. Witnesses: as
above.

191. 25 June 1810. WILLIAM WARWICK and wife, LEANNA, to BENJAMIN
      ESSEX...$2500 #15 where WILLIAM WARWICK lives. Third street
and first alley. Witnesses: PETER DUDLEY, GEORGE CALLAWAY, EDMOND J.
NORVELL.

192. 25 June 1810. BENJAMIN ESSEX to THOMAS WIATT and WILLIAM
      NORVELL to secure WILLIAM WARWICK...$1.00; lot above. Witnesses:
as above.

194. 6 June 1810. JONATHAN LYNCH and wife, MARY, to JOSEPH MOSBY...
      $200; lot opposite THOMAS W. COCKE. Lines: fourth street,
SAMUEL IRVINE. Witnesses: THOMAS STEWART, JAMES ADAMS, HARRISON
RATCLIFF.

195. 16 June 1810. WADDY TATE and wife, ELIZA, Petersburg, Georgia,
      to GEORGE CABELL, SR...$1215. #53. Lines: third street,
third alley, 55, 51, 49. Witnesses: THOMAS W. COEKE, JONATHAN
SAUNDERS, JER. KYLE, CHARLES HOYLE, WILLIAM WORD, J. WRIGHT,
WILLIAM J. CABELL.

197. 25 July 1810. MICHAEL ROHR, Amherst County, releases right
      to #65 bought by my wife, MARY, from JONATHAN LYNCH, SR...
JONATHAN LYNCH to convey to trustees for my wife and heirs. If
done, I release all rights. Witnesses: JOHN ROBINSON, THOMAS
WIATT, JOSEPH JOHNSON.

198. 5 September 1810. HENRY and POLLY MEREDITH, his wife, to
     SAMUEL FISHER...$850; lot occupied by SILAS HESTON. Lines:
seventh alley and fourth street, WILLIAM EDENFIELD, WASHINGTON LAMBETH.
Bought from JONATHAN LYNCH and wife, MARY, 29 August 1810. Witnesses:
WILLIAM NORVELL, SILAS HESTON, E. B. NORVELL. Memo: HOWELL LEWIS
states that HENRY MEREDITH sold it to him and conveyance is at his
request. Witnesses: as above.

199. 27 August 1810. JONATHAN LYNCH and wife, MARY, to EDWARD
     DUFFELL...$500 #70 one-fourth acre; one-half in old part
of town and one-half in new part--opposite 68 where HENRY DAVIS
lives--third street, sixth alley. Witnesses: RICHARD and WILLIAM
THURMON, PETER DUDLEY, HENRY PRIDDY.

200. 18 July 1810. JONATHAN LYNCH and wife, MARY, to JAMES MALLORY...
     $350 near head of horse ford branch. Lines: third alley,
old brick yard where WILL (HILL?) GEORGE formerly lived, fifth
alley, two acres. Witnesses: THOMAS STEWART, MORE BARRICKS,
CHARLES C. and EDWARD LYNCH.

201. 29 August 1810. JONATHAN LYNCH, SR. and wife, MARY, to HENRY
     MEREDITH...$300. Lines: fourth street, seventh alley,
WILLIAM EDENFIELD, WASHINGTON LAMBETH, fourth street. Witnesses:
HOWELL LEWIS, SAMUEL FISHER, CHARLES C. LYNCH.

203. -- November 1810. CALEB TAIT and wife, ANN, to WILLIAM
     STEEN...$1000.00. Lines: BENJAMIN and JONATHAN PERKINS on
second street, JAMES DUFFELL--15, 13. Witnesses: JAMES WADE,
SAMUEL SCHOOLFIELD, GEORGE LEE, ANN signs as NANCY.

204. -- November 1810. CALEB TAIT and wife, ANN, to WILLIAM
     STEEN...$500; one-third of one-half acre; #17; held equally
with JAMES CALLAWAY, deceased. JAMES STEPTOE and TAIT brought
from Lynchburg trustees; JAMES CALLAWAY is called JR. hereinafter.
Witnesses: as above.

206. 3 November 1810. CALEB TAIT and wife, NANCY, to JONATHAN
     and BENJAMIN PERKINS...$4000; #13; second street and first
alley; 15 of BENJAMIN ESSEX. Witnesses: RICHARD POWELL, CHRISTOPHER
LYNCH, WA DUNNINGTON.

207. 9 November 1810. JONATHAN and EDWARD LYNCH, administrators
     of JONATHAN C. LYNCH...have slave, BOB, by descent from my
son, JONATHAN C., who died intestate--about 30. Persuaded that
freedom is natural right of fellow creatures. BOB was tried and
acquitted; emancipation.

207. 6 September 1810. CHRISTOPHER JOHNSON BEAUCOCK, Campbell
     County, SAMUEL and WADDY BEAUCOCK, Ohio, to JONATHAN CABELL,
JR...they are children of NANCY BEAUCOCK, formerly JOHNSON, and
heir of CHRISTOPHER JOHNSON, deceased. $30; #12; second street.
Lines: JONATHAN WARD, SAMUEL IRVINE. Signed BOWCOCK and BOCOCK.
Witnesses: W. RADFORD, B. A. WINSTON, RICHARD RAMSEY, JONATHAN T.
WRIGHT, JONATHAN RICHARDSON.

208. 31 October 1810. HENRY PRIDDY to WILLIAM TARDY...$220; lease;
     tenement and half lot. Lines: WILLIAM WARD, Main Street.
Leased from JAMES GRAHAM, 1 May 1811 for eight years and three
months. $25 per year. Witness: WILLIAM RADFORD.

209. 21 August 1810. THOMAS BURGESS and wife, BETTY, to JOSEPH
     NEEDHAM...$100 west side third street, part of 82. Lines:
JOSEPH NEEDHAM, ARCHER COOPER. Bought from WILLIAM WALLACE and
wife, 7 August 1809. Witnesses: JACOB OGLESBY, WILLIAM WARD,
WILLIAM TARDY, E. B. NORVELL.

211. 6 October 1810. ISAAC PIDGEON, EDWARD LYNCH and wife, MARY,
Lynchburg; JESSE WILLIAMS and wife, SARAH, Stokes County,
North Carolina, to RICHARD THURMON...$3000.00 part of #6. Lines:
second street, Water Street, 8. Witnesses: WILLIAM DAVIS, PETER
DUDLEY, FIELDING BRADFORD, THOMAS W. COCKE.

213. No date. Inventory of DR. JONATHAN C. LYNCH...many medical
books--$785.96½. SETH WARD, JONATHAN WIATT, THOMAS WIATT,
WILLIAM DAVIS; reference to annexed order--notherein.

214. 30 October 1810. JONATHAN LYNCH and wife, MARY, to WILLIAM
MITCHELL, Bedford County...$300; south side Horseford branch;
southeast courses of Water Street; second alley. Witnesses:
THOMAS WIATT, WILLIAM DAVIS, SETH WARD.

215. 9 November 1810. JONATHAN LYNCH and wife, MARY, to GEORGE
CABELL...L25. Lines: CABELL's house, alley by JONATHAN
LYNCH's house, THOMAS MORRISON's unimproved lot.

216. 1 October 1810. JAMES STEWART and wife, NANCY B.; RODERICK
TALIAFERRO and wife, SUSAN, to JAMES DUFFEL...L750; part of
#13. Bought by TALIAFERRO, STEWART and Company--two of partners--
from WIATT and NORVELL--they bought out partner, ZACH TALIAFERRO--
opposite HIGGINBOTHAM BROWN and Company--formerly ROBERT RIVES and
Co. store--one-fourth. Witnesses: REUBEN MITCHELL, CHRIS WINFREE,
WILLIAM THURMON, ALEXANDER TOMPKINS.

217. 21 December 1810. JAMES CAMPBELL's inventory by Lynchburg
Sergeant, THOMAS W. COCKE...$65.42.

218. 22 October 1810. JONATHAN R. DAWSON and wife, SALLY L.,
formerly BEUCOCK, Amherst County, to JONATHAN J. CABELL, JR...
she is daughter of NANCY BEAUCOCK, formerly JOHNSON, and heir of
CHRISTOPHER JOHNSON; $10; interest in lot on second street; #12.
Lines: JONATHAN WARD, SAMUEL IRVINE, 10, second alley. Witnesses:
B. A. WINSTON, OWEN OWENS, GEORGE MC DANIEL, RICHARD D. RAMSEY,
WILLIAM BURD, ROBERT RUTHERFORD.

219. 18 December 1810. WILLIAM NORVELL and wife, ANN, to WILLIAM
MORTON...$1100; opposite MARTIN's WH. Bought from JONATHAN
HUBBARD. Lines: Lynch Street, second alley--towards Spring WH.
Ground descends and not responsible for variations. Witnesses:
JONATHAN BULLOCK, WILLIAM DAVIS, JAMES STEWART. Dower relinquished
to WILLIAM MORGAN and JAMES STEWART on same date.

221. 18 December 1810. WILLIAM MORTON and wife, ANNE, to JONATHAN
LYNCH, JR. and THOMAS WIATT to secure WILLIAM NORVELL...$1.00;
lot above. Witnesses: as above and ANNE relinquished dower to
WILLIAM MORGAN and JAMES STEWART on same date.

224. 10 October 1810. SAMUEL SCOTT and wife, ANN, 29 May 1810...
dower relinquished to M. LAMBETH and JONATHAN LYNCH, JR. on
this date.

225. 10 October 1810. SAMUEL SCOTT and wife, ANN, 29 May 1810, to
ISAAC PIDGEON...dower relinquished--also EDWARD LYNCH and
JESSE WILLIAMS were grantees.

227. 18 January 1811. GUSTAVUS M. WARE to WALTER COX, Washington D.C...
power of attorney by WARE.

227. 9 October 1810. CALEB TAIT and wife, ANN, to PETER DETTO...
L190 paid by DETTO; #55; fourth street and third alley; 51;
49; 53. Witnesses: WILLIAM DAVIS, JONATHAN M. GORDON, THOMAS W.
COCKE.

229. 1 February 1811. JONATHAN LYNCH and wife, MARY, 27 August 1810,
to EDWARD DUFFEL...release of dower to WILLIAM MORGAN and
JONATHAN SCHOOLFIELD.

230. 17 December 1810. WADDY TATE and wife, ELIZA E., Elbert
    County, Georgia, to GEORGE CABELL, SR., 16 June 1810...dower
relinquished to JONATHAN WATKINS and W. HATCHER, Georgia Justices
of the Peace.

231. 6 February 1811. ALEXANDER BRIDGLAND and wife, HARRIET
    SUSANNA, 14 July 1807, to BENJAMIN COFFMAN, Botetourt County...
relinquishment of dower by wife of BRIDGLAND to JONATHAN MURRELL
and GEORGE ROBERTS, Lynchburg Justices of the Peace.

232. 23 January 1811. GEORGE CALLAWAY to GEORGE W. LAMBETH...$300.
    Lines: seventh alley, SAMUEL IRVINE. Witnesses: SAMUEL
WIATT, E. B. NORVELL, THOMAS W. COCKE, CHARLES G. COBBS.

233. 24 December 1810. EDWARD LYNCH and wife, MARY, Lynchburg;
    JESSE WILLIAMS and wife, SARAH, Stokes County, North Carolina
to ISAAC PIDGEON...$1000; part of #6. Lines: second street; Water
Street; WILLIAM DAVIS; SAMUEL ANTHONY. Witnesses: JAMES C. MOORMAN,
THOMAS STEWART, HENRY DAVIS. 234 dower relinquished by both wives
to WILLIAM MORGAN and JONATHAN SCHOOLFIELD.

235. 24 December 1810. ISAAC PIDGEAON and JESSE WILLIAMS and wife,
    SARAH, Stokes County, North Carolina, to EDWARD LYNCH...$1000;
part of 6; THURMOND and WILLIAM DAVIS added to lines. Witnesses:
as above; SARAH relinquished dower as above.

237. 25 May 1810. JONATHAN LYNCH and wife, ANNE, to DAVID SAUNDERS,
    Bedford County...$5000; #4. Lines: Water and second street.
Witnesses: FRANCIS GRAY, SHUBEL BARNARD, GEORGE MC DANIEL, BENJAMIN
PERKINS.

238. 1 March 1811. JAMES GILLIAMS and wife, SALLEY, to WILLIAM
    RADFORD...L60 one-eighth acre next to WILLIAM RADFORD and one-
fourth of #--. Lines: 68, third street, GILLIAM, SAMUEL SCOTT.
Witnesses: WASHINGTON LAMBETH, GEORGE K. LAMBETH, JOSEPH BURGESS.

239. 22 February 1811. JONATHAN LYNCH and wife, MARY, and Lynchburg
    trustees to GEORGE K. LAMBETH...$400; 91. Lines: eighth
alley, Lynch street, COL. JONATHAN WIATT, SAMUEL J. HARRISON.
Witnesses: JONATHAN M. GORDON, CHRISTOPHER WINFREE, WILLIAM SNEAD,
BERNARD LAMBETH, DAVID F. MASON, WILLIAM SUMPTER, B. LAMBETH.
Trustees: JONATHAN LYNCH, JR., WILLIAM DAVIS, THOMAS WIATT, S. J.
HARRISON, EDWARD LYNCH, WILL NORVELL.

240. 12 March 1811. JAMES STEWART and wife, NANCY B., RODERICK
    TALIAFERRO and wife, SUSAN, 1 October 1810, to JAMES DUFFELL...
#13; relinquishment of dower by wives to WILLIAM MORGAN and JONATHAN
SCHOOLFIELD.

241. 12 March 1811. EDWARD LYNCH and wife, MARY, JESSE WILLIAMS
    and wife, SARAH, to ISAAC PIDGEON, 6 October 1810, and
RICHARD THURMOND...dower relinquished as above.

242. 4 March 1811. CHARLES JOHNSON and wife, MARY, to JAMES C.
    MOORMAN...$800 #60 where CHARLES JOHNSON lives. Witnesses:
THOMAS WIATT, PHILLIP ROHR, NELSON BAILEY. Memo: Deed of Trust
by CHARLES JOHNSON, 14 June 1809, to THOMAS HIGGINBOTHAM and JOHN
MURRELL to secure WILLIAM BROWN and Company and to secure THOMAS
HIGGINBOTHAM and Company, 14 March 1810, to JONATHAN MURRELL and
ARCHIBALD ROBERTSON...$1.00 paid by JAMES C. MOORMAN--paid and
released. D. S. GARLAND for WILLIAM BROWN and Company; other
creditors signed.

243. No date. Fire company--Act: 7 January 1784; over forty
      residents of any town may form company; have bought engine
and have advised five companies and have incorporated. Signed:
WILLIAM DAVIS, JONATHAN LYNCH, JR., JAMES STEWART, WILLIAM MORGAN,
JONATHAN MURRELL, JONATHAN SCHOOLFIELD, GEORGE ROBERTS, GEORGE
MC DANIEL, EDWARD LYNCH, THOMAS WIATT, G. K. LAMBETH, WILL NORVELL,
JAMES MALLORY, RODERICK TALIAFERRO, JAMES DUNNINGTON, PETER DUDLEY,
THOMAS HIGGINBOTHAM, CHRIS WINFREE, JAMES DUFFELL, RICHARD THURMOND,
JR., JONATHAN PERKINS, HENRY DAVIS, CHRISTOPHER ANTHONY, JR.,
JONATHAN J. CABELL, THOMAS W. COCKE, EDWARD DUFFIELD, JONATHAN
SAUNDERS, PETER TOEL, SAMUEL SCHOOLFIELD, BENJAMIN ESSEX, DAVID
KYLE, PHILIP ROHR, THOMAS S. MC CLELLAND, SETH WARD, GEORGE
GWATHMEY, WILLIAM THURMON, WASHINGTON LAMBETH, JAMES GILLIAM,
WILLIAM RADFORD, WILLIAM GRANT, ABNER ANTHONY, ANDREW JAMESON,
A. ROBERTSON, JONATHAN THURMON.

244. 9 May 1811. THOMAS W. COCKE qualified as Sergeant of
      Lynchburg...Bondsman: CHARLES HOYLE, P. TOEL, ROWLAND JONES,
D. W. COCKE, SAMUEL IRVINE, PETER DUDLEY, SAMUEL J. HARRISON.

245. 8 April 1811. CALEB TAIT and wife, NANCY, -- November 1810,
      to WILLIAM STEENE...dower relinquished to JONATHAN SCHOOLFIELD
and WILLIAM HEATH.

246. 8 April 1811. CALEB TAIT and wife, NANCY, to WILLIAM STEENE,
      -- November 1810...dower relinquished as above.

247. 8 April 1811. CALEB TAIT and wife, NANCY, to PETER DETTO,
      9 October 1810...relinquished as above.

248. 8 April 1811. CALEB TAIT and wife, NANCY, 3 November 1810, to
      BENJAMIN PERKINS...relinquished as above.

249. 21 December 1810. CHRISTOPHER JOHNSON BEAUCOCK, Campbell
      County, SAMUEL and WADDY BEAUCOCK, Ohio, JONATHAN R. DAWSON
and wife, SARAH L., formerly BEAUCOCK, Amherst County, heirs of
NANCY BEAUCOCK, deceased, who was daughter of CHRISTOPHER JOHNSON,
deceased, to THOMAS HUMPHREYS...L5-6-8 one-fourth acres #34.
Lines: Lynch Street, half of 34 owned by ACHILLES DOUGLAS who sold
to THOMAS HUMPHREYS: 36, 62. Formerly that of CHRISTOPHER JOHNSON.
Witnesses: CALEB TAIT, HENRY DAVIS, WILLIAM DUNNINGTON, S. MAYNARD,
JAMES DUNNINGTON, WAT. DUNNINGTON.

250. 21 May 1811. DAVID MOORE to JAMES C. FISHBACK, Nelson
      County...lease--one-fourth of lot. Lines: second street,
MRS. MARY ROHR, part of 65--thereon DAVID MOORE has built large
brick house and occupied by him and CHARLES Y. JOHNSON. Inside to
be furnished, front windows painted, good stable to be built with
ten stalls, house is on #65 and fifth alley, DAVID MOORE may make
brick on lot. Ten years at $400 per year. Witnesses: J. W.
DIBRELL, JONATHAN PERKINS, W. SAUNDERS, WILLIAM M. CLARK, FRANCIS J.
DENT (?).

257. 2 May 1811. WILLIAM B. BROWN and wife, ELIZA R., King William
      County, to WILLIAM S. REID...$250; #93--property of NELSON
DAVENPORT, deceased, and sold by decree: SAMUEL IRVINE versus
them. REID bought at sale. Witnesses: E. GREGORY, MONTAGUE
WILLIAMS, JAMES BENAGH. Order to WILLIAMS, FENDALL GREGORY, and
JAMES RUFFIN, King William, as to dower. Released to first two.

259. 16 May 1811. DAVID CRAWFORD, Amherst County, 1; ELIZABETH
      CRAWFORD, Lynchburg, 2; THOMAS W. COCKE, 3...ELIZABETH is
widow of DAVID CRAWFORD, Amherst, and mother of DAVID CRAWFORD.
She released interest to children and they will pay her $200 per
year for support. DAVID's part is L10; $1.00; two slaves, JACOB
and MOLLEY, to be hired to humane masters. Revert to DAVID.
Witnesses: ETHELBERT CARROLL, H. DAVIES, CHARLES DEISON (?).

261. 6 May 1811. Acknowledgement of deed in King William by
     WILLIAM B. BROWN and wife, ELIZA R., to WILLIAM S. REID...
ROBERT POLLARD, Clerk.

261. 2 July 1811. STITH MEAD and wife, PRUDENCE W., Campbell
     County, to HOLLAND MC TYREE, Richmond County, Georgia...$400;
lot in Augusta, Georgia--#70. Lines: Green Street, Jackson
Street, part of 72 conveyed to MARY MURPHY where Methodist meeting
house now stands. Dower relinquished to WILLIAM HEATH and JONATHAN
SCHOOLFIELD. Note: Amherst data has much on STITH MEAD and wife--
see deeds in particular.

264. 15 June 1811. SAMUEL IRVINE and wife, ANN F., to WILLIAM
     ROYALL...L1000--bonds and tobacco; #10. Lines: Lynch Street,
second alley, 12, 2. Witnesses: E. P. HUGHES, THOMAS HUMPHREYS,
GEORGE W. RONALD, ABRAM R. NORTH, JONATHAN F. LAMB. Dower relinquished
to JONATHAN MURRELL and GEORGE ROBERTS.

266. 4 July 1811. SAMUEL SCHOOLFIELD believes that freedom and
     liberty are natural rights of all mankind--frees mulatto,
BRIDGETT, from 1 January next.

266. 8 December 1810. JULIUS CURLE to JONATHAN BULLOCK to secure
     WILLIAM NORVELL...$1.00; two slaves--DANIEL, about 27 and
AMEY about 18. Witnesses: RICHARD CHILTON, S. J. HARRISON,
JONATHAN M. GORDON.

268. -- May 1811. JONATHAN LYNCH and wife, MARY, to JONATHAN
     BULLOCK...$400 two acres on hill adjacent road by PIDGEON's
tanyard to JONATHAN RICE--square between fourth and sixth alley
and eighth and ninth streets. Witnesses: GEORGE ROBERTS, THOMAS
STEWART, EDWARD LYNCH.

269. 15 March 1811. WILLIAM NORVELL and wife, NANCY, to LUKE
     VALENTINE...L122. Lines: grantor on Lynch Street and second
alley, near slaughter house, WILLIAM MORTON. Dower relinquished
to WILLIAM HEATH and JONATHAN SCHOOLFIELD.

271. 15 March 1811. LUKE VALENTINE and wife, PAULINA, to RODERICK
     TALIAFERRO and JONATHAN LYNCH to secure WILLIAM NORVELL...$1.00;
lot above. Witnesses: WILLIAM RADFORD, WILLIAM MITCHELL, S. WIATT,
W. DAVIS. Dower relinquished to Justices of the Peace above.

274. 9 May 1811. ELISHA PERKINS and wife, ELIZABETH, Bedford
     County, to JESSE WILLIAMS, Stokes County, North Carolina...
$500 #100. Lines: eighth alley and Lynch Street, RODERICK
TALIAFERRO. Witnesses: J. LINCH, JR., CHRISTOPHER LYNCH, JOHN
SAUNDERS, RICHARD PERKINS, MICAJAH T. WILLIAMS.

275. 24 December 1810. ISAAC PIDGEON, EDWARD LYNCH and wife,
     MARY, Lynchburg, JESSE WILLIAMS and wife, SARAH, Stokes
County, North Carolina, to SAMUEL ANTHONY...$1000 southeast end
of #6. Lines: second street, WILLIAM DAVIS. Witnesses: JAMES C.
MOORMAN, THOMAS STEWART, HENRY DAVIS. Dower relinquished by both
to JONATHAN SCHOOLFIELD and JONATHAN MURRELL.

278. 26 July 1811. MORRIS and DUNNINGTON and SARAH MORRIS to
     THOMAS COHEN...$500 west side fourth street. Lines: WILLIAM
BROWN, JAMES DUFFEL (late BENJAMIN SCHOOLFIELD's), fifth alley.
Bought by S. MORRIS and DUNNINGTON from JONATHAN LYNCH, SR. and
wife, MARY, 6 February 1809. Witnesses: ALBON MC DANIEL, BENJAMIN
PERKINS, WASHINGTON DUNNINGTON.

279. 26 July 1811. THOMAS COHEN and wife, MARY, 1; ROBERT MORRIS
     and JAMES DUNNINGTON, merchants, 2; THOMAS S. MC CLELLAND, 3...
$1.00; lot above. Witnesses: BENJAMIN PERKINS, ALBON MC DANIEL,
WA DUNNINGTON.

280.   14 March 1811.   CULWELL WILLIAMSON to JESSE WILLIAMS, Stokes
       County, North Carolina...$2000 #64.   Lines: second street,
sixth alley, GEORGE K. LAMBETH, JONATHAN LYNCH, JR., THOMAS
HUMPHREYS.   Witnesses: JONATHAN LYNCH, JR., JAMES MOORMAN, EDWARD
LYNCH, MICAJAH T. WILLIAMS.

281.   8 August 1811.   JONATHAN LYNCH and wife, MARY, to WILLIAM B.
       LYNCH, their son...love and $1.00; #96.   Lines: second
street, sixth alley.   Witnesses: THOMAS STEWART, CHRISTOPHER
LYNCH, JAMES C. MOORMAN.

282.   14 February 1811.   CHARLES DEISON, attorney in fact for
       BENJAMIN COFFMAN, late of Botetourt, to ROBERT MORRIS...$700;
#85.   Lines: second street, seventh alley.   Witnesses: THOMAS W.
COCKE, WILLIAM THURMOND, GEORGE GARRANT.

283.   6 July 1811.   JONATHAN LYNCH and wife, MARY, 3 September
       1808, to WASHINGTON LAMBETH...dower relinquished to WILLIAM
HEATH and JONATHAN SCHOOLFIELD.

284.   11 March 1811.   ALEXANDER BRIDGLAND to WALTER DUNNINGTON and
       THOMAS W. COCKE to secure ROBERT MORRIS...$1.00; #84; house
on said lot and occupied by SOLOMON BRIDGLAND--Lynch mill pond.
Witnesses: HOWELL DAVIES, CHARLES G. COBBS, WILLIAM MITCHELL.

286.   6 July 1811.   WASHINGTON LAMBETH and wife, ELIZABETH, to
       WILLIAM C. CONNER...$750 where WASHINGTON LAMBETH lives.
Lines: fourth street, fifth alley, BENJAMIN SCHOOLFIELD, WILLIAM
EDENFIELD, FISHER.   Witnesses: CHRISTOPHER WINFREE, J. WRIGHT,
WILLIAM B. LYNCH, PETER DETTO.   Dower relinquished to WILLIAM HEATH
and JONATHAN SCHOOLFIELD.

288.   7 July 1811.   WASHINGTON LAMBETH, 13 September 1808, to
       THOMAS W. COCKE and RODERICK TALIAFERRO, to secure HENRY DAVIS
and Company, THOMAS HIGGINBOTHAM and Company, HIGGINBOTHAM, BROWN
and Company, DAVID and MAYNARD...release; paid.   Witnesses: as
above.

289.   6 August 1811.   DAVID SAUNDERS and wife, LOCKEY, Bedford
       County, to JONATHAN SAUNDERS, their son...love and $1.00;
northwest part of #4.   Lines: Water Street, second street.
Witnesses: JAMES DUNNINGTON, WA DUNNINGTON, B. A. WINSTON.   Note:
in one or two places I have put MATTHEW DUNNINGTON, but later data
shows him to be WALTER DUNNINGTON.   He usually signed WA DUNNINGTON.

290.   11 March 1811.   ROBERT MORRIS and wife, SARAH, to ALEXANDER
       BRIDGLAND...$400 #84 house thereon on second street; occupied
by SOLOMON BRIDGLAND.   Towards Lynch Mill pond.   Witnesses:
THOMAS W. COCKE, WA DUNNINGTON, WILLIAM MITCHELL.

291.   8 August 1811.   BENJAMIN ESSEX and wife, ANN, to SAMUEL
       SCHOOLFIELD...$2300; #15.   Lines: house, JAMES DUFFEL, first
alley.

291.   8 August 1811.   SAMUEL SCHOOLFIELD to THOMAS HIGGINBOTHAM
       to secure BENJAMIN ESSES...lot above and $1.00.

293.   -- August 1811.   BENJAMIN PERKINS and JONATHAN PERKINS to
       SAMUEL SCHOOLFIELD...$500; #13.   Lines: WILLIAM STEEN,
second street, 15.

294.   -- August 1811.   JONATHAN LYNCH and wife, MARY, to WILLIAM
       COBBS...#233.33.   Lines: MILBY COTTINGHAM, fifth alley,
sixth street.   Witnesses: WILLIAM DAVIS, JR., EDWARD LYNCH, JACOB
OGLESBY.

295. 11 March 1811. LORENZO DOW, Coventry, Connecticut, to STITH
    MEAD...$200 Spartansburg, South Carolina, district--South
Carolina grant of 2 April 1804...Fork of Island Creek; Spears--800
acres. Witnesses: JAMES WADE, JONATHAN PERCIVAL, ANN WADE. Note:
DOW was a Methodist minister--as was MEAD. See my Amherst deeds for
more. Also consult the work of my late friend, ALFRED PERCY and
his treatment of DOW in his Amherst County Story.

295. 22 April 1811. JAMES WADE and wife, ANN, to FRANCIS HARRIS...
    L45; part of #69. Lines: third street, BENJAMIN VAWTER,
grantor, CHARLES MITCHELL. Witnesses: WILLIAM SUMPTER, ROBERT
KINCAID, BENJAMIN VAWTER.

296. 22 April 1811. JAMES WADE and wife, ANN, to BENJAMIN VAWTER...
    L62-7-6; part of 69. Lines: third street, WILLIAM MURRELL,
FRANCIS HARRIS, MITCHELL, JONATHAN MURRELL. Witnesses: WILLIAM
SUMPTER, ROBERT KINCAID, FRANCIS HARRIS.

297. -- August 1811. SAMUEL JOHNSON, acting trustee for SAMUEL
    JOHNSON and CHARLES MOORMAN, acting trustee for DAVID JOHNSON,
deceased, who in life was administrator of CHRISTOPHER JOHNSON, JR.,
deceased; CHARLES and THOMAS JOHNSON, executors of DAVID JOHNSON,
Campbell County, to CHARLES JOHNSON. CHARLES made Deed of Trust
to SAMUEL JOHNSON and CHARLES MOORMAN in Campbell County--#60 where
CHARLES lives. Conveyed to JAMES C. MOORMAN, 4 March 1811. MARY,
wife of CHARLES, obtained injunction to prevent sale by trustees
and since dissolved. CHARLES has paid in. Witnesses: THOMAS
JOHNSON. Witnesses: WILLIAM DAVIS, THOMAS S. MC CLELLAND,
CHRISTOPHER ANTHONY, JR., WILLIAM NORVELL.

298. -- August 1811. CHARLES JOHNSON and wife, MARY, did convey
    on 4 March 1811, to JAMES C. MOORMAN a lot and tenement: #60...
reference to deed above; $1.00 to JAMES C. MOORMAN of "some rights".
Witnesses: as above. Received of JAMES C. MOORMAN, 17 August 1811.
L89-9-4. Witnesses: as above.

298. -- September 1811. Relinquished to S. KING and SAMUEL SCOTT
    of dower by POLLY MEREDITH, wife of HENRY, as to deed of
5 September 1810, to SAMUEL FISHER.

299. 5 September 1811. Relinquished by MARY LYNCH, wife of
    JONATHAN, as to deed to GEORGE ROBERTS and RODERICK TALIAFERRO,
6 March 1811...deed to WILLIAM S. REID--ROBERTS and TALIAFERRO are
Justices of the Peace.

300. 7 October 1811. HUGH MORGAN and wife, JUDITH, Campbell
    County, to EDWARD LLOYD, Campbell County...$500; northwest
part of 58; occupied by HARRY HILL. Lines: fourth alley, third
street, JONATHAN BURGESS, CHARLES JOHNSON--now JAMES C. MOORMAN.
Witnesses: WILLIAM NORVELL, WILLIAM B. LYNCH, JACOB OGLESBY.

301. 6 April 1811. CALEB TAIT, 1; THOMAS HIGGINBOTHAM and
    JONATHAN CABELL, 2; CHARLES CLAY, 3...$1.00; lot
and two tenements occupied by WIATT and ROHR and JONATHAN CABELL--
upper end. Lines: HENRY MOORMAN. Witnesses: THOMAS S. MC CLELLAND,
RICHARD THURMON, JR., J. WRIGHT.

302. 27 October 1811. CHARLES C. LYNCH to SAMUEL J. HARRISON...
    $3069; one-half acre lot on second street; #30. Northwest
part; includes brick office occupied by SAMUEL WIATT. Witnesses:
G. A. ROSE, J. BENAGH, FRANK S. GRAY.

303. 27 October 1811. SAMUEL J. HARRISON and wife, SALLY, to
    CHARLES C. LYNCH...$2500; #94 on second street; occupied by
CHRISTOPHER ANTHONY, JR. Witnesses: as above.

304. 23 September 1811. ISAAC PIDGEON to JAMES DUFFIELD...L150;
    part of #6. Lines: second street, Water street, WILLIAM DAVIS.
Witnesses: JAMES C. MOORMAN, PETER DUDLEY, EDWARD LYNCH.

304. -- December 1811. ISAAC PIDGEON to JONATHAN POE...lease for
      seven years from June next; tenement; tanyard and house
occupied by ISAAC PIDGEON.

305. 10 October 1811. GEORGE D. WINSTON and wife, DOROTHEA,
      signed D. S. WINSTON, to SAMUEL J. HARRISON...$1500 #44.
Lines: second street, eighth alley, 91, 92. Witnesses: JONATHAN
BULLOCK, T. W. COCKE, WILLIAM HARRISON, THOMAS S. MC CLELLAND,
CHRISTOPHER ANTHONY.

306. -- December 1811. ISAAC PIDGEON to JONATHAN POE...seven year
      lease from 1 June next; seems to be same as previous one on
304, but refers to marble table to be used in tanyard; house--$300
per year. Witnesses: CHRISTOPHER ANTHONY, JR., JOSEPH BOYCE, JR.,
STITH MEAD.

308. 23 September 1811. EDWARD LYNCH and wife, MARY, to JAMES
      DUFFIELD...L500 part of 6. Lines: second street, Water
street, WILLIAM THURMOND, WILLIAM DAVIS. Witnesses: JAMES C.
MOORMAN, PETER DUDLEY, ISAAC PIDGEON.

309. 8 October 1811. RICHARD THURMON, JR. and wife, SARAH, to
      JAMES DUFFELL...$1500; part of 6; lines as above. Witnesses:
JAMES C. MOORMAN, WILLIAM STEENE, JOHNSON TERRELL.

309. 30 December 1811. Relinquished to RODERICK TALIAFERRO and
      JAMES STEWART by SALLY HARRISON, wife of SAMUEL J...deed of
27 October 1811, to CHARLES C. LYNCH.

310. 30 November 1811. JONATHAN LYNCH and wife, MARY, to EDWARD
      WATTS, Campbell County...$300; two acres. Lines: between
eighth and ninth streets, second and fourth alley. Witnesses:
ACHILLES MOORMAN, R. A. WISNTON, RICHARD TYREE, EDWARD LYNCH,
SAMUEL WOOD.

311. 3 August 1811. JULIUS CURLE to JONATHAN BULLOCK...reference
      to Deed of Trust to JONATHAN BULLOCK, 8 December 1810, to
secure WILLIAM NORVELL; three slaves; owes SALLY CURLE, New Kent--
bill of sale on slaves (two); thinks slaves will cover debts $1.00;
three named slaves. Also signed by RICHARDSON TAYLOR. Witnesses:
WILLIAM NORVELL, CHARLES LEWIS, RICHARD TAYLOR, JONATHAN LACY.

313. 30 December 1811. JAMES MARTIN and wife, CAROLINE, Campbell
      County, to HENRY BROWN, Bedford; DANIEL BROWN, Franklin
County; JAMES LEFTWICH, Bedford...$1500; part of 29. Lines:
Main street, TATE (21), JONATHAN SCHOOLFIELD. Mansion and out
houses.

314. 16 September 1811. JONATHAN BURGESS and wife, DRUSILLA, to
      GEORGE COCKRAN...$300; lot whereon ISAAC PIDGEON lives.
Lines: fourth street, sixth alley, PIDGEON. Witnesses: ASA
PLUMMER, JONATHAN JOHNSON, EDWARD LYNCH.

315. 7 January 1812. ROBERT T. MOORE and wife, MARY M., formerly
      COLEMAN, and heir of LINDSAY COLEMAN, Amherst County, Orange
County, to ROBERT MORRIS and JAMES DUNNINGTON, merchants...$2120.
Lines: second street, corner of brick house occupied by WILLIAM
MORGAN as a store and counting house--COLEMAN's brick house--lot
sold to WILLIAM BROWN by LINDSAY COLEMAN and wife, LUCY (recorded
in Campbell County), BROWN, JONATHAN MILLER, third alley. Except
part sold by WILLIAM BROWN, 9 September 1806--where firm lately
built new brick house. Witnesses: THOMAS S. MC CLELLAND, WILLIAM
NORVELL, SILAS HESTON, SAMUEL ANTHONY, JONATHAN COLEMAN, RICHARD
HARRISON, JR., REUBEN COLEMAN. Dower relinquished 31 January 1812
to DAVID S. GARLAND and J. M. BROWN, Amherst County.

317. No date. 1812 year only. JONATHAN LYNCH and wife, MARY, to
     WILLIAM STEENE...$1.00; 61. Lines: grantee, 63, fifth
alley. Precisely as much as STEENE bought from them, 6 June 1808--
part of 63. Witnesses: JONATHAN THURMON, NATHAN DICKS, MICAJAH
LYNCH.

318. 20 January 1812. JAMES C. MOORMAN and wife, JANE, to WILLIAM
     ROBINSON...$500 two tracts; one in Breckinridge County,
Kentucky conveyed to both by EBENEZER PATTON and wife, POLLY,
8 May 1810; 91 acres on Long Lick. Lines: HARRIS survey of 400
acres; tract of 123 acres adjacent. Lines: SCOTT, ADAMS--original
patentees. Note: The MOORMAN family has been quite prominent in
Breckinridge and other counties in my native Kentucky. I recall
going with my brother when he spoke to a Rotary Club in that area
and I met several men by name of MOORMAN. There are sketches of
family in Perrin et al. History of Kentucky, Third Edition.

319. 5 March 1812. JONATHAN LYNCH and wife, MARY, to CHRISTOPHER
     ANTHONY, JR...$400. Lines: fourth street, second alley,
SAMUEL IRVINE. Witnesses: JAMES C. MOORMAN, NATHAN DICKS, EDWARD
LYNCH.

320. 26 December 1811. GEORGE CALLAWAY and wife, MARY ELIZABETH,
     to CHARLES CLAY...$1.00. Lines: PETER DETTO, Cocke Street.
Witnesses: THOMAS MITCHELL, DANIEL BROWN, J. WRIGHT.

321. 18 January 1821. GEORGE K. LAMBETH to WILLIAM BARNARD,
     Campbell County, and SMITH and SHUBAL BARNARD, Lynchburg...
$200. Lines: between fourth and fifth streets, northwest side
of seventh alley, SAMUEL IRVINE.

322. 5 March 1812. GEORGE ROBERTS and JONATHAN LYNCH, JR. as
     to dower by MARY LYNCH, wife of JONATHAN...deed of 22 February
1811, to GEORGE K. LAMBETH; #91.

322. 5 March 1812. Same Justices of the Peace as to MARY LYNCH
     above...2 June 1806, to JAMES STEWART; #56.

323. 6 November 1811. JOSEPH NEEDHAM and wife, MARY, to BENJAMIN
     PERKINS...$620; third street. Bought from WILLIAM WALLACE
and wife and THOMAS BURGESS and wife, BETTY. Witnesses: CHRISTOPHER
LYNCH, RICHARD PERKINS, WILLIAM JOHNSON.

324. 6 November 1811. JONATHAN SCHOOLFIELD and JAMES STEWART as
     to MARY NEEDHAM, wife of JOSEPH...deed of 6 November 1811
above, to BENJAMIN PERKINS.

325. 6 March 1812. JONATHAN LYNCH and wife, MARY, to WILLIAM and
     REUBEN MITCHELL...$770. Lines: east side of Blackwater,
WIATT, NORVELL, HIGGINBOTHAM BROWN and Company lumber house, GEORGE
CALLAWAY. Witnesses: WILLIAM B. LYNCH, THOMAS STEWART, CHRISTOPHER
ANTHONY, JR.

325. 14 October 1811. JONATHAN LYNCH and wife, MARY, to WILLIAM
     and REUBEN MITCHELL...$1700; one acre. Lines: Lynch Street,
second alley. Witnesses: THOMAS STEWART, GEORGE CALLAWAY,
CHRISTOPHER LYNCH.

326. 6 March 1812. SAMUEL FISHER and wife, ELIZABETH, to NICHOLAS
     HARRISON...$1500; house and lot. Lines: WILLIAM EDENFIELD,
WILLIAM C. CONNER, lately occupied by WILLIAM FOWLER. Bought from
HENRY MEREDITH.

327. 7 May 1812. JONATHAN LYNCH and wife, MARY, to MARY TOMPKINS...
     dower of MARY TOMPKINS in lot and house; graveyard lott (sic)
and school house--husband is deceased; decree of Hustings court
for children to sell and pay debt of JAMES TOMPKINS, deceased, to
LYNCH. She has conveyed on even date. Lines: COL. JONATHAN WIATT,
second street. Witnesses: THOMAS WIATT, EDWARD LYNCH, THOMAS STEWART.

328. 7 May 1812. MARY TOMPKINS to JONATHAN LYNCH...consideration:
     lot of 24 feet conveyed by LYNCH and wife to her on even date;
her life interest; dower in estate of late husband, JAMES TOMPKINS.
Lot where husband erected walls of a house; graveyard lott.
Witnesses: as above.

329. 20 April 1812. JAMES GILLIAM to EDWARD PRICE to secure
     CHARLES CLAY who is assignee of JONATHAN MURRELL...$1.00.
Lines: third street and fourth alley; three-fourths of lot bought
from WILLIAM NORVELL; #40. Lines: WILLIAM RADFORD, 38. Witnesses:
CHARLES GILLIAM, JONATHAN VAWTER, RICHARD POWELL, THOMAS HIGGINBOTHAM.

331. 7 May 1812. JONATHAN LYNCH, JR...appointed Sergeant of Lynchburg
     by JAMES BARBOUR, Governor of Virginia. Bondsmen: WILLIAM
DAVIS, JAMES MALLORY, EDWARD LYNCH. WILLIAM NORVELL, Clerk.

332. 5 June 1812. WILLIAM C. CONNER frees because of Christian
     convictions these slaves: TOM, light complexion, about 33 or
34 years of age, middle size, about 5 feet 8 inches. PEGGY, 24 or
25 years of age, dark and middle size; TOM, her child, light, three
or four years old; BEN, dark, about 34 or 35 years of age, stout
and well set, 5 feet 6 or 7 inches. CHASEY, wife of BEN, 36 or
37 years of age, middle size, dark. JENNY, their child, four or
five years of age. ANNE, their child, two or three years. SALLY,
their child, three months old.

333. 4 June 1812. SETH WARD and wife, PATSEY (signed MARTHA) to
     STITH MAYNARD...$700; one third of one half acre; third street;
nearly opposite Bell tavern occupied by NATHANIEL RIVES; #49.
Bought from THOMAS WIATT, where brick stable occupied by JONATHAN W.
BRADLEY stands.

334. 11 May 1812. JONATHAN LYNCH and wife, MARY--error--JR. and
     wife, ANNA, to JAMES C. NEWMAN...$600; #35; second street
and seventh alley.

335. 11 April 1812. BENJAMIN MEHARIS to WILLIAM DAVIS, JR. and
     PETER DUDLEY to secure JONATHAN BULLOCK...$1.00; furniture.
Witnesses: E. B. NORVELL, JONATHAN L. DUFFELL, EDWARD NORVELL.

336. 3 March 1812. JONATHAN LYNCH, SR. to JONATHAN LYNCH, JR. and
     JAMES MALLORY...believed advantageous to Lynchburg citizens
to conduct water to different parts of town to prevent fires--
profitable--KIDD's spring and every other spring--thirty feet square
about each one; to conduct by pipes, tubes or logs through any
land of JONATHAN LYNCH, SR. They will--to give JONATHAN, SR. one
fourth of profits. Tube shall be fixed for use of persons settling
near spring; to keep in good repairs; two years.

337. 28 May 1812. JONATHAN SCHOOLFIELD and ROBERT MORRIS as to
     MARY LYNCH, wife of EDWARD LYNCH...deed--23 September 1811, to
JONATHAN DUFFELL; part of #6.

338. -- November 1811. BENJAMIN SCHOOLFIELD and wife, ANN, to
     JAMES DUFFELL...$400; one-half acre on the hill. Lines:
former lot of GABRIEL JONES, now THOMAS COHEN; sixth alley; street
laid off by JONATHAN LYNCH, WILLIAM BROWN. Witnesses: DAVID F.
MASON, NELSON HUGHES, JONATHAN W. SCHOOLFIELD.

339.   -- 1812. JAMES BROWN and wife, ANNA P., Richmond; ROBERT
       RIVES and wife, MARGARET, Amherst County, and THOMAS HIGGINBOTHAM
to PLEASANT THURMOND...$1.00; half acre lot. Lines: WILLIAM
EDENFIELD, BENJAMIN SCHOOLFIELD (now JAMES DUFFELL). One third of
where HENRY MEREDITH formerly lived. Witnesses: CHRIS WINFREE,
J. WIATT, WILL NORVELL, S. GARLAND, WA DUNNINGTON, JOSEPH KENNERLEY,
THOMAS MITCHELL, NICHOLAS HARRISON.

340.   28 May 1812. ISAAC PIDGEON to CHARLES JOHNSTON, Campbell
       County...$4166.66; two tracts. 1. Three-fourths acres.
Lines: fifth street, sixth alley, dwelling where ISAAC PIDGEON
lives. 2. Northwest tract of sixth alley and fifth street, where
tanyard is located. JONATHAN LYNCH conveyed formerly to ISAAC
PIDGEON sufficiency of water from passing branch. Witnesses:
E. B. NORVELL, WILLIAM DAVIS, THOMAS MITCHELL, THOMAS HIGGINBOTHAM.

341.   6 August 1812. MARY TOMPKINS to Lynchburg Mayor...$30; tract
       lately bought from JONATHAN LYNCH--second street, road
passing from second to Horseford--when not used for public road,
it reverts. Witnesses: JONATHAN M. GORDON, THOMAS WIATT, CHARLES C.
LYNCH.

342.   6 November 1812. GEORGE ROBERTS and WILLIAM ROYALL as to
       MARY LYNCH, wife of JONATHAN...deed of 2 June 1806, to THOMAS W.
COCKE, next to #88.

343.   6 August 1812. JONATHAN LYNCH and wife, MARY, to AGATHA
       DICKS...$1.00. Lines: contemplated seventh street and
third alley.

344.   19 March 1812. JONATHAN COCKE to JONATHAN M. GORDON, Campbell
       County, to secure THOMAS W. COCKE on bond for debt...THOMAS
SCOTT, Powhatan--suit there; RICHARD ELAM also on bond. SCOTT has
sued and THOMAS W. had to pay. $1.00; 300 acres in Louisa. Lines:
NATHANIEL WADE, DR. WALKER, HOWETT, MORRIS ROBERTS. Bought by
JOHN's father, WILLIAM COCKE, SR., from GEORGE HAIDEN and wife,
ELIZABETH, Louisa County. JOHN derived from late father by purchase;
no title sent; to be made by different heirs in various parts of
this country; furniture. Witnesses: W. HARRISON, JAMES MOSELEY,
THOMAS HUMPHREYS. Memo: GORDON may appoint THOMAS W. COCKE as
trustee. Witnesses: as above. If memory serves me correctly,
this is same WILLIAM COCKE from whom I descend. There is suit about
a slave in Louisa, but I have not checked it. Therein my ABRAHAM
BAILEY is shown. He married TEMPERANCE COCKE, daughter of WILLIAM
ABRAHAM and wife had son, DAVID BAILEY, who shows in Henrico when
his parents gave him a slave for his son, JOHNSON BAILEY. DAVID
moved to Charlotte County and gave the slave to his son there.
Another son was shown of ABRAHAM's in Henrico and I may be wrong
in saying only one; may have been several, but I am not consulting
BAILEY notes.

347.   JOHN MILLER--will, also in will book. Wife, MARY, form wife
       of BENJAMIN JOHNSON, to be cared for by THOMAS WIATT and my
beloved daughter, SALLY WIATT; children of WIATT by SALLY, present
wife. Amherst tract about two miles from Madison, about 350 acres,
when the children are of age or married of WIATT's; may sell for
them. Children of ANSELM LYNCH by my deceased daughter, SUCKEY--
CHARLES, HENRY, MARY ANNE, JONATHAN P., SARAH C. and SUSAN LYNCH--
as of age or married. Widow and children of deceased son ELIJAH
MILLER; widow and children of deceased son, JONATHAN MILLER; to
HENRY MILLER for his family; my son, PLEASANT M. MILLER; lot and
houses in Lynchburg occupied by me. Executors: THOMAS WIATT,
PLEASANT M. MILLER, WILLIAM NORVELL. -- March 1812; proof on
5 November 1812. Witnesses: E. B. NORVELL, A. ROBERTSON, JAMES
DUNNINGTON, ANDREW JAMIESON.

348. 31 October 1812. JESSE WILLIAMS and wife, SARAH, Stokes
      County, North Carolina, to JONATHAN M. GORDON...$600; #113.
Lines: Lynch Street, between RODERICK TALIAFERRO and eighth alley.
Witnesses: WILLIAM B. LYNCH, PETER DUDLEY, MICAJAH T. WILLIAMS.

349. 7 July 1812. GEORGE ROBERTS and wife, JOHANNAH, to PHILLIP
      ROHR...L25. Lines: fifth alley, 65, 67, 39, 37--part of 67.
Witnesses: THOMAS H. ROBERTS, JONATHAN R. DAWSON, one illegible
signature.

351. 9 November 1812. JONATHAN LYNCH and wife, MARY, to CHRISTOPHER
      ANTHONY, JR...$250. Lines: second alley, fourth street, fifth
street. Witnesses: JONATHAN LYNCH, JR., NATHAN DICKS, WILLIAM B.
LYNCH, CHRIS LYNCH.

351. 30 November 1812. JONATHAN LYNCH and wife, MARY, to ANSELM
      LYNCH...$10.00. Lines: Lynch street, opposite lot lately
that of JONATHAN MILLER, deceased, third alley. Witnesses: as
above.

351. Memo by clerk--return to clerk of General Court--except the
      deed ROBERTS to ROHR--proved after January 1813; signed by
WILLIAM MORGAN.

353. 4 December 1811. JONATHAN LYNCH and wife, MARY, to ISAAC
      PIDGEON...$100. Lines: sixth alley, ISAAC PIDGEON's tanyard.
Witnesses: JONATHAN LYNCH, JR., WASH LAMBETH, WILLIAM B. LYNCH,
BYROM LEA. Note: Another 353 out of place after 354.

354. 3 October 1812. WILLIAM WORD to JONATHAN LYNCH, JR...power
      of attorney--amount due from THOMAS MILES as tenant; JONATHAN L.
MORELAND as tenant--where WILLIAM WORD lately lived. Witnesses:
WILLIAM JOHSNON, PETER DETTO, WILLIAM TARDY.

353. 4 January 1813. (out of place--my error) SETH WARD and wife,
      MARTHA, to CHARLES JOHNSTON, Campbell County...$6000; #31 or
WARD's tavern; one-half acre. Witnesses: JAMES T. WRIGHT, JONATHAN M.
OTEY.

355. 11 December 1812. JAMES C. MOORMAN and wife, JANE, to CALEB
      TAIT...$1000.00 tract in Bourbon County, Kentucky on Hunston
(sic); fork of Licking--this is really Hinkston Creek--my father was
born in Bourbon--JONATHAN FULTON DAVIS. 443 acres. Part of grant
of MICAJAH CALLAWAY. Lines: BUFORD, MARSHALL, save twenty-two
acres in dispute; laid off by RICHARD HIGGINS and excepted in deed
from JONATHAN CALLAWY by attorney, THOMAS TODD. Witnesses:
JONATHAN LYNCH, JR., CHARLES DEISON, BACON TAIT.

356. 11 December 1812. CALEL TAIT and wife, NANCY, to JAMES C.
      MOORMAN...$4000 #21. Lines: second street, first alley,
HENRY MOORMAN--includes two tenements of the large brick building
next to first alley. Witnesses: as above.

356. Memo: JAMES C. MOORMAN has bought the two lover tenements in
      large brick building above and agrees that CALEB TAIT shall
keep lover one occupied by DAVID and WILLIAM KYLE until 1 February
1815; will then deliver to JAMES C. MOORMAN; also to keep one
occupied by TAIT and HUMPHREYS until 10 December next; no date;
acknowledged, 7 January 1813.

357. 10 December 1812. BENJAMIN PERKINS to RICHARD PERKINS...$1500.
      Lines: third street, Cocke Street, to ground sold by
BENJAMIN PERKINS to REUBEN PERRY; #32 bought from JOSEPH NEEDHAM.
Witnesses: CHRIS LYNCH, BOOKER SHELTON, EDMOND J. NORVELL.

357. 18 January 1813. JAMES STEWART and ROBERT MORRIS as to JUDITH
      MORGAN, wife of HUGH MORGAN, to EDWARD LLOYD...7 October 1811;
#58.

358.   20 August 1812.   JONATHAN LYNCH and wife, MARY, to JOAB
       WATSON...$450.   Lines: fourth street, fourth alley.
Witnesses: J. LYNCH, JR., JAMES C. MOORMAN, EDWARD LYNCH.

359.   -- January 1813.   SAMUEL SCHOOLFIELD to JONATHAN M. GORDON,
       JOSEPH CARSON and RODERICK TALIAFERRO...to free two boys,
OSBORN and WINSTON, when 21; $2.00 and the boys. OSBORN was eight
on 1 August 1811; WINSTON was six on 19 January 1812. SAMUEL
SCHOOLFIELD is to retain them, but trustees are to see that they
get freedom when 21.

360.   23 January 1813.   JONATHAN LYNCH, SR. and wife, MARY, to
       WILLIAM B. BARTEE...$220 tract between fifth or seventh
alley, tenth and eleventh streets. Laid off--JONATHAN LYNCH, JR.,
surveyor. Witnesses: JAMES C. MOORMAN, THOMAS STEWART, EDWARD
LYNCH.

361.   -- December 1812.   ROBERT MORRIS and JAMES DUNNINGTON,
       merchants of MORRIS and DUNNINGTON, 1; WILLIAM NORVELL, 2;
WILLIAM WARWICK, Amherst County, 3...$1.00; tract with brick
tenement occupied by WILLIAM MORGAN and ARCHIBALD ROBERTSON and
Company. Joins JONATHAN MILLER, deceased.

NELSON COUNTY, VIRGINIA

ABSTRACT OF WILL BOOK A OF NELSON COUNTY, VIRGINIA

1. EDMUND COFFEY. September 23, 1807; July 25, 1808. Witnesses: DANIEL MC DONALD, JNO. BARNETT. Of Amherst County--it must be remembered that he wrote the will when the division of Amherst and Nelson had not been made. Wife, NANCY; my children: EDMUND, WILLIAM, REUBEN, EMELIA, NANCY and POLLY are to share alike; having respect to sums advanced to son, EDMUND, and daughter, EMELIA--slaves to children and their children. Wife to administrator with sons, EDMUND, WILLIAM and REUBEN. Page 2 has administratrix bond by wife to Nelson Justices of the Peace: JAMES MONTGOMERY, SHELTON CROSTHWAIT, WILLIAM HORSLEY and NELSON ANDERSON on probate date. Her bondsmen: JNO. MASTERS, JAMES MURPHY, JNO. CAMPBELL. SPOTSWOOD GARLAND, Clerk of Court.

3. JOSEPH SHELTON. Sheriff's bond, June 27, 1808. Commission of June 21, 1808. Bondsman: JAMES WOODS, LANDON CABELL, SPOTSWOOD GARLAND. WILLIAM H. CABELL, Governor. Pages 3 and 4 have several bonds by same men for various duties of the office.

5. SAMUEL FOX. May 18, 1808; September 26, 1808. Witnesses: HUDSON MARTIN, SR. and JR., STEPHEN MARTIN. Of Amherst County--wife, ELIZABETH, at her request gets 500 acres where I live in lieu of dower; also stock and furniture. Son, BARTLETT (BARTTELOT?) is bound to me for purchase of mill seat and land next to CHARLES BRIDGWATER; he is to pay balance and BRIDGWATER is asked to convey to BARTLETT (plain here). He also gets fifty acres called HULCEY's tract and next to land of my wife and that of AUGUSTINE SMITH. My son, JNO. FOX--forty acres--of HULCEY tract on Indian branch which I got from AUGUSTINE SMITH. Sons, WILLIAM and JOS. FOX--about 100 acres between them. Sons, SAMUEL and RICHARD FOX get land bought from CAPTAIN JAMES MARTIN--about 100 acres between them. My daughter, ANN FOX; my daughter, SUSANA, wife of DANIEL CARY. GEORGE MARTIN gets no part as his wife, SALLY, my daughter is now dead and she long since got her share. Executors: wife and sons, SAMUEL, RICHARD and BARTLETT FOX. Page 7 administrator's bond by BARTLETT and SAMUEL FOX on probate date. Bondsmen: HUDSON MARTIN. To Justices of the Peace: WILLIAM CABELL, WILLIAM HARRIS, WILLIAM LOVING, JNO. MOSBY.

8. JAMES THOMPSON. Inventory August 23, 1808. Comm.: JAMES STEVENS, JNO. DILLARD, SAMUEL SPENCER. Slaves: L1070; other items: L280-15-3. Furniture, etc.: L1113-10-0.

10. SAMUEL FRANKLIN. Tobacco Inspector--CAMDEN's Warehouse--to Gov. WILLIAM H. CABELL, October 24, 1808, under appointment of September 30, 1808. Bondsman: JAMES CUNNINGHAM.

11. STEPHEN WATTS. Tobacco Inspector at CAMDEN's Warehouse, October 24, 1808, under appointment date as above to Gov. WILLIAM H. CABELL. Bondsman: NORVEL SPENCER.

11. WILLIAM CLASBY. Tobacco Inspector at Tye River Warehouse; dates as above. Bondsman: THOMAS WILSON.

12. GUTRIDGE THURMOND, SR. November 9, 1808; November 28, 1808. Witnesses: JAMES ROBINSON, JNO. BAYLEY, SAMUEL BAILEY, HARMON GENTRY. Sons: THOMAS, JNO., BENJAMIN, GUTRIDGE; daughters: BETSY and FRANKEY THURMOND, WINIFRED CHEATHAM, POLLY BALL. Wife, CATHERINE. Administrators: son-in-law, WILLIAM BALL, JR. and son, THOMAS THURMOND. Page 13--they made bond on probate date. Bondsman: JNO. and SAMUEL BAILEY, TERRISHA BAILEY. Justices of the Peace: WILLIAM HARRIS, WILLIAM H. DIGGS, SHELTON CROSTHWAIT, JNO. MOSBY.

14. CHARLES EDMUNDS. Tobacco Inspector, October 24, 1808--Tye River Warehouse. Bondsman: JAMES HUGHES. Bond to Gov. WILLIAM H. CABELL; appointed September 30, 1808.

14. ELIZABETH LOVING. November 23, 1805; November 28, 1808.
    Witnesses: none. Widow of WILLIAM LOVING. Daughter, SALLY
LOVING; daughter, PEGGY LOVING--if SALLY and PEGGY are without issue,
then their shares to my daughters MARY STAPLES and SUKEY VAUGHAN or
female representatives. Bond owed to JNO. HARTGROVE for benefit of
my deceased daughter, NANCY. Her daughter is now under control of
my daughter, PEGGY, and if HARTGROVE removes her, she gets no sum.
My daughter, LUCY TALIAFERRO. I owe $200.00 to store of TALIAFERRO
and LOVING. Executors: my son, JNO. LOVING, and my friend, CHARLES
TALIAFERRO.

16. WILLIAM PAMPLIN. Tobacco Inspector, CAMDEN's warehouse to
    GOV. WILLIAM H. CABELL. Bondsman: MICAJAH PENDLETON.

16. SARAH BALL. Relinquishes right to administrate estate of
    deceased husband, WILLIAM BALL, and asks that CAPTAIN JESSE
JOPLING serve in her stead, December 27, 1808. Witnesses: JNO.
FERGUSON, LEWIS BALL, JAMES B. FERGUSON, WILLIAM BALL, JR.

17. JESSE JOPLING. Qualified as administrator of estate of WILLIAM
    BALL, December 27, 1808. Bondsmen: ANDERSON and ELIJAH
PETERS. Justices of the Peace: WILL LOVING, JNO. DILLARD, NELSON
ANDERSON, and GEORGE W. VARNUM.

17. ANDREW WARE (WEIR). Qualified as guardian of ANDREW WARE,
    orphan of ROBERT WARE, December 26, 1808. Bondsman: ALEXANDER
MC ALEXANDER. Justices of the Peace: WILL LOVING, NELSON ANDERSON,
JESSE JOPLING and GEORGE W. VARNUM.

18. MARY MARTIN. July 17, 1808; September 26, 1808. Witnesses:
    HUDSON MARTIN, AZARIAH MARTIN and GIDEON MARTIN. Widow of
SHERAD MARTIN. Grandson, REUBEN MARTIN; daughter, MARY MARTIN;
son, SHEROD MARTIN. Executors: MARY and SHEROD MARTIN, my daughter
and son.

18. MARY and HUDSON MARTIN. Qualified to administrate estate of
    MARY MARTIN with MARY as administratrix. Bondsman: HUDSON
MARTIN. Justices of the Peace: WILLIAM LOVING, GEORGE W. VARNUM,
NELSON ANDERSON and JAMES LOVING, JR.

19. FRANCIS NEIGHBOURS. ABRAM NEIGHBOURS bonded to administrate
    estate, January 23, 1809. Bondsman: JAMES MURPHY.

20. EDMOND COFFEY. Inventory of estate, November 28, 1808. No
    total, but one bear trap in list. Comm.: DANIEL MC DONALD,
JOS. BURGHER and DAVID CLARKSON.

21. JUDITH TALIAFERRO. JONATHAN HORSLEY, JR. bonded to administrate
    estate. Bondsman: WILLIAM HORSLEY, March 27, 1809.

22. WILLIAM BALL. Inventory on Thursday, January 5, 1809. No
    total. Com.: BRANSFORD WEST, JNO. FARIS, ABSALOM JOHNSTON and
JNO. FARRAR. Recorded on Monday, March 27, 1809.

23. GUTRIDGE THURMOND. Inventory on Fryday (sic), December 9, 1808.
    L1172-9-6. Comm.: JNO. S. DAWSON, TERISHA BAILEY, TERISHA
TURNER. Recorded on Monday, March 27, 1809.

26. WILLIAM FITZPATRICK. Relinquishment to administrator by REBECCA
    FITZPATRICK, April 15, 1809. Witnesses: SAMUEL BRIDGWATER,
THOMAS WEIR and THOMAS FITZPATRICK.

27. WILLIAM FITZPATRICK. Made bond to administrator of estate of
    WILLIAM FITZPATRICK, April 24, 1809. JNO. W. HARRIS also
qualified and their bondsman was JNO. E. FITZPATRICK.

28. WILLIAM FITZPATRICK. Inventory on May 4, 1809. Comm.:
    SAMUEL and NATHANIEL BRIDGWATER and THOMAS WARE.

29. SAMUEL FOX. Inventory--no total, January 14, 1809. Comm.:
AZARIAH MARTIN, MICHAEL MC MULLEN, and ROBERT HENDERSON.

30. MARY C. BRITTAIN (BRITTON). JNO. HARGROVE and SHELTON CROSTHWAIT
bonded on May 22, 1809 for JNO. HARGROVE as guardian of MARY C.
BRITTAIN, orphan of CHARLES BRITTON.

31. JAMES MORRISON. Administrator's Bond by ELIZABETH MORRIS to
administrator, May 22, 1809. Bondsman: NELSON CRAWFORD.

32. JAMES MONTGOMERY. County surveyor bond under Governor's
commission of July 29, 1808. Bondsman: MATTHEW HARRIS and JNO.
JACOBS, JR. S. GARLAND, Clerk.

32. JAMES WOOD. Coroner Bond, August 22, 1808. Commission from
Governor on July 29, 1808. Bondsman: JOS. SHELTON, S. GARLAND.

33. NELSON ANDERSON. Coroner Bond--same dates as item above.
Bondsman: JAMES MURPHY and STEPHEN WATTS.

34. PARMENAS BRYANT. Constable Bond, June 27, 1808, for two years.
Bondsmen: WILLIAM TEAS and JNO. BRYANT.

34. JNO. BARNETT. Constable Bond, same date as above and term.
Bondsmen: NATHAN BARNETT and JAMES MONTGOMERY.

35. THOMAS CHILDRESS. Constable Bond, same data as above items.
Bondsman: GEORGE VAUGHAN.

35. JEREMIAH YAGER. Constable Bond, July 25, 1808, for two years.
Bondsman: JAMES HIGGINBOTHAM.

36. NATHANIEL HARLOW, JR. Constable Bond. Bondsman: HUDSON
MARTIN, JR. and WILLIAM LEE HARRIS.

36. WILLIAM CUNNINGHAM. Constable Bond, August 22, 1808. Bondsman:
JAMES PAMPLIN.

37. RICHARD MURROW. Inventory, January 20, 1809. Total: L74-5-4½.
Comm.: THOMAS BIBB, JR., ELIZHA PETERS and JAMES MARTIN.

37. MARY MARTIN. Inventory on Fryday (sic), April 14, 1809. Comm.:
CHARLES BRIDGWATER, WILLIAM SMITH and JOS. TOMS (?).

38. JAMES MORRISON. Inventory--many slaves--order of May court,
1809. Done on June 2, 1809. Comm.: NATHAN CRAWFORD, HAWES
COLEMAN and SAMUEL BRIDGWATER.

41. THOMAS E. FORTUNE. Constable Bond on June 26, 1809, for two
years. Bondsmen: JAMES LOVING and ZACH. FORTUNE.

41. HENRY BIBB, JR. Constable Bond, June 27, 1809. Bondsman:
JAMES STEVENS.

42. POLLY T. HILL. Guardian Bond--WILLIAM B. HARE qualified as
guardian and she was orphan of NATHANIEL HILL, deceased.
Bondsman: LANDON CABELL.

42. JAMES THOMPSON. Administrator's Bond, August 22, 1808. JNO.
THOMPSON, JR., qualified. Bondsmen: JNO. THOMPSON (M) and
CHARLES WATTS. Note: I think that this is JNO. THOMPSON, JR. may
be the one who later came to Amherst and was a large land owner.
His will mentions that he wants to be buried in Nelson on certain
estate with parents. I note that this other JNO. THOMPSON employs (M)
by his name to distinguish him, but don't know just what the M stands
for in this case.

43. WILLIAM ALFORD. LITTETIA ALFORD, July 18, 1809, relinquished
     right to administrator of estate of WILLIAM ALFORD and asked
that WILLIAM HOLLINSWORTH will be appointed. Witness: WILLIAM H.
DIGGES. WILLIAM HOLLANDSWORTH (note difference in spelling) qualified
on July 24, 1809. Bondsman: JNO. LOVING.

45. HENRY ROBERTS. Administrator's Bond by FANNY ROBERTS, July 24,
     1809. Bondsmen: JNO. ROBERTS, MATT. HARRIS.

46. JESSE MAYS. Inventory, August 28, 1809. JAMES DILLARD,
     CHARLES WATTS, JNO. THOMPSON.

47. STEPHEN WATTS. Tobacco Inspector at CAMDEN's Warehouse,
     September 25, 1809. Bondsman: THOMAS TRIPLET.

48. LAVENDER LONDON and NORVEL SPENCER. September 30, 1808. Original
     enclosed to auditor for them as additional inspectors at Tye
River Warehouse to GOV. JNO. TYLOR (sic).

48. CHARLES and ROWLAND EDMUNDS. September 25, 1809, as above
     under blank date commission in 1808.

49. SAMUEL FRANKLIN and JNO. MARR. Tobacco Inspector at CAMDEN's
     Warehouse on September 25, 1809, under commission of blank
date, 1808.

50. NICHOLAS CABELL. June 7, 1809; October 24, 1809. Witnesses:
     RO. IRVING, RO. FRANKLIN, LANDON CABELL, WILLIAM H. CABELL.
Witnesses to codicil: JAMES VIGUS, JR. and others above with exception
of LANDON CABELL. Wife, PEGGY R. CABELL; daughter, ELISABETH H.
CABELL--a secretary willed to me by my father, and books, but few
reserved for my mother and sister. Until my son, NATHANIEL, is of
age. I am bound to my mother, HANNAH CABELL, each year for her life-
time--L20 also due from my brother, WILLIAM, and transferred to him.
Payments are to be made each year from proceeds of my warehouse,
fishery, and slave hires. FRANCIS may choose to take one-third of
my land at twenty-one. Guardians for my daughter. Both of my children
to be suitably educated and prepared for learned professions. If
any slaves are obnoxious or disagreeable--such refractory slaves are
to be sold. Mention of lots at Warminster and agreement with legatees.
Administrators and guardians: wife and friends, SAMUEL M. VENABLE,
WILLIAM W. WATKINS, WILLIAM L. WOMACK, BENJAMIN CARRINGTON and my
brother, GEORGE CABELL. Codicil, June 18, 1809: Slave also to
ELIZABETH H., in addition to lands; a girl. Same for son, NATHANIEL
FRANCIS. Warehouse, mill, and ferry boat may need repairs. Mention
of mother's annuity. Page 55 Administrator's Bond for WILLIAM W (M?)
WATKINS and WILLIAM L. WOMACK, October 23, 1809. Bondsmen: WILLIAM
CABELL and RO. RIVES.

57. Widow of DAVID ENIX, SARAH ENIX. Awarded dower by court in
     378 acres--back line of JESSE FIDLER's Spring; line of BETHEL
LIVELY, November 18, 1809. Comm.: JAMES MURPHY, JNO. HIGGINBOTHAM,
BRANSFORD WEST.

58. GEORGE LOVING. Tobacco Inspector as one of inspectors at Tye
     Warehouse. October 27, 1809. Bondsman: JAMES LOVING, JR.

59. JAMES TURNER. Tobacco Inspector at Swan Creek Warehouse,
     November 27, 1809. Bondsman: JNO. LOVING.

59. WILLIAM L. WATTS. Tobacco Inspector at CAMDEN's Warehouse,
     November 27, 1809. Bondsman: MICAJAH PENDLETON.

60. DAVID P. HOWARD. December 26, 1809. WILLIAM A. HOWARD qualified
     as guardian. DAVID was orphan of JNO. HOWARD, deceased.
Bondsman: WILLIAM F. CARTER.

61. WILLIAM ALFORD. Inventory August 10, 1809. Total: $866.33.
     Recorded on December 26, 1809.

64.   JNO. STAPLES, JR. Administrator's Bond on February 26, 1810
      for WILLIAM STAPLES to administrator. Bondsman: SAMUEL STAPLES.
He is not called JR. here, but on page 65 he is so called in inventory:
L137-9-0. March 3, 1810. Comm.: GEORGE VAUGHAN, THOMAS BIBB,
ABRAHAM WARWICK.

66.   WILLIAM H. DIGGS. Commissioner of Revenue--to GOV. JNO. TYLER,
      March 25, 1810. Bondsmen: JOS. SHELTON and RICHARD PHILLIPS.

67.   ASA VARNUM. March 26, 1810. To manufacture tobacco at his home
      in Cabellsville. Bondsmen: JNO. LOVING and SPOTSWOOD GARLAND.

68-70. Various bonds relating to duties of Sheriff. JOS. SHELTON,
        Sheriff, January 9, 1810. Bondsmen: HUDSON MARTIN and JAMES
WOODS.

71ff. I regret to state that pages 74 and 75 are missing from this
       interesting item. Someone has noted this, but I have not been
able to locate them. The Nelson Supervisors are working on plans
now (January, 1964) to enlarge the record room and other parts of their
building. This is greatly needed and it may be that this will enable
me to get at many records stashed away in a huge cabinet in the base-
ment. The light is very poor and things are crowded in the area.
New space will doubtless make many original records more easily availa-
ble. The record begins thus: "Following is list of a manuscript in
an old prayer book and also sundry other papers belonging to estate
of GEORGE STONEHAM, deceased, which was filed in the clerk's office
by JNO. LOVING by court permission. The data follows: GEORGE
STONEHAM was born April ye 13th 1736, MARY STONEHAM was born October
ye 16th 1737; ELIZABETH STONEHAM was born January ye 27 ----; HENRY
STONEHAM was born April ye 16th, 1764; ANN STONEHAM was born ye
June 24th, 1765; GEORGE STONEHAM and MARY, his wife, was married in
the year of our Lord, 1760. GEORGE STONEHAM, JR. was born 21st September
1766. MARY STONEHAM, JR. was born September 13, 1768, MARY STONEHAM
died in the year of our Lord, 1768. GOERGE STONEHAM and MARY STONEHAM,
his wife, was married in the year of our Lord, 1760 December the 5th.

      Copy of a bond given by GEORGE STONEHAM and T. DUNNAWAY to
      executors of WILLIAM GOODRIDGE, deceased. "Astate"--GEORGE
STONEHAM, Caroline County and THOMAS DUNNAWAY, Lancaster County, to
RICHARD and GEORGE GOODRIDGE, executors of last will of WILLIAM
GOODRIDGE--L80--November 26, 1771. The will was recorded in Lancaster
County and devised to GEORGE STONEHAM one sixth part of the "na buuts"
of his negroes and other personal property. STONEHAM is to deliver
to his children, had by MARY, daughter of GOODRIDGE, as they come of
age. Witnesses: RICHARD MITCHELL and HENRY TAPSCOTT. Taken July 5,
1792. Signed: RICHARD GOODRIDGE.

72.   Received of GEORGE STONEHAM in full for all debts from beginning
      of the world to now, June 25, 1800. Signed by ELIJAH MAYS.
Witness: WILLIAM H. DIGGS. Same page: received by MARY STONEHAM
from GEORGE STONEHAM all that is due me, January 28, 1804. Witness:
JAMES KIDD. Same page: another receipt by ELIJAH MAYS for all that
GEORGE STONEHAM owes me, August 15, 1792.

73.   Slave Sale. WILL and BEN--to GEORGE STONEHAM by ELIJAH MAYS,
      August 15, 1792. Witnesses: BYRON STONEHAM and WILLIAM ALFORD.

73.   MARY STONEHAM of Amherst sells slave, LARK, about ten, to
      GEORGE STONEHAM, December 24, 1792. Witnesses: ELIJAH MAYS,
AMBROSE CAMPBELL.

74 and 75. Missing, as stated.

76.   HENRY STONEHAM, Amherst, sells slave, LETT, to GEORGE STONEHAM,
      July 5, 1785. Witnesses: STEPHEN WATTS and CHARLES STATHAM.
Ordered that papers in prayer book be filed.

77.   WILLIAM CUNNINGHAM. Constable Bond, June 25, 1810. Bondsman:
      VALENTINE HYLTON.

78. THOMAS FORTUNE. Constablë Bond, June 25, 1810. Bondsman:
JAMES STEVENS.

78. ISAAC SMITH. Constable Bond, June 25, 1810, to GOV. JNO. TYLER.
Bondsmen: HENRY SMITH and WILLIAM MURRILL.

79. JNO. BARNETT. Constable Bond, June 25, 1810. Bondsmen:
DAVID R. CLARKSON and JNO. JACOBS.

80. NATHANIEL HARLOW, JR. Constable Bond, June 25, 1810. Bondsmen:
WILLIAM LEE HARRIS and JNO. E. FITZPATRICK.

81. REBECCA TURNER. Administrator's Bond for TERISHA TURNER, JR.
to administrator, June 25, 1810. Bondsmen: JAMES TURNER,
WILLIAM H. MOSBY, ALEXANDER ROBERTS. JAMES B. EDWARDS, Deputy Clerk.

83. JNO. PARSONS. Guardian Bond by WILLIAM ALLEN as guardian,
August 27, 1810. Bondsman: WILLIAM BAILEY. Orphan of SALLY
PARSONS, deceased.

83. JOS. SHELTON. Sheriff Bond, June 25, 1810. Bondsmen: HUDSON
MARTIN and JAMES WOODS.

84. SAMUEL BRIDGWATER. Administrator's Bond, July 23, 1810.
HANNAH BRIDGWATER and JNO. M. MARTIN qualified to administrator.
Bondsmen: JOS. ROBERTS and NATHANIEL BRIDGWATER.

85. SAMUEL BRIDGWATER. June 2, 1810; July 23, 1810. Witnesses:
BURGESS WITT, JNO. TOOLER, NATHANIEL BRIDGWATER, HUDSON MARTIN.
Wife, HANNAH--house and slaves; my two youngest children: JOSIAH
BRIDGWATER and POLLY WARE BRIDGWATER; bequests to JNO. JOPLING WOOD
and ELIZABETH WARE PAGE, wife of EDWARD PAGE. My daughter, POLLY WARE,
when of age or married. Executors: wife and friend, JNO. MASSIE
MARTIN and my son, JOSIAH. Note: his wife was HANNAH WOOD who gave
her own consent when bond was secured in Amherst on April 24, 1789.
She was a widow. JOS. LOVING, Surety. I find no marriage in Amherst
for an ELIZABETH WARE WOOD to a PAGE, but my guess is that she was
probably a child of his wife by her previous marriage. The use of
JNO. JOPLING WOOD for one legatee causes one to think that he was
HANNAH's son by her first marriage. If so, it is probable that she
was the HANNAH JOPLING, Spinster, who was licensed to marry RICHARD
WOOD, bachelor, in Amherst, January 5, 1785. WILLIAM WRIGHT, JR. was
surety. Her father, JOSIAH JOPLING, gave his consent and groom's
father, JOSIAS WOOD, also consented. This is not a dogmatic conclusion
on my part, though, for my Amherst will data shows an Administrator's
Bond for a RICHARD WOODS (sic) in 1829.

86. SAMUEL BRIDGWATER. Inventory, August 3, 1810--$3931.57.
JOS. ROBERTS, MICHAEL WOODS, NELSON CRAWFORD.

89f. HUDSON MARTIN. Sheriff Bonds, November 26, 1810. Bondsmen:
JAMES WOODS, WILLIAM CRAWFORD, NELSON CRAWFORD, JR., NELSON
ANDERSON, HUDSON MARTIN, JR.

91. SAMUEL STAPLES. Administrator's Bond, November 26, 1810, for
WILLIAM STAPLES to administrator. Bondsmen: JNO. BIBB, STEPHEN
BOWLES, RICHARD BRYANT.

93. SUSANNA KEY. July 6, 1810; Ocotber 22, 1810. Witnesses:
NELSON ANDERSON, ELISHA FORTUNE, RO. H. ANDERSON, ZACH. NEVIL.
Son, DABNEY KEY; daughters: ELIZABETH, BARBARA, EFFY, PENNY KEY--
PENNY appears to be ONEY a bit later--land bought from ELISHA PETERS.
Grandson, TANDY KEY. Executors: friends: JAMES MURPHY and NELSON
ANDERSON.

93. SUSANNA KEY. Administrator's Bond by JAMES MURPHY and NELSON
ANDERSON, probate data.

94. CHARLES EDMUNDS and ROWLAND EDMUNDS. September 24, 1810, for
CHARLES EDMUNDS as Tobacco Inspector at CAMDEN's Warehouse.

95. STEPHEN WATTS and LAVENDER LONDON. September 24, 1810 for
STEPHEN WATTS as Tobacco Inspector at CAMDEN's Warehouse.

95. SAMUEL FRANKLIN and JNO. MARR. September 24, 1810 for SAMUEL
FRANKLIN at CAMDEN's Warehouse.

96. WILLIAM L. WATTS and VALENTINE HYLTON. September 24, 1810
for WILLIAM L. WATTS as Tobacco Insepctor at CAMDEN's Warehouse.

97. SAMUEL STAPLES. Inventory, January 14, 1811. L475-3-0.
JAMES STEVENS, JR., WILLIAM PURVIS, THOMAS BIBB, JR.

98. THOMAS FITZPATRICK. August 15, 1809; January 28, 1811.
Witnesses: JAMES WOODS, WILLIAM SMALL, WILLIAM FITZPATRICK,
NATHANIEL BRIDGWATER. Daughter, JANE; son, MOSES; daughter, POLLEY;
daughter, SALLEY; son, ALEXANDER; sons, JNO., WILLIAM, BRECKENRIDGE,
THOMAS, when of age. If any die without lawful issue. Wife, FRANKEY--
until youngest child is of age. Lands to wife. My daughters, when
of age or married. Executors: wife and MOSES and THOMAS when of age.

101. THOMAS FITZPATRICK. Administrator's Bond by FRANCES FITZPATRICK
on probate date. Bondsmen: JNO. E. FITZPATRICK, THOMAS
FITZPATRICK, and JOS. ROBERTS.

102. THOMAS PATTON. January 11, 1811; February 25, 1811. Witnesses:
THOMAS EWERS, WILLIAM BRIDGWATER, THOMAS WARE. Wife, JUDITH;
my brothers and sisters or heirs. Executor: wife and friend, JAMES
WOODS.

103. THOMAS PATTON. Administrator's Bond by JUDITH PATTON on probate
date. Bondsmen: THOMAS WEIR, THOMAS EWERS, WILLIAM BRIDGWATER.

104. JOS. SHELTON. Escheator Bond, January 28, 1811. Bondsmen:
JOS. ROBERTS, JNO. E. FITZPATRICK, WILLIAM WRIGHT, S. GARLAND.

105. WILLIAM H. DIGGS. Coroner Bond, January 28, 1811. Bondsman:
RICHARD PHILLIPS.

106. HENRY BIBB, JR. January 28, 1811. Bondsman: JNO. E. FITZPATRICK
and EDWARD HARRIS.

106. JAMES TURNER. Tobacco Inspector at SWAN's Warehouse. January 28,
1811. Bondsman: ELISHA TURNER.

107. JAMES REID. Guardian Bond, February 25, 1811. MICHAEL WOODS
qualified as guardian. Bondsman: JAMES LOVING, JR. Orphan of
JNO. N. REID.

108. THOMAS PATTON. Inventory, March 20, 1811, JUDITH PATTON,
executrix. No total. NATHAN CRAWFORD, HUDSON MARTIN, THRUSTON
or THURSTON J. DICKINSON.

109. JOHN and JOSHUA HARRIS. Guardian Bond, March 25, 1811. JNO.
BURK qualified as guardian. Bondsman: STEPHEN HENDERSON,
THOMAS MATTHEWS and WILLIAM BURK. Orphans of SAMUEL HARRIS, deceased.

109. PEGGY FITZPATRICK. Guardian Bond, March 26, 1811. JNO. E.
FITZPATRICK qualified as guardian. Bondsman: JAMES STEVENS.
Orphans of JANE BAILEY. Note: CHARLES BAILEY and JANE FITZPATRICK,
spinster, got bond in Amherst, February 7, 1800. WILLIAM FITZPATRICK,
surety, and father. He calls her "JANA." Certificate by minister,
REV. WILLIAM CRAWFORD.

110. WILLIAM LYON. March 10, 1811; Monday, April 22, 1811. Witnesses:
     THOMAS EWERS, JESSE GENTRY, HANNON (?) GENTRY, HUDSON MARTIN.
Wife, SALLY--land where I live; my two sons, JAMES and GUTRIDGE LYON.
Daughter, SALLY, until married. My nine children: ELIZABETH GENTRY,
JNO. LYON, FRANCES BOYD, SALLY LYON, WILLIAM LYON, JAMES LYON, MARY
THURMAN (ANDERSON written above line), GUTRIDGE LYON and NANCY BOYD.
Later it is MARY THURMAN ANDERSON and husband, JNO. ANDERSON.
Executors: wife and son, JAMES and GUTRIDGE LYON, but he is referred
to in one place as GUTRIDGE THURMOND.

112. WILLIAM LYON. Administrator's Bond. SALLY LYON, JAMES LYON
     and GUTRIDGE LYON (signed JR.) qualified to administrator on
probate date. Bondsman: HUDSON.

113. WILLIAM CLASBY. Tobacco Inspector at Tye River Warehouse,
     November 26, 1810. Bondsman: THOMAS CLASBY.

114. JESSE MAYS. Administrator's Account--no administrator named,
     from November 2, 1809--not set forth as legatees, but these
family names appear: ROBERT, ELISHA, AUSTIN and LEWIS MAYS. Recorded
June 25, 1810.

115. GEORGE BLAINE. May 28, 1811; May 29, 1811. Witnesses: SOLOMON
     MATTHEWS, WILLIAM LOVING, RODERICK L. TALIAFERRO and NELSON
WRIGHT. Wife, RACHEL; to Overseers of Poor of Nelson County--my
plantation at death of wife--if without issue. Executors: FREDERICK
CABELL, JAMES LOVING, son to JNO. LOVING, and ABRAHAM B. WARWICK.

118. JESSE MAYS. Debts due estate--CHARLES MAYS from August 4,
     1809; JOS. MAYS. Recorded June 25, 1810. Margin notes that
it should have been recorded on page 114.

119. DANIEL LEEBRICK. Ord. Bond in county, May 27, 1811. Bondsman:
     WILLIAM MURRILL.

119. NELSON CAMPBELL. Ord. Bond at Lovingston, May 28, 1811.
     Bondsman: NATHAN BARNETT.

120. RODERICK L. TALIAFERRO. Ord. Bond at Lovingston, May 29, 1811.
     Bondsman: THOMAS COCKE (COCKE?).

121. DANIEL LEEBRICK. Ord. Bond in county, August 27, 1811.
     Bondsman: EDDY FORTUNE.

121. RODERICK L. TALIAFERRO. December 25, 1810, ord. bond at
     Lovingston. Bondsman: SP. GARLAND.

122. WILLIAM TURNER. Guardian Bond, May 28, 1810. TERISHA TURNER,
     JR. qualified as guardian. Bondsman: TERISHA TURNER. Orphan
of JAMES TURNER.

123. WILLIAM BALL. Ord. Bond at home in county, July 21, 1809.
     Bondsman: JESSE JOPLING.

123. JAMES LOVING. Ord. at Loving's Gap, August 28, 1809. Bondsman:
     SAMUEL LOVING.

124. DANIEL LEEBRICK. Ord. Bond at home in County, August 28, 1809.
     Bondsman: THOMAS CHILDRESS.

124. JAMES LOVING. Ord. Bond at his lot in county, February 26,
     1810. Bondsman: JNO. LOVING.

125. GEORGE W. VARNUM. Ord. Bond in county, February 26, 1810.
     Bondsman: S. GARLAND.

125. JAMES MARTIN. Ord. Bond to GOV. WILLIAM CABELL, May 28, 1810.
     Place in county. Bondsman: N. ANDERSON.

126. JNO. WRIGHT. Ord. Bond, May 28, 1810, at Lovingston. Bondsman:
JNO. E. FITZPATRICK.

126. JAMES MARTIN and JNO. JACOBS, JR. January 22, 1810. Ord. Bond
for JAMES MARTIN at KEY's Gap.

127. EDWARD LEWIS. Ord. Bond at Warminster, December 24, 1810.
Bondsman: JAMES MURPHY.

127. CLAYTON C. HARRIS. Constable Bond, June 26, 1811. Bondsman:
MATT. HARRIS.

128. CHARLES C. PATTERSON. Constable Bond, June 24, 1811. Bondsman:
JNO. R. SCRUGGS.

128. NICHOLAS CABELL. Inventory, November 15, 1809. No total,
but long. WILLIAM M. WATKINS and WILLIAM L. WOMACK.

134. WILLIAM H. LEIGH. Constable Bond, July 22, 1811. Bondsman:
TERISHA TURNER.

135. SHADRACK HENDERSON. May 27, 1810; August 26, 1811. Witnesses:
DAVID RICHARDSON, CHARLES HENRY, JNO. PATRICK. Wife, MAY;
daughters, SALLY MARTIN, BARBARY MARTIN, MARY TISDEL, NANCY KERBY,
LUCY BEAVER. Sons, JOS., JNO., deceased--his heirs, WILLIAM.
Executors: son, WILLIAM, and friend, ALLEN SNELL.

136. DAVID CLARKSON. Administrator's Account by DAVID R. and JAMES
CLARKSON. Amherst taxes; WILLIAM CRAWFORD for preaching sermon
at funeral; JESSE CLARKSON for brandy; WILLIAM CLARKSON for "porke."
Legatees due $2452.26. Returned August 28, 1811--GEORGE WILLIAMS,
JAMES MONTGOMERY, WILLIAM B. JACOBS.

138. SAMUEL FRANKLIN. Tobacco Inspector at CAMDEN's Warehouse,
September 23, 1811. Bondsman: WILLIAM STAPLES.

139. DRURY BELL. Tobacco Inspector at CAMDEN's Warehouse, September 23,
1811. Bondsman: STEPHEN WATTS.

139. WILLIAM L. WATTS. Tobacco Inspector at CAMDEN's Warehouse,
September 23, 1811. Bondsman: VALENTINE HYLTON.

140. CHARLES and SAMUEL EDMUNDS. September 23, 1811 for CHARLES
EDMUNDS as Tobacco Inspector at Tye River Warehouse.

140. CHRISTIAN and WILLIAM FOSTER. Guardian Bond, September 23,
1811--SAMUEL TURNER qualified as guardian. Bondsman: TERISHA
TURNER. Orphans of JAMES FOSTER, deceased.

141. LUCAS POWELL. ELIZABETH POWELL relinquished administrator on
September 22, 1811. Witnesses: LUCAS and NORBORN POWELL (B
middle initial).

141. LUCAS POWELL. Administrator's Bond by NATHANIEL POWELL and
JAMES MURPHY, September 23, 1811. Bondsmen: JNO. THOMPSON (M),
THOMAS HAWKINS, RICHARD PHILLIPS, NELSON ANDERSON.

143. JESSE JOPLINE. Account as Overseer of Poor, August 29, 1810.
WYATT TIRY for ELIZABETH LEGANS; a parishoner, MARY DAWSON--
over her portion. CAPT. MOSBY's statement as to ELIZABETH LEGAN's
account.

144. BEN WRIGHT. Administrator's Account by JNO. CAMDEN, administra-
      tor--to JAMES GREGORY as executor of B. WRIGHT; to STEPHEN
BOWLES for MRS. WRIGHT's coffin (date of December 1, 1807); to SUSANNA
MASSIE, widow, and legatee. To legatees: MOSES WRIGHT, BENJAMIN
CAMDEN, MATILDA CASH (widow). Bond of JESSE WRIGHT, JAMES CAMPBELL,
son of WILLIAM--a note: WILLIAM CAMPBELL, son of HENRY--a note:
note of JNO. WRIGHT; also of BENJ. WRIGHT. Recorded October 28, 1811.

146. LUCAS POWELL, SR. Inventory, October 28, 1811. CHARLES WATTS,
      RICHARD PHILLIPS, WILLIAM S. CABELL, JAMES WELLS, SR.

150. ZACH. NEVIL. Tobacco Inspector at Tye River Warehouse,
      October 27, 1811. Bondsman: NELSON ANDERSON.

151. SAMUEL HANSBROUGH. Tobacco Inspector at Tye River Warehouse,
      October 29, 1811. Bondsman: NELSON ANDERSON.

151. ASA VARNUM. Ord. Bond at his house, October 28, 1811. Bondsman:
      ISAAC WHITE.

152. AUSTIN MAYS. Administrator's Bond, October 28, 1811 for
      SUSANNA MAYS to administrator along with AUSTIN WRIGHT.
Bondsmen: WILLIAM EDMUNDS and CHARLES EDMUNDS.

153ff. JNO. DAWSON. Administrator's Account by JNO. S. DAWSON
      from January 10, 1804. To REV. MARTIN DAWSON for sermon. To
Amherst Clerk DAWSON, legatee. To MARY COLEMAN SORRELL and husband,
JNO. SORRELL, with will attached. Committee: NATHAN CRAWFORD, WILLIAM
HARRIS, ZACH. ROBERTS. By order of Amherst court, October, 1804.
Returned November 16, 1805. Further reports as to legatees: SALLY
DAWSON, JNO. DAWSON, PLEASANT DAWSON, RICHARD ADAMS, CHARLES ADAMS,
MARTIN DAWSON; heirs of P, WHITE, NANCY DAWSON, ABNER FORD. WALTON
LEAK, attoney. If MARY COLEMAN SORRELLS departs this life--widow of
JNO. SORRELLS, legatees to get her portion. November 18, 1805.
Same committee as above.

157. JNO. THOMAS. Administrator's Bond by JANE THOMAS, November 25,
      1811, with ANDREW SINNNAL as bondsman.

159. NATHAN SHIELDS. Administrator's Bond by JAMES SHIELDS,
      November 25, 1811; Bondsman: JAMES MONTGOMERY and GEORGE
WILLIAMS.

160. JAMES TILFORD. Administrator's Account. JNO. MASTERS, administra-
      tor from 1802. Bond in 1811 to POLLEY TILFORD. Names of
ANDREW, NICHOLAS and ELIZABETH TILFORD herein. Comm.: WILLIAM B.
JACOBS, JAMES MONTGOMERY. November 25, 1811.

162. JOHN ROBERTS. Made bond as guardian of his infant children;
      not named. November 25, 1811. Bondsman: JOS. SHELTON and
JNO. HARRIS.

162. JAMES STEVENS, JR. Ord. Bond in Lovingston, November 25, 1811.
      Bondsman: S. GARLAND.

163. RICHARD LIGGON. Constable Bond, November 25, 1811. Bondsman:
      JNO. M. MARTIN.

164. JUDITH TALIAFERRO. Inventory, November 26, 1811. WILLIAM
      PAMPLIN, WILLIAM JORDAN, JAMES CUNNINGHAM.

166. JNO. FARRAR, SR. Constable Bond, November 26, 1811. Bondsmen:
      JNO. DIGGS, JNO. M. MARTIN, HUDSON MARTIN, S. GARLAND.

167. JNO. BETHEL. Administrator's Bond by NELSON ANDERSON.
      November 26, 1811. Bondsman: JESSE A. JOPLING.

168. JNO. THOMAS. Inventory, December 23, 1811: $201.01. JNO. N.
      ROSE, WILLIAM STAPLES, HENRY FRANKLIN.

169. THOMAS FARRAR. October 13, 1811; November 25, 1811. Witnesses:
    SAMUEL IRVIN, SHELTON FARRAR, RO. S. FARRAR. Son, GEORGE;
son, PETER; son, THOMAS; daughter, ELIZABETH P.; son, JOHN, to keep
his brother, THOMAS and S -----ELIZABETH P. with him, if they are
without heirs. Executors: Son, JNO. FARRAR and JNO. S. FARRAR.

170. JOSEPH ROBERTS. December 2, 1811; December 23, 1811. Witnesses:
    RO. KINCAID, MICHAEL WOODS, JAMES LYON, HAWES M. COLEMAN, JAMES
PUGH. Son, ALEXANDER; son, JOHN; son, JOSEPH--Kentucky land; son,
THOMAS--land next to CARPENTER and MICHAEL WOODS and ALEXANDER
MC ALEXANDER. Son, HENRY, Kentucky land; son, JAMES, land on south
side of Lackey's Mt. on Davies Creek--formerly called JNO. HARRIS'
Green Mt.--when of age or married. Son, GEORGE, when of age. Son,
WILLIAM C.; daughter, FLERRY B. ROBERTS, when of age or when married;
daughter, SUSANNA B. HUGHES. My wife, SARAH. My daughters: MARY
CARTER, ELIZABETH SHELTON, NANCY HUGHEY, B. SALLY C. ROBERTS, FLERRY B.
ROBERTS and SUSANNA B. ROBERTS. Executors: wife and ALEXANDER and
THOMAS ROBERTS.

173. JOSEPH ROBERTS. Administrator's Bond--SARAH ROBERTS, December 23,
    1811. Bondsmen: ALEXANDER ROBERTS, MICHAEL WOODS, WILLIAM LEE
HARRIS and WILLIAM H. MOSBY.

174. CHARLES EVANS. Administrator's Bond--AILEY EVANS, February 24,
    1812; Bondsman: GEORGE LOVING.

175. JNO. JACOBS, SR. November 28, 1811; February 24, 1812.
    Witnesses: THOMAS MASSIE, CHARLES BURGHER, EDMOND T. COFFEY,
NELSON MONROE. Advanced in age. Wife, SARAH--260 acres. Son, DAVID;
son, WILLIAM B.; Cub Creek land where WILLIAM dwells and has for some
years. Son, JOHN--Kentucky land; son, PETER C.--land on east side of
Tye and bought of RICHARD TALIAFERRO. Daughters: BETSY CLARKSON and
SUSANNAH HILL and children. Executors: sons, WILLIAM and PETER
JACOBS.

177. JNO. JACOBS, SR. Administrator's Bond by WILLIAM B. JACOBS
    and PETER C. JACOBS on probate date above. Bondsmen: DAVID
and JNO. JACOBS.

178. ELISHA ESTES. January 4, 1812; February 24, 1812. Witnesses:
    RICHARD BREEDLOVE and THOMAS BREEDLOVE. My children; executor
to sell land in Caroline where WILLIAM JOHNSON lives. Daughter,
ELISABETH GOODLOW JOHNSON; my single children; my nephew, TRIPLETT J. (?)
ESTES is to be guardian of my three children: MARY TOMPKINS ESTES,
BENJAMIN TOMPKINS ESTES and ELISHA BLUFORD ESTES. Executors: JAMES
MURPHY, TRIPLETT T. ESTES, JAMES JOHNSON and ABRAHAM B. WARWICK.

180. ELISHA ESTES. Administrator's Bond by JAMES MURPHY and
    ABRAHAM B. WARWICK to administrate estate on probate date.
Bondsman: STEPHEN WATTS.

181. PATSY SIMS. Guardians Account by HUDSON MARTIN, guardian,
    from April 1809. My expenses to the west--$50.00; to Orange;
to Hanover; to Staunton; to MARTIN BRYANT from Greenbrier to Kanawha;
another trip to west--$50.00; MARTIN BRYANT--$15.00 for western
trip; two trips down the country; another western trip; a man to go
to Hanover courthouse. Returned February 24, 1812.

181. JOS. ROBERTS. Inventory January 7, 1812--L1770-10-6. NATHAN
    CRAWFORD, JOS. MONTGOMERY, MICHAEL WOODS.

185. JNO. BRADSHAW. Ord. Bond at Nelson Courthouse in his home,
    February 24, 1812. Bondsman: WILLIAM LOVING.

185. DAVID ENIZ. Guardian Bond by THOMAS NASH, February 24, 1812.
    Orphan of BETSY ENIX. Bondsman: WILLIAM MURRELL.

186. SNOWDEN MADDOX. Ord. Bond, March 23, 1812. Bondsman: RO. L.
    TALIAFERRO.

187. EDMOND T. or F. COFFEY, JR. Constable Bond, January 23, 1812. Bondsman: JAMES MONTGOMERY and JESSE CLARKSON.

188. CHARLES EVANS. Inventory; no total, but long, March 19, 1812. ALEY EVANS, administratrix. JNO. BETHEL, THOMAS BIBB, JNO. BIBB.

191. HENRY DAWSON. Ord. at dwelling in county, March 9 or 11 (?), 1812. Bondsman: WILLIAM LEE HARRIS.

191. MARY TEAS. Administrator's Bond by JNO. BARNETT, April 27, 1812. Bondsmen: JAMES MONTGOMERY and GEORGE WILLIAMS.

193. JOS. ROBERTS. Administrator's Bond by THOMAS ROBERTS as one of the administrators, April 27, 1812. Bondsmen: JNO. W. HARRIS and WILLIAM LEE HARRIS.

194. BENNETT NALLEY. January 20, 1812; May 25, 1812. Witnesses: JNO. DAWSON, JNO. LYON, BENJ. DAWSON. Wife, MARY; daughters: MARY THURMOND, JINNEY; son, THOMAS, who settled on his own or rented land; sons, BENNETT, DENNIS and WILLIAM when 21. Son, SAMUEL, when 21. When children are of age or married. Except THOMAS and MARY "who has already been furnished." Youngest sons, WILLIAM and SAMUEL, when of age. Executors: Friends, BENJ. JOHNSON and THOMAS NALLEY. Page 196 Administrator's Bond by BENJ. JOHNSON on probate date. Bondsmen: JOS. SHELTON and JNO. S. DAWSON.

197. MRS. MOURNING JOWIT. On deathbed requested that slave hires, after expenses, be paid to her daughter, FLETCHER, in trust of HUDSON MARTIN. Recorded May 25, 1812. Attested by NATHAN CRAWFORD.

198. THOMAS FARRAR. Administrator's Bond by JNO. FARRAR, May 25, 1812. Bondsmen: JESSE JOPLING and WILLIAM BALL.

199. SNOWDEN MADDOX. May 25, 1812, ord. bond in house in county. Bondsman: JNO. KIRBY.

200. JAMES STEVENS, JR. Ord. Bond at home in county, May 27, 1812. Bondsman: SPOTSWOOD GARLAND.

201. SAMUEL LEAKE. May 23, 1812, chosen treasurer of Nelson and Albemarle Factory. Bondsmen: MARK LEAKE, WILLIAM LEAKE, JNO. S. FARRAR, JOS. FARRAR, WILLIAM ROBERTSON. Witnesses: LANDON FARRAR, PLEASANT BAYLEY, SHELTON FARRAR.

202. JACOB WHEELER. August 10, 1811; June 22, 1812. Witnesses: THOMAS HENDERSON, JNO. PASTON (?), JNO. HENDERSON. Wife, SARAH--217½ acres; my six children--what they received when married from their father. Son, DANIEL; daughter, MARTHEW DUCKETH HENDERSON and heirs; daughters, ANN, MARY, MILDRED and REBECCA--Montgomery County land--360 acres on Rone (?) Creek. Wife and son, DANIEL, to administrate. Page 203 SARAH WHEELER qualified on probate date. Bondsmen: HUDSON MARTIN, SR. and JR.

204. JNO. FARRAR. Constable, June 22, 1812. Bondsmen: HUDSON MARTIN, JR., SP. GARLAND, SAMUEL LEAKE.

205. HENRY BIBB, JR. Constable Bond, June 22, 1812. Bondsman: JNO. HARRIS.

206. EDMOND COFFEY. Constable Bond, June 22, 1812. Bondsman: JAMES MONTGOMERY.

206. CHARLES C. PATTESON. Constable Bond, June 22, 1812. Bondsman: JNO. and TIMOTHY SCRUGGS.

207. MOSES FITZPATRICK. Constable, June 22, 1812. Bondsman: WILLIAM EDMUNDS.

208. WILLIAM SMITH. Constable Bond, June 22, 1812. Bondsmen:
LEWIS TINDALL and STEPHEN WATTS.

209. BENNETT NALLEY. Inventory, $4723.50, June 22, 1812. JNO. S.
DAWSON, JNO. LYON, ZACH. ROBERTS.

210. ELISHA PETERS. Inventory, February 26, 1812. L778-18-9.
ZACH. NEVIL, SAMUEL HANSBROUGH, ELISHA PETERS.

213. THOMAS FARRAR. Inventory recorded July 27, 1812. L211-7-0.
JNO. S. FARRAR, JOS. FARRAR, RO. S. FARRAR.

214. WILLIAM ALFORD. Administrator's Account by WILLIAM HOLLINGSWORTH;
sale and ALFORD buyers were THOMAS and WILLIAM. Each legatee
got L27-10. Amount of sale: L295-3-7½. Recorded November 2, 1811.
JAMES DILLARD, CHARLES WATTS, WILLIAM H. DIGGES.

215. JAMES GREGORY. Ord. Bond at New Market, July 27, 1812.
Bondsman: CHARLES C. PATTESON.

216. GEORGE W. VARNUM. Administrator's Bond--JAMES M. VARNUM and
SOLOMON MATTHEWS, August 24, 1812. Bondsmen: JAMES LOVING,
JR. and S. GARLAND.

217. WILLIAM HAMNER. Administrator's Bond HENRY (HENLEY?) HAMNER,
SR. and bondsmen were: TERISHA TURNER and SAMUEL LEAKE,
August 21, 1812.

219. GEORGE BLAINE. Inventory, recorded August 25, 1812. Cow and
yearling claimed by PARMENAS BRYANT. NICHOLAS L. MARTIN,
Deputy Sheriff and HUDSON MARTIN, Sheriff. Sales: RACHEL BLAINE
and PARMENAS BRYANT were buyers.

220. WILLIAM, MICHAEL and SALLY BAILEY. Guardian Bond--August 25,
1812--CHARLES BAILEY and THOMAS W. COCKE for CHARLES BAILEY as
guardian of the three who were orphans of CHARLES BAILEY. Note: my
own BAILEY line eludes me back of 1769 in Charlotte. DAVID BAILEY
bought land on Dunnavan Creek in that year. Shortly after turn of
century his heirs are set forth in Charlotte and my HOLCOMB D.
BAILEY is among them. HOLCOMB D. married MARTHA DRINKARD in Prince
Edward. DAVID shows on a bond with ROGER COCKE BAILEY and PETER
COCKE BAILEY in Charlotte, but no relationship is shown. PETER
COCKE BAILEY and HOLCOMB D. BAILEY both appear in Montgomery County,
Tennessee and HOLCOMB D. went on to Callaway County, Missouri. An
article in Hardesty and Brock on the GOODWIN family of Amherst tells
that GOODWIN is descended from the ROGER COCKE BAILEY family of
Charlotte and speaks of family home as Albion Castle; I cannot
locate it. It also stated that this BAILEY stems from one ABRAM
BAILEY who came to what is now Richmond and married TEMPERANCE
COCKE. A slave suit in one Tidewater County deals with ABRAM. I
am unable to tie DAVID into the ABRAM BAILEY line. DAVID had a
son, JOHNSON BAILEY, who seems to have died by time of estate
settlement. HOLCOMB D. had a son, WILLIAM HENRY BAILEY, who married
in Tennessee County above to MARTHA JOHNSON of North Carolina stock.
He did not go to Missouri with his father, but came into Graves
County, Kentucky. His son, BERNARD BASCOM BAILEY married ALICE
BYRD and they were my grandparents.

220. JNO. BARDSHAW. Ord. Bond at Lovingston, August 25, 1812.
Bondsman: CHARLES PERROW.

221. CHARLES PATTERSON. Inventory, March 26, 1812; no total.
WILLIAM CLASBY, JNO. MUNROE, THOMAS HAWKINS.

222. AMBROSE CAMPBELL. December 7, 1811; September 28, 1812.
Witnesses: WILLIAM WRIGHT, ELIJAH MAYS, AUSTIN WRIGHT, JOS.
WHITE, JNO. SETTLES. Wife, MARGARET; son, PETER; daughter, LUCY
CAMPBELL; my following children: RACHEL JUNIUS, FRANCES JUNIUS,
SALLY MILLS, TANDY CAMPBELL, ELIZABETH MAYS; children of my daughter,
POLLY PAGE--to be divided. Executors: Son, PETER, and WILLIAM H.
DIGGES. Page 223 PETER CAMPBELL qualified on probate date. Bondsman:
JAMES EDMUNDS.

225. STEPHEN WATTS. September 28, 1812; Tobacco Inspector at
CAMDEN's Warehouse. Bondsman: THOMAS SPENCER.

225. CHARLES EDMUNDS. Tobacco Inspector at Tye River Warehouse,
September 28, 1812. Bondsman: JAMES HUGHES.

226. ZACH. NEVIL. Tobacco Inspector at Tye River Warehouse.
September 28, 1812. Bondsman: NELSON ANDERSON.

227. RODERICK L. TALIAFERRO. Ord. at Lovingston, September 28,
1812. Bondsman: CHARLES PERROW.

227. LEE W. HARRIS. Revenue Commissioner, September 28, 1812.
Bondsman: THOMAS E. FORTUNE.

228. DANIEL MC DONALD. A page pasted together here--July 30,
1812; October 26, 18--. Witnesses: ABNER FRANKLIN, CHARLES
JONES, DANIEL WADE, WILLIAM HILL, JR., BENJAMIN FITZGERALD. My
daughter, MARGARET JACOBS, and children when of age. Executors:
Friend, DAVID S. GARLAND of Amherst County and my two grandsons,
CHARLES ANDERSON JACOBS and HENRY JACOBS--their minority. If
GARLAND won't act, then JNO. N. ROSE of Amherst County. Page 230
DAVID S. GARLAND qualified on October 26, 1812. Bondsman: SPOTSWOOD
GARLAND.

231. WILLIAM L. WATTS. Tobacco Inspector at CAMDEN's Warehouse,
October 26, 1812. Bondsman: SAMUEL P. LAYNE.

231. AMBROSE CAMPBELL. Inventory, November 19, 1812--$352.83.
ROLAND EDMUNDS, CHARLES WATTS, ELIJAH MAYS, SAMUEL EDMUNDS.

233. JAMES WOODS. Sheriff Bond, November 23, 1812. Bondsman:
WILLIAM HARRIS, HUDSON MARTIN, JOS. SHELTON. Same men and
more bonds on 234 and 235.

236. JACOB WHEELER. Inventory--order of June Court, 1812; recorded
November 16, 1812. $1094.05. THRUSTON I. DICKINSON, JNO. N.
DICKINSON, NATHANIEL HARLOW, JR.

238. POLLY WARE BRIDGWATER. Guardian Bond HANNAH BRIDGWATER
qualified as guardian. Bondsmen: WILLIAM JOPLING, JNO. M.
MARTIN. December 28, 1812. Orphan of SAMUEL BRIDGWATER.

239. DANIEL LEEBRICK. Ord. in county, December 28, 1812. Bondsman:
ELISHA FORTUNE.

239. WILLIAM CRISP. December 28, 1812, ord. at Amherst County Old
Courthouse in Nelson. Bondsman: RICHARD BRYANT. The old
courthouse was in vicinity of hamlet of Colleen in present Nelson.

240. ELISHA ESTES. Administrator's Bond by JAMES JOHNSON, January 25,
1813. Bondsman: JNO. HIGGINBOTHAM.

241. MARY TEAS. Inventory, December 28, 1812. WILLIAM B. JACOBS,
JNO. JACOBS and LANDON H. BRENT.

242. WILLIAM RYAN. Ord. at Cross Roads near Tye River, January 25,
1812. Bondsman: STERLING CLAIBORNE.

242.	JNO. DAWSON. Administrator's Account by JNO. S. DAWSON--
	obedient to order of Amherst Court of October, 1814. Reported
by WILLIAM HARRIS, NATHAN CRAWFORD and ZACH. ROBERTS, November 18,
1815. L160-0-4. MARY COLEMAN SORREL had life estate and at her
death to descend to JNO. DAWSON and heirs. Support of MARY SORREL
from November 18, 1805 to May 3, 1810. Land not yet divided among
legatees. September 23, 1812. JAMES WOODS, ZACH. ROBERTS, WILLIAM
HARRIS. Note: discrepancy in dates so recorded.

243.	CHARLES C. PATTESON. Ord. at home near Variety, January 25,
	1813. Bondsman: JNO. SCRUGGS.

244.	HENLEY DRUMMOND estate. Report on order of December 2, 1812.
	Widow, MARY B. DRUMMOND and each child. What ZACH. DRUMMOND
has to his account. Parts of ZACH., FRANCES, HENLEY, CHARLES DRUMMOND.
Land adjoins JAMES PAMPLIN's old line and VALENTINE HYLTON. ZACH
owes M. B. DRUMMOND in settlement. Recorded March 22, 1813.
F. CABELL, MARTIN WILSON, NATH. OFFUTT.

246.	GUTRIDGE THURMOND. Administrator's Bond by WILLIAM BALL,
	March 22, 1813. Bondsmen: JESSE JOPLING, JOS. FARRAR.
Witnesses: IRA GARRETT.

247.	SAMUEL EDMUNDS. January 8, 1812; March 22, 1813. Witnesses:
	JNO. LOVING, SPENCER FAULKNER, JAMES HARVIE, RO. MAYS. Wife,
ALEY; son, CHARLES. Sons: WILLIAM, ROLAND, JNO., SAMUEL. Daughters:
JANE MAYS, MARY KENNEY, ALCEY NEVIL in trust of friend, WILLIAM H.
DIGGES, and sons, ROWLAND and SAMUEL. Any children borne to ALCEY
NEVIL. Grandson, SAMUEL, son of my son, JNO. EDMUNDS. Bequest to
JANE LONDON. Executors: sons, ROWLAND and SAMUEL and friend,
WILLIAM H. DIGGES. Here is another guessing game. Was SAMUEL's
wife, ALEY, the widow of AUGUSTINE WRIGHT and was JANE LONDON her
daughter by him? ALCEY WRIGHT qualified as administratrix of
AUGUSTINE in July of 1777 in Amherst. This estate is still to be
worked out for the indexer made an error in noting administratrix's
division of estate and I have yet to find it, but feel that it is
bound to be in an early book since he indexed it. If this is the
same ALEY or ALCEY, she did not remain a widow very long. In
September of 1777 ALSE WRIGHT, widow, married SAMUEL EDMUNDS in
Amherst. LAVENDER LONDON married JANE WRIGHT in 1800 and SAMUEL
EDMUNDS, JR. was his surety. She was over 21 at marriage. This
is NOT a dogmatic assumption on my part. Page 249 ROWLAND, SAMUEL
EDMUNDS, LEWIS TINDAL and ZACH. NEVIL made Administrator's Bond on
probate date for ROWLAND and SAMUEL EDMUNDS to administrate the
estate.

250.	CHILDRIS SMITH. January 21, 1813; March 23, 1813. Witnesses:
	JNO. and REBECCA JOPLING. Son, FIELD SMITH; daughter,
JANEY SMITH; daughter, BETSY WILSON. My two sons and three daughters.
To WILLIAM BANTON and LITTLE BERRY SMITH. This is so recorded,
but not clear as to all of children. Page 251 FIELDS SMITH and
WILLIAM BAILEY made Administrator's Bond on probate date for FIELD
SMITH.

252.	BERDIT SKINNER. Administrator's Bond for WILLIAM H. DIGGES
	and NANCY SKINNER to administrator, April 26, 1813. Bondsman:
SPENCER FAULKNER.

254.	CHILDRESS SMITH. Inventory--FIELDING SMITH (note new spelling
	here), April 26, 1813. HENRY or HARVEY SMITH, HUDSON MARTIN,
WILLIAM LANKFORD.

255.	BURDIT SKINNER. Inventory--$518.81. May 24, 1813. SAMUEL
	EDMUNDS, JR., ROLAND EDMUNDS, JAMES EDMUNDS. Note: Here, too,
we have different spellings of SKINNER's first name. This is as con-
fusing as the CORTLAND SKINNER in Madison and ESTILL who is an
ancestor of my wife's. I have never established his lineage, but the
name is used by a Tory family of SKINNERS in New York. The name is
spelled CORTLAND, COURTLAND, COTNEY, etc. in Kentucky data.

257. CHARLES C. PATTESON. Ord. at home in county, May 24, 1813.
      Bondsman: WILLIAM RYAN.

258. WILLIAM RYAN. Ord. at home in county, May 24, 1813. Bondsman:
      CHARLES C. PATTESON. This seems to be a case of "you scratch
my back, and I'll scratch yours."

259. JNO. F. ROBERTSON. Ord. Bond at Warminster, May 24, 1813.
      Bondsman: W. I. or J. ROBERTSON.

260. JNO. SPITFATHAM. Ord. at Warminster, May 24, 1813. Bondsman:
      JAMES JOHNSON.

261. DANIEL LEEBRICK. Ord. Bond at house in county, May 25, 1813.
      Bondsman: PARMENAS BRYANT.

262. JAMES JOHNSON. Qualified as guardian of CHRISTOPHER T. ESTES,
      orphand of ELISHA ESTES, May 24, 1813. Bondsman: WILLIAM J.
or I. ROBERTSON.

262. GEORGE HYLTON. February 21, 1811; March 22, 1813. Witnesses:
      GEORGE C. THOMAS, SUSANNAH THOMAS, ZACH. DRUMMOND, WILLIAM and
REES CUNNINGHAM. To MARY W. GILBERT--110 acres for life where she
lives; then to GEORGE HYLTON, son to VALENTINE HYLTON, and to JANE C.
HYLTON. My brother, JAMES HYLTON--land next to WALKER's old field;
my brother, SAMUEL; my brother, NEWMAN; to NED HYLTON; to HANNER
ALLEN; to JESSE JOPLING; to GEORGE ALLEN; to VALENTINE and JEREMIAH
HYLTON, sons of my brother, LIGAH HYLTON; to JESSE HYLTON, son of
my brother, JAMES HYLTON; to JNO. SCRUGGS who married BETSY HYLTON.
Executors: VALENTINE and JEREMIAH HYLTON, sons of my brother,
JAMES HYLTON, and ARCHIBALD HYLTON, son of my brother, LIGA HYLTON.
Page 264 VALENTINE and JER. HYLTON made Administrator's Bond on
probate date. Bondsmen: FREDERICK CABELL, STEPHEN WATTS, SAMUEL
ARRINGTON, JAMES CUNNINGHAM and JAMES WATTS.

266. NANCY DUNWOODY. In presence of SAMUEL MC ALEXANDER and ANDREW
      WEIR said that she intended that JNO. MC NIGHT should have bed
and furniture which he lay in and notes on SAMUEL MC ALEXANDER and
JOS. MARTIN. The rest of her estate to be divided among (?) JNO.
LOBBAN. Witnesses: WILLIAM ROBERTSON, SAMUEL MC ALEXANDER, ANDREW
WEIR, JR. March 22, 1813. Also spelled DUNWIDDY in some places.
Page 266 JNO. LOBBAN and JNO. M. MARTIN made Administrator's Bond
on July 26, 1813, for JNO. LOBBAN. Her name is spelled ANN DINWIDDIE
here.

268. JAMES LOVING, JR. Ord. at home in county, July 26, 1813.
      Bondsman: RODERICK L. TALIAFERRO.

269. DANIEL MC DONALD. Inventory; no total, November 7, 1812.
      THOMAS JONES, CHARLES JONES, JAMES CLARKSON.

270. JAMES GREGORY. Ord. bond at dwelling in county, August 23,
      1813. Bondsman: JORDAN EDMUNDS.

271. SAMUEL EDMUNDS. Inventory $3829.50, August 23, 1813. JNO.
      DILLARD, STEPHEN WATTS, CHARLES WATTS.

272. ANNE DUNWIDDIE. Inventory, JNO. LOBBAN administrator, August 23,
      1813. HUDSON MARTIN, NELSON CRAWFORD, JAMES LOBBAN.

273. WILLIAM HAMNER. Inventory, no total; September 27, 1813.
      HENLEY HAMNER; administrator; SPOTSWOOD GARLAND, Clerk.

274. CHARLES EDMUNDS. Tobacco Inspector at Tye River Warehouse,
      September 27, 1813. Bondsman: LAVENDER LONDON.

275. WILLIAM L. WATTS. Tobacco Inspector at CAMDEN's Warehouse,
      September 27, 1813. Bondsman: VALENTINE HYLTON.

275. ZACH. NEVIL. Tobacco Inspector at Tye River Warehouse,
      September 27, 1813. Bondsman: JESSE JOPLING.

276. STEPHEN WATTS. Tobacco Inspector at CAMDEN's Warehouse,
      September 27, 1813. Bondsman: SAMUEL LOVING.

277. ROBT. FRANKLIN. Administrator's Bond by JNO. FRANKLIN to
      administrator, September 27, 1813. Bondsman: JNO. HIGGINBOTHAM.

279. JNO. DODD. March 29, 1803; October 25, 1813. Witnesses:
      JNO. BALLARD, MOSES HUGHES, JAMES and BENJAMIN HUGHES. Wife,
      MARTHA; son, JOSIAS; daughter, SARAH LEE; to JOS. DODD--$1.00;
      daughter, ELIZABETH DODD; daughter, MARY DODD--while single; son,
      WILLIAM; daughter, PHEBE WITT; daughter, NANCY LEE. Executor:
      son, WILLIAM DODD. Page 281 WILLIAM DODD qualified on probate date;
      bondsmen: JAMES HUGHES and THOMAS GOODWIN.

282. CHARLES L. BARRETT. Ord. at Greenway, October 25, 1813.
      Bondsman: S. CLAIBORNE.

283. LUCY TINDAL. Administrator's Bond by LEWIS TINDAL, October 25,
      1813. Bondsman: ZACH. NEVIL.

285. SALLY SPENCER. Administrator's Bond by STEPHEN WATTS to
      administrator, October 25, 1813. Bondsman: CHARLES L. BARRETT.

286. JNO. BETHEL. Inventory, December 3, 1811--$1683.93. JAMES
      MURPHY, SAMUEL HANSBROUGH, ELISHA PETERS.

288. JNO. DODD. Inventory--no total--November 22, 1813. MOSES
      HUGHES, SR. and JR., BENJAMIN HUGHES.

289. CRAWFORD PUCKETT. Administrator's Bond by JACOB PUCKETT.
      Bondsman: THOMAS E. FORTUNE.

290. MARK LIVELY. Administrator's Bond by ELIZABETH LIVELY,
      November 22, 1813. Bondsmen: PLEASANT BAILEY and JESSE
      JOPLING.

292. JAMES WILLS, JR. Administrator's Bond by JNO. WILLS and
      RO. J. KINCAID, November 22, 1813.

294. JAMES STEVENS. October 14, 1796; November 22, 1813. Witnesses:
      WILL CABELL, LANDON CABELL, JAMES MURPHY, HEZ. HARGROVE,
      JNO. THOMPSON, JR., JNO. STAPLES. Of Amherst County--son, JAMES--mill
      tract--line of WILLIAM LOVING, deceased; land hereinafter devised to
      GEORGE LOVING and SAMUEL SPENCER. Son, JNO. GRIFFIN STEVENS; my
      daughters: MOLLY JOPLING, BETHELAND PENN, ELIZABETH THOMPSON. My
      wife, BETHELELAND; daughter, ANNE SPENCER--land next to HEZ. HARGROVE;
      WILLIAM LOVING, RO. HARRISON, WILLIAM FURBUSH, deceased, and mill
      tract. Daughter, SARAH JOPLING; grandson, JAMES STEVENS JOPLING;
      grandson, JAMES STEVENS, son of my son, JAMES. If son, JNO. GRIFFIN
      STEVENS, leaves no issue. If my daughter, MOLLY JOPLING, is without
      issue. Executor: son, JAMES STEVENS. Codicil: grandson, JAMES
      STEVENS, son of JNO. G. STEVENS; grandson, SAMUEL STEVENS, son of
      JAMES STEVENS, JR.; granddaughters: SALLY and BETHELELAND PENN,
      children of my daughter, BETHELELAND PENN, deceased. My daughter,
      ELIZABETH THOMPSON; my friend, SPOTSWOOD GARLAND. Slave devised to my
      daughter, ANNE SPENCER; the children of my daughter, ELIZABETH; ANNE
      SPENCER gets a slave in lieu of first one. Codicil written on
      March 24, 1810. Witnesses: S. GARLAND, WILLIAM VAUGHAN, JNO.
      BROOKS. Codicil of November 7, 1813, and witnesses: BEN BRADSHAW,
      JAMES S. PENN, S. GARLAND. Land of JNO. G. and wife descends at
      deaths to their children. If daughter, MOLLY JOPLING, dies before
      husband, THOMAS JOPLING. My daughter, MILDRED LOVING. Son, JAMES, JR.
      and his daughters, MILDRED and ELIZABETH. Page 300 SPOTSWOOD GARLAND
      qualified to administrate on November 23, 1813. Bondsman: RO. RIVES.

300ff. JAMES WOODS. Sheriff Bonds, November 23, 1813. Bondsmen: DAVID R. PATTESON, JOS. SHELTON, SPOTSWOOD GARLAND.

304. JAMES STEVENS. Inventory, December 2, 1813--called SR. L1791-19-0. SOLOMON MATTHEWS, RO. J. KINCAID, JAMES WILLS, HEZEKIAH HARGROVE. Recorded February 28, 1814.

305. MARK LIVELY. Inventory January 1, 1814. JNO. FARRAR, WILLIAM BALL, S. (L) FARRAR. Recorded February 26, 1814.

306. CHARLES RODES. Inventory and sale. THOMAS MARTIN, executor, November 26, 1812. Family buyers: DAVID, CHARLES and THOMAS RODES. Recorded February 28, 1814.

307. JNO. BETHEL. Administrator's Account by NELSON ANDERSON, administrator--to MARY BETHEL, her third; son, JNO. BETHEL, JR. Recorded February 28, 1814.

308. BURDIT SKINNER. Administrator's Account by WILLIAM H. DIGGS, administrator--to MRS. SKINNER; RICHARD SKINNER--his part of wheat; STEPHEN WATTS, administrator of WILLIAM SPENCER; NANCY SKINNER; WILLIAM H. DIGGS as agent for WILLIAM C. JOHNSON, March 28, 1814. RICHARD PHILLIPS, ROLAND EDMUNDS, WILLIAM HARGROVE.

310. JAMES WILLS, JR. Inventory December 25, 1813, court order-- $126.97. ABRAHAM SEAY, JR., JOEL PONTON, JNO. WRIGHT, THOMAS E. FORTUNE.

311. MOURNING JOUITT. Sale by JNO. M. MARTIN; negroes hired by direction of PETER CARR, an executor of JNO. JOUITT, deceased, before her will was proved and administrator appointed. Report by MARTIN of September 30, 1813--negroes hired during her lifetime. NATHAN CRAWFORD, administrator of MOURNING JOUITT, May 23, 1814.

312. WILLIAM BOWMAN. February 4, 1804; June court, 1814. Witnesses: JNO. FARRAR, JR., THOMAS FARRAR, PETER FARRAR. Wife, SARAH-- Rockfish land in Albemarle and on branch named Canoe. Son, JOHN; son, RALPH--land in Amherst County to sons, SHEROD and GILBERT BOWMAN on branch called Jollares (?). Buckingham land to son, WILLIAM, and where he lives. Daughter, ELIZABETH FOWLES; daughters: MARY WILKERSON, ALLSE BABER, LUCY WILKERSON, SARY BURKS, NANCY BOWMAN, SUSANNA BOWMAN and REBECCA, the one that's silly. Wife, SARAH, to administrate, along with sons, RALPH and SHEROD BOWMAN.

313. CRAWFORD PUCKETT. Inventory, January 19, 1814. A. and JAMES MC ALEXANDER, JNO. FORTUNE.

313. JACOB MASENCUP. June 13, 1814; July 25, 1814. Witnesses: CHARLES MC CUE, JNO. DETTOR, JACOB WEIR. Wife, CATHERINE--where I live. Son, JOHN. Estate of my brother, JOHN, and money coming to me--he was of Pennsylvania. Daughter, MARY GRASS (?)--fifteen acres of the forest tract and home where she lives along line of PETER TRANGER. Wife to administrate.

314. GEORGE HYLTON. Inventory below the home tract--Island Plantation; many slaves at $18,314.96. Recorded July 25, 1814. NATHANIEL OFFUTT, HENRY H. WATTS, MICAJAH PENDLETON. On page 316 is Administrator's Account by JER. and V. HYLTON from November 10, 1813--expenses of V. HYLTON at Amherst; references to Nelson, New Market, Buckingham and Fluvanna. JEREMIAH had expenses to Bedford--or should say, from there to Nelson, July 21, 1814, record for report. FREDERICK CABELL, CHARLES S. BARRETT.

318. JNO. MC CUE, SR. April 3, 1802; August 22, 1814. Witnesses: BIXZL (?) W. TAXWELL, SR., WILLIAM BOYD, MOSES MC CUE, JNO. MC CUE, JR. Of Amherst County. Son, CHARLES, has endeared himself to me by filial attention and he gets all. Seventy-one acres where I live. Claims of RO. HENDREN and wife, MARY, or DAVID MC CUE or any other of my children shall be null. CHARLES gets all and is to administrate.

319. JAMES T. HUBBARD. Administrator's Account by JAMES BULLOCK
      from November 10, 1812. To MRS. HUBBARD expenses of taking
slaves to Buckingham Courthouse; her plantation in Nelson; SUSAN
HUBBARD's bond: L538-0-1. Page 320--committee appointed by
Buckingham Court, July 1, 1813--L49-15-4 due administrator who
admitted sale of several slaves in trust and intestate to secure
JESSE HIGGINBOTHAM on deed of record in Buckingham. HUBBARD to
PECE (?) PAGE--in Superior Chancery at Richmond--negroes named; one
with only one arm. Comm.: RO. SHANE, BOLLING BRANCH, SAMUEL
JONES. September 26, 1814. ROLFE ELDRIDGE, CC.

320. WILLIAM L. WATTS. Tobacco Inspector at CAMDEN's Warehouse,
      September 26, 1814. Bondsman: VALENTINE HYLTON.

321. CHARLES EDMUNDS. Tobacco Inspector at Tye River Warehouse,
      September 26, 1814. Bondsman: WILLIAM EDMUNDS.

321. STEPHEN WATTS. Tobacco Inspector at CAMDEN's Warehouse,
      September 26, 1814. Bondsman: SAMUEL LOVING.

322. ZACH. NEVIL. Tobacco Inspector at Tye River Warehouse,
      September 26, 1814. Bondsman: JESSE JOPLING.

323. PATRICK HENRY, JR. Administrator's Account of--ELVIRA ANN
      HENRY, SR., guardian of ELVIRA ANN HENRY, JR. From September 24,
1804. EDMOND WINSTON's account--dower slaves. Campbell County land
tax; Island rented to JOEL YANCEY. FAYETTE HENRY for corn in 1812.
L1093-17-9. SR. is mother of JR. and PATRICK HENRY, JR. was husband
of SR. and father of JR. October 24, 1814. JNO. HIGGINBOTHAM and
NELSON ANDERSON.

328-330. LANDON CABELL. Sheriff Bonds, November 28, 1814. Bondsmen:
      WILLIAM CABELL and RO. RIVES.

331. CORNELIUS NEVIL. Inventory--$3564.00, May 22, 1815. JAMES
      DILLARD, JNO. THOMPSON, CHARLES WATTS.

332. SARAH SPENCER. Inventory, L150-5-6, May 22, 1815. JNO. and
      JAMES DILLARD, CHARLES WATTS.

332. JOSEPH LOVING. Inventory, April 15, 1815--$5292.58. WILLIAM H.
      DIGGES, STEPHEN WATTS, WILLIAM HARGROVE.

335. NATHANIEL HARLOW. June 16, 1802; May 23, 1815. Witnesses:
      JAMES BROOKS, RICHARD RICHEDSON, EDMOND PAGE, CHARLES SMITH.
Wife, FANNY--where I live. Lines of JAMES WOODS on south of Lynch
Creek to tract bought of CLAUDIUS BUSTER; sixty-seven acres bought
of SHEROD MARTIN. Son, NATHANIEL--land bought of JNO. MURRELL and
part of which HUDSON MARTIN is to make title for me. Daughter-in-
law, ANNE HARLOW. My other children: WALTER H., REUBEN, WILLIAM,
AUGUSTINE, MORDECAI, JOHN, SUSANNA WEST, ELIZABETH ROBERSON, FANNY
HARLOW, and POLLY HARLOW. My six sons and four daughters. SUSANNA
WEST's part in trust of my sons, WILLIAM and NATHANIEL and at her
death to my sons. If ELIZABETH, FANNY and POLLY are without issue.
Executors: sons: REUBEN, WILLIAM and NATHANIEL. The will was
opposed by LARKIN MILLER, but admitted. NATHANIEL relinquished
right to administrate in person. WILLIAM HARLOW qualified.
Bondsmen: NATHANIEL HARLOW, THRUSTON J. DICKINSON, CHARLES SMITH.

337. WILLIAM HARRIS. January 3, 1815; June 26, 1815. Witnesses:
      WILLIAM LEE HARRIS, LEE W. HARRIS, VINCENT MARKS, HENRY BIBB,
JR. Proved by WILLIAM LEE and LEE W. HARRIS and HENRY BIBB, JR. My
wife, ELIZABETH--house where I live and 400 acres; also many slaves
named. Daughter, MARY SHELTON, and husband, JOS. SHELTON. Daughter,
ELIZABETH COLEMAN and husband, JOS. COLEMAN. Daughter, FANNY NICHOLAS,
and husband, LEWIS NICHOLAS. Son, WILLIAM B. HARRIS--tract called
GILMORE's (?)--1379 acres. Son, JNO. W. HARRIS--plantation where I
live--1379 acres excepting 49½ acers next to JNO. DIGGES and subject
to devise made to my wife. Have recently sold 98 acres to JNO. WOODS

and recorded so JNO. W. actually gets 1175 acres. Daughter,
JUDITH WHARTON, and husband, WILLIAM WHARTON, and their children,
WILLIAM and ELIZABETH WHARTON. Daughter, LUCINDA DIGGES--trustees:
WILLIAM B. and JNO. W. HARRIS and JNO. MOSBY. Slaves loaned to my
daughter, CAROLINE COLEMAN, and any children. Grandson, WILLIAM H.
DIGGES. Friend, LOWZEL (?) WOODFOLK of Kentucky to sell my Kentucky
land. He names several slaves to be freed at death of wife and they
may work certain lands of mine and of my son, WILLIAM B. HARRIS.
Executors: friend, JNO. MOSBY, and son, WILLIAM B. and JNO. W.
HARRIS.

Note: The compiler of this data is a Kentuckian and is able
to spot many families when he encounters them in Virginia data.
RAILEY's fine History of Woodford County has much on this WOOLFOLK
family. SOWEL WOOLFOLK is listed in the 1810 census as SOWEL and
is probably the man listed above. RAILEY thinks that he married a
MARY HARRIS in Virginia and had a son named JOS. HARRIS WOOLFOLK.
CLOUGH HARRIS married a daughter of SOWEL WOOLFOLK and her name was
MARTHA M. HARRIS. JOS. HARRIS WOOLFOLK had a son named JNO. HARRIS
WOOLFOLK. The name of HARRIS is employed in other lines as well.
One is cited to page 396 of RAILEY's work.

341. SHEROD MARTIN. Appears to be JR., but not so signed--April 3,
       1813; August 28, 1815. Witnesses: NANCY MARTIN, RO. BROOKS,
THOMAS ALEXANDER. Mother, MAGGY MARTIN; my youngest brother,
TIPSON (?) MARTIN, when twenty-one. Executor: JEFFREY MARTIN.

342. VALENTINE HYLTON. September 9, 1815; September 25, 1815.
       Witnesses: JAMES CUNNINGHAM, SR. and JR., WILLIAM CUNNINGHAM,
JER. W. HYLTON. My wife and children are to live with her father
and friend, and lands are to be rented to defray expenses. After
debts are paid, she may desire to stay at home. Children are to be
educated and cared for until twenty-one. Children are: GEORGE,
LUCY JANE and JAMES DILLARD HYLTON. Wife, JANE C.--suit pending
between representative of SAMUEL ALLEN versus estate of GEORGE HYLTON,
deceased, for negroes and I am executor and legatee of GEORGE
HYLTON. My brother, JNO. HYLTON, and my sister, KETURAH CREGG (?).
Executors: JAMES S. or L. DILLARD and WILLIAM L. WATTS.

345. WILLIAM BOWMAN. Inventory--Ocotber 31, 1814. Long and many
       slaves. No total. BRANSFORD WEST, WILLIAM JOHNSON, SR. or
JR. (?), JAMES TURNER. Recorded September 25, 1815.

348. WILLIAM BALL. Administrator's Account by JESSE A. JOPLING,
       administrator. To LEWIS BALL for his part of tobacco in 1808
as overseer. VALENTINE BALL to go to LEWIS BALL's--cash. SARAH
BALL's order to REBECCA DAMRON. Amherst and Nelson surveys.
WILLIAM BALL, SR. Bond of ALCEY BALL, WILLIAM, SAMUEL, FERGUS,
SARAH BALL, ALCEY BALL, JAMES JOPLING, JAMES BALL, LUCINDA BALL,
BENJAMIN JOHNSON--for amount from estate of GUTRIDGE THURMOND.
ROBERT LEWIS for bond. Many names in accounts. Total: $9464.06--
charged to widow. September 25, 1815. ZACH. NEVIL, NELSON ANDERSON.

354. JAMES WILLS. Administrator's Account by JNO. WILLS (MILLS?)
       administrator October 21, 1815. RO. J. KINCAID, SOLOMON MATTHEWS,
THOMAS E. FORTUNE.

355. WILLIAM HAMNER. Inventory, October 23, 1815. L92-14-6.
       WILLIAM, CHARLES and JOEL SMITH.

356. JOHN FITZPATRICK. July 1, 1812; September 25, 1815. Witnesses:
       MOSES and THOMAS FITZPATRICK, JAMES WOODS. Codicil on August 27,
1815. Witness: JAMES WOODS. Wife, FRANCES; eldest son, THOMAS;
second son, JNO. E.; eldest daughter, BETSY HUGHES; third son,
ALEXANDER; estate of my brother, WILLIAM; my second daughter, SALLY B.
BRADFORD. Third daughter, JINNEY HUGHES; fourth son, WILLIAM; fifth
son, JAMES. Executors: THOMAS and JAMES FITZPATRICK. Codicil: trust
for my daughter, SALLY B. BRADFORD. Horse and money for FRANCES WITT
revoked for I have bought it for her. Note: he does not give her

94

place as to age, but named his children as: THOMAS, JNO. E., BETSY, ALEX., SALLY, JINNEY, WILLIAM, FRANCES and JAMES.

359. VALENTINE HYLTON. Inventory, October 12, 1815. No total.
STEPHEN WATTS, WILLIAM PAMPLIN, JAMES CUNNINGHAM, SR. and JAMES DILLARD and WILLIAM L. WATTS, executors. Recorded November 27, 1815.

360. JNO. GRIFFIN. March 30, 1815; November 27, 1815. Witnesses: HENRY T. HARRIS, BENJ. HARRIS, WILLIAM WRIGHT, M. C. NAPER.
Land on south side of road running from COL. SHELTON's quarter to BENJ. HARRIS--to my son, HARRISON GRIFFIN. Land on north side to daughters, CHARLOTTE and HANNAH. My sons, LINDSEY and HARRIS, are to administrate. All of my children are to assist.

361. THOMAS WRIGHT. Inventory. $63.00, Ocotber 18, 1815. SAMUEL EDMUNDS, JAMES ROSSEN (?), ELIJAH MAYS.

362-364. LANDON CABELL. Sheriff Bonds, November 27, 1815. Bondsmen: RO. RIVES and WILLIAM CABELL.

365. JACOB DAVIS. Inventory. $32,690. December 18, 1815. SAMUEL IRVIN, BENJ. JOHNSON, GEORGE NOVELL.

367. CAROLINE HARRIS. November 15, 1815; January 22, 1815.
Witnesses: NATHAN and JNO. LANKFORD, HARRISON GRIFFIN.
Brother, BENJ. HARRIS--land divided to me by commissioners from my father's estate--180 acres and next to JNO. W. HARRIS, WILLIAM and ELIZABETH WHARTON, BENJ. HARRIS, NANCY HARRIS and ZACH. ROBERTS.
My sister, SOPHIA TATE--gets named slaves; also to her children. My niece, ELIZA BARRET, while she is single and to be given good English education by SOPHIA. My sister, NANCY HARRIS; my nephew, MATT. ROBERTS, and his son, ZACH. ROBERTS. Personal estate from my father and now in possession of my mother. My sister, PERMELIA JACOBS.
Executors: my brothers, JNO. and BENJ. HARRIS.

368. AUGUSTINE SHEPHERD. April 22, 1815; January 22, 1816.
Witnesses: WILLIAM B. HARRIS, JNO. PUGH, ELIZABETH HARRIS.
Sister, SUSANNA ROBERTS and children: HENRY G. and SARAH ANN ROBERTS when of age or married; the rest of her children. Executors: JNO. M. MARTIN, NICHL. L. (?) MARTIN, and JOS. C. ROBERTS--friends.
Page 369 Administrator's Bond on probate date by JOS. C. ROBERTS.
Bondsmen: WILLIAM LEE HARRIS and WILLIAM B. HARRIS.

371. CAROLINE HARRIS. Administrator's Bond JNO. H. HARRIS, HENRY T. HARRIS, and JNO. DIGGS for two HARRIS men, January 22, 1815.

372. WILLIAM HARRIS. Administrator's Bond. JNO. MOSBY, WILLIAM B. HARRIS, JNO. W. HARRIS, LANDON CABELL and WILLIAM H. DIGGES, June 26, 1815, for MOSBY and two HARRIS men.

373. NATHANIEL HARLOW. Administrator's Bond, May 23, 1815, WILLIAM HARLOW, NATHL. HARLOW, THRUSTON J. DICKERSON, and CHARLES SMITH for WILLIAM HARLOW to administrator.

375. RICHARD HAYS. Administrator's Bond, May 22, 1815, THOMAS HAYS and DAVID R. CLARKSON for THOMAS HAYS to administrator.

376. DAVID HUNTER. Administrator's Bond, August 28, 1815. RO. N. HUNTER and bondsmen: LAVENDER LONDON and DAVID HUNTER.

378. JACOB DAVIS. Administrator's Bond. MARY DAVIS, SAMUEL IRVIN and JNO. NOWELL, November 27, 1815, for MARY DAVIS.

379. PETER PRICE. Inventory--$1568.25, February 26, 1816. JAMES CUNNINGHAM, WILLIAM PAMPLIN, WILLIAM CUNNINGHAM.

380. WILSFORD (WILFORD) LANGFORD. Administrator's Bond (mark of Winnery) WINFRED LANGFORD and WILLIAM LANGFORD, February 27, 1815 for WILSFORD LANGFORD.

384. NATHANIEL HARLOW. Inventory--WILLIAM HARLOW, executor. No
total. Returned March 25, 1816. HUDSON MARTIN, WILLIAM
SMITH, CHARLES SMITH. Slaves in hands of JNO. HARLOW. Slaves in
hands of JNO. WARE and JAMES ROBERTSON and titles in dispute as
to these last two holders.

386. JNO. SAVAGE. Administrator's Bond--NANCY SAVAGE, JNO. SPENCER,
and JESSE SAVAGE, March 25, 1816--also WILSON C. (?) SAVAGE
on bond for NANCY SAVAGE.

388. WILLIAM PRICE. Ord. Bond at Greenway, March 25, 1816.
Bondsman: JOS. HORSLEY.

389. JAMES BRENT. Inventory, March 21, 1816--$10,182.59. THOMAS
COLEMAN, JNO. MARR (?), JAMES MONTGOMERY.

390. JNO. SAVAGE, SR. March 11, 1815; March 25, 1816. Witnesses:
JAMES GREGORY, CHARLES G. PATTERSON, CHARLES EVANS and JUDITH
PATTERSON. Wife, NANCY; daughter, PERLINA HUNTER, wife of DAVID
HUNTER. THOMAS L. (?) SAVAGE, MOSES P. SAVAGE--my two sons. My
two sons, JESSE and CANDALL SAVAGE. My children: SUSANNAH GILMORE,
GEORGE SAVAGE, JESSE SAVAGE, WILLIAM SAVAGE, JAMES SAVAGE, CANDALL
SAVAGE, WILSON L. SAVAGE, PERLINA HUNTER, THOMAS L. SAVAGE, MOSES P.
SAVAGE and JNO. SAVAGE. JNO. gets only five shillings. Executors:
TERISHA TURNER, WILLIAM H. DIGGS, LAVENDER LONDON.

392. JOS. LOVING. Administrator's Bond, February 27, 1815, for
SAMUEL LOVING to administrate along with ROSE or ROSEY LOVING.
Bondsman: BENJAMIN TALIAFERRO.

394. THOMAS WRIGHT. Administrator's Bond, June 26, 1815, for
JAMES MURPHY to administrate. Bondsman: S. GARLAND.

395. SHERAD MARTIN. Administrator's Bond JOS. and JNO. N. MARTIN
and THRUSTON J. DICKERSON, March 27, 1815, for JOS. MARTIN
to administrate.

397. FRACIS C. PHILLIPS. Administrator's Bond May 22, 1815.
GEO. PHILLIPS with bondsman: JNO. CARTER (so signed, but
CARR in bond.)

398. PETER PRICE. Administrator's Bond. SARAH PRICE, October 23,
1815. Bondsmen: ISAAC RUCKER and FRANCIS PRICE.

400. PEGGY CRISP. Administrator's Bond. May 22, 1815. LUCY
CRISP. Bondsman: JAMES MURPHY.

402. VALENTINE HYLTON. Administrator's Bond, September 25, 1815.
JAMES S. DILLARD and WILLIAM L. WATTS. Bondsmen: SAMUEL
TURNER, STEPHEN WATTS, SAMUEL LOVING.

403. THOMAS R. DRAKE. Administrator's Bond, July 25, 1814.
NANCY DRAKE. Bondsman: JNO. JACOBS.

405. WILLIAM BALLOW. Administrator's Bond October 23, 1815.
HOWARD BALLOW. Bondsman: NATHANIEL OFFUTT.

407. JNO. W. RICE. Administrator's Bond, February 27, 1815.
MICHL. WOODS. Bondsman: JOS. SHELTON.

408. HARRISON GRIFFIN. Administrator's Bond, November 27, 1815.
HARRISON GRIFFIN and LANDING GRIFFIN. Bondsmen: WILLIAM
WRIGHT and BENJAMIN HARRIS.

410. JNO. FITZPATRICK. Administrator's Bond, September 25, 1815.
FRANCIS, THOMAS, and JAMES FITZPATRICK. Bondsmen: MICHL.
WOODS and WILLIAM FITZPATRICK.

412. JNO. BROOKS. Ord. bond in house where he lives at Lovingston, February 27, 1816. Bondsman: JAMES GARLAND, JR.

413. HUDSON MARTIN. Ord. bond at house in County, January 22, 1816. Bondsman: JNO. MOSBY.

414. RICHARD BURCH. Ord. at Lovingston, February 28, 1814. Bondsman: SOLOMON MATTHEWS.

414. RICHARD BURCH. Ord. at Lovingston, May 23, 1814. Bondsman: THOMAS E. FORTUNE.

415. JNO. SPITFATHAM. Ord. at Warminster, May 23, 1814. Bondsman: JAMES GREGORY.

416. CHARLES L. BARRETT. Ord. Bond at Greenway, May 23, 1814. Bondsman: VALENTINE HYLTON.

417. WILLIAM RYON. Ord. Bond in County, May 23, 1814. Bondsman: STERLING CLAIBORNE.

418. CHARLES C. PATTERSON. Ord. Bond at house in County, May 24, 1814. Bondsman: WILLIAM RYAN.

419. NATHANIEL OFFUTT. Ord. at Newmarket, November 28, 1814. Bondsman: RICHARD PHILLIPS.

420. WILLIAM BIBB. Ord. Bond at Newmarket, March 27, 1815. Bondsman: JNO. JACOBS.

421. JAMES LOVING. Ord. Bond at his house in County, March 28, 1815. Bondsman: RICHARD BURCH.

422. RICHARD BURCH. Ord. Bond at Lovingston, May 22, 1815. Bondsman: SOLOMON MATTHEWS.

422. JNO. SPITFATHAM. Ord. Bond at Warminster, May 23, 1815. Bondsman: EZEKIEL EAST.

423. WILLIAM RYAN. Ord. Bond at Pea Licker, May 23, 1815. Bondsman: CHARLES C. PATTERSON.

424. CHARLES C. PATTERSON. Ord. Bond at his own house. June 26, 1815. Bondsman: REUBEN BARTES.

425. NATHANIEL OFFUTT. Ord. at New Market, June 26, 1815. Bondsman: JNO. THOMPSON.

426. CHARLES EDMUNDS. Tobacco Inspector at Tye Warehouse, September 25, 1815. Bondsman: MOSES HUGHES.

427. JAMES TURNER. Tobacco Inspector Swan Creek Warehouse, September 25, 1815. Bondsman: JNO. HIGGINBOTHAM.

427. STEPHEN WATTS. Tobacco Inspector at CAMDEN's Warehouse, September 25, 1815. Bondsman: SAMUEL LOVING.

424. WILLIAM L. WATTS. Tobacco Inspector at CAMDEN's Warehouse, September 25, 1815. Bondsman: JAMES DILLARD.

429. ZACH. NEVIL. Tobacco Inspector at Tye River Warehouse, September 25, 1815. Bondsman: JNO. HIGGINBOTHAM.

430. FRANCIS W. L. TURNER. Tobacco Inspector at Swan Creek Warehouse, April 24, 1815. Bondsman: REUBIN B. PATTISON.

431. JAMES TURNER. Tobacco Inspector at Swan Creek Warehouse, February 27, 1815. Bondsmen: WILLIAM J. ROBERSTON and JESSE JOPLING.

432. JAMES TURNER. Tobacco Inspector at Swan Creek Warehouse,
      July 25, 1814. Bondsman: SAMUEL TURNER.

432. BENJAMIN T. ESTES and ELISHA B. ESTES. Guardian's Bond,
      March 28, 1814. ABRAHAM B. WARWICK. Bondsman: ZACH. NEVIL.
Orphans of ELISHA ESTES.

432. JAMES STEVENS, JR. Tobacco manufacturing at place where
      JAMES STEVENS, SR. formerly lived, February 28, 1814.
Bondsman: CHARLES PERVIS.

434. CHARLES L. BARRETT. Tobacco manufacturing at Greenway,
      October 25, 1813. Bondsman: STEPHEN WATTS.

435. HENRY BIBB, JR. Constables Bond, February 28, 1814.
      Bondsman: LEE W. HARRIS.

435. HENRY BIBB. Constable, March 29, 1814. Bondsman: LEE W.
      HARRIS.

436. JNO. BARNETT. Constables Bond, August 22, 1814. Bondsman:
      JNO. JACOBS.

437. HENRY BIBB, JR. Constables Bond in 1st Hundred, July 25,
      1814. Bondsman: SPOTSWOOD GARLAND.

438. DAVID J. CLARK. Constables Bond, November 27, 1815. Bondsman:
      PETER C. JACOBS.

439. EDMOND F. COFFEE. Constable Bond, 2nd Hundred, June 27, 1814.
      Bondsman: JAMES MONTGOMERY.

440. CHARLES FLOOD. Constable Bond 1st Hundred, June 27, 1814.
      Bondsman: THOMAS FITZPATRICK and LEE W. HARRIS.

441. CHARLES C. PATTISON. Constable Bond 1st Hundred, June 27,
      1814. Bondsmen: SAMUEL ARRINGTON and JNO. SCRUGGS.

441. JNO. FARRAR. Constable Bond, July 25, 1814. Bondsmen:
      WILLIAM H. FARRAR, THOMAS THURMOND, NELSON BETHEL, WILLIAM H.
SHELTON and S. GARLAND.

442. MARY MARTIN. Administrator's Bond, November 28, 1814. Bond
      made by WILLIAM WRIGHT to administrator. Bondsman: LEE W.
HARRIS.

444. EDMOND H. HASSON. Administrator's Bond, May 23, 1814.
      Bondsman for HENRY J. or T. HARRIS to administrator was
THOMAS MC CLELAND.

445. THOMAS FITZPATRICK. Administrator's Bond, May 23, 1814.
      Bondsman for MOSES FITZPATRICK to administrate were WILLIAM
LEE HARRIS, EDWARD HARRIS and MATTHEW HARRIS.

447. CORNELIUS NEVIL. Administrator's Bond, July 23, 1814.
      ZACH. NEVIL qualified with ROWLAND EDMUNDS. Their bondsman
was LEWIS TINDILL.

448. WILLIAM BOWMAN. Administrator's Bond, July 25, 1814. GILBERT
      BOWMAN qualified. Bondsmen: JESSE JOPLING, NATHAN HARDING
and RALPH BOWMAN.

450. JAMES BRYANT. Administrator's Bond, March 28, 1814. JNO.
      BRYANT qualified. Bondsman: PARMENAS BRYANT.

451. SARAH SHEPHERD. Administrator's Bond, November 28, 1814.
      ALEX. ROBERTS, JOS. ROBERTS and GEORGE PAGE qualified.
Bondsmen: EDWARD HARRIS and JAMES WOODS.

453. JAMES WRIGHT. Administrator's Bond, November 28, 1814. ELIZABETH WRIGHT qualified. Bondsman: JAMES EDMUNDS.

454. HENRY ROBERTS. Inventory--$6566.00, May 10, 1816. JNO. and JNO. W. HARRIS and EDWARD HARRIS.

456. WILLIAM RYAN. Ord. Bond at Cross roads above Tye River, May 27, 1816. Bondsman: JESSE CLARKSON.

457. HUDSON MARTIN. Ord. Bond at own house in County, May 27, 1816. Bondsman: JNO. MOSBY.

Readers will note that items jump from 1814 to 1816. There is no explanation given in book, but I made a careful check and this is the way that data reads. BAILEY FULTON DAVIS.

458. JOS. MAYS. Ord. Bond at house in County, May 27, 1816. Bondsman: JAMES N. EDMUNDS.

460. JNO. W. REID. Inventory, August 25 (?), 1815; recorded May 27, 1816. No total. JOS. MONTGOMERY, NATHAN BRIDGWATER and DAVID WITT.

461. JNO. GRIFFIN. Inventory; no total; met at house of deceased. Recorded May 27, 1816. ZACH. ROBERTS, WILLIAM RIGHT, JNO. ROBERTS.

463. RO. FRANKLIN. Administrator's Account at New Market, December 26, 1815. JNO. FRANKLIN, administrator. L356-2-3. NATHANIEL OFFUTT, JAMES GREGORY.

465. MARY MARTIN. Inventory, no total, recorded May 27, 1816. AND. (?) WRIGHT, MATTHEW HARRIS, A. MC ALEXANDER.

465. RICHARD BURCH. Ord. at house occupied by him in County. May 29, 1816. Bondsman: JAMES GREGORY.

466. JNO. SPITFATHAM. Ord. at Warminster, June 24, 1816. Bondsman: JNO. HOUSEWRIGHT.

467. DAVID R. CLARKSON. Constable's Bond, 2nd Hundred, June 24, 1816. Bondsman: JAMES HUGHES.

468. EDMOND F. COFFEY. Constable's Bond, June 24, 1816. Bondsman: JAMES MONTGOMERY.

468. CHARLES FLOOD. Constable's Bond, 1st Hundred, June 24, 1816. Bondsmen: THOMAS FITZPATRICK and LEE W. HARRIS.

469. CHARLES C. PATTESON. Constable's Bond, 1st Hundred, June 24, 1816. Bondsman: THOMAS E. FORTUNE.

470. WILSON LEE SAVAGE. Administrator's Bond, June 24, 1816. NANCY SAVAGE qualified. Bondsman: JAMES GREGORY.

471. HENRY SETTER (?). Guardian's Bond, June 24, 1816. JAMES HUGHES qualified. Bondsman: THOMAS FITZPATRICK. No other data. The clerk and his deputy examined this item and they, too, were at a loss as to proper spelling. It is not indexed under any name approaching this interpretation.

472. LANDON CABELL. Sheriff--bond as to poor to raise proper rates, June 24, 1816. Bondsman: NELSON ANDERSON, JAMES GREGORY.

473. JNO. BLAINE. Administrator's Bond, July 22, 1816. ALEX. BLAIN qualified. Bondsman: NATHAN BLAIN and RO. J. KINCAID. Pages have been re-numbered by someone with pencil just here and there are two 474 pages; second is in original ink.

474. JAMES H. BLAIN et al. Guardian's Bond, July 22, 1816.
      ALEX. BLAIN qualified as guardian with RO. J. KINCAID as
bondsman. Wards: JAMES H., FREDERICK R., LUCINDA L. D. BLAIN,
orphans of JNO. BLAIN.

474. CRAWFORD PUCKETT. Administrator's Account by JACOB PUCKETT,
      administrator. L45-1-4 plus debt owed estate of L3-0-5.
JACOB and SAMUEL PUCKETT both owed estate. July 20, 1816. JAMES
SHIELDS, A. MC ALEXANDER and JAMES H. BURTON, comm.

475. JNO. FITZPATRICK. Inventory; no total, August 24, 1816.
      NATHANIEL BRIDGWATER, DAVID WITT, JAMES WOODS.

476. GUTRIDGE THURMOND. Administrator's Accounty, WILLIAM BALL,
      administrator. August 26, 1816. Paid to BENJAMIN, JNO.
FRANCIS, and THOMAS THURMOND's bond due November 14, 1814. L77-19-10.
JESSE JOPLING, NELSON ANDERSON, JNO. S. DAWSON.

479. JAMES SMILEY. Ord. bond in County, August 26, 1816. Bondsman:
      JAMES GREGORY.

480ff. WILLIAM H. DIGGES. Sheriff Bond, August 26, 1816. Bondsman:
      JNO. HARRIS, JNO. THOMPSON, JNO. DILLARD, JNO. MOSBY, JNO.
DIGGS, STEPHEN WATTS, JAMES MONTGOMERY.

483. CHARLES EDMUNDS. Tobacco Inspector at Tye River Warehouse,
      September 23, 1816. Bondsman: LAVENDER LONDON.

484. ZACH. NEVIL. Tobacco Inspector at Tye River Warehouse,
      September 23, 1816. Bondsman: SAMUEL LOVING.

485. STEPHEN WATTS. Tobacco Inspector at CAMDEN's Warehouse,
      September 23, 1816. Bondsman: DRURY BELL.

485. WILLIAM L. WATTS. Tobacco Inspector at CAMDEN's Warehouse,
      September 23, 1816. Bondsman: SAMUEL LOVING.

486. JNO. CHRISTIAN. Tobacco Inspector at CAMDEN's Warehouse,
      September 23, 1816. Bondsman: STEPHEN WATTS.

487. JOS. G. and PETER LILLY. Administrator's Bond, September 23,
      1816. Bondsman for RO. GARLAND, administrator was SPOTSWOOD
GARLAND.

488. WILLIAM H. GAYLE et al. Guardian's Bond, October 28, 1816.
      WILLIAM B. HARE, qualified as guardian of WILLIAM H. and
BENLG. (?) GAYLE, orphans of JNO. GAYLE, deceased, and FRANCES
GAYLE. Bondsman: JOSEPH C. CABELL and THOMAS T. (?) MC CLELLAND.

488. JAMES SPENCER. Ord. Bond near Amherst Old Courthouse,
      October 28, 1816. Bondsman: STERLING CLAIBORNE.

489. RICHARD LIGGIN. Nuncupative will--Tell JOHN MARTIN the will
      I made to be allowed and divide the little property among the
three children of my sister, ANNE CRAWFORD--FRANCIS, JUDITH and
HENRY AARON H. MORRISON. Witness: HOLEMAN JOPLING. Proved on
October 28, 1816, by AARON H. MORRISON. JOPLING witnessed it on
September 8, 1816.

490. RICHARD LIGGIN. Administrator's Bond, October 28, 1816.
      NELSON CRAWFORD qualified. Bondsmen: PETER C. JACOBS and
AARON H. MORRISON.

491. NATHAN BARNETT. June 20, 1816; October 28, 1816. Witnesses:
      S. P. GARLAND, M. C. NAPER, LEVI OWENS. My children: JAMES M.
and POLLY BARNETT. My younger children by my last marriage being
already provided for. My brother, JNO. BARNETT, and THOMAS E. FORTUNE,
to administrate. Proved by GARLAND and NAPIER. JNO. BARNETT
qualified on probate date. Bondsmen: LANDON H. BRENT and EDMOND F.
COFFEY.

492. JESSE EMMERSON. Administrator's Bond, October 28, 1816.
      HENRY EMMERSON qualified. Bondsman: TERISHA TURNER.

495. JESSE MAYS. Administrator's Bond--SUSANNA MAYS qualified to
      administrate on October 28, 1816. Bondsmen: JAMES EDMUNDS
and LAVENDER LONDON.

496. CAROLINE HARRIS. Inventory, September 9, 1816. $2589.00.
      JNO. DIGGS, HARRISON GRIFFIN, NATHAN LANGFORD.

497. ANDREW WRIGHT. November 15, 1816; November 28, 1816.
      Witnesses: RO. J. KINCAID, WILLIAM WRIGHT, JAMES H. BURTON,
M. C. NAPIER. Wife, LUCY--land on south side of Davis Creek--bought
of legatees of PETER MARTIN, deceased, and then divided. My children:
BENJAMIN, ANNE WRIGHT, ESTER M. WRIGHT, POLLY WRIGHT, MATILDA
WRIGHT, MALINDA WRIGHT, PEGGY WRIGHT, SALLY BOLLING, LUCY KIDD. My
granddaughter, ELIZABETH FORTUNE. Executors: BENJAMIN CHILDRESS
and BENJAMIN WRIGHT.

498. SARAH and GRIZZLE C. SLAUGHTER. Guardian's Bond, December 23,
      1816. FRANCIS SLAUGHTER qualified as guardian of her children,
named above. Bondsman: STERLING CLAIBORNE.

499. ANDREW WRIGHT. Administrator's Bond--BENJAMIN WRIGHT qualified
      to administrate, December 23, 1816. Bondsmen: JNO. WILLS,
LEVI OWENS, JNO. WRIGHT, J. GARLAND.

500. MARTHA HANSBROUGH. Administrator's Bond, SAMUEL HANSBROUGH
      qualified, January 27, 1817. Bondsman: JAMES MURPHY.

501. BENJAMIN MOSBY. Revenue commissioner, February 24, 1817.
      Bondsman: WILLIAM B. HARRIS.

502. HENRY DAWSON. Ord. Bond at own house in County, February 24,
      1817. Bondsman: WILLIAM LEE HARRIS.

502. JNO. SPENCER. Ord. Bond at own house on Tye River, March 24,
      1817. Bondsman: CHARLES PERROW.

503. JNO. HOWELL. Administrator's Bond, March 24, 1817. SYLVANUS
      MEEKS qualified to administrate. Bondsman: JNO. JACOBS.

505. RO. WRIGHT. Inventory, May 27, 1817. $4708.50 and carried
      forward for $4714.75. HENRY DAWSON, THOMAS E. FORTUNE and
JAMES H. BURTON.

507. ELIJAH MAYS, JR. Ord. Bond on lands of ELIJAH MAYS, SR.
      Bondsman: ELIJAH MAYS, May 26, 1817.

508. CORBIN BRYANT et al. Guardian's Bond--RICHARD BRYANT qualified
      as guardian of RICHARD BRYANT, May 27, 1817. Bondsman:
PARMENAS BRYANT. Wards were CORBIN, SOPHIA, JUDITH and ELIA BRYANT.

509. WILLIAM H. DIGGES. Sheriff's Bond, June 23, 1817. Bondsman:
      ZACH. NEVIL and HENRY T. HARRIS.

509. JESSE PAMPLIN. April 23, 1817; July 28, 1817. Witnesses:
      HENLEY DRUMMOND, WILLIAM CUNNINGHAM, JAMES and REES CUNNINGHAM.
My sister, JUDITH PAMPLIN--effects in hands of ABRAHAM STRATTON.
Executors: WILLIAM PAMPLIN and RO. L. COLEMAN.

510. GEORGE GREGORY. Guardian's Bond--HENRY TURNER qualified as
      guardian on July 28, 1817. Orphan of JNO. GREGORY. Bondsman:
SAMUEL TURNER.

510. MARTHA JOHNSON. Administrator's Bond. WILLIAM H. JOHNSON
      qualified, July 28, 1817. Bondsmen: WILLIAM PAMPLIN and
WILLIAM CUNNINGHAM.

511. JESSE PAMPLIN. Administrator's Bond. July 28, 1817. WILLIAM
     PAMPLIN qualified. Bondsmen: WILLIAM JOHNSON and WILLIAM
CUNNINGHAM.

512. JAMES THOMPSON. Administrator's Account by JON (sic) THOMPSON,
     administrator, November 30, 1816. To JAMES THOMPSON, JR.; by
BARTLETT THOMPSON. Comm.: JNO. HAYNES, JAMES GWATKIN, JNO. H. OTEY.

515. LUCAS POWELL. Administrator's Accounty by NATHANIEL POWELL
     and JAMES MURPHY, administrators, from July 31, 1812. Bond
of ELIZABETH POWELL, BENJAMIN POWELL, LUCAS POWELL. SEYMOUR POWELL
for ticket; wrong charges--from STAUNTON. June 23, 1817. NELSON
ANDERSON, THOMAS S. MC CLELLAND, Comm.

518. JAMES SPITFATHAM. Ord. Bond at Warminster, August 25, 1817.
     Bondsman: JNO. HOUSEWRIGHT.

519. AUGUSTINE HARLOW. Inventory, August 25, 1817. Eleven acres;
     also $100 in his father's estate. No committee set forth.

519. LUCY REINS. Guardian's Bond, August 25, 1817. JNO. QUICK
     qualified as guardian of above; no parent set forth. Bondsman:
JNO. CRITZER.

519ff. WILLIAM H. DIGGES. Sheriff's Bond, August 27, 1817.
     Bondsmen: STEPHEN WATTS, JNO. MOSBY, H. T. HARRIS, RO.
GARLAND, S. CLAIBORNE.

522. HENRY DAWSON. Ord. Bond at own house called the Redhouse,
     May 27, 1817. Bondsman: SP. GARLAND.

523. JNO. BROOKS. Administrator's Bond--MILDRED BROOKS, September 22,
     1817. Bondsman: NATHANIEL POWELL.

524. MRS. HANNAH CABELL. April 10, 1817; September 22, 1817.
     Witnesses: EDWARD A. CABELL, ABRAM J. CABELL, NICHOLAS C.
CABELL, WILLIAM H. CABELL. Proved by ABRAM and NICHOLAS CABELL.
JOS. C. CABELL qualified. Bondsmen: RO. RIVES on probate date.
My son, GEORGE CABELL. Daughter, MARY ANN CARRINGTON. My children
and grandchildren. Shortly after death of my brother, COL. EDWARD
CARRINGTON, I conveyed to his widow, ELIZA, all of my interest in
his estate. Daughter, MARY ANN, at death of her husband. My sons,
WILLIAM H. and JOS. C. CABELL. Son, NICHOLAS, deceased. Any
children of my daughter, MARY ANN; my grandchildren, HANNAH H. and
SARAH E. HARE. I release all claims against WILLIAM B. HARE.
BENJAMIN CARRINGTON, husband of my daughter, MARY ANN. Executors:
sons, WILLIAM H., GEORGE, and JOSEPH C. CABELL, and son-in-law,
WILLIAM B. HARE and friend, LANDON CABELL.

527. CHARLES EDMONS. Tobacco Inspector at Tye River Warehouse.
     September 22, 1817. Bondsman: LAVENDER LONDON. Two pages
numbered 527.

527. ZACH. NEVIL. T' at Tye River Warehouse. September 22, 1817.
     Bondsman: JESSE JOPLING.

527. STEPHEN WATTS. Tobacco Inspector at CAMDEN's Warehouse,
     September 22, 1817. Bondsman: SAMUEL LOVING.

528. WILLIAM L. WATTS. Tobacco Inspector at CAMDEN's Warehouse,
     September 22, 1817. Bondsman: SAMUEL LOVING.

529. JAMES CHRISTIAN. Tobacco Inspector at CAMDEN's Warehouse,
     September 22, 1817. Bondsman: WILLIAM C. (?) WATTS.

529. MRS. HANNAH CABELL. Inventory--$3415.00. HILL CARTER, WILLIAM
     SALE, ALEX. P. MARR, JNO. THOMPSON, JR. October 27, 1817.

530. WILLIAM TURNER. Administrator's Bond, October 27, 1817.
    TERISHA TURNER qualified. Bondsmen: ALEX. ROBERTS and
TERISHA BAILEY.

531. JEREMIAH HYLTON. No date--Power of attorney by him as resident
    of Bedford County to WILLIAM L. WATTS as surviving executor of
GEORGE HYLTON, deceased. WATTS is to collect any debts due me in
Amherst and Buckingham. Witnesses: S. GARLAND, ROBT. TINSLEY,
JAMES CHRISTIAN.

532. MARTHA JOHNSON. Inventory, September 6, 1817--about $1000.00.
    WILLIAM PAMPLIN, JAMES and WILLIAM CUNNINGHAM.

533. ROBT. PAGE and wife, MARY. Adair County, Kentucky--power of
    attorney to son, GEORGE W. (?) PAGE, Nelson County, Virginia
on May 28, 1817, to sell their lands in Nelson and Albemarle. ISAAC
CALDWELL, Deputy Clerk--Adair County, Kentucky. NATHAN MONTGOMERY,
Presiding Magistrate.

534. Out of place. See after 450: HAGGARD item.

536. ANDREW WRIGHT. Inventory, December 28, 1816--$4322.00.
    JAMES WRIGHT, HENRY DAWSON, JAMES H. BURTON, BENJAMIN WRIGHT,
administrator. JNO. WRIGHT, son of RO. bought rye at sale.

538. JNO. MOSS. Ord. at tavern owned by OWENS and HARGROVE in
    Lovingston, December 22, 1817. Bondsman: STERLING CLAIBORNE.

539. JNO. BROOKS. Inventory, December 22, 1817. No total. RO. J.
    KINCAID and JNO. WRIGHT.

540. ELIZ. STEVENS. Guardian's Bond, January 26, 1818--ELIZ. and
    SAMUEL STEVENS; ELIZABETH guardian of above as ward. Orphan
of JAMES STEVENS.

534. JNO. HAGGARD and wife, MARY. Clark County, Kentucky--power of
    attorney to ALEX. ROBERTS, Nelson County, Virginia to sell
Taylor Creek land; part of former property of AUGUSTINE SHEPHERD,
deceased. Delivered to ROBERTS, August 15, 1843. Dated November 1,
1815. JAMES P. BULLOCK, Clark County, Kentucky, Clerk. THOMAS
SCOTT, Presiding Justice.

540. JNO. CRITZER. Administrator's Bond--SUSAN CRITZER, January 26,
    1818. Bondsman: JNO. CRITZER.

541. PETER CAMPBELL. Administrator's Bond--JAMES P. GARLAND,
    January 26, 1818. Bondsman: RICHARD PHILLIPS.

542. JESSE PAMPLIN. Inventory, January 26, 1818. One man about 22
    at $500.00; also blankets (old--four), boat cover, etc.
JNO. HORSLEY, JR., WILLIAM CUNNINGHAM.

453. MARY B. DRUMMOND. Administrator's Bond--ZACH. T. DRUMMOND.
    SAMUEL LOVING, and STERLING CLAIBORNE, February 23, 1818, for
ZACH. T. DRUMMOND.

1. 28 June 1808. NATHL., WILLIAM, JR., GEORGE HILL, JNO.
PERKINS HILL, WILLIAM RYAN and wife, BETSY, THOMAS R. DRAKE
and wife, NANCY, JNO. JACOBS and wife, LUCY and POLLY T. HILL,
children of NATHL. HILL and some are married as above, to THOMAS
MASSIE...all parties in these deeds are of Nelson unless otherwise
shown (B.F.D.)--to THOMAS MASSIE, 29 September 1809--L718-10; part
of tract of NATHL. HILL, deceased. Lines: top of the mountain,
JAMES DICKIE, Thoroughfare branch 280 acres. Witnesses: DANIEL
MC DONALD, P. RYAN, JAMES MORE, ETTA EVERETT, MARBELL EASTHAM,
JESSE JONES, CHAPPEL DAVENPORT, NATHAN LANKFORD. SPOTSWOOD GARLAND,
Clerk of Court.

2. 29 February 1808. SAMUEL FRANKLIN, Amherst County, to
ANDREW WHITE, Bent Creek, Buckingham County...to secure
THOMAS HIGGINBOTHAM and Company, Bent Creek. To W. KYLE for
ANDREW WHITE, 24 October 1808--and HIGGINBOTHAM, BROWN and Company,
Bent Creek; five shillings; slaves named and ages. Witnesses:
RO. HORSLEY, WILLIAM H. WILLS, SHADRACK CARTER.

3. 24 June 1808. JAMES SPEARS, Buckingham County, to GEORGE
HYLTON...$1.00 two acres surveyed 3 May 1780; small island
in Fluvanna River and south side Allen's Island. Witnesses:
SAMUEL FRANKLIN, ZA. T. DRUMMOND, STEPHEN WATTS, VAL HYLTON, WILLIAM
CARTER.

4. 30 November 1807. DAVID OWENS to MICHL. WOODS and JAMES H.
BURTON...to secure CHARLES SMITH, executor of CHRISTOPHER
SMITH; ALEX. MC ALEXANDER, bondsman. JNO. MOORE, Deputy Sheriff
versus DAVID and LEVI OWENS; $1.00--to A. MC ALEXANDER, 30 January
1810--plantation on the mountain. Lines: CABELL, JNO. FORTUNE,
furniture, stock. Witnesses: JNO. and JANE MC ALEXANDER.

5. 30 May 1808. JNO. WRIGHT, commonly designated waterman--see
index on his name for comments--to ASA VARNUM...$1.00; to
secure GEORGE W. VARNUM; slave. Witnesses: WILLIAM H. SHELTON,
MARTIN WILSON, RO. NIMMO, PARMENAS BRYANT.

6. 1 April 1806. JAMES STEVENS, JR., Amherst County, ELISHA
PETERS, Amherst County, 2; JAMES MURPHY and RO. RIVES,
Amherst County, 3...JAMES STEVENS, JR. owes ELISHA PETERS; $1.00;
150 acres in Amherst County. Lines: RO. RIVES, GEORGE LOVING,
JAMES STEVENS, SAMUEL LOVING, deceased, JNO. STAPLES, THOMAS BIBB.
B(ought) from WILLIAM FURBUSH, wagons, horses; 14 slaves. Witnesses:
GEORGE PURVIS, GEORGE LOVING, LANDON E. and WILLIAM E. RIVES.

7. 28 May 1808. WILLIAM THARP, Amherst County, to LEE W.
HARRIS, Amherst County...to RIVES MURPHY and Company,
26 September 1808; debt to said county; $1.00; 54 acres. Lines:
ALEX. MC ALEXANDER--cattle. Witnesses: JNO. E. FITZPATRICK,
JAMES WILLS, JR., CHARLES FLOED, WILLIAM LEE HARRIS, HENRY EMMERSON.

8. 6 November 1807. RICHARD C. POLLARD to ZACH ROBERTS, Amherst
County, to secure WILLIAM BROWN and Company, Warminster...to
JNO. LOVING per order from ZACH ROBERTS, 30 May 1809--$1.00 six
slaves. WILLIAM M. BAILEY is bondsman for debt; may sell at ACH.
Witnesses: THOMAS BERRY, WILLIAM CAMP, JUDITH H. MARTIN. Memo:
also mulatto boy, ORNAGE. Witnesses: BERRY and CAMP.

9. 22 August 1808. ELISHA ESTES to RO. MOORE...to SAMUEL JONES,
27 March 1809--six shillings; slaves; to secure SAMUEL JONES.

10. 26 February 1808. WILLIAM THORPE to HENRY T. HARRIS...to
HENRY T. HARRIS, 24 October--six shillings, 22 acres, to
secure NATHAN BARNETT--bought from NATHAN BARNETT who bought from
WILLIAM BARNETT. Witnesses: REUBEN HARRIS, CHARLES FLOOD, HENRY
DAWSON, HENRY BIBB, JR., LEE W. HARRIS.

11. 28 June 1808. JNO. SAVAGE, SR. to ANDERSON MOSS...L400-15;
     slave. Witnesses: WILLIAM HALL, JAMES HALL, JNO. SAVAGE, JR.

12. 21 August 1808. WILLIAM CABELL to SHELTON CROSTHWAIT...five
     shillings; privilege to conduct water for distillery and tan
yard from branch on CABELL's tract--late in occupation of HECTOR
CABELL and near SHELTON CROSTHWAIT's mill on RUCKER's run--pipes--
BETHEL's path.

13. 25 July 1808. CAMPBELL GOODE, WILLIAM DAVIS and wife, BETSY,
     formerly GOODE, WILLIAM CAMPBELL and wife, SALLY, formerly
GOODE, JESSE HOUCHINS and wife, MARY ANN, formerly GOODE, WILLIAM,
DANIEL, PHOEBE and JOS. GOODE, JACOB PECK and wife, SUSANNAH,
formerly GOODE, heirs of DANIEL GOODE, the Elder, Amherst County,
deceased...to DAVID S. GARLAND. DANIEL died many years ago,
intestate, and owned tract on north borders Piney; 133 acres patent.
1 June 1782; $30; one-ninth part.

14. 20 January 1808. REUBEN T. MITCHELL to NATHAN HARRIS...six
     shillings--to JNO. MOSBY, 26 June 1809--141 acres Rockfish.
Lines: ALEX. ROBERTS, JAMES TURNER, HENRY EMMERSON, JNO. TURNER,
TERISHA TURNER, MARTIN DAWSON; slaves; to secure WILLIAM H. MOSBY
who is bondsman to WILSON C. NICHOLAS. Witnesses: HENRY T. and
LEE W. HARRIS, WILLIAM H. COLEMAN.

15. 24 February 1808. MATT. HARRIS, 1; HAWES COLEMAN, HUDSON MARTIN,
     JR. and THRUSTON J. DICKERSON, 2; THOMAS GOODWIN, 3...$1.00
300 acres on Rockfish in Amherst County and where MATT. HARRIS
lives. Lines: COL. JOS. SHELTON, CLOUGH SHELTON, deceased;
WILLIAM LEE HARRIS. Witnesses: HUDSON MARTIN, NATHAN CRAWFORD,
JNO. RUCKER, JNO. W. MARTIN. Memo: THOMAS GOODWIN received L50
of debt on 1 April. Witness: JUDSON MARTIN.

17. 5 August 1808. GEORGE MARTIN and wife, SALLY, to NATHL.
     HARLOW...to NATHL. HARLOW, JR., 25 March 1811--L21-13; tract
devised to GEORGE MARTIN by father, SHEROD MARTIN--one acre. Lines:
Big road, grantor, HUDSON MARTIN, JNO. COLES, deceased. Witnesses:
WILLIAM and AUGUSTIN HARLOW, HUDSON MARTIN, JR., GIDEON MARTIN, JR.,
EDWARD W. JOPLING.

19. 9 April 1808. LEWIS NEVIL, Buckingham County, to CORNL.
     NEVIL...CORNL. NEVIL has paid RO. RIVES and Company, assignees
of CLOUGH SHELTON and Company--slaves; furniture. Witnesses:
JAMES NEVIL, THOMAS BIBB, JR.

19. 8 June 1808. JNO. MOORE and wife, BETSY, to REUBEN MICHEL...
     L7-14-6--to JNO. BURKS, 27 March 1809--two acres. Lines:
the road. Witnesses: MICHL. WOODS, WILLIAM H. LEIGH, MICHL.
DAWSON, JNO. PERKINS.

20. 11 July 1808. JOS. SMITH and wife, PATIENCE, to JNO. SHEPHERD...
     $200 150 acres Rockfosh. Lines: DAVID GARLAND, WILLIAM
MOSBY. Witnesses: JNO. SCRUGGS, DAVID FERGUSON, JNO. LANHAM.

22. 4 May 1808. ALEX. B. ROSE to GEORGE WILLIAMS...to DANIEL
     MC DONALD, 5 May 1809--to secure DANIEL MC DONALD; $1.00;
slaves. Witnesses: EDWARD H. CARTER, CHARLES C. CARTER, JNO.
EUBANK, JR., JNO. EDWARDS.

23. 26 September 1808. JESSE MAYS to JAMES VIGUS and RO. FRANKLIN,
     Warminster...to J. MURPHY, 18 August 1809--to secure JAMES
MURPHY and Company in suit in District Court in Charlottesville;
debt to MURPHY BROWN and Company; $1.00; 150 acres where JESSE MAYS
lives. Lines: JAMES DILLARD, JNO. DILLARD, JOS. MAYS, SR.; slave.
Witnesses: RO. MOORE, JNO. CABELL, JER. YAGER.

25. 29 March 1808. ELISHA ESTES to RO. MOORE and JAMES VIGUS...
     $1.00--to RO. MOORE, 5 June 1809--to secure WILLIAM BROWN
and Company, Warminster--Rucker's Run. Lines: ABRAHAM WARWICK,
THOMAS STATHAM, WILLIAM BREEDLOVE--573 acres where ELISHA ESTES
lives. WILLIAM BROWN and Company by RICHARD POWELL. Witnesses:
JAMES MURPHY, JNO. HIGGINBOTHAM, A. B. WARWICK, JER. YAGER, RO.
IRVING.

26. 23 September 1808. HUDSON M. GARLAND to THOMPSON NOEL...to
     THOMPSON NOEL, 26 May 1809--$1.00; debt due SPOTSWOOD GARLAND,
bondsman--Sllen Bugg, District Court in Charlottesville--slave and
three children.

27. 24 September 1808. ELISHA ESTES to JAMES MURPHY, 2; JAMES
     VIGUS, 3...debt due WILLIAM BROWN and Company: PLEASANT
CREWS District Court; SHELTON CROSTHWAIT; MURPHY and Company; $1.00;
Rucker's Run 573 acres. Lines: ABRAM WARWICK, deceased, WILLIAM
BREEDLOVE, JAMES WOOD, ELIJAH STATON, DANIEL MC COY; slaves; stock.

30. 4 March 1808. RANSOM MURROW, WILLIAM and BLUFORD MURROW to
     WILLIAM F. CARTER...to JAMES MURPHY, 21 November 1805--RO.
RIVES is security for RANSOM MURROW to PARMENAS BRYANT, administrator
of RICHARD MURROW; owes MURPHY BROWN and Company; $1.00; all rights
in late father's estate by RANSOM MURROW and WILLIAM MURROW. Lines:
RO. RIVES, ELISHA PETERS, WILLIAM CABELL--late HECTOR CABELL,
deceased; horse--late that of RICHARD MURROW and bought by WILLIAM
MURROW. To sell at ACH.

31. 15 October 1808. RO. DINWIDDIE conveyed to HUDSON MARTIN
     and JAMES WOODS 200 acres in trust to secure NATHAN CRAWFORD,
14 October 1807; recorded 19 October in Amherst County. Release.
Witnesses: HUDSON MARTIN, JR., WILLIAM B. JACOBS, HAWES COLEMAN,
BENJ. HUGHES.

32. 20 April 1808. SAMUEL COLEMAN, Casey County, Kentucky, to
     WILLIAM COFFEY...L40 Ivy Creek; branch of Tye; 100 acres--
surveyed for GEORGE HAYS, --50-1--and 50 acres surveyed for THOMAS
HAYS, 13 February 1766--adjacent both sides creek. Lines: JOS.
BURGER, NELSON MONROE, RICHARD L. ELLIS. Witnesses: JAMES MOUNT,
LANDON H. BRENT, JAMES GILES.

32. 25 July 1808. CAMPBELL GOODE, WILLIAM DAVIS and wife, BETSY,
     formerly GOODE, WILLIAM CAMPBELL and wife, SALLY, formerly
GOODE, JESSE HOUCHINS and wife, MARY ANN, formerly GOODE, WILLIAM,
DANIEL, PHOEBE, JOS. GOODE, JACOB PECK and wife, SUSANNAH, formerly
GOODE, heirs of DANIEL GOODE, the Elder, late of Amherst County, to
DAVID S. GARLAND...$30 to each; north borders Piney 133 acres.
DANIEL GOODE, died intestate years ago owning said tract.

34. 25 May 1808. WILLIAM PAMPLIN and wife, MARY, to MICAJAH
     PENDLETON...L90 two acres mill tract on Elk Creek in Amherst
County and Nelson. Lines: WIDOW ALLEN, GEORGE HYLTON.

35. 15 October 1808. JNO. ROBERTS, JR. to MICHL. WOODS...to
     THOMAS ROBERTS, 23 October 1809--to secure THOMAS ROBERTS;
$1.00; slave. May sell at SAMUEL BRIDGWATERS and the Redhouse.
Witnesses: WILLIAM LEE HARRIS, LEE W. HARRIS, JOS. ROBERTS.

35. 14 September 1808. JESSE S. PROFFITT to WILLIAM F. CARTER...
     $1.00; stock; furniture; to secure MURPHY BROWN and Company.
Witnesses: JAMES GREGORY, JNO. CREWS, JNO. HARGROVE, CHARLES
EDMUNDS.

36. 1 October 1808. JNO. CARR to THOMAS E. FORTUNE...to THOMAS E.
    FORTUNE, 22 February 1809--to secure JOS. ROBERTS, bondsman,
to WILLIAM PATTERSON and JNO. MC BRYDE, assignees, versus ROBT.
HORSLEY; six shillings. 54 acres north side Tye and located by
JNO. CARR in treasury office warrant; 98 acres south side Tye and
bought from ROBT. HORSLEY by JNO. CARR in Amherst County; 173 acres
north side south prong of Tye. May sell at MAJOR MASSIE's Mill or
at Nelson CH. Witnesses: S. GARLAND, GEO. W. VARNUM, J. HENDERSON,
A. B. SNEAD, WILLIAM KENNEDY, CHARLES PERROW.

38. 8 November 1808. JOS. LOVING and wife, ROSE, to NELSON
    CLARKSON, Campbell County...to JOS. LOVING, 26 June 1809--
horses exchanged--tract as JOS. LOVING's share from WILLIAM LOVING,
deceased, in Green County, Kentucky. Witnesses: SAMUEL EDMUNDS, JR.,
JOHN LOVING, JAMES LOVING, JR., S. GARLAND.

39. 3 November 1807. SARAH ENOCKS, wife of DAVID ENOCKS, deceased,
    to JESSE FIDLER...L 25; dower in Rockfish tract. Lines:
WILLIAM BALL, JESSE A. JOPLING, MARK LIVELY, JNO. SNIDER. Witnesses:
JNO. FARRAR, PETER FARRAR, SHELTON FARRAR.

39. 3 November 1808. ALEX. B. ROSE, 1; THOMAS HIGGINBOTHAM,
    THOMAS S. MC CLELLAND, ARCHELAUS MAYS, Lynchburg, 2; CHARLES
CLAY, Bedford, 3...$1678.38 due CHARLES CLAY; $1.00--2530 acres on
Tye and Hatt. Lines: THOMAS MASSIE, DAVID S. GARLAND, THOMAS
FITZHUGH, HENRY ROSE, PHILLIP RYAN. Devised from JNO. and CHARLES
ROSE; slaves. Witnesses: JNO. ROBINSON, G. A. ROSE, WILLIAM J.
LEWIS, PATRICK ROSE, ASA VARNUM, RO. RIVES, JNO. N. ROSE, S. GARLAND,
ASA VARNUM, CHARLES PERROW, JAMES MURPHY.

41. 28 November 1808. RIVES MURPHY and Company, Warminster, to
    ZACH FORTUNE...$300 80 acres north fork Davis Creek. Lines:
JOS. ROBERTS, ZACH FORTUNE, JOS. SHELTON, grantors--part of 260 acres
where WILLIAM HARRIS (Green Mt.) now lives--conveyed to DANIEL
HIGGINBOTHAM in Deed of Trust, 2 July 1803, from WILLIAM HARRIS to
secure company. Sold by WILLIAM HARRIS to company.

42. 28 November 1808. SAMUEL EDMUNDS, JR. to JNO. LOVING to secure
    WILLIAM WRIGHT...six shillings; two slaves. To sell at old
ACH and New Market. Witnesses: SPENCER FAULCONER, JAMES WOODS,
H. M. GARLAND.

43. 4 Ocotber 1808. MARY NEVIL and -- NEVIL, wife of CORNL.
    NEVIL, to JNO. SYME...$2000--to W. S. CABELL, 30 January 1809
412 acres. Lines: JAMES MURPHY, ZACH NEVIL, CHARLES YANCY, THOMAS
KEY, ELISHA PETERS, WILLIAM DIXON. Witnesses: WILLIAM H. DIGGES,
ROWLAND EDMUNDS, THOMAS BIBB, JR.

44. 4 March 1808. RANSOM MURROW, WILLIAM and BLUFORD MURROW to
    WILLIAM F. CARTER to secure PARMENAS BRYANT, administrator of
RICHARD MURROW; MURPHY BROWN and Company; RO. RIVES, bondsman...$1.00;
WILLIAM and RANSOM's interest in father's tract. Lines: RO. RIVES,
ELISHA PETERS, WILLIAM CABELL (late HECTOR CABELL), deceased,
BLUFORD's mare--late that of RICHARD MURROW. Witnesses: JAMES
GREGORY, JOS. HARGROVE, JNO. HARGROVE, WILLIAM L. BALL.

45. 26 November 1808. THOMAS SPRADLING and wife, NANCY, to
    WILLIAM JORDAN...L65 Elk Island Creek--65 acres. Lines:
WILLIAM VIA, GEORGE HYLTON, grantee. Witnesses: WILLIAM HORSLEY,
RO. HORSLEY, SALLY HORSLEY.

46. 31 October 1808. SAMUEL DIXON to JNO. DIXON...L100 south
    fork Rockfish. Lines: WILLIAM DIXON, SR., NORBORN THOMAS,
THOMAS CHILDRESS, ELISHA PETERS, JNO. FARIS--sold to them jointly
by NORBORN THOMAS in 1805--recorded Amherst County. Witnesses:
JNO. HARGROVE, JAMES DICKSON--signed DICKSON.

47. 28 November 1805. JNO. BETHEL to wife, MARY...where I live
     on north side TINSLEY's Mt. Lines: JNO. BETHEL, JR., ABRAM
WARWICK, deceased, JAMES MARTIN, HECTOR CABELL, deceased; furniture.
Witnesses: GEORGE W. VARNUM, THOMAS ALFORD.

48. 1 May 1808. GEORGE WOODY, Amherst County, to WILLIAM H.
     SHELTON...L2-17-5 mare and colt. Witnesses: LEE W. HARRIS,
HENRY EMMERSON, WILLIAM MC ALEXANDER.

48. 26 September 1808. GEORGE LOVING and wife, MILDRED, to
     MURPHY BROWN and Company, Warminster...L122-2 434 acres Tye.
Lines: WILLIAM CLASBY and including tract. GEORGE LOVING bought
from THOMAS LAIN. Witnesses: JNO. JACOBS, JAMES DICKSON, PETER
CAMPBELL, WILLIAM BIBB.

49. 9 November 1808. LEWIS GILLESPIE to SAMUEL and JOS. DICKISON
     to secure WILLIAM DICKISON, SR...to SAMUEL DICKISON, 24 August
1810; six shilliqgs; slave girl. Witnesses: CHARLES CHRISTIAN,
JAMES and JNO. DICKISON.

50. 23 August 1808. JOSHUA HARRIS to JOS. SHELTON and JAMES H.
     BURTON to secure WILLIAM DOUGLAS...$1.00; furniture, etc.
Witnesses: JNO. P. HOPE, ELIZABETH SHELTON, THOMAS BARRY, WILLIAM H.
SHELTON, RO. KINCAID.

51. 25 January 1809. SALLY MAYS, widow of JOS. MAYS, to son,
     ROBERT MAYS, for managing my dower estate by will...ten
shillings; slaves; use of tract where I live. Witnesses: ISAAC
WHITE, GEORGE MAYS.

52. 21 January 1809. SAMUEL EDMONDS, SR. and wife, ALICE, to
     ROWLAND EDMONDS...to ROWLAND EDMONDS by GEORGE MAYS, 10 January
1816--$1.00 eight acres. Lines: grantee. Witnesses: WILLIAM H.
DIGGES, SAMUEL EDMUNDS, JR., CHARLES TOWNSEND.

53. 4 June 1808. DAVID OWENS to JNO. MC ALEXANER (note: should
     be MC ALEXANDER) to secure MARY NEVIL...$1.00; stock. To
JNO. MC ALEXANDER, 5 June 1809. Witnesses: JNO. HORSLEY, JR.,
JACOB PUCKETT, SR. and JR.

54. 27 March 1808. WILLIAM CAMDEN to HENRY SCHROEDER, Baltimore...
     L100 72½ acres. Lines: SUSANNA SPRADLING, GEORGE SHRADER,
GEORGE HYLTON, WEBSTER heirs. To JNO. ROSE, 23 April 1810--also
spelled SHROEDER--probably SHRADER.

55. 29 November 1808. JEFFRY MARTIN and wife, NANCY, to RICHARD
     RICHARDSON, Albemarle...L80 220 acres. Lines: grantee.
Witnesses: NATHL. HARLOW, JR., LEE W. HARRIS, JNO. E. FITZPATRICK,
JNO. HENDERSON, AUGUSTINE SHEPHERD.

56. 29 November 1808. Order to Nelson Justices of the Peace as
     to above deed...NATHAN CRAWFORD and HUDSON MARTIN, SR. and JR.

57. 22 March 1808. ALEX. B. ROSE to JAMES FREELAND and ARCHIBALD
     AUSTIN, Buckingham, to secure SAMUEL JONES...five shillings.
2500 acres on Tye and Hatt. Lines: THOMAS MASSIE, THOMAS FITZHUGH,
HENRY ROSE, EDMOND WILCOX, deceased, DAVID S. GARLAND, NATHNL. HILL,
deceased--where ALEX. B. ROSE lives. Witnesses: THOMAS N. EUBANK,
JNO. MOORE, LEE W. HARRIS, MICAJAH CAMDEN.

58. 9 September 1808. WILLIAM VIA and wife, PHEABY, to WILLIAM
     CAMDEN...L100 72½ acres--left to WILLIAM VIA by father.
Lines: SUSANNAH SPRADLING, GEORGE SHRADER, GEORGE HYLTON, WEBSTER
heirs. Witnesses: LEROY CAMDEN, MICAJAH PENDLETON, HIRAM MC GINNIS,
JNO. WHITEHEAD.

59. 13 October 1808. GEORGE MARTIN and wife, SALLY, to NATHL.
     HARLOW, JR...L6-1-7 two acres. Lines: grantee, HUDSON MARTIN,
grantor, Big Road, WILLIAM A. HARLOW was a witness; also DAVID
SHIELDS, REUBEN HARLOW, NANCY HARLOW, HUDSON MARTIN, JR.

61. 1 November 1808. NICHL. CABELL to JOS. C. CABELL, Warminster...
     rent; nine acres in town. Lines: Swan Creek, JNO. PATTESON--
ten years at $19.50 per year. Witnesses: RO. MOORE, GEORGE
CABELL, RICHARD POWELL. Note: I have commented on Warminster in
Amherst data. CABELL had visions of establishing a large place on
the James, but his dreams did not materialize. My wife and I drove
up to see the site one afternoon and it is just a country store
site.

62. 1 November 1808. NICHL. CABELL and wife, PEGGY R., to
     JOS. C. CABELL, Warminster...L386-13; lots 36 and 34--7½ acres
on Main Street. Witnesses: JNO. HIGGINBOTHAM, SAML. J. CABELL, JR.,
GEORGE CABELL, JR., WILLIAM B. HARE, WILLIAM H. and LANDON CABELL.

63. 27 February 1809. Order to Justices of the Peace: ABRAM B.
     WARWICK and RICHARD POWELL...NICHL. CABELL and wife, PEGGY R.,
1 November 1808, to JOS. C. CABELL 7½ acres; done, 1 March 1809.

64. 5 August 1808. Order to JAMES MONTGOMERY and WILLIAM B.
     JACOBS...NATHL. HILL, WILLIAM HILL, JR. and wife, SUSANNAH,
GEORGE and JNO. P. HILL, JNO. JACOBS, JR. and wife, LUCY, WILLIAM
RYAN and wife, ELISABETH, THOMAS R. DRAKE and wife, NANCY, and
POLLY T. HILL, 28 June 1808, to THOMAS MASSIE; done, 1 February
1809.

65. 22 September 1808. ALEX. B. ROSE to JNO. NICHOLAS ROSE...
     $441; two slaves. Witnesses: EDWARD H. CARTER, JNO. MITCHELL.

66. 31 December 1808. NATHL. HARLOW, SR. and wife, FANNY, to
     NATHL. HARLOW, JR...to JR., 25 March 1811--$1.00 and love
for their son 575 acres on Rockfish at foot of Blueridge; bought
from JNO. MURRELL in life and two small tracts bought from HUDSON
MARTI. Lines: JAMES WOODS, HUDSON MARTIN, ANN DINWIDDIE.
Witnesses: HUDSON MARTIN, SR. and JR., JNO. WOODS, WILLIAM
WEATHERWED, RO. DINWIDDIE, T. J. DICKINSON.

67. 10 October 1808. PRESLEY RAINES to RO. FRANKLIN and JAMES
     VIGUS...to WILLIAM CABELL, 7 July 1812--to secure MURPHY
BROWN and Company; six shillings; wagon; stock. Witnesses:
W. F. CARTER, SAMUEL STEVENS, GEORGE LAVENDER, JNO. SYME, BENJAMIN
BROWN.

69. 27 April 1809. CHARLES TOWNSEND to JAMES LOVING and THOMAS E.
     FORTUNE to secure PETER CAMPBELL and GEORGE W. VARNUM...$1.00;
stock; linen. Witnesses: JNO. STEWART, S. GARLAND, CHARLES G.
PERROW.

70. 22 May 1809. HENRY WOODS to JNO. THOMPSON and wife, REBECCA
     EDWARDS...$110 55 acres of survey of 5 March 1805 on Piney.
Lines: CHARLES IRVING, deceased, DANIEL GOODE, deceased. Patent
to HENRY WOODS at Richmond, 13 November 1808.

71. 22 November 1808. JNO. CAMDEN and wife, ONEY, N. County, to
     DAVID JACOBS...L1250 tobacco and one bay mare 54 acres on
Little Cub; branch of Tye. Lines: JAMES BROWN's former survey.
Witnesses: JAMES MONTGOMERY, JNO. BARRETT.

72. 22 May 1809. WILLIAM HOLLANDSWORTH (HOLLINGSWORTH) and wife,
     FANNY, to RO. RIVES...L282 265 acres. Lines: TERISHA TURNER
(formerly WILLIAM CRISP), Spencer's road, WILLIAM LOVING, deceased,
WILLIAM LOVING, JR., grantee, Bob's Creek, RO. HARRISON's former
line. Witnesses: JAMES MURPHY, HENRY BIBB, JR., DANIEL NASH,
NELSON HARGROVE.

73. 9 November 1808. HENRY CAMPBELL to LANDON CABELL and JOS. C.
     CABELL to secure WILLIAM B. HARE...$1.00; tobacco at Tye and
Swan Creek bought; HENRY CAMPBELL made Deed of Trust on residence,
28 October 1803, and deemed insufficient; four negroes; wagon;
horses. Witnesses: THOMAS HARVIE, STEPHEN EWERS, LEWIS DAVIES.

75. 25 October 1808. JNO. WRIGHT to SHELTON CROSTHWAIT and NATHL.
     OFFUTT to secure AUGUSTINE WRIGHT...six shillings; wagon;
horses; stock; furniture. Witnesses: MATT. HIGHT, JNO. EDMUNDS,
JR., ANDREW FOGUS.

76. 11 March 1809. WILLIAM ALLEN to RO. FRANKLIN and WILLIS
     WILLS, Warminster, to secure MURPHY BROWN and Company...six
shillings; 122 acres; Dutch freek. Lines: THOMAS NASH, grantor,
JNO. MOSBY, SPARKS MARTIN. Witnesses: GEORGE VAUGHAN, ABSALOM
JOHNSON, JAMES VIGUS, JR., RO. IRVING.

77. 16 December 1808. MOSES MAYS and wife, LUCY, to WILLIAM
     CLASBY...to WILLIAM CLASBY, JR., by SR., 14 June 1818--$1.00
52 acres south side of Cedar Creek. Lines: grantor--part of a
tract. Witnesses: RO. COLEMAN, RO. H. COLEMAN, JOS. and WILL
LOVING. Order to WILLIAM H. DIGGES and WILLIAM and JOS. LOVING
as to relinquishment of dower; done by both LOVINGS, same date.

79. 19 April 1809. JOS., RO. and SAMUEL HORSLEY to WILLIAM
     HORSLEY...L120 all interest in Nelson tracts; 200 acres on
James River devised by our father, WILLIAM HORSLEY, to MARTHA
HORSLEY, deceased--our mother, and at her death to his six sons:
WILLIAM, JOS., RO., SAMUEL, JNO. and NICHL. HORSLEY; 200 acres
adjacent--devised by ROBERT HORSLEY to brothers, WILLIAM and JNO.--
both dead; 60 acres on James--part of Rich Branch tract and
adjacent first 200 acres above on westerly end. Lines: GEORGE
HYLTON. Witnesses: RICHARD PHILLIPS, N. C. HORSLEY, SAMUEL
BRANSFORD, MICAJAH PENDLETON, ANDREW W. WHITE, GEORGE W. KYLE,
WILLIAM J. FREELAND, JNO. HORSLEY, JR.

81. 26 May 1809. FRANCIS WEST to RO. FRANKLIN and JAMES VIGUS,
     Warminster...execution in County Court in hands of LEE W.
HARRIS, Deputy Sheriff, for JOS. SHELTON, Sheriff; debt to JAMES
MURPHY and Company; five shillings, 214 acres Swan Creek. Lines:
JAMES TURNER, NORBORN THOMAS, GEORGE CABELL, BRANSFORD WEST; stock;
furniture. Witnesses: THOMAS HARGROVE, LEE W. HARRIS, RO. IRVING,
JAMES STEVENS, JR., JER. YAGER.

82. 30 January 1809. Order to WILLIAM H. DIGGES and JOS. LOVING...
     MARY NEVIL, CORNL. NEVIL and wife, AILSEY, 4 October 1808,
to JNO. SYME--412 acres, 30 January 1809. Done as to AILSEY, 2 May
1809.

83. 25 November 1808. RICHARD POLLARD to RO. POLLARD, Richmond...
     L1000; named slaves; furniture. Witnesses: JNO. CAMP,
WILLIAM CAMP, JOSHUA PHILLIPS.

83. 28 June 1809. ELISHA PETERS and wife, CINTHA, to SUKEY KEY...
     $30; no acres. Lines: JNO. SYME, THOMAS KEY on south side
old Glade road. Witnesses: NELSON CAMPBELL, JAMES MURPHY, TIMOTHY R.
RYAN.

84. 17 December 1808. RICHARD CLARK, trustee of DAVID OWENS, to
     MURPHY BROWN and Company...Deed of Trust, 4 August 1806, by
DAVID OWENS to RICHARD CLARK; sold, 30 November last, to grantee
at $150--339 acres where DAVID OWENS lives; bought from WALLER FORD.
Witnesses: ANDREW WHITE, GEORGE W. KYLE, WILLIAM PAMPLIN, PETER
PIERCE.

85. 7 June 1809. EDDY FORTUNE to WILLIS H. WILLS and NATHL.
     OFFUTT...to JAMES MURPHY, 27 November 1809; to secure
SHELTON CROSTHWAIT; $1.00; 81 acres on Tye. Lines: WILLIAM
ALFORD, WILLIAM HOLLANDSWORTH, JOS. LOVING--lately bought from
WILLIAM W. KEY; slaves; stock. Witnesses: GEORGE D. TYLER, JNO.
STEIGEL, FRED. FULTZ.

87. 26 June 1809. Order to Justices of the Peace as to JOS.
     LOVING and wife, ROSE, 8 November 1808, to NELSON CLARKSON...
tract in Green County, Kentucky; done, 24 June 1809, by WILLIAM H.
DIGGES and SHELTON CROSTHWAIT.

89. 1 July 1809. (There is no page 88 in book) DAVID S. GARLAND,
       Amherst County, to DAVID R. CLARKSON...L50 200 acres upper
Tye. Lines: JAS. HATTER, JNO. M. HATTER, THOS. PHILLIPS, JNO.
MASTERS, TILFORD, NICHL. MORAN, WILLSON NICHOLAS, JNO. C. HATTER.
Witnesses: JAS. GARLAND, CHAS. A. JACOBS, THOMPSON NOEL.

90. 24 July 1809. ABRAHAM B. WARWICK to ELISHA PETERS...$1.00;
       seventy acres by patent. Lines: JAS. MARTIN.

91. 24 July 1809. THOS. MASSIE, JOS. SHELTON, RO. RIVES, GEO. W.
       VARNUM, JNO. DILLARD, SHELTON CROSTHWAIT, JON. HARRIS, JOS.
ROBERTS, SR., LOVINGSTON trustees to RO. KINCAID...Act of Assembly,
24 January 1809, to establish town on lands of JAS. LOVING and they
were appointed trustees to lay off thirty acres in half acre lots;
did so; sold, 18 May last--as directed--to sell at doors of Amherst
County and Nelson after due notice--No. 32--eighty-six yards long
and thirty-two yards broad; south by Main; west by Spring Street;
west by No. 31; east by Front Street. L12-3.

92. 24 July 1809. Same trustees to JOS. SHELTON...L8-8; lot 31;
       to build dwelling house--twelve foot square; brick or stone
chimney--within five years.

94. 24 July 1809. WM. EDMUNDS and wife, POLLY, to JNO. JACOBS,
       JR...L103-7-4 EDMUNDS of Amherst County; sixty-eight acres
Tye bought from WM. HILL, JR. Lines: grantee; THOS. MASSIE;
THOS. R. DRAKE.

95. 4 May 1809. WM. W. KEY and wife, ELIZ., to EDDY FORTUNE...L80
       81 acres Tye. Lines: WM. ALFORD, WM. HOLLANDSWORTH, JOS.
LOVING. Witnesses: WILLIS H. WILLS, JAS. THOMPSON, SHELTON
CROSTHWAIT. ELIZ. relinquished dower to ABRAHAM WARWICK and
SHELTON CROSTHWAIT, Justices of the Peace, on same day.

97. 3 April 1809. JNO., TANDY and JOSHUA KEY, executors of
       MARTIN KEY, to JNO. FITZPATRICK...L250 333 acres Davis
Creek. Lines: RO. WRIGHT, JON. LOVING, JAS. WRIGHT, THOS.
MONTGOMERY. Witnesses: WA--(?) KEY, J. W. WOOD, JESSE B. and
JESSE KEY--TANDY KEY and JOSHUA KEY acknowledged deed in Albemarle,
1809, JNO. NICHOLAS, Clerk. August, 1809.

98. 27 February 1809. JESSE PROFFITT to SHELTON CROSTHWAIT to
       secure ABRAHAM WARWICK...SYLVANUS BRYANT, bondsman; $1.00;
bay horse bought from ABRAHAM WARWICK. Witnesses: JNO. LOVING,
RO. MOORE, JNO. BIBB.

99. 27 December 1808. TERISHA TURNER to JAS. TURNER...L120 200 acres
       both sides Rockfish. Lines: HENRY EMMERSON, WM. MARTIN,
WM. MOSBY, CONRAD MOWYER, BENJ. PAYNE, down creek to junction with
the MAGANS(?). Witnesses: TERISHA TURNER, MATT. LANGFORD, HENRY
TURNER, CHAS. LANGFORD.

100. 25 July 1809. SHELTON CROSTHWAIT and wife, ELIZ., to MURPHY
       BROWN and Company...L12500 Rucker's Run--bought from JAS. P.
COCKE, mills, distillery, tanyard--760 acres--500 acres of it
bought from JNO. EDMUNDS; also lot on Tye near New Market with
lumber house lately occupied by SHELTON CROSTHWAIT; slaves, stock,
etc. Witnesses: JAS. GREGORY, NATHL. OFFUTT, WILLIS H. WILLS,
S. GARLAND, CHAS. PERROW, JNO. EUBANK, ELIZ. relinquished dower,
5 August 1809, to WM. H. DIGGES and ASA VARNUM.

102. 28 August 1809. SHELTON CROSTHWAIT and WM. H. DIGGES to AAS
       VARNUM...$40 1600 square yards; Cabellsville--No. 30; recorded
in Amherst County plat.

103. 12 July 1808. MARY TEAS to JNO. BURNETT, friend...power of
       attorney to recover slaves in Virginia or elsewhere to which
I am entitled. Witnesses: JESSE CLARKSON, GEO. WILLIAMS.

104. 2 May 1809. WM. HILL, JR. and wife, SUSANNAH, to WM. EDMUNDS,
      Amherst County...to WM. EDMUNDS, 25 February 1810--L103-7-4;
68 acres Tye. Lines: JNO. JACOBS, JR., THOS. MASSIE, THOS. R.
DRAKE, grantor--lot 8 in division of NATHL. HILL, deceased.
Witnesses: WM. COFFEY, JR., PETER RIPPETOE, NELSON CLARKSON, HENRY
RYAN.

105. 25 September 1809. JOS. BURGHER and wife, MOLLY, to WM.
      COFFEY, SR...to WM. B. JACOBS, 2 October 1809--L300; 260 acres
south borders Tye. Lines: JNO. JACOBS, THOS. MASSIE, NELSON
MONROE, a branch.

107. 25 January 1809. NICHL. CABELL and wife, PEGGY, to JESSE
      JOPLING...L160-13 378 acres. Lines: JNO. SNYDER, grantee,
BETHEL LIVELY, WM. BALL--former tract of DAVID ENIX and where he
last resided. Witnesses: RO. MOORE, WILLIS H. WILLS, JERE YAGER,
G. CABELL, JR.

108. 25 September 1809. JNO. JARVIS and wife, MARY ANN, to WM.
      JOHNSON...L140 three adjacent tracts Rucker's Run. 52 acres.
Lines: CHAS. STEWART, SAML. LOVING, to grantor's house; 123 acres.
Lines: where grantor lives and bought from JOS. TUCKER, CHAS.
PERROW--formerly WM. CRISP; grantee; SAML. LOVING. Thirteen acres
adjacent 123 acres; bought from THOS. HAWKINS--plat and survey of
18 May 1790. 188 acres.

110. 21 August 1809. DAVID CLARKSON to JNO. MASTERS...sent to
      WM. B. COFFEY's administrator, MORRIS COFFEY, 5 May 1848--
owns estate, MELAND(?)--L40 Elk Creek of Tye--40 acres. Lines:
grantee, WILSON C. NICHOLAS, grantor, a branch.

111. 13 May 1809. GIDEON MARTIN and wife, POLLY, to HUDSON MARTIN,
      JR...L200; 100 acres. Lines: STEPHEN MARTIN, deceased.
Witnesses: HENRY BIBB, JR., WM. LEE HARRIS, JNO. E. FITZPATRICK,
JNO. GOODWIN, PETER C. JACOBS. Dower relinquished to NATHAN
CRAWFORD and HAWES COLEMAN on same day.

114. 1 July 1809. JAS. LOVING and wife, NANCY, to WM. CABELL,
      NATHAN CRAWFORD, WM. HARRIS, HUDSON MARTIN, SAML. J. CABELL,
JOS. SHELTON, JAS. WOODS, WM. LOVING, LANDON CABELL, WM. B. HARE,
ALEX. B. ROSE, WM. H. DIGGES, JOS. LOVING, JAS. MONTGOMERY, THOS.
MASSIE, WM. JACOBS, WM. HORSLEY, JESSE A. JOPLING, WM. B. HARRIS,
JOS. C. CABELL, JNO. S. DAWSON, NELSON ANDERSON, ASA VARNUM, JAS.
MURPHY, JNO. DILLARD, ALEX. B. WARWICK, JNO. JACOBS, GEO. W. VARNUM,
RICH. POWELL, HAWES COLEMAN, JAS. LOVING, SHELTON CROSTHWAIT, JNO.
MOSBY, HUDSON MARTIN, JR., son of HUDSON, SR., RO. RIVES, JNO.
DIGGES, Justices of the Peace...Act of Assembly, 31 December 1808,
to fix permanent seat of justice for Nelson County--fixed where his,
JAS. LOVING's land is located, near his spring--if he will donate
two acres--having courthouse near his house--$1.00; one lot near
center of Lovingston and laid off by commissioners--where public
buildings are to be erected. Witnesses: JNO. BROOKS, JACOB
PUCKET, JNO. MC ALEXANDER.

115. 1 July 1809. THOS. MASSIE, JOS. SHELTON, RO. RIVES, GEO. W.
      VARNUM, JNO. DILLARD, SHELTON CROSTHWAIT, JNO. HARRIS, and
JOS. ROBERTS, SR., Lovingston trustees...Act of Assembly, 24 January
1809, establishing town on lands of JAS. LOVING, and trustees
appointed--three lots in town: 1, 2, and 6. One and two join.
Lines: Main Street on south, Front Street on west, Pleasant Street
on north, street around public square on north, Back Street on east,
alley on south; lot 5--sold to THOS. E. FORTUNE on west. Lot
entered on map of town sold to FORTUNE and by him resold to
GEO. W. VARNUM for $225.00.

117. 15 July 1809. JNO. FORTUNE to JAS. LOVING, JR. and ASA VARNUM
      to secure debts...$1.00; three slaves named and ages. Signed
also by GEO. W. VARNUM. Witnesses: JNO. BARNETT, CHAS. FLOED,
WM. MC CALEB.

119. 23 October 1809. THOS. JOPLING and wife, MOLLY, to RALPH
    and JNO. JOPLING, NANCY WEST, wife of BRANSFORD WEST, SARAH
BALL, widow of WM. BALL, KATH. THURMOND, widow of GUTRIDGE THURMOND,
JANE JOPLING, Nelson County, WM. and BENJ. JOPLING, North Carolina,
DANL. JOPLING and PATSY THOMAS, wife of MICHL. THOMAS, Albemarle
County, MICHL. THOMAS, RALPH THOMAS, BETSY FERGUSON, wife of DANL.
FERGUSON, children of MARY THOMAS, deceased, and late wife of RALPH
THOMAS, and formerly MARY JOPLING, Nelson County...tract bought by
RALPH JOPLING, late of Amherst County, and father of parties--
except children of MARY THOMAS-- and he was their grandfather;
conveyed to THOS. JOPLINE, agent of RALPH JOPLING, by COLBERT BLAIR,
Burke County, North Carolina, 8 October 1789. RALPH JOPLING by will
of 28 June 1791, in Amherst County; devised tracts to be equally
divided to sons, RALPH and JAS. (will says Buckingham County, North
Carolina--B. Davis)--since dead; intestate; no issue--$21 to carry
out will; in proportion to grantees--two tracts--save one twelfth--
Burks County, North Carolina. 323 acres. Lines: Both sides Muddy
fork of Lower creek, ELIAS and AMBR. POWELL, the road, EDWD. WILSON,
DOUGLAS, a branch. 150 acres adjacent. Lines. ELIAS POWELL, old
mill seat, DOUGLAS, a branch. One-twelfth to each of parties.

122. 27 September 1808. THOS. ALFORD and wife, FRANCES, to CHAS.
    FLOED...to CHAS. FLOED, 11 July 1811--L100 50 acres south
borders Rucker's Run. Lines: BERDIT SKINNER, WM. DIGGS, TERISHA
TURNER, WM. ALFORD--deeded to THOS. ALFORD by JNO. ALFORD. Witnesses:
WM. H. DIGGES, BURDIT SKINNER.

123. 22 May 1809. REUBEN T. MITCHELL and wife, MILLY, to JNO.
    BURKS...L9 two acres. Lines: the road. Witnesses: JESSE
JOPLING, JNO. TURNER, RO. L. FARRAR, SAML. SCRUGGS, JNO. WILLS,
HENRY SMITH, ISAAC SMITH, WM. WALKER.

124. 25 November 1809. JNO. W. HARRIS to JOS. SHELTON...to CAMPT.
    JNO. W. WITT, 4 May 1844--L112-10; 37½ acres south side
Rockfish; part of tract of BENNETT JOPLING and bought from him.
Lines: CAPT. MATT. HARRIS, grantee, north side Rockfish.

125. 25 August 1809. HAWES COLEMAN, MATT. HARRIS, MICHL. WOODS
    and JOS. ROBERTS, commissioners, to DAVID WITT, JR...decree
to sell tract of LITTLEBERRY WITT, deceased; sold, 17 June 1809, for
L90; Rockfish. Lines: JOS. ROBERTS--two acres. Witnesses:
WM. LEE HARRIS, BURGESS WITT, JESSE JOPLING.

126. 26 September 1809. Order to WM. B. and JNO. JACOBS as to
    MOLLY BURGHER, wife of JOS., 25 September 1809, to WM. COFFEY...
done, 26 October 1809.

127. 20 December 1809. JAS. WALTERS and wife, LYDIA, to JAS.
    MAYS...L110 71 acres bought borders Tye. Lines: JNO. DILLARD,
grantee.

128. 21 September 1809. WM. HARRIS (GM--sic) to LEE W. HARRIS...to
    LEE W. HARRIS, 4 July 1810--to secure RIVES MURPHY and Company
from July 2, 1803. 190 acres north fork Davis where WM. HARRIS
lives; entire tract. Lines: ZACH FORTUNE, JOS. ROBERTS, stock.
Witnesses: WM. LEE HARRIS, THOS. FORTUNE, ZACH and ELIZ. FORTUNE.

129. 15 January 1810. JNO. CLARKSON and wife, NANCY, JAS. CLARKSON
    and wife, MARIAH, Albemarle, to SAML. PARRISH...$200; two
shares as heirs of DAVID CLARKSON, deceased. North courses from
old dwelling house--No's 4 and 5; blank acres. Witnesses: JAS.
MONTGOMERY, JNO. JACOBS, JR., JESSE CLARKSON.

130. 22 January 1810. JNO. SPARROW, NATHL. OFFUTT, and RO.
    FRANKLIN, latter two as grantees...to secure MURPHY BROWN and
Company--to JAMES MURPHY, 6 November 1816--$1.00; stock; furniture;
tools. Witnesses: EDMD. LANIER, L. C. RIVES, F. CABELL.

132. 11 January 1810. DAVID CLARKSON and wife, REBECCA, ELIZ.
CLARKSON, widow of DAVID CLARKSON, deceased, JAS. EAST and
wife, BETSY, formerly CLARKSON--scratched and PATSY signs--SAML.
PARISH and wife, JANE, formerly CLARKSON--heirs of DAVID CLARKSON,
to JAS. CLARKSON, Albemarle...$600--Tavern plantation on Tye.
Witnesses: EDMD. COFFEY, JAS. MONTGOMERY, JNO. JACOBS, JR., WM.
COFFEY, JNO. HUGHES, DANL. WADE.

133. 15 January 1810. Order to JAS. MONTGOMERY and JNO. HACOBS,
JR. as to above...done, 15 January 1810.

134. -- December 1809. THOS. PRATT, JR., to MICHL. WOODS...L50
140 acres Rockfish borders, part of tract conveyed to THOS.
PRATT, JR. by SR. and wife, ELIZ. Lines: south side of Mt.,
grantee, DAVID WITT, JOS. MONTGOMERY. Witnesses: HENRY DAWSON,
CLAYTON C. MONTGOMERY, NATHAN BARNETT, JOS. ROBERTS.

136. 10 May 1808. JNO. SNIDER and wife, NANCY, to their daughter,
SALLY FARRAR...love and $300; 132 acres in Amherst County on
Bar Branch. Lines: DAVID ENIX, grantor, JNO. HARDING, EDWD.
HARDING. Witnesses: JNO. FARRAR, JR., RO. S. FARRAR, JESSE FILDER.

137. 12 December 1809. THOS. PRATT, JR., to JOS. MONTGOMERY...
L22-4; 70 acres Rockfish. Lines: top of the mountain,
grantee, HAWES COLEMAN, MICHL. WOODS. Conveyed by THOS. PRATT, SR.
to JR.; on grantee's side of the mountain. Witnesses: MICHL.
WOODS, CLAYTON C. MONTGOMERY, NATHAN BARNETT, JOS. ROBERTS.

138. 9 November 1809. JNO. THOMPOSN, merchant, and wife, REBECCA,
to DAVID S. GARLAND...to DAVID S. GARLAND, 25 June 1810;
returned, 29 December 1812, to DAVID S. GARLAND--L1200 two adjacent
tracts north side Piney--535 acres. 480 acres of it bought from
estate of CHAS. IRVING, deceased. Fifty-five acres bought from
HENRY WOODS. Lines: DANL. GOODE, deceased. Witnesses: DANL.
HIGGINBOTHAM, THOMPSON NOEL, THOS. ALDRIDGE.

140. 15 January 1810. DAVID WOEN and wife, PATSY, to JNO.
FORTUNE...L50 50 acres north prong Rucker's Run. Lines:
both. Witnesses: THOS. E. FORTUNE, AUSTIN SEAY, NANCY MC ALEXANDER.

141. 9 February 1810. ALEX. B. ROSE to ANDREW MORGAN...stock at
EDWARDS and ROSE ISLE house; furniture; books; blacksmith
tools; anvil and bellows; crops. L150. Witnesses: WM. M. MORGAN,
BENJ. H. MORGAN, ALEX. MARR, DAVID MORGAN.

142. 23 October 1809. JNO. TURNER and wife, ELIZ., to HENRY and
SAML. TURNER...L200 385 acres Rockfish. Lines: Rich Cove
Creek, WM. LEIGH, HENRY TURNER, the branch, top of the Little
Mountain, TERISHA TURNER. Witnesses: TERISHA TURNER (2), MATT.
LANGFORD, EDWD. HARRIS, JNO. MOSBY, JNO. DIGGS--last two as Justices
of the Peace, too.

145. 23 October 1809. JNO. TURNER and wife, ELIZ., to HENRY and
SAML. TURNER...L200 tract and mill on Cove Creek; 80 acres.
Lines: SAML. ANDERSON at first branch below mill; Spring branch;
HENRY TURNER, Sr.; MARTIN DAWSON. Justices of the Peace as above.

148. 26 February 1810. JNO. MONROE to children: FANNY, SARAH,
MARY, ANDREW, JANE, ELIZ. and JNO. MONROE...slaves, stock,
furniture, tools. Note: this is the family of one of my members,
MRS. ED GILL, North Main Street, Amherst, Virginia, 24521. She
has worked hard on this line, but lacks confirmation on statement
in Hardesty and Brock that it is the same family as that of
PRESIDENT MONROE. If any reader has proof, I suggest that contact
be made with MRS. GILL.

149.   26 February 1810. THOS. MASSIE, JOS. SHELTON, RO. RIVES,
        GEO. W. VARNUM, JNO. DILLARD, JNO. HARRIS, JOS. ROBERTS, SR.,
Lovingston trustees, to GEO. YOST...reference to act of 24 January
1809; on lands of JAS. LOVING; thirty acres to be laid off for
permanent seat of justice and town--half acre and lots and streets;
to be called Lovingston when done; Lot 30. Lines: No. 39 of
ALEX. MC ALEXANDER, Spring Street, Pleasant Street, Front Street.
Must build within five years--dwelling house--twelve foot square;
brick or stone chimney.

151.   20 August 1809. Trustees as above, plus SHELTON CROSTHWAIT,
        to JNO. WRIGHT...Lot 3; 64 yards long and 38 yards broad.
Lines: Main Street, No. 4, Front Street, to build as above.

153.   9 March 1807. MARY TILMAN, formerly DOSWELL, Hanover County,
        to JOS. W. HENDRICK and wife, MARY DRUMMOND, Hanover...to
MR. GOODWIN by WM. H. COLEMAN, April 1810 (?)--$5.00 and maternal
love; one-fourth of Amherst County tract by will of THOS. DOSWELL,
Hanover--devised to MARY. Witnesses: WM. HARRIS, NATHL. POPE,
THOS. W. CLAYBROOK, JNO. BURNLEY. Hanover: WM. POLLARD, Clerk,
by THOS. POLLARD, Deputy. Recorded: Nelson, 25 March 1810.

155.   9 March 1807. MARY TILMAN, as above, to her children:
        JNO. DOSWELL TILMAN and NANCY DANIEL TILMAN...$5.00; one
moiety of tract as her inheritance from father, THOS. DOSWELL,
Hanover; one-half of remaining one-half. Witnesses: as above.

158.   20 January 1810. GEO. HYLTON to VALENTINE HYLTON...$1.00;
        358 acres. Lines: RICH. WOOD, WM. PAMPLIN, JAS. PAMPLIN,
DRUMMOND, WM. JORDAN. Witnesses: ZA. DRUMMOND, WM. CUNNINGHAM,
MICAJAH PENDLETON, SAML. FRANKLIN, SPOTSWOOD GARLAND, Clerk.
To WM. DILLARD, 7 April 1831.

160.   6 January 1810. JAS. PAMPLIN and wife, MARY, to JAS.
        CUNNINGHAM...L20 25 acres north branch Elk Island Creek.
Witnesses: WM. HORSLEY, ZA DRUMMOND, WM. CUNNINGHAM, VAL. HYLTON.

161.   6 January 1810. JAS. PAMPLIN and wife, MARY, and RACHEL
        PAMPLIN to MARY B. DRUMMOND...to her by JNO. HORSLEY, 28 May
1811--L240 110½ acres north borders Elk Island Creek. Witnesses:
as above.

163.   1 March 1810. MOSES MARTIN and wife, ELIZ., Rockbridge
        County, to DANL. MC DONALD...to him, 27 August 1810--$500
north border Tye, Cub Creek. One of three tracts. 121 acres
surveyed 1 November 1788. Lines: JNO. JACOBS, WM. COFFEY, his
own. Part of 150 acres between above and Cub Creek bought from
JAS. MOORE. Witnesses: JNO. SMITH, WM. SALE, DUDLEY SANDIDGE.

165.   12 March 1810. BARTLETT FOX and JNO. FOX and wife, LUCY,
        to JNO. TOMS...L110; tract by will from our father--89 acres.
Lines: JAS. MARTIN, now AUG. SMITH. Witnesses: HUDSON MARTIN,
JR., JOS. TOMS, SAML. HOLCOMB, LARKIN MILLER. Justices of the
Peace--two HUDSON MARTIN.

168.   1 October 1809. WM. LEE HARRIS to LEE W. HARRIS and HENRY
        BIBB...$50 105 acres. Lines: JNO. HARRIS, deceased. Tract
bought by WM. LEE HARRIS from COL. WM. CABELL, JNO. TOOLEY.

169.   21 April 1810. BENEDICT LANHAM and wife, PENELOPE, to DAVID
        FERGUSON...20 shillings; 60 acres Kirby Creek. Lines: JOS.
SMITH, JOS. MATTHEWS. Witnesses: JOS. SMITH, WM. LANHAM, ELIJAH
PUGH, JNO. LANHAM.

169.   25 April 1810. BENEDICT LANHAM and wife, as above, to WM.
        LANHAM...20 shillings; 143 acres; Kirby Creek. Lines: DAVID
FERGUSON, CORNL. MURRELL, a lane, TOBY's branch, JOS. SMITH.
Witnesses: JOS. SMITH, DAVID FERGUSON, JNO. LANHAM.

116

170.   17 November 1809.   STEVEN MARTIN to HUDSON MARTIN, JR....
       $80; his share; from his father, STEVEN MARTIN, SR.; Rockfish.
Lines: CHAS. BRIDGWATER, ROBT. HENDERSON. Father died intestate.
Witnesses: JNO. M. MARTIN, THRUSTON J. DICKINSON, DAVID SIMS,
JOS. MARTIN.

171.   12 October 1809.   REUBEN T. MITCHELL and wife, MILLY, to
       SAML. SCRUGGS and JNO. SCRUGGS...to SAML. SCRUGGS, 4 November
1824--L200 both sides Rockfish 140 acres. Lines: MARTIN DAWSON,
DUNMORE DAMRON, HENRY EMMERSON, mouth of Rock Branch, TERISHA
TURNER, JNO. TURNER, ALEX. ROBERTS. Witnesses: JNO. WILLS,
SAML. S. SCRUGGS, WM. SCRUGGS, NANCY SCRUGGS, ISAAC SMITH, JNO.
JOPLING.

173.   21 April 1810.   BENEDICT LANHAM and wife, PENELOPE, to
       JNO. LANHAM...20 shillings; sixty acres. Lines: WM. LANHAM,
Kirby Creek, CONRAD MOYWER, WM. MOSEBY, JOS. SMITH, TOBEY's Branch.
Witnesses: JOS. SMITH, DAVID FERGUSON, WM. LANHAM.

174.   9 January 1810.   SKYLER BARNETT, attorney-in-fact for THOS.
       FITZPATRICK, to MOSES HUGHES, SR...power of 18 November 1809,
in Madison County, Kentucky--to sell interest in tract of WM.
FITZPATRICK, deceased--interest conveyed to HUGHES, but does not
extend to rights of widow of WM.--RACHEL FITZPATRICK. Witnesses:
H. T. HARRIS, WM. LEE HARRIS, JAS. HUGHES, HENRY BIBB, JR.

175.   29 November 1809.   SAML. J., WM. and LANDON CABELL to THOS.
       MASSIE...to him, 28 June 1813--L75; half acre lot in New
Market--joins Tye Warehouse; no. 9. Lines: Main Street, Lot 10
of RO. RIVES and Company. Sold by WM. CABELL, deceased, to
WM. SPENCER and by him to RIVES and Company; by them to PARMENAS
BRYANT and by him to MASSIE. It is alleged that WM. CABELL made
no deed. Witnesses: WM. BRYANT, JAS. GREGORY, CHAS. EDMUMDS,
WM. DIXON, SYLVANUS BRYANT.

176.   23 April 1810.   Order to HILL CARTER and JNO. N. ROSE, Amherst
       County Justices of the Peace, as to WM. CAMDEN and wife,
ISBELL, 27 March 1808, to HENRY SHRADER...72½ acres; done, 2 May
1810.

178.   13 January 1810.   ALEX. FITZPATRICK, son of JNO., and wife,
       REBECCA, to MOSES HUGHES...L85; interest in estate of WM.
FITZPATRICK--not as to dower of RACHEL, widow, of WM. Witnesses:
HENRY T. HARRIS, JNO. EUBANK, WM. LEE HARRIS, NATHAN CRAWFORD,
HUDSON MARTIN, Justices of the Peace as to last two.

180.   11 March 1810.   HAWES COLEMAN, guardian of infants of JANE
       BAILEY, formerly FITZPATRICK, heir of WM. FITZPATRICK, to
MOSES HUGHES, SR...L75. Witnesses: HENRY T. HARRIS, WM., THOS.,
and MOSES FITZPATRICK, NATHL. BRIDGWATER.

181.   23 April 1810.   THOS. MASSIE, JOS. SHELTON, RO. RIVES,
       GEO. W. VARNUM, JNO. DILLARD, JNO. HARRIS, JOS. ROBERTS, SR.,
Lovingston trustees, to THOS. MC CALEB...Lots 18 and 19; $40.
Lines: Lot 20, Front Street, Second Street, lot 18, alley, lot 17.

183.   29 December 1809.   MINOS WRIGHT to NATHL. OFFUTT and RO.
       FRANKLIN to secure MURPHY BROWN and Company...$1.00; stock;
furniture; crops. Witnesses: JESSE S. PROFFITT, LANDON C. RIVES,
RO. HOOD, GEO. D. TYLER.

185.   11 December 1809.   PETER FARRAR and wife, SALLY, to DRURY
       SHEPHERD...to DRURY SHEPHERD, 22 December 1811--L132 132 acres;
patent, 3 August 1796, to JNO. SNIDER. Lines: DAVID ENIX, JNO.
SNIDER, Bar Branch, JNO. HARDING, EDWD. HARDING. Witnesses:
JNO. FARRAR, RO. S. FARRAR, LANDON FARRAR.

186. 28 May 1810. JNO. MOSBY to JNO. MOORE...$100; to JNO. MOSBY,
      23 November 1813--150 acres. Lines: DR. WM. MARTIN,
REUBEN T. MITCHELL, DUNMORE DAMRON. Recorded from JNO. MOSBY as
trustee for me in Deed of Trust; sold to HENRY EMMERSON--JNO. MOORE.

188. 9 January 1810. JNO. FITZPATRICK and wife, JANE, JAS. CLARKE
      and wife, SARAH, WM. FITZPATRICK and wife, FANNY, to MOSES
HUGHES, SR...L225; interest in tracts of WM. FITZPATRICK. Lines:
SAML. BRIDGWATER, THOS. FITZPATRICK, son of JNO., JOS. LIGON,
deceased, CLOUGH SHELTON, deceased. Three-eighths. Witnesses:
HENRY T. HARRIS, JNO. WOOD, WM. LEE HARRIS, JAS. HUGHES.

189. 26 May 1810. EDWD. HARDING and wife, POLLY, to DRURY SHEPHERD,
      Albemarle...to DRURY SHEPHERD, 22 December 1817--L284 142 acres
south fork Rockfish. Lines: grantor, MURPHY BROWN and Company,
formerly CORNL. THOMAS, WM. JOHNSON, deceased, WM. BALL, JNO. SNIDER.
Witnesses: JAS. MURPHY, LANDON C. RIVES, RO. MOORE, WM. WHEELER,
HUGH WHITE.

191. 11 December 1809. CLAYTON C. MONTGOMERY and wife, MARY, to
      WM. LOBIN...to WM. LOBIN, 23 March 1812--L450 179½ acres
north fork Rockfish. Lines: JOS. MARTIN, JAS. BROOKS, JNO.
SHIELDS, ALEX. SHIELDS. Witnesses: JAS. WOODS, JAS. LOBBAN,
JNO. LOBBAN, JR., WM. WEATHER---?, WM. BRIDGWATER. NATHAN CRAWFORD
and JAS. WOODS, Justices of the Peace.

194. 28 October 1809. HENRY SMITH to WM. LEE HARRIS to secure
      JOS. SHELTON...$1.00; two slaves. Witnesses: WM. H. SHELTON,
HENRY T. HARRIS, LEE W. HARRIS, NATHAN BARNETT.

196. 19 April 1810. JOS. MONTGOMERY to JNO. FITZPATRICK...L75
      58 acres Rockfish. Lines: grantor, DAVID WITT, THOS.
FITZPATRICK, grantee. Witnesses: HUDSON MARTIN, SAML. BRIDGWATER,
JAS. FITZPATRICK.

197. 18 June 1810. DAVID WITT, JR. to WM. WOOD...$80 40 acres.
      Lines: both. Witnesses: DAVID WITT, SR., WM. WITT, RICHARD
WOOD.

199. 4 October 1809. GEO. HYLTON to WM. O. MURRAY...L142 3/9;
      three slaves; for benefit of SALLY LEWIS, wife of CHAS. A.
LEWIS, and children. Witnesses: VAL. HYLTON, ZACH and JAMES N.
NEVIL.

200. 24 June 1810. JNO. BETHEL and wife, JANE, and BENJ. HARRIS
      and wife, MARY, Albemarle, to JNO. WALTERS...$7.50 per acre;
112 acres. Talow's Creek, branch of Rockfish. Part of former tract
of COL. CHISWELL. Lines: THOS. ROBERTS, WM. SMITH.

202. 7 June 1810. JAS. WILLS, JR. to RO. FRANKLIN and NATHL.
      OFFUTT...to RO. FRANKLIN, 30 January 1812--to secure MURPHY
BROWN and Company. $1.00. 400 acres. Lines: JAMES STEVENS, SR.,
JAS. THOMPSON, slaves. Witnesses: JAS. B. EDWARDS, LEE W. HARRIS,
RO. KINCAID, BENJ. BONDURANT, CHAS. PERROW, GEO. D. TYLER, RICH.
BRYANT.

204. 13 March 1810. WM. CAMPBELL and wife, ELIZ., Attorney-in-fact
      for brother, JNO. CAMPBELL, JACOB PUCKETT and wife, ELIZ.,
formerly CAMPBELL, to JAMES MONTGOMERY...nine acres; interest in
tract or share of CLARY CAMPBELL--legatee of JNO. CAMPBELL. Lines:
JNO. MARR, HENRY ROSE, PEGGY CAMPBELL's lot. Surveyed by RICH. S.
ELLIS. $21. Witnesses: JNO. BARNETT, JNO. JACOBS, JR., WM. B.
JACOBS.

205.   25 June 1810. RO. ROSE and wife, MARY S. H., Fauquier
       County, to DAVID S. GARLAND...L50,000 tobacco 662 2/3 acres.
North borders Hatt. Part of tract of JNO. ROSE, deceased, and
RO. is a son and this is his share conveyed. Lines: HENRY ROSE,
JNO. CAMPBELL, deceased, JAS. MONTGOMERY, GEO. WILLIAMS--line
between HENRY and RO. ROSE in their father's estate. EDWD. DIGGS,
JR., WM. HERNER, GEO. B. PUCKETT, Fauquier Justices of the Peace--
done by first two. H. R. CAMPBELL, Clerk.

209.   13 January 1810. ALEX. FITZPATRICK, son of WM., to THOS.
       FITZPATRICK, son of JNO...L75; interest in estate of WM.
FITZPATRICK, deceased; subject to dower of REBECCA FITZPATRICK.
Witnesses: H. HARRIS, ALEX. FITZPATRICK, JNO. EUBANK, JAS. HUGHES,
SAML. BRIDGWATER, MATT. HARRIS.

211.   25 June 1810. JAS. LOVING, son of WM., and wife, NANCY, to
       RODERICK L. TALIAFERRO...L90; part of tract where WM. VAUGHAN
lives. Lines: grantor, old road, CHAS. PERVIS, JAS. STEVENS, JR.,
main road, SPOTSWOOD GARLAND 80 acres. Survey by GEO. W. VARNUM.

212.   25 June 1810. WM. VAUGHAN and wife, ELIZ., to ROD. L.
       TALIAFERRO...L60; tract above. Note: see will of WM. LOVING
in Amherst; RODERICK gets share of ELIZ. VAUGHAN at her death.
ELIZ. was daughter of WM. LOVING. They grant him this tract for
love and affection.

214.   25 June 1810. ANN, JNO., NELSON, CHAS. PHILLIPS, SUSANNA
       STATHAM, POLLY JOHNSON to WM. DAWSON as "legatees"...$200
119 acres two adjacent tracts of 78 and 41 acres. Lines: MATT.
PHILLIPS, MATT. HARRIS, DANL. MOSBY. RO. JOHNSON also signed.

216.   25 June 1810. RO. ROSE and wife, MARY S. H., Fauquier County,
       to ANDREW MORGAN...$200 74 acres south Tye; lot from estate
of JNO. ROSE--"The Commons." Lines: ALEX. ROSE, THOS. FITZHUGH's
lot, PAT. ROSE, HENRY ROSE. EDMD. DIGGES, JR. and WM. HORNER,
Justices of the Peace.

219.   23 July 1810. NATHL. HILL to JNO. JINKINS...L92 76 acres;
       part of tract of NATHL. HILL, deceased. Lines: JAS. DICKEY,
THOROUGHFARE.

221.   16 June 1810. TANDY KEY, Albemarle, to JNO. E. FITZPATRICK...
       TANDY KEY in own right and attorney-in-fact for THOS., JNO.,
MARTIN, JOSHUA, WM. B. KEY, JNO. WHITE, JR. and wife, PATSY,
JOSIAH DANIEL and wife, ELIZ., WALTER and JAS. KEY--heirs of MARTIN
KEY, deceased, Albemarle. L250 333 acres by will.

222.   23 July 1810. DAVID S. GARLAND and wife, JANE H., Amherst
       County, to JNO. MARR...L100 666 acres Hatt Creek. Bought
from RO. ROSE, heir of COL. JNO. ROSE. Lines: HENRY ROSE, JNO.
CAMPBELL, deceased, JAS. MONTGOMERY, GEO. WILLIAMS.

222.   (Two such pages) Nelson Court, 1809 SHELTON CROSTHWAIT,
       JOS. SHELTON, WM. H. DIGGES, GEO. W. VARNUM, JNO. MOSBY,
appointed commissioners to lay off two acres for permanent site of
justice; SPOTSWOOD GARLAND, Clerk--done in Lovingston, 22 July
1810; near center; deed from JAS. LOVING--page 225--plat and
reference to 5:270. Public lot--off of Main Street--100 yards
square. GEO. W. VARNUM, Surveyor.

226.   26 July 1810. WM. LOVING and wife, SARAH, to RO. RIVES...to
       WM. LOVING, 2 October 1810. $1300 1797 acres south side
Rucker's Run and both sides of Bob's Creek. Lines: grantee, GEO.
LOVING, Spencer's road.

228.   2 May 1809. PETER CAMPBELL to WM H. DIGGES to secure JOS.
       LOVING...six shillings; slave; still; crops; stock. Witness:
SAML. EDMUNDS, JR.

230. 23 July 1810. Order to WM. H. DIGGES and JOS. LOVING...
      WM. EDMUNDS and wife, POLLY A., to JNO. JACOBS, 24 July 1809;
68 acres. Done, 24 July 1810.

232. 16 August 1810. JOS. SHELTON to JACOB YOST...$120; lot 31 in
      Lovingston. Lines: Front Street, DR. RO. KINCAID, Spring
Street, Pleasant Street. Witnesses: RO. J. KINCAID, WM. H. SHELTON,
THOS. COCKE.

233. 16 August 1810. JACOB YOST to WM. H. SHELTON to secure JOS.
      SHELTON...$1.00; lot above. Witnesses: JAS. and THOS. COCKE,
RO. KINCAID.

234. 21 August 1810. LEWIS DAVIS and wife, ELIZ., to JNO.
      CAMPBELL...to him, 24 July 1826--L405 200 acres; part of
former tract of THOS. PENN. Lines: Main Road, DR. HARE. Witnesses:
WILLIS H. WILLS, SAML. STAPLES, RO. FRANKLIN.

236. 30 April 1810. JNO. LOVING and wife, ELIZ., to WM. H.
      COLEMAN...to WM. H. DIGGES--no date--$400; headwaters of
Bob's Creek. Lines: Spencer's road, RO. RIVES, TERISHA TURNER,
WM. H. DIGGES, MATT. HARRIS, WM. LOVING--318 acres. Also tract on
same creek. Lines: MATT. HARRIS, HAWES COLEMAN, WM. H. DIGGES
205 acres. Witnesses: WM. WRIGHT, JOS. LOVING, WM. H. DIGGES,
WM. C. JOHNSON, RICH. PHILLIPS. Margin: page 239 item should be
here. WM. H. DIGGES and JOS. LOVING, Justices of the Peace.

239. 24 May 1810. ALEX. B. ROSE to RO. H. ROSE, Orange County, and
      HILL CARTER of Amherst County...$1.00; bond due CHAS. CLAY,
Bedford County; 2750 acres Roseisle; many slaves. Witnesses:
JNO. BRAIDY (? or BRIADY?), BENJ. H. MORGAN, JNO. MITCHELL, DAVID
MORGAN.

242. 27 August 1810. ANDREW MORGAN and wife, MARY, to THOS.
      MASSIE...$74 74 acres Tye; allotted to RO. ROSE, Fauquier,
as heir of COL. JNO. ROSE--The Commons; bought from RO. ROSE by
ANDREW MORGAN; ALEX. B. ROSE, THOS. FITZHUGH, PAT. and HENRY ROSE.
Witnesses: DAVID R. CLARKSON, RO. GARLAND, NATHAN CRAWFORD, LANDON
CABELL, BENJ. H. MORGAN.

244. 28 November 1809. PRESLEY RAINES to NATHL. OFFUTT and RO.
      FRANKLIN to secure MURPHY BROWN and Company, WM. C. JOHNSON,
JAS. SHIELDS, WM. WRIGHT, LEE W. HARRIS, EDWD. CARTER, WM. WATSON...
$1.00; stock; furniture. Witnesses: JESSE S. PROFFITT, JAS. MAYS,
JR., JAS. GREGORY.

246. 24 September 1810. THOS. CHILDRESS and wife, BETSY, to JAS.
      MURPHY and CHAS. CHRISTIAN to secure (?) them; $250; 230 acres
south Rockfish. Lines: CUTHBERT WEBB, THOS. JOPLING, deceased.
To CHAS. CHRISTIAN, 27 September 1810.

248. 8 August 1810. JNO. GRIFFIN to JOS. SHELTON...L5 south side
      main road from Loving's Gap to Rockfish; part of tract. Ten
acres. Lines: both, Three Chopt, SHEROD GRIFFIN. Witnesses:
WM. HARRIS, JR., JAS. MC ALEXANDER, JNO. B. FITZGERALD.

249. 25 September 1810. JNO. DILLARD and ASA VARNUM as to REBECCA
      THOMPSON, wife of JNO...9 November 1809, to DAVID S. GARLAND--
535 acres.

250. 17 October 1810. JNO. SYME and wife, NANCY (signed ANN J.),
      to ZACH NEVIL...$1500 south Rockfish; 412 acres. Bought from
CORNL. NEVIL and residence of late COL. JAS. NEVIL. Lines: JAS.
MURPHY, grantee, CHAS. YANCY, THOS. KEY, ELISHA PETERS, WM. DICKSON,
NORBORN THOMAS. Witnesses: NELSON ANDERSON, ELISHA PETERS, ELISHA
FORTUNE.

251.	20 September 1810.	STEPHEN WATTS to WM. LAWSON WATTS...five
	shillings.	130 acres north side and adjacent Buffaloe.
Lines:	HIGGINBOTHAM's road, grantor, JOS. SEAY, JAS. SEAY.	CHAS.
CHRISTIAN ran line in presence of JAS. and JOS. SEAY.

252.	29 December 1809.	JNO. HORSLEY, Campbell County, to GEO.
	HYLTON...to C. L. CHRISTIAN, 24 May 1813--L150 113 acres;
part of Rich Branch tract.	Witnesses:	MICAJAH PENDLETON, JNO.
LAVENDER, RO. HORSLEY, JESSE PAMPLIN.

253.	20 October 1810.	THOS. S. MC CLELLAND, trustee for CHAS.
	CLAY and ALEX. B. ROSE, Lynchburg, to GEO. CABELL, Lynchburg...
Two Deeds of Trust to THOS. S. MC CLELLAND, THOS. HIGGINBOTHAM, and
ARCHIBALD MAYS by ALEX. B. ROSE, 30 May 1808, and 3 November 1808;
sold fifth day this instant and CABELL bought at $12,700; Tye and
Hatt; 2530 acres.	Lines:	THOS. MASSIE, DAVID S. GARLAND, THOS.
FITZHUGH, HENRY ROSE, PHILIP RYAN.

254.	15 October 1810.	WM. SMALL and wife, SARAH, to DAVID WITT...
	L300 100 acres.	Lines:	MICHL. WOODS, THOS. FITZPATRICK,
NATHL. BRIDGWATER, grantee--where WM. SMALL lives.	Witnesses:
DAVID WITT, JR., BURGESS WITT, JNO. SMALL.

255.	22 October 1810.	JNO. BETHEL to SUSAN ELLIOT, natural
	daughter of my wife, MARY (formerly ELLIOT)...love and $100;
slave bought from JAS. MURPHY, stock, furniture, another slave.

256.	18 July 1810.	WM. H. DIGGES and ELIJAH MAYS to MARY
	STONEHAM...GEO. STONEHAM owed her from 14 May 1790; Deed of
Trust in Amherst County, 25 June 1801 or about that time--to
grantors; 150 acres where GEO. then lived.	Lines:	WM. H. DIGGES,
JOS. LOVING, MINOS WRIGHT, SAML. EDMUNDS, MOSES MAYS, AMBR.
CAMPBELL.	Sold, 7 October 1809; advertisement in Lynchburg Star;
MARY bought at L127-6-7.

257.	27 August 1810.	Order to Amherst Justices of the Peace:
	EDMD. T. COLEMAN and BENJ. TALIAFERRO as to ELIZ. MARTIN,
wife of MOSES, 1 March 1810, to DANL. MC DONALD for 261 acres...
done, 18 September 1810.

258.	26 May 1810.	JNO., SYLVANUS, WM., BENJ., JAS., POLLY, NICHL.
	MARTIN, a son of BETSY MARTIN, and REBECCA MARTIN, the mother,
to HUDSON MARTIN, JR...L164 100 acres; tract of STEPHEN MARTIN,
deceased, on Meriwether Branch.	Lines:	grantee, RO. HENDERSON,
CHAS. BRIDGWATER.	Witnesses:	THRUSTON J. DICKINSON, DAVID SIMS,
JR., JNO. R. MARTIN, REUBEN HULETT, SHEROD MARTIN, JR., RO. HENDERSON.

259.	22 Ocotber 1810.	ACHILLES WRIGHT and wife, NANCY, to WM.
	HARGROVE...L145 three adjacent tracts on Tye--385 acres where
ACHILLES WRIGHT lives.	Lines:	JOS. LOVING, SAML. EDMUNDS, WM.
CLASBY.	Witnesses: WM. H. DIGGES, JOS. LOVING, REUBEN BATES, PETER
CAMPBELL.	WM. H. DIGGES and JOS. LOVING, Justices of the Peace.

261.	25 September 1809.	NATHAN BARNETT to RO. FRANKLIN...to JAS.
	MURPHY, 14 October 1811, to secure MURPHY BROWN and Company.
Five shillings.	435 on Rockfish.	Lines:	JNO. E. FITZPATRICK,
JAS. WRIGHT, WM. WRIGHT, where NATHAN BARNETT lives and bought
from JAS. MC ALEXANDER.	Witnesses: CHAS. PERROW, ZACH NEVIL,
JAS. GREGORY, CHAS. EDMUNDS.

263.	16 November 1810.	WM. WARDER, Barren County, Kentucky,
	attorney-in-fact for BENJ. TEMPLE DICKINSON, same Kentucky
county, 19 June 1809, power given...$1100 to THURSTON J. DICKERSON
(sic); named slaves in hands of THURSTON J. DICKERSON.	Witnesses:
HUDSON MARTIN, NICHL. L. MARTIN.

264.	19 June 1809.	Power of attorney by BENJ. TEMPLE DICKINSON,
	Barren County, Kentucky, to WM. WARDER, same county...to collect
from THURSTON DICKERSON.	WM. LOGAN, Clerk.	HENRY MILLER, Justice of
the Peace.

265.   30 October 1810. Order to JESSE JOPLING and A. B. WARWICK...
       JNO. SYME and wife, ANN J., to ZACH NEVIL, 11 October 1810;
done 28 November 1810.

266.   22 September 1810. JANE RHEA and her son, ARCH. RHEA,
       Rockbridge, to RO. MC CORMACK...to him, 22 March 1811--L18
126 acres by survey of 22 December 1785--Blue Mountains on Pond
River; branch of Tye. Lines: JAS. TILFORD. Witnesses: EDMD.
TANKERSLEY, JNO. RHEA, WM. RHEA, RO. RHEA; November 5, 1810,
certified by A. REID, Rockbridge Clerk.

267.   17 September 1810. ANDREW MORGAN to RO. MC CORMACK, Rockbridge...
       $90 270 acres--head of Pond Run; north branch of north fork
Tye. Lines: ARCH RHEA, deceased, top of Blue Ridge. Witnesses:
as above.

268.   3 January 1811. ALEX. B. ROSE to ALEX. F. ROSE, Westmoreland...
       $4300; slaves. Witnesses: JNO. N. ROSE, JNO. BRADY, S.
GARLAND, GEO. YOST.

269.   20 October 1810. LEWIS MAYS and wife, LUCY, SARAH MAYS,
       widow of JOS. MAYS, to RO. MAYS...consideration: one slave
boy--interest in 385 acres by will of JOS. MAYS--to widow for life
and then to two sons, MOSES and LEWIS MAYS. Seven acres sold to
SPENCER and EDMUNDS. Witnesses: REUBEN BATES, CORNL. NEVIL,
PETER CAMPBELL, WM. H. DIGGES and JOS. LOVING, Justices of the
Peace (last two).

271.   1 Ocotber 1810. SAML. W. ANDERSON, SR., Albemarle, to SAML.
       BAILEY...$200 109 acres south side Buck Creek Mountain,
Hickory Creek. Lines: WM. MORRISON, deceased, RICH. HARE.
Witnesses: TERISHA BAILEY, THOS. and JNO. THURMOND.

272.   31 August 1818. ALEX. F. ROSE, executor of DR. HENRY ROSE,
       to JNO. NICHL. ROSE...DR. HENRY ROSE by FAIRFAX will directed
sale of Nelson County tracts; sold at ACH, 20 August 1810; subject
to dower; $4165; 1170 acres. Lines: ALEX. B. ROSE, PHILLIP RYAN,
RO. ROSE, JESSE CLARKSON, RO. ROSE, JNO. CAMPBELL, JNO. PANOCK--
Hatt Creek. Witnesses: L. CLARKSON, CHAS. R. ROSE, EDMD. LANIER,
CHAS. MOORE, ANDREW SKINNELL, WM. B. JACOBS, D. MC DONALD, JNO.
HIGHT, HENRY MASSIE, HENRY JACOBS, WM. W. CAMDEN.

273.   29 September 1810. JNO. NICHL. ROSE and wife, MARY, Amherst
       County, to ALEX. F. ROSE...$4165--to THOS. MASSIE, 26 March
1811--1170 acres Hatt. Witnesses: as above, subject to dower.

275.   2 January 1811. ALEX. F. ROSE and wife, MILDRED (middle
       name seems to be WASHINGTON), Westmoreland, to THOS. MASSIE...
$7005; part of tract of COL. JNO. ROSE--came to DR. HENRY ROSE by
descent--1401 acres. Lines: JONES, Hatt Creek, BIBEY. Witnesses:
as above.

276.   18 January 1811. JNO. MC ALEXANDER and wife, NANCY, to JACOB
       PUCKET...$600 137 acres south borders Davis Creek. Lines:
ALEX. MC ALEXANDER. Witnesses: HENRY BIBB, JR., GEO. W. VARNUM,
RO. KINCAID. VARNUM and ASA VARNUM, Justices of the Peace.

278.   15 January 1811. JNO. MC ALEXANDER and wife, NANCY, to JAS.
       MC ALEXANDER...to JAS., 4 November 1817--$100; Long Branch;
branch of north fork Davies Creek; 130 acres. Lines: grantor,
ALEX. MC ALEXANDER. Witnesses: GEO. W. VARNUM, HENRY T. HARRIS,
HENRY BIBB, JR. Justices of the Peace as above.

280.   25 January 1811. THOS. MASSIE and wife, SALLY, to WM. B.
       JACOBS...to W. W. MASSIE, executor of D. JACOBS, 25 July 1836--
L1180; Fairfield tract on Tye. 354 acres. Lines: JOS. BURGHER--
measured by REID. Witnesses: HENRY MASSIE, JNO. EUBANK, JNO.
JACOBS, PETER C. JACOBS, JAS. CLARKSON.

281. 28 January 1811. JAS. HUGHES and wife, JANE, to BENJ. HUGHES...
five shillings. Eighty acres. Lines: MOSES HUGHES, grantor.

282. 9 August 1808. SAML. W. ANDERSON, Albemarle, to his son,
JNO. ANDERSON...love and $1.00; 120 acres on Hickory Creek.
Patent, 10 July 1802, to SAML. W. ANDERSON. Lines: PERRIN FARRAR,
deceased, GEO. BLAIN, SAML. S. ANDERSON, JNO. BAILEY, SAML. PERKINS.
Witnesses: JAS. LYON, THOS. THURMOND, TERISHA BAILEY.

283. 5 November 1810. NATHAN CRAWFORD to RO. DINWIDDIE...to
MICHL. WOOD, 7 May 1812--L5 130 acres north borders south fork
Rockfish; part of 230 acre patent to NATHAN CRAWFORD, 18 July 1798.
Lines: JAS. FLACK, SAML. DINWIDDIE, deceased, grantee. Witnesses:
AARON H. MORRISON, MOSES FITZPATRICK, NELSON CRAWFORD.

284. 5 November 1810. RO. DINWIDDIE and wife, ANNE, to MICHL.
WOODS...margin as above--L1000 610 acres borders of south
fork Rockfish--various deeds and some from father, RO., by will.
Lines: NATHAN CRAWFORD, down the mountain, REV. WM. CRAWFORD,
JAS. MORRISON, deceased, ANNE DINWIDDIE, tract bought from JAS.
HUNDLEY, tract bought from NATHAN CRAWFORD--all in Nelson. Witnesses:
AARON H. MORRISON, MOSES FITZPATRICK, NELSON CRAWFORD, JOS.
MONTGOMERY. NATHAN CRAWFORD and HUDSON MARTIN, JR., Justices of
the Peace.

287. 28 August 1810. JESSE CLARKSON, 1; JAS. CLARKSON, Albemarle, 2;
JNO. EUBANK, HUDSON MARTIN, JR. and JNO. M. MARTIN, 3...to
JAS. CLARKSON, 21 November 1817--$1.00; slaves. Witnesses: JAS. P.
GARLAND, JNO. BARNETT, HUDSON M. GARLAND.

288. 22 January 1811. JAS. THOMPSON to JAS. STEVENS, JR. and
SPOTSWOOD GARLAND for benefit of wife and children...six
shillings; slaves; stock; furniture--wife, ELIZ. Witnesses:
THOS. JOPLING, MOLLY JOPLING, MARIAH DAVIS.

290. 15 September 1810. HENRY CAMPBELL to LANDON CABELL to secure
WM. B. HARE...$1.00; tract where HENRY CAMPBELL lives and
bought from HARE in 1803; slaves. Witnesses: SAML. W. D. REID,
THOS. HARVIE, JAS. THOMPSON.

291. 27 November 1810. JESSE JOPLING and JAS. MURPHY, overseers
of the poor, to WM. MURREL...order of 26 February 1810, to
bind out poor boy, JAS. MC QUEEN; parents can't support him;
until 21; also joins trade.

293. 7 October 1810. THOS. S. MC CLELLAND to ALEX. B. ROSE...
Deed of Trust to secure CHAS. CLAY--Rose Isle--slaves in
Deed of Trust to THOS. S. MC CLELLAND, THOS. HIGGINBOTHAM and
ARCH. MAYS: TAYLOR versus ROSE--Staunton Chancy. Witnesses:
CHAS. HOYLE, CABL. JONES.

293. 20 August 1810. JESSE ALLEN and wife, NANCY, Buckingham,
to MICAJAH PENDLETON...$1144 208 acres north borders Elk
Island Creek. Lines: RICH. WOOD, WM. JOURDAN, DAVID ROSS, CHAS.
CHRISTIAN, grantee. Witnesses: WM. H. DIGGES, R. PHILLIPS, DAVID G.
DAVIDSON, ABRAHAM STRATTON. Buckingham Justices of the Peace--not
named.

295. 17 Ocotber 1810. ROD. MC CULLOCH, surviving executor of
WM. HORSLEY, Amherst County, to WM. HORSLEY...by will to
sell--L221-5 300 acres on James; patent 20 July 1780. Lines:
JNO. HORSLEY, JAS. FREELAND, deceased, GEO. HYLTON, WM. HORSLEY,
deceased. Also 250 acre patent 20 July 1780. Lines: same as
above--save for JNO. HORSLEY. Witnesses: JNO. HORSLEY, SR. and
JR., LEWIS TINDALL, JOS. HORSLEY, N. C. HORSLEY, R. W. CHICK.

298. 2 August 1810. JAS. WOOD, Amherst County, to ELIJAH STATON...
L150 200 acres south fork Rockfish. Lines: ELISHA PETERS,
JNO. FARIS. Witnesses: THOS. CHILDRESS, JNO. DICKSON, SAML.
WOOD, DANL. MC COY.

299. 1 September 1810. JAS. STEWART, JR. to RO. RIVES and JAS.
MURPHY...$1000 and $1.00; 600 acres. Lines: SPOTSWOOD
GARLAND, WM. VAUGHAN--where JAS. STEWART lives. Witnesses: RO.
FRANKLIN, JNO. RYAN, CHAS. WATTS, JAS. DILLARD.

300. 4 January 1811. RO. JONES, Orange County, to THOS. JONES,
Nelson, to secure CHAS. JONES, GEO. WILLIAMS and JAS.
MONTGOMERY...$1.00 1100 acres where THOS. JONES lives. Witnesses:
JAS. HAMNER, JAS. SUDDARTH, BENJ. FITZGERALD.

302. -- February 1811. ZACH NEVIL and wife, NANCY, to JAS.
MURPHY...L250 151 acres south side Rockfish branch. Lines:
grantor, the road, WM. H. CABELL, JAS. MURPHY.

304. 25 February 1811. PATRICK ROSE to CHRISTIAN FLOYD, about
thirty and daughter of SARAH FLOYD...freedom. Witnesses:
C. P. TALIAFERRO, JNO. N. ROSE.

305. 25 March 1811. RICH. BREEDLOVE and wife, MILLY, to ELISHA
PETERS...$200 100 acres, branches south fork Rockfish--part
of former tract of HENRY KEY and conveyed to MILLY KEY.

306. 1 March 1811. JESSE SAVIDGE to RO. FRANKLIN and ZACH FORTUNE
to secure EDDY. (?) FORTUNE and JNO. SAVIDGE, JR...$1.00;
slave; furniture; stock. Witnesses: RO. H. ANDERSON, RANDOLPH
PROFIT, ROWLAND PROFIT.

307. 7 September 1810. PETER RIPPETOE and wife, SARAH, to JAS.
CLARKSON...L291-1-4 south side Cub; north border of Tye;
280 acres. Lines: STEWART (?) heirs, NICHOLAS, DANL. MC DANIEL.
Witnesses: DANL. MC DONALD, WM. HILL, JR., DAVID S. GARLAND,
BENJ. FITZGERALD, PETER CLARKSON, PETER RIPPETOE, JR.

309. 17 October 1810. ROD. MC CULLOCH, surviving executor of
WM. HORSLEY, Amherst County, to JAS. LYLE, Chesterfield and
town of Manchester...to TARLTON SAUNDERS, agent for LYLE's administrator, 30 December 1820--L162--LYLE as agent of HENDERSON MC CAUL
and Company and FLIPPEN and Company--headborders Mobley Creek;
south borders Owen; patent 22 June 1789. Lines: WM. HORSLEY,
deceased, JOS. MIGGINSON, GEO. HILTON, JAS. FREELAND, deceased,
Migginson's road. Witnesses: N. C. HORSLEY, R. W. CLICK, JNO.
HORSLEY, JR., WM. HORSLEY.

310. 25 March 1811. NICHL. HORSLEY to GEO. HYLTON...L150 113 acres;
part of Rich Branch tract. Lines: grantee, WM., RO. and
JNO. HORSLEY.

311. 25 March 1811. JAS. WILLS, SR. and wife, MILDRED, to JAS.
WILLS, JR., their son...love and $1.00; 200 acres borders
Rucker's Run. Lines: ZACH FORTUNE, JAS. STEVENS, where JR. lives
and has deeded to RO. FRANKLIN and NATHL. OFFUTT in Deed of Trust.

312. 26 March 1811. HUDSON MARTIN, JR. and wife, MARY ANN, to
JNO. N. DICKINSON...to T. J. DICKINSON, 24 May 1816--$5.00;
300 acres; survey of 18 April 1768--Meriwether's Branch of Rockfish.
Lines: JAS. MARTIN, JR. Granted to RO. JOHNSON by patent,
14 July 1780.

314. 25 March 1811. JESSE JOPLING and JAS. MURPHY, Overseers of
the Poor, to WM. HALL, Amherst County...to bind out bastard
boy, WILLIS WILLIAMS, son of DEBORAH WILLIAMS, who can't support
him--sixteen years old--until 21; to learn trade of a hatter.

315.	23 September 1810.	PHILLIP RYON to son, SAML. RYON...love
	and $1.00; fifty acres Cook Creek. Lines: NICHL. MORAN,
deceased, JAS. TILFORD, deceased--taken up by DR. MC LAIN--secured
to me by patent. Witnesses: JNO. STEWART, GEO. RULEY, SAML.
STEVENS.

316.	23 February 1811.	WM. W. RICHARDSON and wife, NANCY D.,
	Hanover, to JAS. DOSWELL, Hanover...$1.00; one-fourth of
tract on Tye; devised by THOMAS DOSWELL, deceased, by will to
daughter, MARY DOSWELL, and by her transferred to daughter, NANCY D.
THILMAN, now RICHARDSON--deed of gift--197¼ acres. Witnesses:
THOS. DOSWELL, CHAS. B. PICKETT, WM. ELLIS. Hanover, 5 March 1811,
proved. WM. POLLARD, Clerk.

317.	15 October 1810.	JNO. GRIFFIN to WILSON CARY NICHOLAS,
	Albemarle...to H. GRIFFIN, 24 February 1817--$1.00; 430 acres
south side Rockfish. Lines: JOS. SHELTON, JOS. PHILLIPS, MATT.
HARRIS, deceased--where he lives--possessed on 26 July 1806;
except tract sold (?0 : south side road from MATT. HARRIS' ford
to Nelson Courthouse. Witnesses: WM. H. SHELTON, HARRISON GRIFFIN,
BENJ. CHILDERS.

318.	22 April 1811.	HUDSON MARTIN, JR. and wife, MARY ANN, to
	JAS. LOBAN...to him, 26 May 1817--$800 114 acres. Lines:
EDWD. COLE, the border, the river, WM. SUDDARTH, AZARIAH MARTIN,
CHAS. BRIDGWATER, grantor.

319.	18 April 1811.	AZARIAH MARTIN and wife, POLLY, to HUDSON
	MARTIN, JR...$250 35 acres. Lines: road, CHAS. BRIDGWATER,
grantee, SHEROD MARTIN. Witnesses: JAS. LOBBAN, WM. FARRAR,
LARKIN MILLER, JOS. TOMES.

320.	22 April 1811.	SAML. PERKINS and wife, FRANCES, to JNO.
	ROBERTS...$35 two tracts on Hickory; border of Rockfish.
Part of tract patent to JNO. FARRAR 56 acres. 1. Twenty acres.
Lines: grantor, JOSIAH CHEATHAM. 2. Thirty-six acres. Lines:
RICH. HARE, grantee.

322.	24 May 1810.	JAS. LOVING, 1; CHAS. PERROW, 2; JAS. LOVING,
	JR. and THOS. E. FORTUNE, 3...$1.00; tract devised to him
by father, JNO. LOVING, deceased. South side Loving's Gap; reference
to Amherst County court; slaves; stock. Witnesses: RO. KINCAILD,
NATHAN BARNETT, JNO. MATTHEWS.

324.	18 January 1811.	JOS. SMITH and wife, PATIENCE, to REUBEN T.
	MITCHELL...to REUBEN T. MITCHELL, 28 April 1812--$500 340 acres
Rockfish. Lines: WM. SMITH, SAML. H. SCRUGGS, Tripple Fall Creek,
FIELD SMITH, DAVID S. GARLAND, JNO. SHEPHERD, WM. HIBBS. Witnesses:
JNO. SHEPHERD, JANE MURRELL, SR. and JR.

325.	29 May 1811.	WM. WRIGHT to NATHAN BARNETT...Ten dollars per
	acre for 91 acres. South border of south fork Davies Creek.
Lines: WM. FORBUS, grantee, HENRY DAWSON, JNO. E. FITZPATRICK,
JOS. SHELTON, grantor. Witnesses: WM. DOUGLASS, WM. TERRY, HENRY
DAWSON.

326.	29 May 1811.	NATHAN BARNETT to WM. DOUGLASS, Albemarle, and
	town of Warren to FLEMING GARLAND, 25 January 1813...to secure
THOS. WHITE, Richmond. $1.00 two tracts on Rockfish. 1. Bought
from WM. WRIGHT 91 acres. Lines: JOS. SHELTON, grantor's residence.
2. Bought from WM. FORBUS twenty acres; adjacent 1. Witness:
JNO. M. MARTIN.

328.	26 March 1811.	LANDON CABELL and ABRAHAM B. WARWICK as to
	RICH. BREEDLOVE and wife, MILLY, 25 March 1811...to ELISHA
PETERS--100 acres.

329.   18 December 1810.   PARMENAS BRYANT to WM. H. DIGGES...to
       WM. H. DIGGES, 21 February 1812--to secure creditors; one
WM. C. JOHNSON; $1.00; slaves--three.

330.   25 January 1809.   JOS. W. HENDRICK and wife, MARY D., Hanover,
       to JAMES DOSWELL, Hanover...$1.00; headborders Tye in Amherst
County (sic) one-fourth interest; devised by will of THOS. DOSWELL,
Hanover, to daughter, MARY DOSWELL, and she transferred to us by
deed of gift--497¼ acres by Council survey.   Hanover, 25 January
1809; WM. POLLARD, Clerk.

331.   20 April 1811.   Order to JNO. POLL and JONATHAN CLARK, Barren
       County, Kentucky, Justices of the Peace, as to JOS. W.
HENDRICK's wife, MARY D., as to deed above; done, 11 May 1811;
WM. LOGAN, Clerk in Kentucky County; THOS. DICKINSON, first Justice
of the Peace; recorded Nelson, 24 June 1811.

334.   24 June 1811.   WM. DAVIS and wife, BETSY, formerly GOODE,
       Bath County, to DAVID S. GARLAND...L9; one-ninth of 133 acres;
north side Piney and adjacent; tract of DANIEL GOODE, SR.; patent
1 June 1782; BETSY is an heir.   Acknowledged in Nelson.

334.   24 June 1811.   JNO. MATTHEWS and wife, MARY ANN, to REUBEN
       MARTIN, Albemarle...L550; 200 acres both sides Dutch Creek.
Lines: WM. BAILEY, JNO. JOPLING, WM. DICTION (?), JNO. WATKINS.
Witnesses: DUNMORE DAMERON, JNO. MATTHEWS, JR., TANDY PASSON (?).

335.   8 May 1811.   JAS. LYLE, Manchester, sur. partner of HENDERSON
       MC CAUL and Company, to WM. CLASBY...to WM. CLASBY by STEPHEN
WATTS, 27 August 1811--L99-5-5; 200 acres Tye.   Lines: ARTHUR
ROBINSON, WM. TYREE.   Bought by -- GATEWOOD from THOS. WILTSHIRE;
reference to GATEWOOD's deed to ALEX. STEWART and by ALEX. STEWART
to LYLE.   Witnesses: JNO. P. SCRUGGS, CHAS. C. PATTERSON, DAVID
HUNTER, JR.

337.   22 June 1811.   WM. SMITH, overseer, to DAVID S. GARLAND...
       six shillings; debt due; beds; crops; fowles (sic) on GARLAND's
plantation.   Witness: WILLIS BROWN.

338.   31 December 1810.   SAML. P. LAYNE and wife, NANCY, to JNO.
       PAMPLIN...L60 72½ acres.   Witnesses: WM. WOOD, ALEX. and
RICH. WOOD.

339.   22 June 1811.   ABRAHAM B. WARWICK to ELISHA PETERS...L7
       Rucker's Run on Fenley's Mt., part of tract patent to
ABRAHAM B. WARWICK and ELISHA PETERS, assignee.   Lines: RICH.
MURRY, grantee, HECTOR CABELL, the road, grantor, DANL. MC COY.

340.   12 June 1811.   NATHAN BARNETT to JOS. SHELTON, HENRY T. HARRIS
       and RO. FRANKLIN...to secure debtors; $1.00; 435 acres.
Lines: JNO. E. FITZPATRICK, JNO. MILTON, JNO. WRIGHT, PETER MARTIN,
COL. JOS. SHELTON--where NATHAN BARNETT lives and bought from JAS.
MC ALEXANDER; slaves; interest in estate of MATT. HARRIS, deceased.

342.   20 July 1811.   MARTHA JOHNSON to son, JNO. H. JOHNSON...stock,
       furniture.   Witnesses: DAVID HUNTER, BENJ. JOHNSON (?).

342.   25 June 1810.   JNO., ANN, NELSON, CHAS. PHILLIPS, SUSANNA
       STATHAM, POLLY JOHNSON, to WM. DAWSON...$500; 119 acres in
two adjacent tracts 78 acres and 41 acres.   Lines: MATT. PHILLIPS,
MATT. HARRIS, DANL. MOSBY--as heirs of MATT. PHILLIPS.   Signed
also by THOS. STATHAM and RO. JOHNSTON (sic).

344.   -- July 1811.   ZACH NEVIL and ABRAHAM B. WARWICK to ELISHA
       PETERS...by court order they advertised lands of RICH. MURROW,
deceased, and sold on seventeenth instant to ELISHA PETERS at $230.22.

345. 1 April 1811. Plat: order to set aside dower of SARAH
       BALL, widow of WM. BALL...dwelling house and 200 acres where
WM. BALL resided. CHAS. CHRISTIAN, surveyor. JAS. MURPHY, ZACH
NEVIL, NELSON ANDERSON, committee. Plat shows lines of JESSE
JOPLING, mouth of Shop Branch, Briney Branch.

346. 1 July 1811. ALEX. WRIGHT to JNO. WRIGHT to secure JAS.
       WRIGHT...$1.00; stock. Witnesses: ABRAHAM SEAY, JR., HENRY
BIBB, JR., THOS. WILSON.

347. 15 August 1811. FRANCIS W. S. TURNER to JOS. C. CABELL...
       $104.50 near Warminster and joins grantee on northeast; plat
by RO. SHIELDS--to JOS. C. CABELL, 24 July 1820. Lines: both,
Fluvanna River--17½ acres. Witnesses: RO. SHIELDS, JAS. VIGUS,
JR., W. C. MAUPIN, WM. J. ROBERTSON. Plat.

349. 21 March 1811. RICHARDSON ALPHIN to RO. FRANKLIN and FRED.
       CABELL to secure JAS. GREGORY...$1.00; slave boy about two
years old, TOM. Witnesses: RO. W. CARTER, CHAS. C. PATTERSON,
ELIJAH STATON.

350. 24 August 1811. RO. RIVES to ELISHA PETERS...L6 eight acres
       Joe's Creek. Lines: grantee, a branch.

351. 26 August 1811. THOS. MASSIE, JOS. SHELTON, RO. RIVES,
       GEO. W. VARNUM, JNO. DILLARD, RO. KINCAID, JNO. HARRIS,
JOS. ROBERTS, surviving trustees of Lovingston, to SOLOMON MATTHEWS...
lot 33; 76 yards by 32 yards north of Main; west by Spring Street;
south by lot 34; east by Front Street. L21.

353. 16 August 1811. WM. HORSLEY, MICAJAH PENDLETON and wife,
       MARY, JOS. and RO. HORSLEY, RICH. PHILLIPS and wife, MARTHA,
JNO. HORSLEY, JR. and NICHL. C. HORSLEY to JUDITH HORSLEY...love
and $1.00; slave, JEFF. Witnesses: WM. L. BELL, DAVID G. DAVIDSON,
WM. SHEREMAN.

354. 26 March 1811. Order to Amherst County Justices of the Peace
       as to JOHN NICHL. ROSE and wife, MARY, 29 September 1810, to
ALEX. F. ROSE...117 acres; done by DAVID S. GARLAND and HILL CARTER,
26 August 1811.

355. 4 June 1811. Wilkes County, Georgia--certified that ASA
       VARNUM of Virginia married ANNA MOORE, Wilkes County, Georgia,
and she owned twelve named slaves and ages...A. LIPHAM, GEO. JOHNSON,
HOLEMAN FREEMAN, Justices of the Peace. JNO. HALEDAY, Clerk.

356. 5 August 1811. JNO. MITCHELL to his son, ARCELAUS MITCHELL...
       $100; crops. Witnesses: S. and JAS. GARLAND, JR.

357. 27 February 1811. JAS. WILLS, JR. to ABRAHAM B. WARWICK and
       JNO. WILLS...$1.00 to secure debts; slave; stock; furniture.
Witnesses: VINCENT MARKS, GEO. BUTLER, JNO. BUTLER.

358. 16 August 1811. JNO. HORSLEY, JR. to WM. HORSLEY...L600;
       one-third interest in 200 acres devised by WM. HORSLEY to
six sons--River tract; one-third devised by RO. HORSLEY to WM. HORSLEY,
deceased; one-third of adjacent tract of sixty acres--Rich Br.
tract. Witnesses: BENJ. POWELL, JR., DRURY BELL, JOS. HORSLEY,
WM. BELL.

359. 28 October 1811. HUDSON MARTIN, JR. to JOS. HAWKINS,
       Lexington, Kentucky...power of attorney as to wife of MARTIN--
MARY ANN, who owns Kentucky land; she is daughter of EDWD. HAWKINS,
deceased. May sell tract.

360. 23 September 1811. JESSE JOPLING and JAS. MURPHY, overseers
       of the Poor, to JACOB YOST...bind out JAS. BRYANT, a poor boy;
son of NANCY, who can't support him; age of -- until 21; wagon maker
trade.

361. 4 September 1811. JNO. TOOLEY and wife, MILLEY, to WM. WOOD...
       L120 100 acres. Lines: WM. LEE HARRIS, CLOUGH SHELTON,
deceased, grantee. Witnesses: WM. LEE HARRIS, POLLY N. HARRIS,
LEE W. HARRIS, SAML. WOOD, WM. PERRY, MATT. HARRIS. Dower relinquished,
28 October 1811. WM. HARRIS and JNO. DIGGES, Justices of the Peace.

363. 18 September 1811. SAML. EDMONDS, SR. to granddaughter,
       SAMARIA LEWIS NEVIL, and grandson, SAML. EDMONDS NEVIL,
children of CORNL. and ALICE NEVIL...when of age; slaves. Witnesses:
JEFF. S. (L) EDMONDS, SAML. EDMONDS, JR., JAS. SWINNEY, WM. WRIGHT.

364. 24 August 1811. SAML. ARRINGTON to his children: WOODROW,
       SAML. L., POLLY, ELIZ. and WILLIS ARRINGTON...love and $5.00;
slaves to each one--names and ages. Witnesses: WM. and SHADRICK
CARTER.

365. 10 October 1811. CORNL. NEVIL to RO. FRANKLIN and NATH.
       OFFUTT...$1.00--slave boy about 15. Witnesses: JEFF. L.
EDMONDS, THOS. BIBB, SR., REUBEN BATES.

366. 11 August 1811. BENJ. POWELL to ABRAHAM POWELL, Bedford
       County...L150 interest in estate of BENJ. POWELL's father,
LUCAS POWELL, by will--if he dies intestate. Witnesses: S. GARLAND,
JAS. GARLAND, JR., CHAS. PERROW.

367. 17 September 1810. ANDREW MORGAN to JABETH DAVIS...$100 130
       acres on Blue Ridge; head borders north fork Tye. Lines:
DAVID TILFORD, DOWLES and DRUMMOND, TILFORD's mill. Conveyed by
ARCH. RHEA, 8 April 1798. Witnesses: EDMD. TANKERSLEY, JNO.,
WM. and RO. RHEA.

369. 9 October 1811. JAS. THOMSON and wife, WINIFRED, to WM. B.
       HARE...$400 100 acres. Lines: PHILIP DAVIS--where he lives;
bought from EBENEZER HAYCOCK. Witnesses: SOL. DAY, THOS. HARVIE,
BENJ. HARE, JAS. KNIGHT.

370. 28 October 1811. JNO. MORRISON and wife, POLLY, to ZACH.
       ROBERTS...$126 twenty-one acres. Lines: both, main road,
branch below, ZACH. ROBERT's dwelling house.

370. 25 October 1811. JAS. LOVING, JR. and wife, NANCY, to
       GEO. W. VARNUM...$399.84 headborders Rucker's Run--part of
town of Lovingston. Lines: northwest corner lot 33 at Spring
Street, across (sic) Mt., JAS. STEVENS, SR., JAS. LOVING, SR.,
main road from Lovingston to Loving's Gap--six lots--52 acres.
W. S. GARLAND, HENRY BIBB, JR., SAML. LEAKE, RO. J. KINCAID.

372. 28 October 1811. WM. HARRIS, 1; BENJ. HARRIS, 2; HARRISON
       GRIFFIN, 3...to HARRISON GRIFFIN 20 July 1821; L25-13-10;
crops; furniture.

374. 28 October 1811. JOS. SHELTON and GEO. W. VARNUM as to FANNY
       FITZPATRICK, wife of WM., to MOSES HUGHES, SR., 9 January
1810; order to quiz SARAH CLARKSON, wife of JAS., too.

375. 12 October 1811. JAS. WILLS, JR. to GEO. W. VARNUM and JAS.
       GARLAND, JR...to secure HENRY BIBB, JR.; $1.00; 154 acres.
Lines: grantor, JAS. STEVENS, SR., JAS. THOMPSON, deceased, JAS.
WILLS, SR., bought from JNO. SEAY. Witnesses: CHAS. PERROW,
DANL. PERROW, W. B. TYLER, JAS. S. PENN.

376. 22 October 1811. JOSIAH SMITH to HUDSON MARTIN to secure
       JOS. TOMS...HUDSON MARTIN as trustee of WM. WOODS, 11 March
1811, to secure JOSIAH SMITH on debt due WM. WOODS--100 acres.
Bought by SMITH from WOODS, Rockfish. Devised to JOSIAH SMITH by
father--north side. Lines: AUGUSTINE SMITH, JOS. TOMS, HENRY
MC LEAN. Paid and released. Witnesses: JNO. M. MARTIN, SAML.
HOLCOMB, E. S. WARE.

128

377. 22 April 1806. OBADIAH MARTIN, JR. and wife, ELIZ., to
     HUDSON MARTIN, JR...L414-14 207½ acres Meriwether's Branch
of Rockfish--formerly that of JNO. MARTIN, deceased, and given by
him to son, OBADIAH. OBADIAH MARTIN sold to JNO. MARTIN, deceased,
father of OBADIAH MARTIN, JR. who died intestate. Lines: JNO.
COLES, GIDEON and GEORGE MARTIN. Witnesses: REUBEN HARLOW, STEPHEN
MARTIN, SYLVANUS MARTIN, NATHL. HARLOW, JR., NATHAN CRAWFORD, HUDSON
MARTIN--last two as Justices of the Peace as to ELIZ., 17 October
1806. Lincoln County, Kentucky, acknowledged by OBADIAH MARTIN
and wife--THOS. MONTGOMERY, Clerk. Recorded in Kentucky, 19 December
1810; HERBERT KING, Justice of the Peace.

381. 30 April 1811. EDDY FORTUNE to RO. FRANKLIN and NATHL.
     OFFUTT...$1.00 slave and children; stock. Witnesses:
RO. W. CARTER, ROWLAND PROFFITT, FLEMING EDMUNDS.

382. 26 March 1811. Order to WM. S. STONE, DABNEY HERNDON and
     THOS. GOODWIN (GOODRUM), Fredericksburg Justices of the
Peace, as to ALEX. F. ROSE and wife, MILDRED, W., 2 January 1811,
to THOS. MASSIE...1401 acres. Done by first two, 29 August 1811.

383. 10 May 1811. ANN W. ROSE, Westmoreland, to ALEX. F. ROSE,
     same county...she is entitled to dower in Nelson tract of
DR. HENRY ROSE, Fairfax County, her deceased husband--descended to
husband from COL. JNO. ROSE of Roseisle--$800 for interest.
Witnesses: DANL. CARMICHAEL, HENRY GERALD LETNZ, JNO. STARKE.
JNO. FOX, Clerk.

384. 27 November 1811. RODERICK L. TALIAFERRO and wife, ELIZA C.,
     to SPOTSWOOD GARLAND...$900 Rucker's Run; bought from JAS.
LOVING, JR. and WM. VAUGHAN and wife, 25 June 1810. Surveyed by
CAPT. GEO. W. VARNUM; eighty acres. Lines: JAS. LOVING, old
road, CHAS. PURVIS, JAS. STEVENS, JR., main road, along tract bought
by SPOTSWOOD GARLAND from JAS. STEVENS. Witnesses: GEO. W. VARNUM.

386. 23 December 1811. HENRY T. HARRIS and RO. FRANKLIN, trustee
     of JNO. and BENJ. HARRIS, MURPHY BROWN and Company, NATHAN
BARNETT to JNO. HARRIS, Albemarle...Deed of Trust by BARNETT to
HENRY T. HARRIS and RO. FRANKLIN, to secure BROWN and Company--
bond to ABRAHAM MARTIN; deed of 12 June 1811; sale to HENRY T.
HARRIS and RO. FRANKLIN, 28 October 1811; JAS. MURPHY bought at
$1200 and consents for NATHAN BARNETT to sell to secure MURPHY.
JNO. HARRIS agrees to buy at $1000; 435 acres. Lines: JNO. E.
FITZPATRICK, JNO. MELTON, JOS. SHELTON. Bought by county from
JAS. MC ALEXANDER and where NATHAN BARNETT lives.

387. 23 October 1811. JANE GARLAND, Albemarle, to SAML. HOLCOMB...
     L30 two tracts on south borders north fork Rockfish. Sixty
acres and forty acres adjacent. Lines: SAML. FOX, JNO. N. DICKERSON,
ROBT. HENDERSON. Witnesses: JNO. TOMBS, JOS. TOMBS, RO. BROOKS.

388. 20 September 1811. JACOB KINNEY, Augusta, and JAS. HAYS,
     Albemarle, executors of JAS. FLOOD or FLACK (?) to JOS.
TOMBS...L100 100 acres north borders Rockfish. Lines: HENRY
MC CLAIN, grantee, AUG. SMITH, JNO. TOMBS. Witnesses: RO. BROOKS,
JNO. TOMBS, C. YANCY, SAML. HOLCOMB.

389. 24 June 1810. JNO. BETHEL and wife, JANE, BENJ. HARRIS and
     wife, MARY, Albemarle, to JNO. WALTERS...$7.50 per acre;
112 acres Taylor Creek, border of Rockfish. Part of tract of
COL. CHISWELL. Lines: THOS. ROBERTSON, WM. SMITH.

390. 16 December 1811. GEO. YOST and wife, PEGGY, to SAML.
     MC CALEB...$210 lot 30 Lovingston. Lines: lots 31 and 29--
half acre. Witnesses: HENRY BIBB, JR., CHAS. PERROW, HUDSON MARTIN,
JR., JAS. S. PENN.

391. 16 December 1811. SAML. MC CALEB to RO. J. KINCAID and
      CHAS. PERROW to secure HENRY BIBB, JR...$1.00 Lovingston lot
bought from GEO. YOST. Witnesses: GEO. YOST, HUDSON MARTIN, JR.,
JAS. S. PENN.

392. 23 December 1811. BENJ. HARRIS and wife, MARY, Albemarle,
      to WM. SMITH...L204 68 acres east Rockfish and Taylor Creeks.
Lines: THOS. ROBERTSON, EDWD. COLES, WM. B. HARRIS.

394. 23 December 1811. PHILIP RYAN, SR. to WM. RYAN...love and
      $1.00 200 acres south borders Hat. Lines: THOS. JONES,
THOS. MASSIE, GEO. CABELL--occupied by PHILIP RYAN, SR. Witnesses:
JNO. THOMPSON, JR., JNO. HENDERSON, SAML. MC CALEB.

394. 9 December 1811. JAS. LOVING, JR. to SAML. MC CALEB...$30;
      lots 7 and 8 in Lovingston. Witness: CHAS. PERROW.

395. 22 December 1811. JOEL PONTON to JNO. SEAY...$20 two acres
      Rucker's Run. Lines: ABRAHAM SEAY, SR. Witness: CHAS.
PERROW.

396. 29 October 1811. DAVID BROWN to CHAS. PERROW...to SOLOMON
      MATTHEWS, 17 November 1812--to secure SOL. MATTHEWS $1.00;
stock; furniture--may sell at the Tavern in Lovingston. Witnesses:
ROD. L. TALIAFERRO, JAS. GARLAND, JAS. S. PENN, S. GARLAND.

397. 15 July 1811. JAS. CLARKE, deceased, married SARAH FITZPATRICK,
      daughter of WM. FITZPATRICK, and she had title to one-eighth
or Rockfish tract. CLARKE sold to MOSES HUGHES and died before
SARAH relinquished dower as heir of WM. FITZPATRICK, deceased.
Certified in Shelby County, Kentucky: WM. TAYLOR and OBADIAH CLARKE,
Justices of the Peace. JAS. CRAIG, Clerk. JACOB CASTLEMAN,
Presiding Justice of the Peacd. Note: Many years ago I released
the index to the Sixth Edition of Perrin, Battle and Kniffin--
History of Kentucky--which covers Shelby County, Kentucky (where I
was reared). I see a number of CLARKS in the index, but have not
looked them up at this time. I note that two CLARK women married
into MEEKS and SMOOT families and both are found in Amherst and
Nelson Counties. GEO. WILLIS' History of Shelby County, Kentucky
lists a JNO. CLARKE in the first will book and four make CLARK or
CLARKES in early marriages. Several CLARKS also show in his early
tax lists, but a quick glance reveals no FITZPATRICKS. I had a
CLARK family in my first Shelby County church at Clay Village and
one of them, LESTER CLARK, was a deacon. His sister, SARAH, was
in my 1925 high school class at Shelbyville High School.

398. 22 November 1811. JANE FITZPATRICK, wife of JNO., relinquished
      dower to one-eighth of Rockfish tract to MOSES HUGHES. She
was in Pulaski County, Kentucky: FRANCIS CLARKE and JOS. PORTER,
Justices of the Peace. WM. FOX, Clerk; JNO. NEWBY, Presiding
Justice of the Peace.

399. 19 December 1811. JNO. LOVING and wife, ELIZ., to JAS. SEAY...
      L159-12 133 acres north side and joining Buff. Lines: mouth
of Raven Creek, Higginbotham's road. Witnesses: CHAS. L. CHRISTIAN,
STEPHEN WATTS, WM. H. DIGGES, JAS. LOVING, SOL. MATTHEWS, JAS.
STEVENS, JR., S. GARLAND. Dower relinquished to JOS. LOVING and
WM. H. DIGGES, 15 February 1812.

401. 28 May 1811. Order to GEO. W. VARNUM and WM. HEMPLEY...JAS.
      PAMPLIN and wife, MARY, and RACHEL PAMPLIN, 6 January 1810,
to MARY B. DRUMMOND. Done as to MARY, 7 October 1811.

402. 5 August 1811. JOS. SHELTON to WM. H. SHELTON, his son, to
      CLOUGH SHELTON, 3 December 1821...$1.00; 197 acres on Davis
Creek; bought from WM. BONES. Lines: JAS. WRIGHT, NATHAN BARNETT,
grantor.

403. 20 August 1811. JAS. LIVELY and wife, KETURAH, to STEPHEN
CAMPBELL, Augusta...$10.00; paid by RO. CAMPBELL for lotter
ticket, No. 66, in MATT. WATSON's lottery. It drew the tract
herein--315 acres; part of tract--Surry County, North Carolina, on
Mitchell's River--415 acres bought from TOBIAS REDCROSS (?) MARGHA,
16 February 1805. Margin: Ought not to have been recorded.
Witnesses: SOL. MATTHEWS, RO. H. and NELSON ANDERSON.

404. 22 February 1812. JNO. BAILEY and wife, FRANCES, and SAML.
ANDERSON to SAML. PERKINS and wife, FANNY...$40 forty acres
Hickory Creek. Lines: JNO. ANDERSON. Witnesses: JNO. LYON,
TERISHA BAILEY, SAML. BAILEY, THOS. THURMOND. To DR. DL. WATSON,
present owner, 1855.

405. 4 February 1811. ELISHA ESTES to NELSON ANDERSON, ABRAHAM B.
WARWICK and RO. FRANKLIN to secure JAS. WILLS, SR...sent to
JAS. MURPHY by WM. C. JORDAN, 5 August 1813--also other creditors;
$1.00; 573 acres Rucker's Run. Lines: WARWICK, THOS. STATHAM--
where ELISHA ESTES lives; former Deed of Trust to RO. MOORE to
secure WM. BROWN and Company--sold by RO. MOORE to CHAS. YANCY,
Buckingham--$160 over debt due BROWN and Company--they released
rights; slaves; stock; crops, etc. Witnesses: WM. PURVIS, NATHL.
OFFUTT, GEO. D. TYLER, WM. GOWING.

407. 27 November 1811. JAS. WILLS, SR. to JR., his son...love and
$1.00; Rucker Run tract. L:10 feet below mill now occupied
by JR.; ten feet of mill dam of SR. now occupied by HENRY BIBB, SR.,
ZACH FORTUNE, JR.--33 acres and mill race. Witnesses: JNO. BROOKS,
NELSON CAMPBELL, NORBORN B. POWELL, CHAS. TOWNSEND.

407. 27 November 1811. JAS. WILLS, JR. to SOL. MATTHEWS and
RO. J. KINCAID to secure GEO. W. VARNUM...$1.00; tract above.
Witnesses: NORBORN B. POWELL, JNO. BROOKS, RO. C. CUTLER, HUDSON
MARTIN, JR.

409. 1 July 1811. JNO. SCRUGGS to RO. FRANKLIN and FRED. CABELL
to secure JAS. GREGORY...$1.00; slave girl about ten in possession
of GREGORY. Witnesses: SAML. SPENCER, JNO. STEWART, WM. BRYAN.

410. 12 September 1805. GEO. PAGE, Bedford, to ARCH. MC DONALD
and wife, MARY ANN...L340 164 acres east Rockfish--bought
from THOS. HERD, 2 August 1779. Lines: ARCH WOODS former line.
Witnesses: HUDSON MARTIN, AUG. SHEPHERD, RO. PAGE, JNO. HARLOW,
JAS. WOOD. Dower released on same day to MARTIN and WOOD.
Recorded in Nelson, 24 February 1812. MARTIN and SHEPHERD as
witnesses.

412. 9 October 1811. WM. TEASE to CHAS. PERROW...power of attorney
to manage for my family. Witnesses: ELEANOR PERROW. To
CHAS. PERROW, -- March 1819.

413. 5 October 1811. AUG. SHEPHERD to GEO. PAGE...L70 twelve
acres Rockfish; part of tract devised to MRS. SARAH SHEPHERD
by husband, AUG. SHEPHERD, deceased. She had life estate and then
to grantor. Lines: road from her place to JNO. ROBERTS over the
mountain; grantee. To GEO. PAGE, 12 August 1819. Witnesses:
JNO. M. MARTIN, JOS. C. ROBERTS, LINSEY GRIFFIN.

414. 19 December 1811. JNO. LOVING and wife, ELIZ., to JNO.
DILLARD...L420 298½ acres south side and joining Tye. Lines:
LAVENDER LONDON, Buff. Witnesses: WM. H. DIGGES, JOS. LOVING,
STEPHEN WATTS, CHAS. L. CHRISTIAN. Dower relinquished, 15 February
1812, to WM. H. DIGGES and JOS. LOVING.

415. 10 August 1811. ALEX. MC ALEXANDER to JNO. MC ALEXANDER...to
him, 6 October 1818--$1.00. Tract on south Davies Creek.
Lines: NATHAN BARNETT, JNO. MELSON, ROBT. WRIGHT, LEE W. HARRIS--
111 acres.

416. 15 August 1811. ALEX. MC ALEXANDER to WM. MC ALEXANDER...
      ninety acres--not recorded, 23 April 1810--to ALEX., 22 March
1820; head of Rucker's Run--part of 149 acres. Lines: JOEL
PONTON, NICHL. CABELL, deceased, JAS. WILLS, JR.

417. 20 February 1812. HENRY BIBB to LEE W. HARRIS to secure
      HENRY BIBB, JR. and JAS. STEPHENS, JR. et al...$1.00; stock;
furniture; crops.

418. 29 November 1810. PHILIP DAVIS and wife, SARAH, to WM.
      CAMPBELL, son to GEO., Amherst County...to JNO. H. CAMPBELL,
12 April 1824, for WM. CAMPBELL; $315 189 acres; half of tract
granted to PHILIP DAVIS, assignee of PHILIP BUSH, per patent of
9 August 1794. Lines: JAS. THOMPSON, EDWD. MASTERS, DAVID S.
GARLAND. Witnesses: THOS. PENN, GEO. CAMPBELL, JAMES. GARLAND.

419. 27 August 1811. JAS. CLARKSON and wife, MARIA, Albemarle,
      to THOS. JONES...to N. C. CLARKSON, -- December 1835; L420
200 acres Little Hatt Creek; transferred to CHESLEY KINNEY by WM.
BIBB and GEO. GILLESPIE by deed. Lines: CHARLES JONES, GEO.
WILLIAMS, THOS. MASSIE, PHILIP RYAN, grantee. Witnesses: JNO.
BARNETT, ALEX. B. ROSE, ARCHY MITCHELL.

420. 9 December 1811. THOS. HAWKINS, NATHL. POWELL, ABRAHAM
      POWELL, agent for BENJ. POWELL, JNO. THOMPSON, M, agent of
MILDRED TALIAFERRO and LUCAS POWELL, guardian of children of WM.
POWELL, deceased, heirs of LUCAS POWELL, deceased...consideration:
right of dower of widow of LUCAS, ELIZ. POWELL; five slaves.
Witnesses: NORBORNE B. POWELL, JNO. THOMPSON, JR., R. COWPER.

420. 21 February 1812. CATLETT WILLS and wife, LUCINDA B. --
      ABRAHAM WARWICK, late of Amherst and grandfather of LUCINDA B. --
by will, to her as daughter of ABRAHAM's son, BEVERLY WARWICK,
deceased...ABRAHAM B. WARWICK was her guardian--to account. Before
marriage, LUCINDA B. for love of her brother, NELSON B. WARWICK,
and her sister, CANDICE G. WARWICK--with consent of WILLS--L150 of
her estate--to her uncle, ABRAHAM B. WARWICK, guardian for $1.00.
L75 for brother and sister--each.

423. 28 August 1811. JESSE JOPLING and JAS. MURPHY, Overseers
      of the Poor, to WM. VAUGHAN...bind out CHARLOTTE SMITH, poor
girl--mother, MILLY SMITH, unable to support her. Until 18--to
learn knitting, washing, spinning and sewing.

424. 28 August 1811. Same overseers to WM. VAUGHAN...bind out
      SPENCER SMITH, son of MILLY SMITH; farmer (?).

425. 24 February 1812. Same overseers to CHAS. PERROW...bind out
      WIATT--child of free negro woman, REBECCA--until 21; farmer.

426. 23 March 1812. (Recorded) JAS. LOBBAN to JAS. WOOD and
      JNO. M. MARTIN to secure PETER LE----...$1.00; 114 acres
Rockfish. Lines: CHAS. BRIDGWATER, AZARIAH MARTIN. Bought from
HUDSON MARTIN, JR.

428. 4 December 1811. MATT. HARRIS, JNO. HARRIS, JNO. DIGGES
      to JOS. SMITH...L266-10; order of Amherst County court as to
estate of JNO. HARRIS, Green Mt., deceased. 350 acres. Lines:
grantees, WM. LEE and JAS. HARRIS, JAS. MARTIN, JAS. H. BURTON,
WM. HARRIS, son of JNO., deceased. Witnesses: HENRY DAWSON, WM.
LEE HARRIS, WM. H. SHELTON.

430. 4 March 1802. THOS. MOORE and wife, SALLY, Amherst County,
      BENJ. MOORE and wife, POLLY, Bedford County, RICH. PERKINS
and wife, ELIZ., Fluvanna, HARDIN PERKINS and wife, MILLEY,
Buckingham County, and ANDREW DONALD and wife, SALLY, Bedford, heirs
of WM. MOORE and entitled to one-sixth each--MOORES and females--
and one-twelfth of land...to JNO. MOORE, Bedford $1250--Amherst
County and Albemarle tracts; Hickory; border of Rockfish--901 acres.

Lines: BENNETT NALLY, JAS. THURMOND, PETER LYON, SAML. ANDERSON,
JNO. DAWSON. Dower of LETTISHA MOORE, for life, by will of her
husband, BENJ. MOORE. Witnesses: JNO. ADAMS, JNO. GARROTT, ISAAC
OTEY, MICHL. KIRNIS (?), WM. QUARLES, BENJ. PERKINS. QUARLES and
JACOB KEY, Bedford Justices of the Peace as to SALLY and POLLY
MOORE; SALLY DONALD--order of 7 June 1802, from Amherst County;
done, 17 July 1802. JOSIAH ELLIS and DAVID S. GARLAND, Amherst
County Justices of the Peace, as to THOS. and SALLY MOORE, 7 June
1802; order; done, 2 October 1802. Bedford to Amherst County
certified, 28 February 1803. Fluvanna, 27 October 1806--acknowledged
by RICH. PERKINS; by HARDIN PERKINS, 14 October 1811. Recorded
Nelson, 23 March 1812.

435. 1 January 1812. THOS. STEWART and wife, TIRZAH, Bedford, to
LEONARD HALE...$50 62 acres Stony Creek; branch of Rockfish.
Witnesses: J. S. PENDLETON, T. ALDRIDGE, JAS. GARLAND, SR. and JR.,
HUDSON M. GARLAND, JAS. S. PENN. To JAS. M. MARTIN, 25 November
1812; recorded Nelson, 24 February 1812.

436. 1 January 1812. JNO. ROBERTSON to ELIZ. MERIWETHER ROBERTSON...
love and $1.00; furniture; stock. Witnesses: HARRISON
GRIFFIN, WM. CAMP, WM. LEE HARRIS. To JNO. KIRBEY, 4 July 1818, for
ELIZ.

437. 19 August 1808. RICH. HARE and wife, ELIZ., to JNO. ROBERTS...
to JNO. ROBERTS by his son, 2 May 1827--L42 seven acres Hickory
Creek; border of Rockfish. Lines: both. Witnesses: MATT. HARRIS,
JR., WINGFIELD NORVELL, JNO. THURMOND.

438. 24 February 1812. GEO. VAUGHAN and wife, SUKEY, to WM.
LANGFORD...to him, 27 September 1816--L250 261½ acres Dutch
Creek. Lines: HUDSON MARTIN, LUNSFORD LOVING, JNO. FARIS, JAS.
MATTHEWS, CHAS. STATHAM, WM. MURRILL. Where GEO. VAUGHAN lives.

439. 23 March 1812. GEO. VAUGHAN and wife, SUSANNAH, to WM.
MURRILL...L66-11 60½ acres. Lines: HENRY SMITH, HUDSON
MARTIN, WM. LANGFORD, CHAS. STATHAM, the road, the new shop. South
fork of Rockfish and Dutch.

441. --, 1812. JNO. ANDERSON and wife, POLLY, to JNO. J. WOOD,
Albemarle...to him, 23 November 1812--$100 120 acres Hickory
Creek. Lines: PERRIN FARRAR, deceased, GEO. BLAIN, SAML. ANDERSON,
JNO. BAILEY, SAML. PERKINS. Witnesses: LANDON H. BRENT, N. HARLOW,
JR.

443. 23 March 1812. JAS. CLARKSON and wife, MARIA, Albemarle,
to DAVID and PETER JACOBS...to WM. MASSIE, executor of DAVID
JACOBS, 25 July 1836--$10 ten acres Tye--as heirs of DAVID CLARKSON;
dower reserved. Witnesses: LANDON H. BRENT, JNO. HENDERSON,
WM. RYAN.

444. 25 January 1812. WM. BIBB and wife, POLLY T., to JNO.
JENKINS...L100 95 acres lot 2; assigned to POLLY T. HILL--now
BIBB; part of tract of NATHL. HILL, deceased. Lines: lot 1,
THOS. HARVIE. Witnesses: JAS. MONTGOMERY, JNO. HIGHT, THOS.
MASSIE, JNO. MILLER, CHAPPELL DAVENPORT.

445. 28 June 1808. NATHL. HILL, WM. HILL, JR., GEO. HILL, JNO.
PERKINS HILL, WM. RYAN and wife, BETSY, THOS. R. DRAKE and
wife, NANCY, JNO. JACOBS and wife, LUCY, and POLLY T. HILL, children
of NATHL. HILL, deceased, to THOS. MASSIE...L718-10; part of tract
of NATHL. HILL, deceased. Lines: JAS. DICKIE, the mountain,
thoroughfare branch. 280 acres. Witnesses: DANL. MC DONALD,
P. RYAN, JAS. MOORE, ITHAR (?) EVERETT, MARBELL EASTHAM, JESSE
JONES, CHAPPELL DAVENPORT, NATHAN LANGFORD, LEE W. HARRIS, CLAYTON C.
HARRIS, WM. BREEDLOVE.

447.   26 March 1812.   WM. RYAN and wife, ELIZ. B., to DAVID S.
       GARLAND...ELIZ. B., formerly HILL, L85 85 acres Jackson Creek,
north border Piney, part of tract of NATHL. HILL, deceased, as
heirs. Lines: DAVID S. GARLAND, THOS. HARVEY, JNO. JENKINS, GEO.
HILL.

449.   27 April 1812.   JAS. WOODS and wife, SARAH, to SAML. COLLINS...
       $500 121½ acres south side Rockfish. Lines: CLOUGH SHELTON,
deceased, MOSES HUGHES, SR., deceased, JOS. LIGON, deceased.

450.   15 August 1811.   DAVID CAULDWELL and wife, HANNAH, Rockingham,
       to JACOB SCRIVER...$275 93. 1. Three acres Beaver branch,
north border of Rockfish. Lines: JNO. COFFMAN, JNO. SMITH, JACOB
ARISMAN, FREDERICK WARE. One-third of 280 acres sold by JAS. FLCAK
to JNO. COFFMAN, SR., their father; JNO. COFFMAN, SR. conveyed to
ANDREW COFFMAN in Amherst County. S. M. WILLIAMS, Rockingham Clerk.

452.   25 February 1812.   WM. SMITH and wife, ELIZ., to SAML. PAGE
       and wife, ELIZ...L100 131 acres Rockfish. Lines: AUG.
SHEPHERD, RO. PAGE, WM. SMITH.

453.   1 October 1811.   JAMES LOVING, JR. and wife, NANCY, to CHAS.
       PERROW...$225 26 acres Rucker's Run; part of a tract. Lines:
alley around Lovingston, THOS. COCKE, JAS. LOVING, SR. and JR.

455.   25 April 1812.   SHEROD MARTIN, JR. to WM. LOBBIN...to him,
       2 November 1812; $62; thirteen acres. Lines: grantee.

456.   25 April 1812.   SHEROD MARTIN to JEFFRY MARTIN...$250 62 acres.
       Lines: the road.

457.   2 February 1810.   SAML. FITZPATRICK to THOS. WEIR...to him
       with dower relinquished, 15 November 1818--L70 interest in
estate of WM. FITZPATRICK, deceased; his father, dower of widow,
REBECCA. Witnesses: ALEX. and THOS. FITZPATRICK, JNO. and THOS.
WEIR.

458.   11 December 1811.   WM. H. DIGGES and wife, NEICEY, to REUBEN
       BATES...to him, 22 August 1814--L300 199 acres; two adjacent
tracts on Tye. Lines: old line, MARY STONEHAM, AMBR. CAMPBELL,
BERDET SKINNER--bought from HENRY STONEHAM--20 acres. Lines:
south side road from JNO. THOMPSON, M, to mill--formerly that of
SHELTON CROSTHWAIT, grantor, ELIJAH MAYS, house occupied now by
WM. WRIGHT, crossing road, tract bought from HENRY STONEHAM,
AMBR. CAMPBELL, ROLAND EDMONDS, JOS. WHITE--subject to dower of
COURTNEY WHITE "to one tract." Witnesses: RO. RIVES, PARMENAS
BRYANT, JAS. MURPHY, WM. BIBB.

460.   28 March 1812.   JAS. MARTIN to THOS. BRAMMWEL...$72 twelve
       acres. Lines: grantee--where he lives, Carolina rode (sic),
RO. BROOKS. Witnesses: JACOB SHRIVER, JACOB ARISMAN, FRED. WEIR.

461.   24 April 1812.   SHEROD MARTIN to CHAS. MC CUE to secure THOS.
       BRAMWELL on purchase of twelve acres of JAS. MARTIN...260
acres. Lines: BRAMWELL, FRED. WARE, JNO. THOMPSON, ROBT. BROOKS,
ALEX. SHIELDS, WM. LOBBAN--should JAS. MARTIN confirm title when
of age, now about 18 by 10 August next--then MC CUE to reconvey.
Witnesses: RO. BROOKS, JACOB ARISMAN, RICH. MITCHELL, JACOB SHRIVER.

462.   27 April 1812.   LANDON CABELL to DAVID S. GARLAND...margin:
       see page 479 for memeo--SAML. ROSE, Kentucky, by power of
attorney, 8 September 1805, to LANDON CABELL to sell--493 acres
allotted to children of his father, HUGH ROSE, deceased. SAML.
ROSE's interest in 493 acres of HUGH ROSE--part of tract--divided
to JNO., PATRICK, CHAS. ROSE and children of HUGH ROSE by Amherst
County commissioners.

464. 9 -- 1812. "Between March of Nelson" (sic). PRESLEY RAINES
     to RO. FRANKLIN and NELSON ANDERSON...bond of equal date to
MURPHY BROWN and Company; $1.00; stock. Witnesses: ANDREW N.
FOGUS, WM. J. CABELL, JAS. SMILEY. Recorded, 27 April 1812. To
WM. J. CABELL, 7 July 1812.

465. 1 September 1811. PRESLEY RAINES to RO. FRANKLIN and NATHL.
     OFFUTT--margin as above...to secure MURPHY BROWN and Company;
$1.00; mare--formerly that of RICH. MURROW; horse bought from
WILLIS H. WILLS. Witnesses: RO. JOHNSON, RO. W. CARTER, JOS.
MARVIN (?).

466. 22 April 1812. RO. J. CABELL, attorney-in-fact for MATT.
     JORDAN, Abbeville District, South Carolina, to JOS. EADES,
Albemarle...$600; Albemarle tract on Fluvanna; 227 acres. Lines:
Rock House Branch--part of 1000 acres of MATT. JORDAN, deceased,
Albemarle; share of MATT. JORDAN on division. Witnesses: WM. H.
SHELTON, JAS. STEVENS, JR., JAS. GARLAND, JR., S. GARLAND.

468. 27 March 1812. Abbeville District, South Carolina--MATT.
     JORDAN, SR., Albemarle, deceased, died and share of 227 acres
to MATT. JORDAN, JR. Lines: JAS. FOWLS, JR. is at Abbeville CH,
South Caroline--power of attorney to RO. J. CABELL, of same place;
to receive from JOS. EADES sums for 227 acres. Witnesses: HENRY
LIGON, JAS. KYLE, ANDREW HAMILTON, Justice of the Peace. JAS.
WARDLOW, Clerk, 27 March 1812.

470. 8 September 1805. SAML. ROSE, late of Amherst County, but
     now of Kentucky, to LANDON CABELL...power of attorney to
receive from WM. CABELL and PATRICK ROSE, executors of his father,
HUGH ROSE--to sell tract between or near Fairmount and Roseisle--
former tract of father and uncles. Kentucky: Ohio circuit;
DANL. BARRY, Clerk of Ohio Circuit Court. STEPHEN CLEAVER, Clerk
of Ohio Circuit Court. Recorded Nelson, 27 April 1812. Note: I
presume that this is Ohio County, Kentucky--formed in 1798, BAILEY F.
DAVIS.

471. 23 September 1811. JAS. STEVENS to JNO. BROOKS...$648.75
     92 acres Rucker's Run. Lines: JAS. STEVENS, JR., THOS.
JOPLING, JAS. THOMPSON. Witnesses: SP. GARLAND, JNO. HENDERSON,
CHAS. W. TOWNSEND.

472. 18 April 1812. JAS. STEVENS to SPOTSWOOD GARLAND...to J.
     DILLARD, 5 March 1842--L660-16-6 267 acres Rucker's Run.
Lines: JAS. STEVENS, SR. and JR., JAS. LOVING, S. SPENCER, HEZEKIAH
HARGROVE, JAS. THOMPSON, JNO. BROOKS. Witnesses: JNO. HENDERSON,
JNO. BROOKS, CHAS. W. TOWNSEND.

474. 23 November 1811. JNO. ROBERTSON to JNO. KIRBY...to JNO. F.
     ROBERTSON, 19 September 1819--to secure JNO. F. ROBERTSON,
Manchester, Chesterfield County; WM. J. ROBERTSON, Warminster, Nelson
County; $1.00; stock; furniture (one item shows that a pine chest
has been painted a walnut color so they were evidently at this game
of changing color of wood in those days. B.D.)--long and interesting
list. Witnesses: JAS. VIGUS, JR., RO. SHIELDS, HENRY JACOBS, JNO.
HOUSEWRIGHT.

477. 23 May 1812. WM. BRIDGWATER and wife, SALLY, to THOS. WEIR...
     to him--sent, 13 August 1824--L30 thirty acres south side of
Pilate Mountain; Rockfish.

478. 23 March 1812. Order to Albemarle Justices of the Peace:
     DAVID WOOD and PARMENAS ROGERS...JAS. CLARKSON and wife,
MARIA, 27 August 1811, to THOS. JONES--done, 2 May 1812; to NELSON
CLARKSON, 2 December 1833.

479. 25 May 1812. LANDON CABELL understood that SAML. ROSE meant
     to convey his interest by will of father, HUGH ROSE, and that
of his sister, PAULINA ROSE, deceased. Reference to page 462.

480. 23 March 1812. JNO. HERNDON and wife, MARY, Goochland, to
      DAVID and PETER JACOBS...$10.00; interest in ten acres;
Tye; Mill tract; as heirs of DAVID CLARKSON--save dower. Witnesses:
LANDON H. BRENT, WM. RYAN, WM. BIBB, JNO. HENDERSON.

481. 25 April 1812. HAWES COLEMAN to WM. BIBB...to WM. BIBB,
      6 November 1817--L6 00 Naked Creek; north border of Tye--
part of tract of WM. BIBB, deceased; allotted to TANDY JOHNSON
and wife and by them sold to JAS. WILLS, SR., 210 acres by old
survey, but 216 by later one. Lines: WM. BIBB, deceased--now
HAWES COLEMAN, WM. HOLLANDSWORTH, PARMENAS BRYANT, CONYERS WHITE,
deceased; WM. H. DIGGES.

482. 22 February 1812. THOS. SPENCER and wife, JANE, Buckingham,
      to SAML. and JNO. SPENCER...$1000 south side Tye; mansion
house tract of WM. SPENCER, late of Nelson; 200 acres--given by
SAML. SPENCER, The Elder, by Buckingham will--grandfather of THOS.
SPENCER from larger tract; interest of THOS. by will of his
grandfather. Witnesses: JNO. DILLARD, JOS. LOVING, STEPHEN WATTS,
JNO. LOVING. JNO. DILLARD and JOS. LOVING, Nelson Justices of
the Peace; same date.

485. 22 February 1812. SAML SPENCER, THOS. SPENCER, SAML. TURNER
      and wife, SALLY, formerly SPENCER, JNO., JAS., NORVILLE
SPENCER, JNO. LOVING and wife, ELIZ., formerly SPENCER, heirs of
WM. SPENCER who died intestate and owned considerable land--agreed
to divide. Lots to SAML. SPENCER--mansion house and half of adjacent
tract. THOS. SPENCER--Buckingham tracts--on JAS. and one short
distance from river--west side bought from LITTLEBERRY HUGHES,
Buckingham. SAML. TURNER for wife--half of James River tract;
dwelling house; lower part bought by WM. SPENCER from JOS. MAYO,
agent for RO. MAYO, in Amherst County. JNO. SPENCER--lower end of
mansion house tract and includes his building. JAS. SPENCER--
North Carolina tract in Granville County on Tare River--to him by
WM. in lifetime by deed. NORVILLE SPENCER--three tracts in
Amherst County--part of former tract of late COL. HUGH ROSE--two
to him by WM. and other on east side of ROSE's Mountain--where
NORVILLE SPENCER has house--bought by WM. from SAML. IRVINE. JNO.
LOVING--half tract on James; upper part--west side bought from
JOS. MAYO, agent of RO. MAYO. Witnesses: CHAS. L. CHRISTIAN,
STEPHEN WATTS, JOS. LOVING, JNO. DILLARD.

488. 31 August 1811. HENRY CAMPBELL to RO. FRANKLIN and NATHL.
      OFFUTT to secure MURPHY BROWN and Company...$1.00 Tye and
Piney on Castle Creek; 447 acres. Lines: JNO. CAMDEN, JAS.
DICKEY--bought from DR. WM. B. HARE; slaves; stock. Witnesses:
JNO. SCRUGGS, JESSE PROFFITT, SAML. HANSBROUGH, JAS. SMILEY.

491. 22 May 1812. VALENTINE BALL to ZACH NEVIL to secure JESSE
      JOPLING...JESSE JOPLING on bond for trespass, assault and
battery--ELISHA PETERS versus BALL. $1.00; blank acres--one-eighth
of tract of WM. BALL, deceased; two shares.

493. 22 June 1812. JNO. UTLEY, Fayette County, Kentucky, and wife,
      NANCY, to JAS. CLARKSON, Albemarle...$150 one-tenth interest.
Lines: CHAS. JONES, THOS. JONES, PHILIP RYAN, THOS. MASSIE--200
acres; Tavern tract bought by DAVID CLARKSON from CHESLEY KENNY
and to ten heirs of DAVID CLARKSON. NANCY is an heir. JNO.
HERNDON, attorney-in-fact for JNO. UTLEY. To JNO. HERNDON, 23 June
1812.

494. 22 June 1812. JNO. HERNDON and wife, MARY, Goochland, to
      JAS. CLARKSON, Albemarle...L45; one-tenth of tract above.
MARY is an heir.

495. 26 March 1812. JAS. STEVENS, JR., 1; JNO. HIGGINBOTHAM and
      RO. FRANKLIN, 2; WILLIS H. WILLS, 3...to JNO. HIGGINBOTHAM,
27 July 1812--WILLIS H. WILLS is assignee of JAS. WILLS, SR. $1.00;
slaves. Witnesses: J. GARLAND, THOS. MC CLELLAND, GEO. W. VARNUM.

497.   10 June 1812.   SAML. IRVINE and wife, ANN, daughter of late
        HUGH ROSE, Lynchburg, to DAVID S. GARLAND...$70 sixty acres
from estate of HUGH ROSE and also as heir of PAULINA ROSE, deceased,
daughter of HUGH ROSE; Jackson Creek. Lines: JNO. C. CARTER,
WM. B. HARE, PAT. ROSE, grantee--493 acres; share of HUGH ROSE in
Piney Woods tract. Witnesses: THOS. ALDRIDGE, SAML, EDMUNDS, JR.,
THOS. S. MC CLELLAND.

498.   30 December 1811.   JAS. MONTGOMERY to RO. FRANKLIN and NELSON
        ANDERSON to secure STEPHEN WATTS, administrator of WM.
SPENCER...$1.00; slaves--four. Witnesses: ZACH NEVIL, SAML.
HANSBROUGH, RO. W. CARTER.

499.   28 March 1812.   DAVID R. CLARKSON and wife, REBECCA, and
        ELIZ. MARTIN, Fluvanna, to DAVID and PETER C. JACOBS...to
WM. MASSIE, administrator of DAVID JACOBS, 25 July 1836 (?) L70
72 acres both sides Tye. Lines: HENRY HARPER, WM. COFFEY, JNO.
JACOBS, near mouth of late race of CLARKSON; three shares in mill
tract. Witnesses: WM. B. JACOBS, JNO. JACOBS, JR., SAML. PARRISH.
JNO. JACOBS, JR. and WM. B. JACOBS, Justices of the Peace.

502.   11 December 1811.   REUBEN BATES and wife, NANCY, to CHAS.
        WATTS and RICH. PHILLIPS to secure WM. H. DIGGES...$1.00;
two adjacent tracts on Tye. Lines: MARY STONEHAM, AMBR. CAMPBELL,
BURDETT SKINNER. 199 acres; 18 or 20 acres. Lines: south side
of road from JNO. THOMPSON, M, to the mill--formerly that of
SHELTON CROSTHWAIT, grantor, ELIJAH MAYS, house occupied by WM.
WRIGHT, WM. H. DIGGES, ROLAND EDMUNDS, JOS. WHITE. Bought this
day from WM. H. DIGGES. Witnesses: WM. BIBB, RO. RIVES, JAS.
MURPHY.

505.   10 September 1811.   NATHAN BARNETT to RO. J. KINCAID and
        JAS. GARLAND to secure various bondsmen: JAS. LOVING, JR.,
HENRY BIBB, JR., ZACH FORTUNE, JNO. SEAY to MATT CLAY, assignee
of WM. BARNETT...$1.00; stock; slave; stills. Witnesses: JNO.
BROOKS, JAS. STEVENS, JR., WM. BIBB, THOS. MALLORY.

507.   6 July 1812.   SPOTSWOOD GARLAND and wife, LUCINDA, late ROSE
        and daughter of HUGH ROSE, deceased, and heir of PAULINA
ROSE, to DAVID S. GARLAND...$70 interest in 493 acres; part of
tract of HUGH ROSE--Piney Woods; divided to JNO.: PATRICK and
CHAS. ROSE, children of HUGH ROSE by Amherst County commissioners.

508.   1 July 1812.   WM. H. LEIGH and wife, MILLY, to TERISHA
        TURNER...L112 100 acres Cove Creek. Lines: HENRY TURNER,
SAML. TURNER.

509.   2 April 1812.   TERIL TURNER and wife, POLLY; LEONARD PHILLIPS
        and wife, ELIZA; PAGE DANIEL (DAMERON) and wife, SUSANNAH,
HENRY RITTENHOUSE and wife, PATSEY; JNO. GRAVES and wife, LUCY;
JESSE JOBLIN and wife, REBECCA; NANCY; MILDRED and JUDITH TURNER
to WM. HAMNER, Albemarle--note: LEOND. PHILLIPS is later called
ZACH PHILLIPS and DANIEL is DAMERON--messed up deed...$500; 100
acres. Lines: Cove Creek, BENJ. PAYNE, MATTHEWS, SAML. ANDERSON,
mill tract. Witnesses: SAML., HENRY, TERISHA and WM. TURNER,
WM. H. LEIGH. These signatures appear: LITTLE PAGE DAMERON,
HENRY RITTENHOUSE, JNO. JOPLING, SUSANNAH DAMERON, LEANNA PHILLIPS,
JNO. GROVES, POLLY TURNER, MILDRED TURNER, NANCY TURNER, REBECCA
JOBLING, LUCY GRAVES, PATSY RITTENHOUSE, JUDIAH TURNER.

510.   27 July 1812.   JAS. LOVING, JR. and wife, NANCY, to LUNSFORD
        LOVING...$200 one acre lot in Lovingston: 35 and 36.

511.   21 December 1811.   ALEX. B. ROSE to JNO. MYERS, Amherst
        County...to DAVID S. GARLAND, 10 October 1812--to secure.
THOS. ALDRIDGE and Company. Six shillings; eleven slaves, stock.
Two more slaves. Witnesses: WM. HILL, JR., JNO. BARNETT, JESSE
JONES.

512. 27 April 1812. LANDON CABELL and wife, JUDITH SCOTT CABELL,
      to NATHL. OFFUTT...to him, 10 June 1819--$20 lot in New Market--
82 by 30 yards--east side Tye and not far from its mouth; no. 5--
towards the west. Lines: Lot 6 bought by RO. RIVES and Company
and now NATHL. OFFUTT's. Witnesses: RO. FRANKLIN, WM. J. CABELL,
JNO. SCRUGGS.

513. 24 July 1812. JAS. DILLARD, CHAS. WATTS, WM. H. DIGGES,
      commissioners to sell tract of WM. ALFORD, deceased, to
WM. HOLLINSWORTH...$500 150 acres east borders Tye. Lines:
JOS. LOVING, BURDITT SKINNER, MURPHY BROWN and Company, EDDY
FORTUNE.

514. 25 August 1812. MICHL. WOODS to THOS. REID, Madison County,
      Kentucky...power of attorney to divide and dispose of tract
in Washington County, Kentucky; patent to JNO. and JAS. WOODS.

515. 24 July 1812. WM. HOLLINSWORTH and wife, FANNY, to EDDY
      FORTUNE...L190 150 acres east borders Tye. Lines: see page
      513.

515. 23 June 1812. Order to Goochland Justices of the Peace:
      ARCHL. PERKINS and NAT PERKINS and JAS. CARTER--JNO. HERNDON
and wife, MARY, 23 March 1812, to DAVID and PETER JACOBS...Ten
acres; Tye; mill tract interest. Done by the two PERKINS men,
7 July 1812.

517. 23 June 1812. Order to same Justices of the Peace: JNO.
      HERNDON and wife, MARY, 22 June 1812, to JAS. CLARKSON...one-
tenth of 200 acres. As above, 7 July 1812.

518. 18 March 1812. MICHL. BROCK and wife, ELIZ., to SAML.
      HEIZER, Augusta...to SAML. HEIZER, 25 April 1814--L125-5;
headwaters of Beaver--63 acres. Lines: JNO. THOMPSON, RICH.
MITCHELL. Witnesses: RO. BROOKS, RICH. W. BROOKS.

519. 1 August 1812. HENRY EMMERSON to MICAJAH WHEELER, Albemarle...
      to MICAJAH WHEELER, 21 July 1813--six shillings to secure
debt to MICAJAH WHEELER; slave; stock; tract where HENRY EMMERSON
lives on Rockfish--160 acres. Lines: JAS. TURNER, SAML. SCRUGGS,
DUNMORE DAMERON--"unto the said JAS. OLD" (sic)--to pay OLD.
Witnesses: HENRY T. HARRIS, RO. GARLAND as to OLD.

521. 1 January 1812. JNO. DICKSON to RO. FRANKLIN and NELSON
      ANDERSON...to RO. H. ANDERSON, 25 June 1813--to secure MURPHY
BROWN and Company; $1.00; between 2 and 300 acres. South fork
Rockfish. Lines: NORBORN THOMAS, CHAS. CHRISTIAN, WM. DICKSON,
furniture, stock. Witnesses: RO. W. CARTER, PETER CAMPBELL,
STEPHEN HENDERSON, WM. TYREE, WAT., JAS. GREGORY, JAS. MARTIN,
JNO. BETHEL. Note: I began this page on the morning of 5 June 1968.
My wife and I were at breakfast when the woman with whom she rides
to teach at Amelon, MRS. NELL HARVEY BROCKMAN (MRS. P. D. BROCKMAN),
called to tell of the shooting of SENATOR ROBT. KENNEDY in California.
I am typing with the radio going so that I can hear the latest
news. This act was despicable in every sense of the word. Our
nation cannot stand to be governed by threats and violence and we
pray that somehow we may be able to overcome such an attitude on
the part of the lawless elements.

522. 22 May 1812. WM. CABELL and wife, ANN, to GEO. W. VARNUM...
      $1668 431 acres Joe's Creek and Rucker's Run. Lines:
MURPHY BROWN and Company, RO. RIVES, ELISHA PETERS, the road, on
the mountain, a spring, fork of road. Witnesses: S. GARLAND,
RO. FRANKLIN, EDDY FORTUNE, DANL. LEEBRICK.

524. 3 December ----. Recorded 24 August 1812. JAS. T. HUBARD to
      BENJ. BONDURANT...power of attorney to rent all lands and
receive sums in Amherst County. Witnesses: RO. FRANKLIN and proved
by him.

524. 28 March 1812. EDWD. LEWIS to WILLIS H. WILLS, Warminster...
to JNO. HIGGINBOTHAM, 11 September 1812--and to JAS. FREELAND,
Buckingham, to secure MURPHY BROWN and Company and HIGGINBOTHAM and
BROWN and Company; five shillings, 71 acres. Lines: MACE FREELAND,
two lots. Lines: JNO. PATTESON and AUGUSTINE NORVELL, deceased--
or NOWELL (?), stock, furniture. Witnesses: JOS. BAKER, WM.
KENNEDY, JESSE JOPLING.

526. 17 August 1812. JOS. BAKER to WILLIS H. WILLS and RO. FRANKLIN
to secure MURPHY BROWN and Company...to WILLIS H. WILLS,
1 September 1812--five shillings, furniture. Witnesses: JAS.
VIGUS, JR., JNO. HOUSEWRIGHT, SNOWDEN MADDUX.

527. 29 December 1809. JOS. C. MEGGINSON and wife, SARAH,
Buckingham, to THOS. S. MC CLELLAND, Lynchburg...to THOS. S.
MC CLELLAND, 25 May 1814--$100; 291 acres in two grants of 200 acres
and 91 acres bought from WARREN TALIAFERRO--part of tract to
WARREN TALIAFERRO from his father; also 140 acres--part of said
devised tract; sold by said TALIAFERRO to JOSEPH LYLE and by him
sold to JOS. C. MEGGINSON; not fully surveyed--444 acres on James
above Camden's WH. Lines: Mouth of Mill Creek, CAMDEN, WM. HORSLEY,
deceased, ROBERTSON, JAS. CABELL, SR., J. FLOOD, WM. MEGGINSON,
EDWD. B. CABELL, WM. WATSON. WATSON and FLOOD, Buckingham Justices
of the Peace, 22 June 1810; recorded 23 July 1810.

530. 1 March 1812. REUBEN WOODY, Albemarle, to RICH. PHILLIPS and
ROWLAND EDMUNDS to secure JAS. EDMUNDS, SR...$1.00; slave
about fourteen or fifteen. Witnesses: PETER CAMPBELL, JNO. SUTTLES,
RO. MAYS, DICY WOOD (his mark).

531. 9 March 1812. JNO. SCRUGGS to RO. FRANKLIN and WM. J. CABELL...
to FRED. CABELL, 26 December 1814--to secure FRED. CABELL;
$1.00; girl slave about twelve. Witnesses: HOWARD BALLOWE,
A. N. FOGGS, JNO. STAPLES, JNO. SHELMAN.

532. 17 August 1812. GUSTAVUS A. ROSE, Lynchburg, to DAVID S.
GARLAND...$100 77 acres--as heir of COL. HUGH ROSE, deceased,
and his heir, PAULINA ROSE, deceased--a child, Jackson Creek.
Lines: NNO. C. CARTER, WM. B. HARE, PATRICK ROSE, DAVID S. GARLAND--
493 acres assigned HUGH ROSE as his share of Piney Woods.

533. 9 April 1812. REUBEN MARTIN to JOS. SHELTON to secure JNO.
MATTHEWS...to JNO. MATTHEWS, 9 April 1814--$1.00; 100 acres;
part of tract deeded by MATTH$WS to MARTIN; north side Dutch Creek.
Lines: JNO. WATKINS, WM. BAILEY. Witnesses: WM. LEE HARRIS,
POLLY GLASS (?), JOS. W. SHELTON.

535. 18 July 1812. HAWES COLEMAN, WM. H. COLEMAN and wife, NANCY,
to WM. H. DIGGES...to A. BROWN, 26 June 1852--L1921-10; 405
acres; headborders Bob's Creek. Lines: MATT. HARRIS. WM. BIBB,
LEWIS WHITE, CONYERRS WHITE, deceased, grantee, also 318 acres.
Lines: Spencer's road, RO. RIVES, TERISHA TURNER, grantee, MATT.
HARRIS. Witnesses: JNO. W. HARRIS, THOS. W. and H. M. COLEMAN,
JOS. SHELTON. WM. HARRIS and JOS. SHELTON, Justices of the Peace.

537. 25 August 1812. RO. RIVES and wife, MARGARET, to PETER
VAUGHAN, Culpeper...$1318.50 northeast of Keys' Church.
Lines: grantor, ELISHA PETERS, GEO. VAUGHAN, RICH. BRYANT--219 3/4
acres. Witnesses: RO. FRANKLIN, NELSON ANDERSON, ZACH NEVIL,
WM. S. CABELL.

539. 28 September 1812. JNO. E. FITZPATRICK and wife, REBECCA,
Fluvanna, to LEE W. HARRIS...to JNO. E. FITZPATRICK by
WM. H. MOSBY, 27 October 1813--L536 south fork Davis Creek. 376
acres. Lines: RO. WRIGHT. Bought from TANDY KEY, agent for heirs
of MARTIN KEY, deceased.

540. 25 November 1808. REUBEN B. PATTESON and WM. F. CARTER,
     trustees of CORNL. THOMAS, to MURPHY BROWN and Company...to
J. MURPHY, 21 May 1813--Deed of Trust of 1807 to secure JAS. MURPHY
and Company in Amherst County. Sold, 19 November of this year for
$2622.56--2301 acres, south fork Rockfish. Lines: WM. JOHNSON,
EDWD. HARDING, NORBORN THOMAS, JOS. CABELL, WM. BOWMAN--where
CORNL. THOMAS lives. Witnesses: JAS. POWELL, RO. MOORE, CHAS.
IRVING, RICH. POWELL, THOS. CHILDERS, JER. YAGER.

541. 7 April 1812. PHILIP RYAN to NATHL. HILL, JR. and THOS.
     PENN to secure WM. RYAN...$1.00; furniture; stock. To sell
and pay. Witnesses: JNO. BALLARD, JAS. FULCHER, JAS. BOIEN (?).

542. 20 December 1811. ALEX. B. ROSE to JNO. BARNETT...L100;
     rent for 1812; Rose Isle; above public lane ford on west side
Tye; owes JNO. BARNETT this sum; slaves. Witnesses: WM. HILL, JR.,
JNO. HUGHES, JESSE JONES.

544. 17 August 1812. WALLER FORD, Amelia, to SAML. FORD, Amelia...
     to C. FORD, 26 June 1815--$600 287 acres; 184 acres; 103
acres head borders Davis Creek. Lines: DAVIS--error--no lines--
just Davis Creek. Witnesses: S. GARLAND, JR., WM. H. SHELTON,
JAS. S. PENN, JAS. F. STEVENS.

545. 1 October 1811. JNO. MELTON to THOS. MELTON, his son...love
     and $1.00; head of Dutch--patent to THOS. EADES, 10 July 1766.
Lines: JNO. HUNTER, top of the mountain--142 acres. Witnesses:
HUDSON MARTIN, SOLOMON MATTHEWS, JNO. W. GREEN.

546. 24 October 1812. JEFFREY MARTIN and wife, NANCY, to RO.
     BROOKS...$200 16½ acres forks of the Carolina road near
WM. LOBBAN, up towards Rockfish Gap, ALEX. SHIELDS, road from
Rockfish Gap to Scott's ferry.

547. 26 October 1812. JEFFREY MARTIN and wife, NANCY, to RO.
     EDWARDS...L120 36 acres Michim's river--a new one on me.
Lines: the path. Witnesses: RO. BROOKS, JAS. HAYS, JR., HUDSON
MARTIN, JR.

548. 26 April 1812. JNO. MORRISON and wife, MARY, to JNO. J.
     WOOD...to JAS. BARNETT on order of JNO. J. WOOD, 11 January
1814--$25; no acres; Hickory Creek. Lines: ZACH ROBERTS. Witnesses:
HENRY T. HARRIS, SP. GARLAND, MICHL. WOODS, AARON H. MORRISON.

549. 13 October 1812. WM. CABELL to RICH. BRYANT...to RICH. BRYANT,
     15 September 1813--L365 292 acres Joe's Creek. Lines: old
church road, grantor, MURPHY BROWN and Company, GEO. VAUGHAN at
fork of road to Variety Mills, RO. RIVES. Witnesses: JAS. MURPHY,
CHAS. C. PATTESON, RO. FRANKLIN.

550. -- August 1812. HAWES COLEMAN, MATT. HARRIS, MICHL. WOODS,
     commissioners, to DAVID WITT, JR...tract of LITTLEBERRY WITT,
deceased, then JOS. ROBERTS is named as another commissioner;
sold, 17 June 1809, for L90; Rockfish. Lines: JOS. ROBERTS,
deceased, DAVID WITT, SR., WAN (?) WOODS--200 acres. Witnesses:
N. L. MARTIN, HAWES N. COLEMAN, JNO. FARRAR, SR., WM. LEE HARRIS.

551. 23 November 1812. JNO. MYERS, Amherst County trustee, to
     GEO. CABELL, Campbell County...to GEO. CABELL, 15 May 1814--
Deed of Trust, 27 August 1812, by ALEX. B. ROSE to JNO. MYERS to
secure THOS. ALDRIDGE and Company; six shillings, 140 acres.
Lines: DR. GEO. CABELL--ROSE's share of Piney Commons from estate
of father, JNO. ROSE. Sold for $705.00.

553. 31 March 1812. STERLING CLAIBORNE and wife, JANE, to DAVID S.
     GARLAND...$70 sixty acres; interest in estate of HUGH ROSE
from his father, Piney Woods. Witnesses: T. ALDRIDGE, JAS. S.
PENDLETON, JNO. MYERS.

140

554. 17 November 1812. WM. DIXON, of --, to JNO, ANNE, LUCRETIA,
     SALLY and PEGGY DIXON...love for son, JNO., and his daughters;
$1.00; 460 acres; south fork Rockfish. Lines: ZACH NEVIL, NORBORN
THOMAS, also Dutch Creek tract of 135 acres. Lines: REUBEN and
WM. MARTIN, DUNMORE DAMERON. Signed DICKSON. Witnesses: ANDREW
RUSSELL, WM. H. CARTER. Certified from Washington Court, 23 November
1812.

556. 30 June 1812. JNO. MITCHELL to RO. MITCHELL...$200; crops.
     Witnesses: S. GARLAND, CHAS. TOWNSEND.

556. 28 December 1812. LANDON CABELL and wife, JUDITH S., to
     THOS. MASSIE...to THOS. MASSIE, 28 June 1813--L552 100 acres
by survey of 22 May 1788; north side Priest Mountain and both sides
Crab Tree Branch; borders of Tye and Piney. Lines: Shoe Creek.
Granted to WM. CABELL, 28 June 1789, and devised to LANDON CABELL
by his father, WM. CABELL, by will; also 54 acres by survey of
3 December 1795--head springs of Stoney Creek; branch of Tye and on
top of Big Priest Mountain. Patent to WM. CABELL, 25 August 1797;
also 50 acres; survey of 3 December 1795--both sides of Crab Tree
Creek and includes the great falls thereon. Lines: first tract.
Granted to LANDON CABELL, assignee of WM. CABELL; grant of 25 August
1797; all adjacent. 1104 acres. In Amherst County at the time.
Note: this is the Crabtree Falls tract which is still privately
owned, but the government is trying to negotiate a trade. It is
near the Federal land in the Department of Inferior forest and the
road goes on up to Montebello and then onto the Parkway. These
falls are beautiful and we enjoy going there for hikes and picnics.
One must exercise caution in climbing near the falls for several
people have been killed by falling on slippery rocks. They begin
in a large meadow called Crabtree Meadows and the road to this area
is a very narrow one. I recall going there some years ago and
state troopers were stationed at each end of the road with communica-
tions systems. The speaker at this event proposed that an escalator
be built up one side of the falls.

561. 29 July 1812. WM. R. COPELAND and wife, EMMELLY, Campbell
     County, to DAVID S. GARLAND...$100; Jackson Creek; part of
tract of COL. HUGH ROSE--part of Piney Woods; 77 acres due EMMELLY
as heir of ROSE and PAULINA ROSE, deceased--heir of HUGH ROSE.
To DAVID S. GARLAND, 25 January 1813. Witnesses: JAS. BENAGH,
LITTLETON ROSE, WM. B. LYNCH, CHAS. H. TAIT, CORNL. POWELL.
Certified from Lynchburg, 28 December 1812.

562. 1 December 1812. ELIZ. LIVELY from WM. MARTIN and wife,
     NANCY; FRANCIS SMITH and wife, FANNY; RICH. FOSTER and wife,
LUCY; WM. FOSTER and wife, POLLY; JAMES MATTHEWS and wife, SYNTHA;
JOEL DAVIS and wife, SALLY; JNO. BETHEL and wife, error--no wife,
but the name of ALSEY BETHEL...$130; tract of JNO. BETHEL, deceased,
Rucker's Run of Tye. Lines: JAS. MARTIN, GEO. VAUGHAN, JNO.
BETHEL, JR., JAS. WARWICK--120 acres. Witnesses: NELSON ANDERSON,
CHAS. C. PATTESON, ZACH NEVIL, SAML. LOVING, JAS. MARTIN.

564. 1 October 1812. CHAS. PERROW and wife, ELEANOR, to RO. GARLAND,
     Albemarle...$700 26 acres Rucker's Run; part of tract. Lines:
alley around Lovingston, THOS. COCKE, JAS. LOVING, SR. and JR.
Witnesses: JNO. M. MARTIN, S. GARLAND, THOS. E. FORTUNE.

566. 10 October 1812. JNO. TOMS and wife, SALLY, to JNO. M. MARTIN...
     L100 both sides Pounder Branch; border of Rockfish. Lines:
JAS. MARTIN's old corner, CAPT. JAS. MARTIN's old line--110 acres.
Devised by SAML. FOX to sons, JNO. and BARTLETT FOX, and conveyed
to them to TOMS; also lines of AUG. SMITH, RO. HENDERSON. Witnesses:
HUDSON MARTIN, JR., SAML. B. DENNEY, WM. FABER, GEO. YOST.

567. 19 January 1813. A. B. WARWICK and JNO. MOSBY as to LANDON
     CABELL's wife, JUDITH SCOTT CABELL, 27 April 1812...lot 5 in
Lovingston to NATHL. OFFUTT. To NATHL. OFFUTT, 19 June 1819.

569.   23 January 1813. THOS. EWERS and wife, ELIZ., to HUDSON
       MARTIN, SR. and JR., NICHL. L. MARTIN...to NICHL. L. MARTIN,
28 February 1848--$350 80 acres both sides Rockfish below ford. Lines:
MAJOR JAS. WOODS, grantor, present ford, the road, old road.
Witnesses: JNO. S. SNELL, WM. LEE HARRIS, JNO. HARRIS, MATT. HARRIS.

570.   26 August 1812. PLEASANT DAWSON and wife, SALLY, Albemarle,
       to HUGH WHITE...to HUGH WHITE, 22 March 1813--L150; one-
eighth share; 512 acres on Hickory Creek. Lines: HENRY TURNER,
MARTIN DAWSON, JNO. L. DAWSON, ZACH ROBERTS. Tract of JNO. DAWSON,
deceased--as heirs. Witnesses: JNO. L., BENJ. and NELSON DAWSON.

571.   8 November 1812. JNO. STEVENS to RO. FRANKLIN and NELSON
       ANDERSON to secure MURPHY BROWN and Company...$1.00; slave
about forty and one eighteen years old. Witnesses: S. GARLAND, JR.,
JNO. WRIGHT, JOS. SHELTON, JOS. HARGROVE.

573.   10 December 1812. PETER CAMPBELL to WM. H. DIGGES and RO.
       FRANKLIN...to LEMUEL TURNER, agent for RO. RIVES, 25 February
1818--to secure MURPHY BROWN and Company; $1.00; 100 acres devised
to PETER CAMPBELL by father, AMBR. CAMPBELL; part of tract.
Lines: REUBEN BATES, ROWLAND EDMUNDS--where PETER CAMPBELL lives.
Witnesses: RO. SHIELDS, RO. H. ANDERSON, JNO. THOMPSON, JR., ELIJAH
MAYS.

574.   9 January 1813. JAS. STEVENS, SR. to SAML. STEVENS, son of
       JNO. STEVENS, JR...grandson; love and L363 paid by SAML. to
MURPHY BROWN and Company for JAS. 600 acres Rucker's Run. Lines:
SP. GARLAND, CHAS. PURVIS, SAML. LOVING, JAS. STEVENS, JR., lands
given to GEO. LOVING by SR. and SAML. SPENCER. Intended to be
left by SR. to JR. in will. Deduct tract sold to SP. GARLAND and
JNO. BROOKS. Witnesses: S. GARLAND, JNO. STEVENS, JNO. HENDERSON,
JNO. CARTER.

576.   9 January 1813. SAML. STEVENS to JAS. STEVENS, JR. and wife,
       ELIZ., and JNO. STEVENS, son of JAS. STEVENS, JR., and wife,
ELIZ...love of SAML. STEVENS for his parents and his brother, JNO.;
six shillings; to comply with request of grandfather, JAS., SR.
200 acres; part of tract conveyed this day by SR.; lower end;
including mill; occupied by JR.; does not include dwelling house
lately occupied by JR. and family, but to have free use of it for
lives--when JNO. is 21--200 acres in lieu of $1000.00. Witnesses:
as above.

578.   25 January 1813. PLEASANT MARTIN, Albemarle, to HUDSON
       MARTIN, JR...$40 part of tract to which PLEASANT MARTIN is
entitled from mother, ELIZ. MARTIN, deceased. Meriwether's Branch--
his share as legatee of STEPHEN MARTIN, deceased.

579.   26 December 1812. WM. HARGRAVE and wife, SUCKEY, to SAML.
       EDMUNDS, JR...to ALEX. BROWN, an executor of SAMUEL EDMUNDS, JR.,
17 December 1824--L300 three adjacent tracts on Tye--385 acres.
Bought from ACHILLES WRIGHT. Lines: JOS. LOVING, WM. CLASBY,
SAML. EDMUNDS, JR. Witnesses: WM. H. DIGGES, JOS. LOVING,
CORNL. and JAS. NEVIL; JOS. LOVING and WM. H. DIGGES, Justices of
the Peace, 23 January 1813.

581.   19 January 1813. JAS. STEVENS, SR. to GEO. LOVING and wife,
       MILDRED, daughter of JAS. STEVENS, SR...love and $1.00; Rucker's
Run where GEO. LOVING lives. Lines: RO. RIVES, HEZ. HARGROVE,
tract formerly occupied by JAS. STEVENS, JR.; 200 acres. Witnesses:
CHAS. PERROW, THOS. JOPLING, JNO. STEWART.

582.   19 January 1813. JAS. STEVENS, SR. to SAML. SPENCER and wife,
       ANN, daughter of JAS. STEVENS, SR...love and $1.00; 200 acres.
Lines: GEO. LOVING, HEZ. HARGROVE, tract occupied by ELIZ. THOMPSON,
wife of JAS.--who is now in service of U.S.; SP. GARLAND. Witnesses:
CHAS. PERROW, THOS. JOPLING, JNO. STEVENS.

583. 4 November 1812. JAS. STEVENS, JR. to SAML. STEVENS...L145;
slave boys. Witnesses: JORDAN EDMUNDS.

584. 4 December 1812. JNO. BETHEL to CHAS. C. PATTESON...$100; to
CHAS. C. PATTESON, 9 May 1818, 14 3/4 acres both sides Rucker's
Run. Lines: grantor, MURPHY BROWN and Company, Nelson and
Albemarle Union Factory just below it. Witnesses: RO. FRANKLIN,
ELISHA FORTUNE, JNO. SHELMAN, WM. MARTIN.

585. 25 January 1813. JAS. MURPHY and JESSE JOPLING, overseers
of the poor, to WM. MORGAN...bind out JESSE FITZGERALD, infant
bastard of RACHEL FITZGERALD--boot and shoemaker art which MORGAN
follows--until 21.

586. 22 February 1813. RICH. WOOD and wife, AUCKEY, to VAL.
HYLTON...$285 57 acres. Lines: grantee.

587. 4 January 1813. JNO. W. and HENRY M. GREEN, WM. CRISP and
wife, ELIZ., and ABIGAIL GREEN to RICH. GILLIAM, Buckingham...
to JNO. W. GREEN, 9 October 1813--L103-17-6 138½ acres in Buckingham.
Lines: JNO. BUNDRAM, MOSES FLOOD. Witnesses: ARTHUR H. POLLARD,
WM. ALLEN, GEO. MARTIN.

588. 2 January 1810. JNO. WATKINS to WILLIS H. WILLS and RO.
FRANKLIN to secure MURPHY BROWN and Company...five shillings
Dutch Creek. Lines: JNO. MATTHEWS, WM. BAILEY, DUNMORE DAMERON
eighty acres where JNO. WATKINS lives; stock. Witnesses: RICH.
POWELL, RO. MOORE, WM. BAILEY, ABSALOM JOHNSON.

590. 17 June 1811. JAS. JOPLING, Albemarle, HAWES COLEMAN,
LEWIS NICHOLAS and ZACH. ROBERTS, commissioners to BRANSFORD
WEST...Amherst County decree, November, 1801: THOS. JOPLING et al.
versus JAS. JOPLING, surviving executor of THOS. JOPLING et al.--
tracts not devised by THOS. JOPLING to be sold; JAS. JOPLING
bought at L13-one tract west--buys at L13; ten shillings. Thirty
acres south fork Rockfish borders Menasoce's Mt. Witnesses:
WM. BALL, JAS. and JESSE JOPLING.

592. 28 November 1811. HENRY SMITH to LANDON CABELL and WILLIS H.
WHITE to secure MURPHY BROWN and Company...five shillings
south fork Rockfish and Dutch. Lines: GEO. VAUGHAN, HUDSON MARTIN.
Sixty acres bought from DR. WM. MARTIN--145 acres bought from JAS.
TURNER; 390 acres bought from estate of THOS. ANDERSON; 176 acres
bought from LUNSFORD LOVING; 80 acres bought from --; slaves;
furniture. Witnesses: EDWD. LEWIS, SNOWDEN MADDUX, WM. J. ROBERTSON,
JAS. VIGUS, WM. KENNEDY.

594. 6 March 1813. SHEROD GRIFFIN and wife, POLLY, Bedford, to
JOS. SHELTON...L110 103½ acres south borders Rockfish.
Lines: MATT. HARRIS, deceased, grantee, WILSON C. NICHOLAS, THOS.
LOCKETT. Witnesses: ROD. L. TALIAFERRO, HARRISON GRIFFIN,
AMADIAH GRIFFIN, WM. LEE, BENJ. HARRIS.

594. 22 March 1813. WM. BREEDLOVE and wife, MARY BREEDLOVE, to
JNO. BUSTER, Albemarle...$450 150 acres. Lines: LANDON
CABELL, ELISHA PETERS, deceased--where WM. BREEDLOVE lives. To
JNO. BUSTER, 4 December 1817.

595. 22 March 1810. JNO. FARIS and wife, MARY, to JNO. WINGFIELD,
Albemarle...L240-10 275 acres. Lines: JNO. SNIDER, JESSE
JOPLING, WM. HORSLEY, FRANCIS WEST--Rockfish--where JNO. FARIS
lives.

596. 14 December 1812. ANDREW HART and wife, ELIZ., Albemarle, to
WM. SUDDARTH, Albemarle...L800 200 acres Rockfish. Lines:
CAPT. AZARIAH MARTIN, HUDSON MARTIN, JAS. LOBNAN, EDWD. COLES,
WM. HARRIS, CHAS. SMITH. Witnesses: E. L. WILLIAMS, WM. MOORE,
RICH. SUDDARTH, JAS. SUDDARTH, JR., JNO. R. MARTIN.

597. 30 November 1812. JNO. TURNER and wife, LUCY, to NATHAN
      BLAIN, Albemarle...L300 200 acres both sides Rockfish.
Lines: HENRY EMMERSON, WM. MARTIN, WM. MOSBY, CONRAD MOWYERS,
BENJ. PAYNE, Cove Creek. Witnesses: JNO. PLEASANTS, CLAIBORNE
GENTRY, JNO. HENDERSON.

598. 13 November 1812. JAS. TURNER and wife, LUCY, to NATHAN
      BLAIN, Albemarle...L32-10 32 acres. Lines: MATT. HARRIS,
deceased, WM. TURNER. Witnesses: as above.

599. 1 September 1812. JESSE H. WALKER, Buckingham, to JNO. H.
      JOHNSON...$2500; slaves; stock. Witnesses: ALEX. J. TURNER,
WM. CUNNINGHAM, CHAS. L. BARRETT, WM. PAMPLIN.

600. 19 January 1813. RO. RIVES, JAS. MURPHY, JNO. HIGGINBOTHAM
      to NATHL. OFFUTT...L45 three lots in New Market; east side
Tye and not far from its mouth--6, 7 and 8. Lines: lot 5--given
by WM. CABELL to LANDWON CABELL and now that of NATHL. OFFUTT.
Witnesses: RO. FRANKLIN, JAS. SMILEY, WM. J. CABELL.

601. 1 January 1813. FRANCES FITZPATRICK to MOSES FITZPATRICK...
      $50 tract of THOS. FITZPATRICK, deceased--east of main road
from HUDSON MARTIN to CH; about 110 acres. Lines: NAT. BRIDGWATER,
SAML. BRIDGWATER, deceased, JNO. FITZPATRICK. Witnesses: WM.
EDMUNDS, JAS. N. EDMONDS, MOSES HUGHES, SR. (JR.).

602. 1 September 1810. ALEX. F. ROSE, executor of HENRY ROSE, to
      THOS. MASSIE...$74 74 acres; part of Piney Commons--allotted
to HENRY ROSE on division of late COL. JNO. ROSE. Witnesses:
STERLING CLIABORNE, JNO. N. ROSE, DAVID S. GARLAND, CHAS. R. ROSE,
HILL CARTER, JNO. JACOBS, JR., WM. P. JACOBS.

603. 22 March 1813. CHAS. C. PATTESON to WILLIS H. WILLS and
      WM. J. CABELL to secure RO. FRANKLIN...$1.00; 14 3/4 acres
both sides Rucker's Run below Nelson and Albemarle Factory--bought
lately from JNO. BETHEL.

604. 4 February 1813. WM. DOUGLAS, Albemarle, to THOS. WHITE,
      Richmond...$551 two tracts Rockfish. One bought by NATHAN
BARNETT from WM. WRIGHT--91 acres. Lines: JOS. SHELTON--where
NATHAN BARNETT lives. Second, bought by NATHAN BARNETT from WM.
FORBUS--20 acres adjacent to one. Deed of Trust by BARNETT to
WM. DOUGLAS, 29 May 1811, to secure WHITE. Sold, 4 February 1813,
at $551. Witnesses: CHAS. R. ROSE, SAML. LEAKE, C. GARLAND.

606. 25 February 1812. AARON COLLINS who married PEGGY CAMPBELL,
      heir of CLARY CAMPBELL, deceased--child of JNO. CAMPBELL,
deceased, and wife, PEGGY, and WM. CAMPBELL to JAS. MONTGOMERY...
$7.50; interest in lot of CLARY CAMPBELL--part of JNO. CAMPBELL
tract. Lines: grantee, JNO. MARR. Witnesses: LANDON H. BRENT,
JACOB PUCKETT, JR., JNO. SHIELDS, JNO. EDWARDS.

607. 7 December 1812. JNO. BETHEL to ANDERSON MOSS...$100 Rucker's
      Run; blank acres. Lines: factory lot, grantor, COL. CABELL.
Witnesses: RO. FRANKLIN, CHAS. C. PATTESON, JNO. CREWS, JNO.
SHELLMAN.

608. 19 January 1813. A. B. WARWICK and JNO. MOSBY as to JUDITH S.
      CABELL, wife of LADON CABELL, 28 December 1812, to THOS.
MASSIE.

609. 10 February 1813. JAS. MONTGOMERY and wife, RACHEL, to THOS.
      MASSIE...$530 Hat Creek. Lines: JOHN MARR, grantee, ANTHONY
MULLINS, RICH. L. ELLIS, grantor--108 acres; 96 acres is part of
tract bought by JAS. MONTGOMERY from JAS. VOSE; rest--allotted CLARY
CAMPBELL from tract of JNO. CAMPBELL, deceased, as legatee. Lines:
JNO. MARR, THOS. MASSIE, ANTHONY NULLINS, RICH. L. ELLIS. Witnesses:
EDWD. C. F. COFFEY, ILLIA EVERITT, JNO. HIGHT, JNO. CAMDEN, SR.

610. 10 February 1813. WM. CAMPBELL and wife, FRANKEY, to JAS.
MONTGOMERY...FRANKEY is heir of CLARA CAMPBELL, who was heir
of JNO. CAMPBELL--$7.50; interest in Hat Creek tract. Witnesses:
CORNL. CAMPBELL, RO. RIVES.

611. 20 January 1813. WM. LEE HARRIS and wife, POLLY, to JAS.
MONTGOMERY...$800; both sides Hatt Creek; 319 acres. Lines:
grantee, JNO. MOORE, JNO. CAMPBELL, deceased, RICH. L. ELLIS. To
WM. LEE HARRIS from trustees of JAS. VOSE, agent: DAVID BULLOCK.
DOBSON land.

612. 23 March 1813. JAS. LOVING, JR. and wife, NANCY, to LUNSFORD
LOVING...$105 25 acres south side Loving's Gap. Lines:
JAS. STEVENS, SR. Witnesses: LANDON CABELL, JNO. MOSBY, ARTHUR H.
POLLARD. LANDON CABELL and JNO. MOSBY, Justices of the Peace.

614. 23 March 1813. JAS. LOVING, JR. and wife, NANCY, to LUNSFORD
LOVING...$25 north side Loving's Gap; as heirs of JNO. LOVING,
deceased. Witnesses and Justices of the Peace as above.

616. 4 November 1812. HUDSON MARTIN, JR. and wife, MARY ANN, to
HENRY BENNER...L472 Meriwether Branch. 118 acres. Lines:
grantor, the road, GEO. MARTIN, RO. HENDERSON, CHAS. BRIDGWATER.

617. 14 April 1813. HENRY BENNER to WM. EDMUNDS...280 acres both
sides south fork Rockfish. Lines: MOSES HUGHES, RICH. LEE
WEST, my own.

618. 22 March 1813. JOS. MONTGOMERY and wife, JANE, BENJ. HARRIS
and wife, MARY, RICH. NETHERLAND and wife, MARGARET, BARBARA
MARTIN, WM. B. HARRIS and wife, ELIZ., heirs of SAML. WOODS, deceased,
to SALLY WHEELER, executrix of JACOB WHEELER, deceased...$99; 66 acres
north fork Rockfish. Lines: RO. HENDERSON. Witnesses: JNO.
HARRIS, N. HARLOW, JR., JAS. MONTGOMERY.

619. 25 December 1812. JNO. DETTOR and wife, ELIZ., Albemarle,
to NICHL. DETTOR...love and $1.00; both sides Patin's branch,
branch of north fork Rockfish; 160 acres. Transferred by JNO.
KNOWLS and wife, SARAH, to JNO. DETTOR, 6 December 1793. Lines:
JACOB RUDASIL, CHAS. RODES, JAS. BROOKS. Witnesses: JNO. NEESE,
SOL. CARY, JACOB S--illegible.

620. 12 April 1813. ROBT. HENDRON and wife, MARY, to RO. MITCHELL...
L50 89 acres headwaters Rockfish. Lines: SAML. HEIZER.
Witnesses: CHAS. MC CUE, SAML. HEIZER, -- illegible.

622. 7 April 1813. JAS. OTEY and CHAS. MARKLE, JR., Bedford
Justices of the Peace, as to POLLY GRIFFIN, wife of SHERAD
GRIFFIN, 6 March 1813, to JOS. SHELTON.

623. 2 June 1812. CHAS. BRIDGWATER and wife, LUCY, to BARTLETT
FOX...L50; mill seat; Meriwether's Creek; border of north
Rockfish; pond and race. Witnesses: HUDSON MARTIN, JR., NICHL.
DETTOR, THOS. C. MULLING (?), JNO. VINES, -- illegible.

624. 18 March 1813. RICH. HARE and wife, ELIZ., to WINGFIELD
NORVELL...$375 Hickory Creek, border of Rockfish. Part of
a tract and where RICH. HARE lives--37 acres. Lines: grantor,
JNO. ROBERTS. Witnesses: MATT. HARRIS, JR., JNO. HARRIS,
JNO. ROBERTS.

This is from the first register and it is a copy. The Clerk does not know what became of original bonds. I am not sure of some names and have put question marks by them. In many cases they did not give date of marriage.

3. 14 September 1810. I. or J. M. ALEXANDER (could be MC ALEXANDER) to THOS. E. FORTUNE...Security: S. GARLAND. WM. WRIGHT, Officiant--in many cases they did not give date of marriage.

5. 13 August 1812. JNO. ALLEN and P. CASHWELL...Security: FLEMING CASHWELL.

SA ALLEN--HEZEKIAH BAILEY. 1 October 7, 1808. Security: WM. ALLEN; note says SUKEY--see original.

L. S. ANDERSON--ANDREW SMITH

ELIZABETH ARISMAN--A. WALLER

5. 25 May 1812. FREDERICK ARNOLD and R. CRITZER...Security: JNO. CRITZER. Officiant: BENJ. BURGHER.

4. 16 December 1811. LEWIS ARRINGTON and S. CARTER...Security: S. CARTER. Officiant: JNO. ALLCOCK on same day. Note: LAWSON ARRINGTON and not LEWIS.

R. AUSTIN--JNO. JOPLING

PATSY BABER--JNO. CRITZER

SALLY BABER--GEO. CRITZER

ANN S. BAILEY--S. S. SCRUGGS

3. 22 October 1810. DAVID BAILEY and NINA BAILEY...Security: WM. BAILEY.

HEZEKIAH BAILEY--see SA ALLEN

L. BAILEY--WM. BAILEY

5. 25 January 1813. M. D. BAILEY and N. C. SCRUGGS. Security: SAML. S. SCRUGGS.

NINA BAILEY--WM. BAILEY

W. BAILEY--WM. SMITH

5. 25 January 1813. WM. BAILEY and L. BAILEY...Security: WM. BAILEY. L. (S.) BALDWIN--M. C. NAPIER

3. 8 February 1811. LEWIS BALL and E. DIXON. Security: JOSEPH DIXON.

M. BALL--B. JOPLING

2. 11 August 1810. GEO. BANTON and SALLY SMITH. Security: THOS. CHILDRESS.

Note: I began this when I had only gone through 1816 so inserts are put in when I got more data. B.F.D.

5. 27 April 1812. JNO. BATES and JUDITH PATTON...Security:
WM. HARLOW. Officiant. BENJ. BURGHER.

L. (S) BECKNAL--N. SNEED

7. 10 December 1814. WM. L. BELL and P. PURVIS. Security:
S. GARLAND. Officiant: WM. WRIGHT 1814.

J. BETHEL--JNO. MURRY

4. 7 November 1811. NELSON BETHEL and BETSY PERKINS. Security:
NATHAN BLAIR.

S. (L) BETHEL--JNO. GUNTER

3. 21 February 1811. WM. BIBB and P. L. HILL. Security:
JNO. P. HILL.

6. 20 May 1813. BENJ. BIBEE and S. MULLINS. Security: GEO.
PACE. Officiant: ANTHONY GIANNIY, same day.

11. 7 June 1818. JAS. M. BISHOP and M. S. SHACKLEFORD. Security:
JNO. SPEARS.

B. BOGLEGUM (? not indexed)--clerks seemed to skip the hard
ones--THOS. TAYLOR

10. 15 December 1816. JNO. BOND and M. SPEARS. Security:
JNO. SPEARS. Officiant: ANTHONY GIANNIY, December 16th.

4. 5 August 1811. WM. BOWLING and PATSY MEEKS. Security:
WM. MEEKS. Officiant: ANTHONY GIANNIY, August 8th.

S. BOWMAN--SAML. HARDING

E. BRADSHAW--JNO. HOUSEWRIGHT

3. 24 February 1811. JNO. BRADY and POLLY EAST. Security:
JNO. BARNETT. Officiant: WM. WRIGHT, February.

ELIZ. BREEDLOVE--THOS. MURRILL

N. BREEDLOVE--WILLIS CASH

E. BRIDGWATER--BENJ. HARDIN

5. 24 April 1812. NATHAN BRIDGWATER and R. CLARK. Security:
J. BRIDGWATER.

M. C. BRITTON--JNO. HARGROVE

1. 3 August 1808. JNO. BROOKS and M. POWELL. Security:
RO. NIMMO. Officiant: WM. WRIGHT.

10. 16 October 1817. R. W. BROOKS and N. M. MORRISON. Security:
JNO. NEESE.

P. BRUNHAM(HUM)--J. HOUSEWRIGHT

5. 16 July 1811. JAS. BRYANT and POLLY W. MEEKS. Security:
RICH. MEEKS. Officiant: ANTHONY GIANNIY, July 18th.

2. 11 November 1809. RICH. BRYANT and C. CRISP. Security:
JNO. CRISP. Officiant: WM. WRIGHT, November, 1809.

S. (?) BURCH--JAS. GARLAND

JANE (JACE?) BURKS--THOS. MATTHEWS

MATA BURNETT--JOSHUA FOSTER

CLA CABELL--JESSE IRVIN

M. CABELL--J. (?) HIGGINBOTHAM

M. E. CABELL--GEO. CALLAWAY

P. R. CABELL--GEO. WHITLOCK

3. 10 April 1811. GEO. CALLAWAY and M. E. CABELL...Security:
THOS. JORDAN.

1. 26 July 1809. CHAS. CALON and S. WILLIAMS. Security:
N. HARLOW, JR.

S. CAMDEN--JNO. HIGHT

S. CAMDEN--JOS. SHIELDS

4. 10 April 1812. WM. CAMP and L. LOVING. Security: WM. MOSS.
Officiant: BENJ. BURGHER.

4. 10 November 1811. WM. CAMP and E. M. GREEN. Security:
JNO. W. GREEN.

C. CAMPBELL--C. CAMPBELL

4. 23 September 1816. S. H. CAMPBELL. Officiant: ALEX. SALE,
26 September.

4. 28 October 1811. C. CAMPBELL and N. CASHWELL. Security:
WM. CASHWELL. Officiant: ALEX. SALE, November 28.

11. 24 November 1817. GEO. CAMPBELL and P. DRAKE. Security:
C. CAMPBELL.

11. 29 March 1818. JESSE CAMPBELL and P. HARVEY. Security:
JAS. W. HARVEY.

10. 29 August 1816. JOEL CAMPBELL and NANCY COFFEY. Security:
EDMUND COFFEY. Officiant: WALTER CHRISTIAN, September 8th.

M. CAMPBELL--J. GREGORY

N. CAMPBELL--JOEL HIGHT

1. 17 January 1809. PETER CAMPBELL and SALLY SMITH (blurred).
Security: REUBEN BATES. Officiant: WM. WRIGHT--I or J SMITH.

R. CAMPBELL--JNO. GREGORY

7. 25 (28?) November 1814. JNO. CARR, JR. and E. DAVIS. Security:
JNO. FITZGERALD. Officiant: ANTHONY GIANNIY, December 5th.

P. CARR--RO. W. FITZGERALD

6. 20 May 1813. JOSHUA CARROLL and S. H. (?) OWEN. Security:
SAML. WOODY.

S. CARROLL--A. PUGH

S. CARTER--LEWIS ARRINGTON

10. 14 December 1816. THOS. CARTER and P. G. SCRUGGS. S. C. C.
PATTESON.

5. 12 August 1812. WM. CARTER and A. HILL. Security: WM. MOSS.
Officiant: BEN. BURGHER.

NANCY CARY--PETER ROBINSON

L. B. CASH--JOSEPH HARGROVE

N. CASH--RO. MITCHELL

2. 15 March 1810. WILLIS CASH and N. BREEDLOVE. Security: JNO. PAINTER.

N. CASHWELL--C. CAMPBELL

P. CASHWELL--JNO. ALLEN

7. 18 March 1814. T. CATLING and BETSY MC CUE. Security: CHAS. MC CUE.

P. CHANDLER--WM. HILL

CATH. CLARK--JNO. MARTIN

R. CLARK--NATH. BRIDGWATER

2. 25 October 1809. RICH. CLARK and MARY WATTS. Security: STEPHEN WATTS. Officiant: WM. WRIGHT, October.

9. 26 August 1816. N. C. CLARKSON and B. HUGHES. Security: JNO. HUGHES. Officiant: JAS. BOYD, September 2nd.

A. CLASBY--JNO. STAPLES

NANCY COFFEY--JOEL CAMPBELL

SALLY COFFEY--TARLTON EAST

4. 28 October 1811. SAML. COLLINS and POLLY HUGHES. Security: MOSES HUGHES. Officiant: WM. CRAWFORD.

9. 6 October 1816. HAWES N. COLEMAN and S. WOODS. Security: JAS. WOODS.

7. 2 June 1814. ROBT. COLEMAN and P. HARRIS. Security: JOS. SHELTON.

7. 27 June 1814. T. (?) W. COLEMAN and M. B. MORRISON. Security: JNO. W. HARRIS. Officiant: BENJ. BURGHER.

6. 26 April 1816. JNO. P. COOLEY and J. THOMPSON. Security: J. THOMPSON. Officiant: BENJ. BURGHER.

1. 3 January 1809. JNO. COSBY and PATSY HARE. Security: LINDSEY GRIFFIN.

4. 26 December 1811. WM. COX and T. WILLIAMS. Security: HUGH SMILEY. Officiant: WM. WRIGHT, December.

2. 8 February 1810. THOS. CREW and DICEY MARTIN. Security: JNO. FORBUS.

POLLY CRITZER--CLIFTON TOMS

C. CRISP--RICH. BRYANT

11. 27 March 1818. GEO. CRITZER and SALLY BABER. Security: ZANEES (?) BABER.

6. 26 April 1813. JNO. CRITZER and PATSY BABER. Security: JNO. SNELL. Officiant: BENJ. BURGHER.

R. CRITZER--FREDERICK ARNOLD

9. 28 August 1816. ROBT. CUNNINGHAM and E. VIA. Security: MARTIN VIA.

6. 14 June 1813. W. CUNNINGHAM and L. MAYS. Security: JAS. MAYS.

11. 26 September 1817. ROBT. C. CUTLER and R. POWELL. Security: S. POWELL. Officiant: JAS. BOYD, October 2nd.

SOPHIA DAMRON--THOS. GLASS

11. 8 October 1817. EDWD. DAVIDSON and M. LAVENDER. Security: N. FORTUNE.

A. M. DAVIS--RICH. HARVEY

E. DAVIS--JNO. CARR, JR.

5. 18 January 1813. WM. DAVIS and P. LIGGIN. Security: WM. BRYANT.

7. 9 May 1814. DAVID G. DAVISON and M. LAVENDER. Security: WM. LAVENDER.

E. DAWSON--ELLIOT ROBERTS

2. 25 December 1809. NELSON DAWSON and SALLY WHITE. Security: JNO. WHITE. Officiant: WM. WRIGHT, January, 1810.

SALLY DAWSON--THOS. B. JOHNSON

1. 25 January 1819. NICHL. DEBTOR and POLLY RODES. Security: JACOB RUDACILL. Officiant: ZACH EMMERSON, January.

8. 11 December 1815. S. B. DENNY and N. LOVING. Security: SAML. STEVENS.

10. 22 January 1817. THRUSTON J. DICKINSON and M. MORRISON. Security: A. H. MORRISON. Officiant: BENJ. BURGHER.

E. DILLARD--HENRY H. WATTS

9. 30 September 1816. JAS. L. DILLARD and N. E. TURNER. Security: EZEK. DAY. Officiant: BENJ. BURGHER.

N. DIQUISOR--JAS. TOMS

E. DIXON--LEWIS BALL

1. 4 May 1809. JNO. DIXON and NANCY WOOD. Security: SAML. WOOD. Officiant: WM. WRIGHT, May, 1809.

P. DRAKE--GEO. CAMPBELL

F. DRUMMOND--JAS. FARIS

P. DUNCAN--LINDSEY PAGE

E. EAGLETON--T. W. M. SMITH

8. 7 October 1815. EZEK. EAST and DOLLY MELTON. Security: JNO. MELTON.

POLLY EAST--JNO. MELTON

POLLY EAST--JNO. BRADY

3. 29 January 1811. TARLTON EAST and SALLY COFFEY. Security: WM. COFFEY. Officiant: ROBT. JONES, 7 February.

E. EDMUNDS--GEO. S. MAYO

I. EDMUNDS--JNO. SHIPMAN

5. 2 February 1813. J. (I) N. EDMUNDS and N. TINDALL. Security:
    S. GARLAND. Officiant: WM. WRIGHT, same day.

6. 30 October 1813. JAS. EDMUNDS and S. FITZPATRICK. Security:
    THOS. FITZPATRICK. Officiant: BENJ. BURGHER.

    P. EDMUNDS--A. G. FOGUS

2. 14 February 1810. WM. EDMUNDS and NANCY PROFFITT. Security:
    H. HOLLOWAY.

    SUSAN ELLIOT--THOS. LINCOUS

8. 7 June 1815. H. EMBERSON and POLLY MATTHEWS. Security:
    JNO. MATTHEWS.

    ----EMBLY--GEO. HIGHT

    P. EMBLY--ZACH PARROCK

    ----EMESLY--NATHAN LANKFORD

    B. ENIX--FLEMING WOODY

    J. R. ESTES--A. B. WARWICK

7. 14 November 1814. JNO. EUBANK and L. (S) PARROCK. Security:
    JNO. WILLS. Officiant: WM. WRIGHT, 1814.

9. 25 February 1816. JNO. EUBANK and CATH. ROSE. Security:
    SP. GARLAND. Note: SP. was SPOTSWOOD GARLAND--early clerk
of Nelson. B.D.

4. 18 December 1811. THOS. EUBANK and J. PARRICK. Security:
    PORTER BIBEE. Officiant: WM. WRIGHT.

    R. EVANS--WM. MARTIN

8. 12 (?) September 1815. JACOB EVILEIZER and LETTY MELTON.
    Security: JESSE MELTON. Officiant: BENJ. BURGHER.

7. 12 October 1814. WM. FABER and I. (J) L. MARTIN. Security:
    T. J. DICKINSON.

7. 12 September 1814. JAS. FARIS and F. DRUMMOND. Security:
    JOS. HORSLEY.

8. 11 November 1815. GEO. FARRAR and F. L. SLAUGHTER. Security:
    WM. GILES.

8. 2 January 1816. JNO. M. FARRAR and N. WHEELER. Security:
    DANL. WHEELER. Officiant: BENJ. BURGHER.

    S. (L) FARRAR--JNO. MAXWELL

7. 25 January 1814. WM. H. FARRAR and ESTHER MC LAIN. Security:
    JNO. MC LAIN. Officiant: BENJ. BURGHER, February 4 (?).

9. 14 November 1816. EDWD. FERGUSON and N. ROBERTS. Security:
    JNO. ROBERTS. Officiant: SAML. DAY, 26 November.

4. 7 November 1811. JAS. B. FERGUSON and R. MATTHEWS. Security:
    JOS. MATTHEWS.

2. 30 November 1809. JNO. FERGUSON and N. SMITH. Security:
    GEO. FARRAR.

2. 20 September 1809. JAS. FITZGERALD and JANE OGLESBY. Security: JNO. FITZGERALD.

2. 22 December 1809. JNO. B. FITZGERALD and E. HARRIS. Security: HARRISON GRIFFIN.

5. 23 November 1812. RO. W. FITZGERALD and P. CARR. Security: JNO. FITZGERALD. Officiant: ANTHONY GIANNIY, December 12th.

1. 4 August 1809. S. L. FITZGERALD and MARY HARPER. Security: BARTLETT FITZGERALD. Officiant: WM. CHRISTIAN.

E. FITZPATRICK--WM. WITT

11. 24 November 1817. G. B. FITZPATRICK and P. FITZPATRICK. Security: JNO. J. WOOD.

7. 10 September 1814. JAS. FITZPATRICK and L. FITZPATRICK. Security: HENRY ROBERTS.

JANE FITZPATRICK and DAVID WITT

L. FITZPATRICK--JAS. FITZPATRICK

6. 4 October 1813. MOSES FITZPATRICK and H. HUGHES. Security: JAS. HUGHES. Officiant: WM. WRIGHT, same day.

P. FITZPATRICK--G. B. FITZPATRICK

S. FITZPATRICK--JAS. EDMUNDS

10. 28 March 1817. CHAS. FLOOD and MILLY SKINNELL. Security: WM. HAWKINS.

PEGGY FLOOD--BENJ. PONTON

L. FLOWERS--SAML. WOODY

M. FLOYD--WM. MULLINS

6. 26 July 1813. A. G. FOGUS and P. EDMUNDS. Security: CHAS. EDMUNDS.

B. FORTUNE--HUDSON SMALL

JANE FORTUNE--JNO. PONTON

7. 18 July 1814. JESSE FORTUNE and SALLY THOMAS. Security: JAS. THOMAS.

P. FORTUNE--LAWRENCE WILLS

P. T. FORTUNE--JAS. MC ALEXANDER

5. 8 July 1812. THOS. FORTUNE and E. WRIGHT. Security: ANDREW WRIGHT.

3. 14 September 1810. THOS. E. FORTUNE and J. (I) M. ALEXANDER (MC ALEXANDER?). Security: S. GARLAND. Officiant: WM. WRIGHT.

C. FOSTER--TERISHA TURNER

1. 3 August 1808. JOSHUA FOSTER and MATA BURNETT. Security: A. MC ALEXANDER.

S. J. FOSTER--SAML. TURNER

SUS FOSTER--JAS. PAGE

10. 23 December 1816. WM. FOSTER and F. B. ROBERTS. Security: HENRY ROBERTS. Officiant: JAS. BOYD, 24th.

9. 26 November 1816. BARTLETT FOX and POLLY LIVELY. Security: WM. LIVELY. Officiant: SAML. DAY, 28th.

NANCY FOX--WM. SMITH

POLLY GARDNER--JNO. WOODY

7. 22 September 1814. JAS. GARLAND and S(?) BURCH. Security: RICH. BURCH. Officiant: WM. WRIGHT, 1814.

1. 17 January 1809. SAML. GERALD and NANCY RAMSEY. Security: WM. RAMSEY.

2. 12 March 1810. THOS. GLASS and SOPHIA DAMRON. Security: WM. ROGERS.

6. 13 July 1813. RO. GOOLSBY and N. TINDALL. Security: JAS. N. EDMUNDS. Officiant: WM. WRIGHT, same day.

C. GORDIN--CHAS. PETERS

11. 19 December 1817. R. GRANT and R. HARRIS. Security: H. GRIFFIN. Officiant: JNO. SHEPHERD, 25th.

S. GRAVES--JAS. LYON

3. 20 November 1810. THOS. GRAVES and I(J) TURNER. Security: TERISAH TURNER.

5. 21 December 1812. J. GREGORY and M. CAMPBELL. Security: JOEL CAMPBELL. Officiant: ANTHONY GIANNIY, 24th December.

5. 8 February 1813. JNO. GREGORY and R. CAMPBELL. Security: JOEL CAMPBELL. Officiant: ANTHONY GIANNIY, 13th February.

E. M. GREEN--WM. CAMP

7. 2 February 1815. DR. GRIFFIN and P. MELTON. Security: WM. MC CALEB. Officiant: JAS. BOYD, -- February.

F. GRIFFIN--JAS. WOOD

8. 31 July 1815. JNO. GUNTER and S. (L) BETHEL. Security: JOEL BETHEL. Officiant: BENJ. BURGHER.

F. HAMLET--JNO. WRIGHT (note: some are spelled HAMBLETT--below)

10. 22 September 1817. JNO. HAMLET and B. LOVING. Security: JNO. BRADSHAW. Officiant: JNO. SHEPHERD, 25th.

S. HAMLET--WM. J. KIDD

LUCY HAMBLETT--W. C. KIDD

2. 19 September 1809. WM. HAMBLET and DICEY WRIGHT. Security: THOS. ROBERTS. WITT--bride.

2. 25 December 1809. RO. HAMBLETON and N. RIPPETOE. Security: PETER RIPPETOE.

10. 22 July 1817. JNO. HAMNER and PATSY SMALL. Security: HENRY ROBERTS. Officiant: JAS. BOYD, 29th.

9. 1 February 1816. SAML. HANSBROUGH and S. (L) LOVING. Security: SAML. LOVING. Officiant: SAML. DAY, same

4. 16 March 1812. BENJ. HARDIN and E. BRIDGWATER. Security: JNO. N. DIXON. Officiant: WM. WRIGHT, March.

11. 14 July 1818. E. HARDING and L. B. WEST. Security: RO. WILBOURN. Officiant: SAML. DAY, 16th.

1. 13 September 1808. SAML. HARDING and S. BOWMAN. Security: N. HARDING.

7. 30 August 1814. WM. HARDING and SARAH WHITE. Security: JNO. WRIGHT. Officiant: WM. WRIGHT, 1814.

6. 26 June 1813. RICH. HARDWICK and P. JOHNSON. Security: SAML. JOHNSON.

PATSY HARE--JNO. COSBY

REBECCA HARE--EDWIN THOMAS

1. 27 May 1809. JNO. HARGROVE and M. C. BRITTON. Security: S. GARLAND. Officiant: WM. WRIGHT, May.

7. 21 March 1814. JOS. HARGROVE and L. B. CASH. Security: RO. MITCHELL. Officiant: WM. WRIGHT, same day. Note: This couple was the parents of SARAH E. HARGROVE who married RUFUS ANDERSON HIGGINBOTHAM and my daughter-in-law, MARY GAYLE PETTYJOHN, wife of my son, THURMAN BLANTON DAVIS--is a descendant. RANDOLPH CASH named SARAH E. HARGROVE as granddaughter, but did not name her mother. (It would appear that all Hargroves were children of Jos. Hargrove and wife, nee Cash. The Hargroves bug me for they should be grandchildren of old Hezekiah who was Revolutionary soldier. Sweeny has data, but can't find any data in Nelson as to heirs. Note that Joseph had son, Hezekiah. B.F.D.)

9. 17 July 1816. N. HARGROVE and L. LOVING. Security: SAML. LOVING.

3. 28 January 1811. WM. HARGROVE and S. WHITE. Security: JNO. HARGROVE. Officiant: WM. WRIGHT, same day.

F. HARLOW--LARKIN MILLER

POLLY HARLOW--JNO. WEIR

MARY HARPER--S. L. FITZGERALD

C. HARRIS(?)--JNO. WOOD

E. HARRIS--JNO. B. FITZGERALD

8. 25 March 1818. JNO. HARRIS and A. STRICKLIN. Security: ABIEL STRICKLIN. Officiant: BENJ. BURGHER.

3. 22 January 1811. LEE W. HARRIS and E. C. SHELTON. Security: JOS. SHELTON. Officiant: WM. WRIGHT, same day.

M. HARRIS--JNO. ROBERTS

M? A. G. HARRIS--ST. GEO. TUCKER

N. HARRIS--ST. GEO. TUCKER

N. HARRIS--JAS. MARTIN

P. HARRIS--DAVID JACOBS

P. HARRIS--RO. COLEMAN

R. HARRIS--R. GRANT

9. 6 June 1816. JNO. HARVEY and S. SANDERS. Security: JNO. SANDERS. Officiant: JNO. SHEPHERD, 30 (?) June.

P. HARVEY--JESSE CAMPBELL

11. 31 March 1818. RICH. HARVEY and A. M. DAVIS. Security: EDMD. DAVIS. Officiant: ANTHONY GIANNIY, same day.

LUCY HATTER--JAS. SNEED

9. 17 August 1816. WM. HATTER and NANCY MEEKS. Security: RICH. MEEKS. Officiant: ANTHONY GIANNIY, same day.

6. 21 March 1813. WM. HAWKINS and C. SKINNER. Security: PRICE SKINNER. Officiant: WM. WRIGHT, same.

6. 1 October 1813. WM. HAYES (HAGER?) and ELIZ. SEAY. Security: JAS. SEAY.

4. 16 December 1811. THOS. HENDERSON and P. SYMES. Security: HUDSON MARTIN, JR.

5. 23 June 1812. WM. HENDERSON and E. MC CLAIN. Security: HENRY MC CLAIN. Officiant: BENJ. BURGHER.

11. 26 January 1818. J. HENDRICK and B. LAINE. Security: WM. HORSLEY.

N. HENLEY--DABNEY KEY

7. 25 November 1814. CHAS. HENRY and P. ISBEL. Security: JOS. ROBERTS.

1. 4 August 1809. JNO. HENSLEY and FRANCES SMITH. Security: JOS. SMITH.

C. HICKOK--THOS. HILL

8. 4 December 1815. J. (I) HIGGINBOTHAM and M. CABELL. Security: S. .J CABELL, JR.

D. HIGHT--WM. MORAN

5. 27 April 1812. GEO. HIGHT and ---WMBLEY. Security: LUKE EMBLEY. Officiant: WM. WRIGHT, same.

8. 28 August 1815. JOEL HIGHT and N. CAMPBELL. Security: H. CAMPBELL.

4. 11 March 1812. JNO. HIGHT and BETSY CAMDEN. Security: JNO. BRADY. Officiant: WM. WRIGHT, March.

M. HIGHT--SHELTON JONES

A. HILL--WM. CARTER

B. HILL--WM. MOSES

P. L. HILL--WM. BIBB

9. 22 January 1816. SAML. HILL and M. OFFLIGHTER. Security: THOS. OFFLIGHTER. Officiant: BENJ. BURGHER.

3. 16 March 1811. THOS. HILL and C. HICKOK. Security: JNO. HICKOK.

4. 24 March 1812. WM. HILL and P. CHANDLER. Security: JNO. FARIS.

2. 12 February 1810. JNO. HOUCHIN and S. JOHNSON. Security: ROWLAND PROFFITT.

11. 19 December 1817. J. HOUSEWRIGHT and P. BRUNHAM. Security: JNO. NANCE.

8. 30 December 1815. JNO. HOUSEWRIGHT and E. BRADSHAW. Security: THOS. WOODY.

P. HOUSEWRIGHT--WM. TRUSLOW

1. 8 November 1808. WM. HUDGINS and SELEY LIGGON. Security: JNO. TYREE.

B. HUGHES--N. C. CLARKSON 9

H. HUGHES--MOSES FITZPATRICK

POLLY HUGHES (?)--THOS. WEIR

POLLY HUGHES--SAML. COLLINS

5. 8 January 1813. DAVID HUNTER and P. SAVAGE. Security: JNO. SAVAGE. Officiant: WM. WRIGHT, same day.

9. 12 November 1816. DAVID HUNTER and P. THOMAS. Security: HENRY THOMAS. Officiant: SAML. DAY, 15th.

11. 24 October 1817. RO. HUNTER and MARY SEAY. Security: NELSON SEAY.

K. INGLE--R. THOMAS

8. 27 June 1815. JESSE IRVIN and CLA CABELL. Security: WM. J. CABELL.

P. ISBEL--CHAS. HENRY

S. JACKSON--JNO. WINTERS

6. 27 December 1813. DAVID JACOBS and P. HARRIS. Security: PETER C. JACOBS.

5. 10 October 1812. LEWIS (RO. L.) JEFFERSON and M. JORDAN. Security: JAS. EDMUNDS.

E. JOHNSON--JNO. MELTON

11. 8 December 1817. F. JOHNSON and C. G. WARWICK. Security: JAS. JOHNSON.

4. 18 November 1811. GEO. JOHNSON and SALLY WOOD. Security: JAS. WOOD. Officiant: WM. WRIGHT, November.

1. 13 December 1808. JNO. JOHNSON and BETH LOVING. Security: SAML. STAPLES. Officiant: WM. WRIGHT, December.

8. 27 December 1815. JNO. H. JOHNSON and N. WALKER. Security: JOS. HORSLEY.

M. JOHNSON--JACOB YOST

N. JOHNSON--WM. MORRIS

P. JOHNSON--ELISHA RIDER

P. JOHNSON--RICH. HARDWICK

PATSY JHONSON--Z. PUGH

POLLY JOHNSON--THOS. THORNTON

S. JOHNSON--JNO. HOUCHIN

3.   7 September 1810. SPENCER JOHNSON and M. THURMOND. Security:
WM. THURMOND.

6.   17 July 1813. STEPHEN JOHNSON and B. PERRY. Security:
JAS. HUGHES. Officiant: WM. WRIGHT, same.

1.   27 June 1808. THOS. B. JOHNSON and SALLY DAWSON. Security:
NELSON DAWSON. Officiant: WM. CRAWFORD, July, 1808.

BETSY C. JONES--W. TRIBLE

10. 7 June 1817. GABL. JONES and MARY KIRBY. Security: CHAPMAN
KIRBY.

8.   24 July 1815. SHELTON C. JONES and M. HIGHT. Security:
THOS. JONES. This one is hard to read, but HARDESTY and
BROCK--see my J will work on Amherst--calls her MONA HIGHT or HITE.

11. 16 December 1817. B. JOPLING and M. BALL. Security: RICH.
BALL. Officiant: JNO. SHEPHERD, 18th.

2.   14 April 1810. JNO. JOPLING and R. AUSTIN. Security:
ANDREW SKINNELL. Officiant: WM. WRIGHT, 12 July.

S. A. JOPLING--NATHL. TOWNSEND

5.   10 October 1802. M. JORDAN--LEWIS (RO. L.) JEFFERSON

J. KEETIN--REUBEN TYREE

C. KENNEDY--WM. WRIGHT

5.   26 June 1812. DABNEY KEY and N. HENLEY. Secuirty: SAML.
HENLEY.

11. 22 December 1817. COLEMAN W. KIDD and S. LOVING. Security:
SP. GARLAND. Officiant: JNO. SHEPHERD, 25th.

3.   30 January 1811. HUDSON KIDD and L. WRIGHT. Security:
ANDREW WRIGHT.

6.   12 July 1813. JNO. KIDD and L. SANDERS. Security: WM. C.
KIDD.

M. A. KIDD--J. D. LANKFORD

9.   8 June 1816. R. N. KIDD and A. WILLOUGHBY. Security: JOSHUA
WILLOUGHBY. Officiant: JNO. SHEPHERD, 9th.

3.   17 October 1811. W. C. KIDD and LUCY HAMBLETT. Security:
WM. HAMBLETT.

6.   23 December 1813. WM. J. KIDD and S. HAMLET. Security:
WM. HAMLET.

11. 24 August 1818. CHAPMAN KIRBY and B. LANGHORNE (?). Security:
THOS. FITZPATRICK. Officiant: JAS. BOYD, 25th.

MARY KIRBY--GABL. JONES

10. 22 September 1817. JOS. KYLE and SIGUS PENN. Security:
THOMPSON NOEL. Officiant: SAML. DAVIDSON, 1 October.

B. LAINE--J. HENDRICK

E. B. LANDCRAFT--HENRY D. ROBERTS

9. 13 February 1816. JAS. LANKFORD and J. MARTIN (MURTIN?).
    Security: WM. MURRILL. Officiant: JNO. SHEPHERD, 14th.

    B. LANGHORNE (?)--CHAPMAN KIRBY

8. 7 (9) October 1815. LEWIS F. LANHAM and A. SANDERS. Security:
    HUDSON WATKINS.

11. 21 January 1818. W. LANHAM and N. MATTHEWS. Security:
    J. MATTHWS. Officiant: JNO. SHEPHERD, 4 March.

1. 27 February 1809. EDWD. LANKFORD and B. MURRILL. Security:
    R. T. MITCHELL.

9. 7 September 1816. J. D. LANKFORD and M. A. KIDD. Security:
    JAS. KIDD. Officiant: J. SHEPHERD, 8th.

    L. LANKFORD--SCRUGGS

2. 25 September 1809. NATHAN LANKFORD and -- EMLEY. Security:
    JNO. EMESLEY. Officiant: WM. WRIGHT, -- September. Note to
see J. EMESLY.

    P. LANKFORD--HUDSON WATKINS

    M. LAVENDER--EDWD. DAVIDSON

    M. LAVENDER--DAVID DAVIDSON

1. 9 January 1809. SAML. B. LAYNE and N. SEAY. Security: JAS.
    SEAY.

10. 11 March 1817. WM. LAYNE and P. SMITH. Security: RO. SMITH.

    JANE LEE--GEO. MORRIS

    P. LIGGIN--WM. DAVIS

    SALLY LIGGIN--WM. DAVIS

    M. LILLEY--JNO. RAMSEY

7. 25 July 1814. THOS. LINCOUS and SUSAN ELLIOT. Security:
    WM. RYAN. Officiant: WM. WRIGHT, 1814.

    J. (I) LIVELY--JOS. TYREE

    POLLY LIVELY--BARTLETT FOX

9. 20 August 1816. WM. B. LIVELY and JANE MARTIN. Security:
    JOS. TYREE. Officiant: SAML. DAY, 23rd.

    L. LOBBAN--M. WALLACE

    B. LOVING--JNO. HAMLET

    BETH LOVING--JNO. JOHNSON

9. 30 October 1816. JNO. LOVING and NANCY SCURY. Check by it
    and not indexed. Security: S. GARLAND.

    L. LOVING--N. HARGROVE

    L. LOVING--WM. CAMP

    N. LOVING--S. B. DENNY

    N. LOVING--SAML. STEVENS

S. (L) LOVING--SAML. HANSBROUGH

S. LOVING--COLEMAN W. KIDD

11. 24 August 1818. P. LOVING and PATSY WEIR. Security: THOS. WEIR. Officiant: JAS. BOYD, 25th.

10. 25 August 1817. JNO. LUCK and LUCY RIVES. Security: JNO. CRITZER.

6. 26 March 1813. JAS. LYON and S. GRAVES. Security: HENRY ROBERTS. Officiant: WM. WRIGHT, same day.

DICEY MARTIN--THOS. CREW

5. 23 November 1812. HEZEKIAH MARTIN and M. WINGFIELD. Security: WM. L. WATTS. Officiant: JNO. ALCOCK, November.

I. (J) L. MARTIN--WM. FABER

6. 1 January 1814. JAMES MARTIN and N. HARRIS. Security: WM. HARRIS.

JANE MARTIN--WM. B. LIVELY

1. 20 (?) August 1809. JNO. MARTIN and CATH. CLARK. Security: WM. C. KIDD.

LUCINDA MARTIN--JNO. WHITE

N. MARTIN--M. PATTESON

P. MARTIN--REUBEN SMOOT

S. MARTIN--H. SUTLER

S. R. MARTIN--DANL. L. PIERCE (?)

6. 7 December 1813. WM. MARTIN and R. EVANS. Security: JNO. BETHEL.

POLLY MATTHEWS--H. EMBERSON

N. MATTHEWS--H. EMBERSON

N. MATTHEWS--W. LANHAM

R. MATTHEWS--JAS. B. FERGUSON

1. 16 February 1809. THOS. MATTHEWS and JACE BURK. Security: JNO. BURK.

8. 21 October 1815. JNO. MAXWELL and S. (L) FARRAR. Security: CHAS. LANKFORD.

8. 1 January 1816. GEO. S. MAYO and E. EDMUNDS. Security: JAS. N. EDMUNDS.

L. MAYS--W. CUNNINGHAM

I. (J) M. ALEXANDER (MC ALEXANDER?)--THOS. E. FORTUNE

9. 10 April 1816. JAS. MC ALEXANDER and P? T. FORTUNE. Security: ZACH FORTUNE.

E. MC CLAIN--WM. HENDERSON

ESTHER MC LAIN--WM. H. FARRAR

5. 28 (?) December 1812. HENRY MC CLAIN and E. TOMS. Security: WM. H. FARRAR. Officiant: BENJ. BURGHER.

2. 15 December 1809. JNO. MC CLAIN and M. WHEELER. Security: DAVID or DANL. WHEELER.

8. 6 April 1815. R. W. MC CLAIN and M. MC CLAIN. Security: JNO. FITZGERALD. No need to index bride.

BETSY MC CUE--T. CATLING

2. 31 July 1810. BENJ. MEDARIS and SALLY WEST. Security: JAS. WEST.

NANCY MEEKS--WM. HATTER

PATSY MEEKS--WM. BOWLING

POLLY W. MEEKS--JAS. BRYANT

DOLLY MELTON--EZEK. EAST

4. 3 June 1811. JNO. MELTON and POLLY EAST. Security: G. LYON.

5. 9 December 1812. JNO. MELTON and E. JOHNSON. Security: THOS. BIBB, JR. Officiant: WM. WRIGHT, same.

LETTY MELTON--JACOB EVILEIZER

P. MELTON--DR. GRIFFIN

10. 22 December 1817. S. MELTON and R. WHEELER. Security: DANL. WHEELER.

3. 11 January 1811. LARKIN MILLER and F. HARLOW. Security: JNO. SNELL. Officiant: BENJ. BURGHER.

5. 22 January 1813. RO. MITCHELL and N. CASH. Security: S. GARLAND. Officiant: WM. WRIGHT, same.

7. 2 March 1814. WM. MITCHELL and SALLY READ. Security: JNO. PUCKET. Officiant: WM. WRIGHT, same.

10. 6 January 1817. WM. MORAN and D. HIGHT. Security: GEO. HIGHT.

T. MONROE--FRANCIS PRICE

MARTHA MONTGOMERY--JNO. TOMPKINS

F. R. MORGAN--NATHAN WILLS

4. 16 December 1811. GEO. MORRIS and JANE LEE. Security: WM. MORRIS.

5. 30 November 1812. WM. MORRIS and N. JOHNSON. Security: WM. ANGUS. Officiant: BENJ. BURGHER.

J. MORRISON--A. RAMSEY

N. MORRISON--THRUSTON J. DICKINSON

M. B. MORRISON--T. (?) W. COLEMAN

N. M. MORRISON--R. W. BROOKS

11. 20 July 1818. DANL. MOSBY and A. M. POLLARD. Security: WM. CAMP. Officiant: JAS. BOYD, 21st.

2. 12 July 1810. JNO. MOSS and MARY H. WATTS. Security:
    EDDY FORTUNE. Officiant: WM. WRIGHT, 23rd.

1. 7 (?) September 1809. WM. MOSES and B. HILL. Security:
    L. PARNELL--hard to read--index has MOSER, also see MOSES.

    B. MOYER--JNO. THURMOND

5. 14 December 1812. JNO. MOYER and A. SMITH. Security:
    FIELD SMITH.

    S. MULLINS--BENJ. BIBEE

9. 3 July 1816. WM. MULLINS and M. FLOYD. Security and Officiant:
    ANTHONY GIANNIY, 4th.

11. 12 April 1818. JNO. MURRAY and J. BETHEL. Security: JNO.
    BETHEL.

    B. MURRILL--EDWD. LANKFORD

1. 17 December 1808. THOS. MURRILL and ELIZ. BREEDLOVE.
    Security: DAVID W. BREEDLOVE.

    J. MURTIN (MARTIN?)--JAS. LANKFORD

    P. NALLY--THOS. THURMON

10. 18 April 1817. M. C. NAPIER and L. (S) BALDWIN. Security:
    HENRY DAWSON. Officiant: JNO. SHEPHERD, 19th.

8. 23 October 1815. I. (J) B. NASH and F. SKINNER. Security:
    THOS. NASH.

    BETSY NEASE--JAS. Y. (?) RODES

    A. NEVIL--GEO. VAUGHAN

    M. OFFLIGHTER--SAML. HILL

9. 14 February 1816. THOS. OFFLIGHTER and P. RIPPETOE. Security:
    SAML. MOSES. Officiant: BENJ. BURGHER.

    JANE OGLESBY--JAS. FITZGERALD

3. 7 (9) December 1810. WM. OLIVER to W. SUTLERS. Security:
    REUBEN BATES. Officiant: WM. WRIGHT, 9th.

    S. H. OWEN (?)--JOSHUA CARROLL

6. 29 October 1813. J. PAGE and F. PUGH. Security: THOS. PUGH.

3. 6 November 1810. JAS. PAGE and SUS FOSTER. Security: SAML.
    TURNER.

1. 7 October 1808. LINDSAY PAGE and P. DUNCAN. Security:
    WM. KENNEDY.

    J. PARRICK--THOS. EUBANK--or L. (S) PARROCK; neither indexed
    on this page. My error: THOS. EUBANK is page 4; JNO. and
L. (S) PARROCK is on page 7--see both.

7. 24 October 1814. ZACH PARROCK and P. EMBLY. Security:
    LUKE EMBLY. Officiant: ANTHONY GIANNIY, 26th.

1. 9 May 1809. CHAS. PARSON and S. SMITH. Security: THOS. NASH.

2. 5 December 1809. TANDY PARSONS and R. WATKINS. Security:
    JNO. MATTHEWS, JR.

E. PATTESON--NELSON SEAY

11. 5 January 1818. M. PATTESON and N. MARTIN. Security: JAS. HUGHES. Officiant: JAS. BOYD, 6th.

JUDITH PATTON--JNO. BATES

JANE PENDLETON--BENJ. POWELL

L. (S) PENDLETON--GEO. THOMPSON

SIGUS PENN--JOS. KYLE

BETSY PERKINS--NELSON BETHEL

NANCY PERKINS--CHAS. WINEBARGER

R. PERKINS--JNO. J. WOOD

S. (L) PERKINS--GEO. WILLIAMS

3. 23 October 1810. CHAS. PERROW and E. TEESE. Security: JNO. LOVING, JR. Officiant: WM. WRIGHT, 26th (?).

B. PERRY--STEPHEN JOHNSON

J. PERRY--WM. THURMOND

1. 17 December 1808. CHAS. PETERS and C. GORDIN. Security: ALBIN GORDIN. Officiant: WM. WRIGHT, December.

4. 26 August 1811. DABNEY PHILLIPS and N. WILLS. Security: SAML. LOVING. Officiant: WM. CRAWFORD.

8. 10 April 1815. E. PHILLIPS and E. STATON. Security: JNO. FITZPATRICK.

F. PHILLIPS--GILES RICHARDSON

9. 4 April 1816. JNO. PHILLIPS and ELIZ. WATT. Security: PHIL GOWING.

11. 13 August 1818. DANL. L. PIERCE (?--not indexed; hard to read) and S. R. MARTIN. Security: HEZ. MARTIN. Officiant: SAML. DAY, 16th.

11. 22 July 1818. W. S. PLUNKET and M. F. SHIELDS. Security: GEO. SHIELDS. Officiant: BOYD, 28th (?).

A. M. POLLARD--DANL. MOSBY

E. C. POLLARD--RODERICK L. TALIAFERRO

7. 16 March 1814. RICH. POLLARD and P. RIVES. Security: L. C. RIVES. Officiant: WM. WRIGHT, same.

2. 23 July 1810. BENJ. PONTON and PEGGY FLOOD

11. 7 July 1818. FLEMING PONTON and LUCY WILLS. Security: JNO. WILLS. Officiant: BOYD, same.

4. 4 March 1812. JNO. PONTON and JANE FORTUNE. Security: JNO. FORTUNE. Officiant: WM. WRIGHT, same.

S. PONTON--A. SEAY

EMMANUEL POOR--R. SMITH

3. 28 October 1811. BENJ. POWELL and JANE PENDLETON. Security: M. PENDLETON. Officiant: WM. WRIGHT, October.

M. POWELL--JNO. BROOKS

R. POWELL--RO. C. CUTLER

6. 22 March 1813. FRANCIS PRICE and T. (?) MONROE. Security: JNO. MONROE.

NANCY PROFFITT--WM. EDMUNDS

8. 2 January 1816. OBADIAH PROFFITT and A. RYAN. Security: PAGE (?) RYAN.

P. PROFFITT--KINDAL SAVAGE

7. 11 February 1814. JNO. PUCKET and E. READ. Security: HENRY READ. Officiant: WM. WRIGHT, 21st (?).

8. 4 November 1815. A. PUGH and S. CARROLL. Security: CHAS. CARROLL.

8. 14 December 1815. Z. PUGH and PATSY JOHNSON. Security: C. JOHNSON. Out of place.

F. PUGH--J. PAGE

7. 26 September 1814. JNO. PUGH and E. WEIR. Security: THOS. WEIR.

P. PUGH--WM. SNEAD

Z. PUGH--out of place--see PUGHS above--after A. PUGH

P. PURVIS--WM. L. BELL

10. 9 September 1817. WM. PURVIS and S. G. STRATON. Security: JAS. JOHNSON.

6. 11 December 1813. A. RAMSEY and J. MORRISON. Security: A. H. MORRISON. Officiant: BENJ. BURGHER.

2. 23 March 1810. JNO. RAMSEY and M. LILLEY. Security: THOS. NALLY.

NANCY RAMSSY--SAML. GERALD

E. READ--JNO. PUCKET

SALLY READ--WM. MITCHELL

8. 2 November 1815. GILES RICHARDSON and F. PHILLIP. Security: RILES RICHARDSON, SR.

7. 2 May 1814. ELISHA RIDER and P. JOHNSON. Security: WM. H. DIGGES. Officiant: WM. WRIGHT, same.

N. RIPPETOE--RO. HAMBLETON

P. RIPPETOE--THOS. OFFLIGHTER

LUCY RIVES--JNO. LUCK

P. RIVES--RICH. POLLARD

8. 25 December 1815. ELLIOT ROBERTS and E. DAWSON. Security: JNO. S. DAWSON.

11. 20 October 1817. HENRY D. ROBERTS and E. B. LANDCRAFT. Security: BENJ. (?) M. HARDIN.

1. 21 February 1809. JNO. ROBERTS and M. HARRIS. Security: H. T. HARRIS. Officiant: WM. CRAWFORD, 1809.

N. ROBERTS--EDWD. FERGUSON

9. 29 January 1816. JNO. ROBERTSON and M. WHEELER. Security: DANL. WHEELER. Officiant: BENJ. BURGHER.

2. 14 December 1809. PETER ROBINSON and NANCY CARY. Security: DANL. CARY. Officiant: ZACH EMMERSON.

D. RODES (?)--DANL. WHEELER

11. 14 February 1818. JAMES Y. (?) RODES and BETSY NEASE. Security: DANL. WHEELER.

9. 8 October 1816. JNO. H. RODES and S. P. SMITH: Security: JNO. M. SMITH.

POLLY RODES--NICHL. DEBTOR

7. 11 April 1814. THOS. RODES and ELIZ. RUDASI. Security: JNO. CRITZER.

CATH. ROSE--JNO. EUBANK

L. ROSE--CHAS. P. TALIAFERRO

ELIZ. RUDASIL--THOS. RODES

A. RYAN--OBADIAH PROFFITT

A. SANDERS--LEWIS F. LANHAM

L. SANDERS--JNO. KIDD

S. SANDERS--JNO. HARVEY

5. 28 November 1812. KINDAL SAVAGE and P. PROFFITT. Security: CHAS. C. PATTERSON. Officiant: WM. WRIGHT, same.

P. SAVAGE--DAVID HUNTER

8. 14 November 1815. -- SCRUGGS and L. LANKFORD. Security: WM. LANKFORD.

5. 5 September 1812. JNO. P. SCRUGGS and S. B. SCRUGGS. Note on bond--index says S. B. SPENCER--see original.

N. C. SCRUGGS--M. D. BAILEY

NANCY SCURY--JNO. LOVING

P. G. SCRUGGS--THOS. CARTER

5. 9 June 1812. S. S. SCRUGGS and ANN S. BAILEY. Security: M. D. BAILEY.

9. 31 January 1816. A. SEAY and S. PONTON. Security: THOS. PONTON.

ELIZ. SEAY--WM. HAYES (HAGER?)

MARY SEAY--RO. HUNTER

N. SEAY--SAML. B. LAYNE

10. 11 January 1816. NELSON SEAY and E. PATTESON. Security:
     JNO. P. SCRUGGS.

 1. 16 October 1808. WM. SETTLES and DUD WRIGHT. Security:
     REUBEN BATES. Officiant: WM. WRIGHT. Index says JUDITH--see
original.

     M. S. SHACKLEFORD--JAS. M. BISHOP

     E. C. SHELTON--LEE W. HARRIS

 4. 21 December 1811. WM. H. SHELTON and B. STEVENS. Security:
     JAS. STEVENS, JR. Officiant: WM. WRIGHT, December.

 6. 18 April 1813. JOS. SHIELDS and S. CAMDEN. Security:
     WM. CAMDEN.

     M. F. SHIELDS--W. S. PLUNKET

 9. 20 April 1816. JNO. SHIPMAN and I. EDMUNDS. Security:
     CHAS. EDMUNDS. Officiant: SAML. DAY, 2 May.

     MILLY SKINNELL--CHAS. FLOOD

     C. SKINNER--WM. HAWKINS

     F. SKINNER--I. B. NASH

     F. L. SLAUGHTER--GEO. FARRAR

     LUCY SLAUGHTER--NORVIL SPENCER

10. 7 August 1817. HUDSON SMALL and B. FORTUNE. Security:
     NICHL. FORTUNE.

     PATSY SMALL--JNO. HAMNER

     A. SMITH--JNO. MOYER

10. 11 August 1817. ANDREW SMITH and L. (S) ANDERSON. Security:
     JACOB ARISMAN. Officiant: BENJ. BURGHER.

     FRANCES SMITH--JNO. HENSLEY

 8. 25 November 1815. JAS. SMITH and P. WILLS. Security:
     S. GARLAND.

     N. SMITH--JNO. FERGUSON

     P. SMITH--WM. LAYNE

     R. SMITH--EMMANUEL POOR

     S. SMITH--CHAS. PARSON

     S. P. SMITH--JNO. H. RODES

     SALLY SMITH--GEO. BANTON

     SALLY SMITH--GEO. BANTON

     SALLY J. (I) SMITH--PETER CAMPBELL

 5. 27 June 1812. T. W. M. SMITH and E. EAGLETON. Security:
     CHAS. PURVIS.

 1. 12 (?) June 1809. WM. SMITH and NANCY FOX. Security:
     BARTLETT FOX.

4. 10 April 1812. WM. SMITH and W. BAILEY. Security: CHAS. PERROW.

8. 27 March 1815. REUBEN SMOOT and P. MARTIN. Security: HEZ. MARTIN.

9. 4 May 1816. JAS. SNEED and LUCY HATTER. Security: BENJ. HATTER.

7. 24 October 1814. N. SNEED and L. (S) BECKNAL. Security: WM. RYAN. Officiant: ANTHONY GIANNIY, 27th.

10. 7 March 1817. WM. SNEED and P. PUGH. Security: JNO. PUGH.

ELIZ. SNIDER--M. THOMAS

M. SPEARS--JNO. BOND

B. SPENCER--JNO. STEWART

2. 1 March 1810. NORVIL SPENCER and LUCY SLAUGHTER. Security: THOS. NASH.

S. B. SPENCER (SCRUGGS)--see JNO. P. SCRUGGS

10. 21 January 1816. JNO. STAPLES and A. CLASBY. Security: WM. CLASBY.

E. STATON--E. PHILLIPS

3. 13 November 1810. GEO. STEPTOE and M. A. THOMAS. Security: GEO. CABELL, JR.

B. STEVENS--WM. H. SHELTON

10. 18 February 1817. JAS. STEVENS and P. THOMPSON. Security: JNO. STEVENS. Officiant: BOYD, 20th.

8. 11 December 1815. SAML. STEVENS and N. LOVING. Security: S. B. DENNY.

4. 13 January 1812. JNO. STEWART and B. SPENCER. Security: R. L. TALIAFERRO. Officiant: WM. WRIGHT, January.

S. G. STRATON--WM. PURVIS

A. STRICKLIN--JNO. HARRIS

9. 24 June 1816. H. SUTLER and S. MARTIN. Security: JAS. HUGHES.

W. SUTLERS--WM. OLIVER

P. SYMS--THOS. HENDERSON

3. 14 January 1811. CHAS. P. TALIAFERRO and L. ROSE. Security: RODERICK TALIAFERRO.

4. 29 July 1811. RODERICK L. TALIAFERRO and E. C. POLLARD. Security: WM. CAMP.

11. 12 August 1818. THOS. TAYLOR and B. BOGLEGUM (?)--not indexed. Security: FLEMING MILLER.

E. TEAS--CHAS. PERROW

2. 8 January 1810. EDWIN THOMAS and REBECCA HARE. Security: WINGFIELD NORVILL.

2. 22 December 1809. M. THOMAS and ELIZ. SNIDER. Security: PETER FARRAR.

M. A. THOMAS--GEO. STEPTOE

P. THOMAS--DAVID HUNTER

7. 18 February 1815. R. THOMAS and K. INGLE. Security: WM. ALLEN.

SALLY THOMAS--JESSE FORTUNE

8. 2 December 1815. GEO. THOMPSON and L. (S) PENDLETON. Security: BENJ. POWELL.

J. THOMPSON--JNO. P. COOLEY

L. THOMPSON--POWHATAN WOODY

P. THOMPSON--JAS. STEVENS

9. 12 March 1816. THOS. THORNTON and POLLY JOHNSON. Security: JNO. MARTIN.

4. 27 January 1812. JNO. THURMOND and B. MOYER. Security: WM. M. BAILEY.

10. 24 March 1817. JNO. THURMOND and N. TURNER. Security: TERISHA TURNER. Officiant: SHEPHERD, 2 April.

M. THURMOND--SPENCER JOHNSON

3. 27 May 1811. WM. THURMOND and J. PERRY. Security: JAS. HUGHES. Officiant: WM. WRIGHT, 1811.

2. 26 March 1810. THOS. THURMOND and P. NALLEY. Security: TERISHA TURNER.

N. TINDALL--RO. GOOLSBY

N. TINDALL--J. (T) N. EDMUNDS

7. 28 March 1814. JNO. TOMPKINS and MARTHA M. MONTGOMERY. Security: JAS. MONTGOMERY.

6. 20 May 1813. CLIFTON TOMS and POLLY CRIDER. Security: JNO. A. SNELL. Officiant: BENJ. BURGHER.

E. TOMS--HENRY MC CLAIN

10. 23 December 1816. JOS. TOMS and N. DIQUISOR. Security: WM. DIQUISOR. Officiant: BENJ. BURGHER.

9. 12 November 1816. NATHL. TOWNSEND and S. A. JOPLING. Security: WM. MURRILL. Officiant: JNO. SHEPHERD, 15th.

4. 27 May 1811. W. TRIBLE and BETSY C. JONES. Security: JNO. M. MARTIN.

11. 23 February 1818. WM. TRUSLOW and P. HOUSEWRIGHT. Security: J. TRUSLER (sic).

I. (J) TURNER--THOS. GRAVES

10. 19 March 1817. ST. GEORGE TUCKER and M. A. G. HARRIS. Security: JAS. T. TALIAFERRO.

N. TURNER--JNO. THURMOND

N. E. TURNER--JAS. L. DILLARD

2. 12 December 1809. SAML. TURNER and S. J. FOSTER. Security:
A. J. S. (?) FOSTER.

6. 6 January 1814. TERISHA TURNER and C. FOSTER. Security:
SAML. TURNER.

3. 22 April 1811. JOS. TYREE and J. (I) LIVELY. Security:
JNO. BETHEL. Officiant: WM. WRIGHT, April.

3. 25 December 1810. REUBEN TYREE and J. KEETIN. Security:
JNO. TYREE. Officiant: JNO. ALLCOCK, December.

3. 27 September 1810. ZACH TYREE and D. WRIGHT. Security:
REUBIN L. TYREE.

B. VAUGHAN--W. VAUGHAN

10. 21 April 1816. GEO. VAUGHAN and A. NEVIL. Security:
CHAS. PERCELL (?).

8. 8 April 1815. W. VAUGHAN and B. VAUGHAN. Security: SAML.
LOVING.

E. VIA--RO. CUNNINGHAM

2. 1 December 1809. JNO. VIA and ANN WRIGHT. Security: JNO.
BERRY.

N. WALKER--JNO. H. JOHNSON

10. 8 April 1817. M. WALLACE and L. LOBBAN. Security: WM. L. (S)
LOBBAN.

7. 11 January 1815. A. WALLER and ELIZ. ARISMAN. Security:
SAML. HAGER (?). Officiant: BENJ. BURGHER.

6. 30 November 1813. A. B. WARWICK and J. R. ESTES. Security:
NELSON B. WARWICK. Officiant: WM. WRIGHT, same.

1. 27 March 1809. A. W. WARWICK and MARY WOODS. Security:
JAS. WOODS. Officiant: WM. CRAWFORD, 1809.

C. G. WARWICK--F. JOHNSON

L. B. WARWICK--CATLETT WILLS

9. 25 November 1816. HUDSON WATKINS and P. LANKFORD. Security:
WM. LANKFORD. Officiant: JNO. SHEPHERD, 29th.

R. WATKINS--TANDY PARSONS

ELIZ. WATT--JNO. PHILLIPS

4. 21 April 1812. HENRY H. WATTS and E. DILLARD. Security:
JNO. N. WILSON.

MARY WATTS--RICH. CLARK

MARY H. WATTS--JNO. MOSS

E. WEIR--JNO. PUGH

6. 22 March 1813. JNO. WEIR and POLLY HARLOS. Security:
N. HARLOW.

PATSY WEIR--P. LOWERY

6. 4 October 1813. THOS. WEIR and POLLY ISTEP (HUGHES)--not indexed for either--illegible. Security: WM. FITZPATRICK. Officiant: BENJ. BURGHER.

L. B. WEST--E. HARDING

SALLY WEST--BENJ. MEDARIS

11. 27 March 1818. DANL. WHEELER and D. RODES (?). Security: BENJ. M. HARDIN.

M. WHEELER--JNO. ROBERTSON

M. WHEELER--JNO. MC CLAIN

N. WHEELER--JNO. M. FARRAR

R. WHEELER--S. MELTON

7. 22 October 1814. JNO. WHITE and LUCINDA MARTIN. Security: JAS. Z. (?) RODES. Officiant: BENJ. BURGHER.

S. WHITE--WM. HARGROVE

SALLY WHITE--NELSON DAWSON

SARAH WHITE--WM. HARDING

10. 28 May 1817. GEO. WHITLOCK and P. R. CABELL. Security: WM. S. CABELL.

7. 26 December 1814. GEO. WILLIAMS and S. (L) PERKINS. Security: B. WILLIAMS. Officiant: ANTHONY GIANNIY, 28th.

S. WILLIAMS--CHAS. CALON

T. WILLIAMS--WM. COX

A. WILLOUGHBY--R. N. KIDD

4. 6 January 1811. CATLETT WILLS and L. B. WARWICK. Security: JAS. MARTIN. Officiant: WM. WRIGHT, January.

1. 7 November 1809. LAWRENCE WILLS and P. FORTUNE. Security: ELISHA FORTUNE. Officiant: WM. WRIGHT, 1809.

LUCY WILLS--FLEMING PONTON

N. WILLS--DABNEY PHILLIPS

5. 26 October 1812. NATHAN WILLS and F. R. MORGAN. Security: S. GARLAND.

P. WILLS--JAMES SMITH

2. 10 February 1810. CHAS. WINEBARGER and NANCY PERKINS. Security: JOSHUA JONES. Officiant: BENJ. BURGHER.

M. WINGFIELD--HEZ. MARTIN

6. 25 December 1813. JNO. WINTERS and S. JACKSON. Security: BURWELL JACKSON. Officiant: WM. WRIGHT, 26th.

DICEY WITT--WM. HAMBLETT

3. 10 September 1810. DAVID WITT and JANE FITZPATRICK. Security: MOSES FITZPATRICK. Officiant: THOS. CRAWFORD (?).

SALLY WITT--WM. WITT

3. 21 November 1810. WM. WITT and SALLY WITT. Security: DAVID WITT. L: BENJ. BURGHER.

3. 4 December 1810. WM. WITT and E. FITZPATRICK. Security: THOS. FITZPATRICK. Officiant: WM. CRAWFORD.

5. 6 March 1813. JAS. WOOD and F. GRIFFIN. Security: DR. GRIFFIN. Officiant: WM. WRIGHT, 6 February 1813 (sic).

6. 24 January 1814. JNO. WOOD and C. HARRIS (?). Security: THOS. FORTUNE.

6. 18 July 1813. JNO. J. WOOD and R. PERKINS. Security: THOS. FORTUNE.

6. 18 July 1813. JNO. J. WOOD and R. PERKINS. Security: SAML. PERKINS.

NANCY WOOD--JNO. DIXON

SALLY WOOD--GEO. JOHNSON

MARY WOODS--A. S. WARWICK

S. WOODS--HAWES N. COLEMAN

3. 1 October 1810. FLEMING WOODY and B. ENIX. Security: DAVID ENIX.

3. 26 February 1811. GEO. WOODY and H. WRIGHT. Security: WM. MC CALEB. Officiant: WM. WRIGHT, same.

4. 23 September 1811. JNO. WOODY and POLLY GARDNER. Security: FLEMING WOODY.

5. 24 December 1812. POWHATAN WOODY and L. THOMPSON. Security: CHAS. THOMPSON.

10. 9 January 1817. RO. WOODY and M. WRIGHT. Security: THOS. FORTUNE. Officiant: JAS. BOYD, same.

10. 4 December 1816. SAML. WOODY and L. FLOWERS. Officiant: SAML. DAY.

ANN WRIGHT--JNO. VIA

D. WRIGHT--ZACH TYREE

E. WRIGHT--THOS. FORTUNE

H. WRIGHT--GEO. WOODY

10. 8 February 1817. JNO. WRIGHT and F. HAMLET. Security: JACOB YOST. Officiant: JAS. BOYD, 9th.

JUDITH (DUD) WRIGHT--WM. SETTLES

L. WRIGHT--HUDSON KIDD

M. WRIGHT--RO. WOODY

3. 11 September 1810. WM. WRIGHT and C. KENNEDY. Security: CHAS. WATTS. Officiant: JNO. ALLCOCK.

3. 12 January 1811. JACOB YOST and M. JOHNSON. S. THOS. MC CABE. Officiant: WM. WRIGHT, same.

I decided that I would continue this work and have gone through page 34 of Nelson register. These are from page 12 and officiants are alphabetized.

19. 6 May 1824. RO. S. ADAMS and LUCY F. LOVING. C. W. KIDD--security--JAMES BOYD, same.

24. 12 February 1828. LORENZO D. AISTROP and SARAH WOODY. S. H. LOVING and CHAS. PERROW, securities.

ELIZ. AKERS--WM. L. (S) JONES

MARTHA A. AKERS--GEO. W. PURVIS

31. 10 June 1833. JAS. ALEXANDER and PATSY MC ALEXANDER. JOS. R. MC ALEXANDER.

30. 24 April 1833. DAVID ALLEN and SALLY JOHNSON. BENJ. JOHNSON. Officiant: JNO. M. JOHNSON, 25th.

HARRIET ALLEN--MOSES I. MAYS

34. 3 February 1836. JESSE I. ALLEN and JANE M. SMALL. BR. FITZPATRICK, Security.

29. 20 March 1832. JNO. ALLEN and SALLY F. CAMPBELL. Security: H. CAMPBELL.

32. 23 May 1834. JNO. ALLEN and ANNA KELLY. Security: WM. ALLEN. Officiant: EDWD. L. WARREN, May.

29. 12 May 1832. JOSHUA ALLEN and POLLY CAMPBELL. Security: DAVID A. ALLEN.

NANCY ALLEN--LOVING T. LANHAM

16. 7 March 1822. SAML. ALLEN and POLLY HIGHT. Security: JNO. HIGHT.

SUSAN ALLEN--JAS. A. CAMPBELL

ELIZ. C. ANDERSON--NELSON CRAWFORD

FRANCES ANDERSON--DAVID DRUMHELLER

G. ANDERSON--A. WOOD

20. 22 August 1825. JAS. ANDERON and POLLY PAXTON. Security: JNO. C. ROBERTSON. Officiant: WM. HAMERSLY, 28th. ANDERSON for groom.

28. 28 April 1831. NATHAN C. ANDERSON and MARTHA I. W. SMILEY. Security: RO. P. SHELTON.

POLLY ANDERON--WOODSON B. FOX. ANDERSON for bride.

31. 29 May 1833. RICH. N. ANDERSON and CATH. GARDNER. Security: WM. J. ROBERTSON.

31. 19 June 1833. THOS. J. ANDERSON and SALLY THOMAS. Security: RO. HALL.

12. 8 September 1818. ROBT. ANDERSON and N. EDMUNDS. Security: SAML. EDMUNDS. Officiant: JAMES BOYD, 17th. Error: ANDREWS and not ANDERSON.

CATH. ARISMAN--HENRY MAYFIELD

18. 12 December 1823. JACOB ARISMAN and BELINDA HALL. Security:
J. MASENCOUP.

MARY ARISMAN--WM. D. SMITH

MARY E. ARMSTRONG--FLOYD L. WHITEHEAD

ELIZ. A. ARRINGTON--WM. LAYNE

14. 4 May 1820. WILLIS ARRINGTON and MARY SPENCER. Security:
J. W. TREVILLIAN.

HANNAH G. AUSTIN--ISAAC PAUL

17. 2 November 1822. JESSE AUSTIN and SALLY JOPLING. Security:
BENJ. JOPLINE. Officiant: EDWD. L. WARREN, 7th.

ELIZ. BABER--THOS. QUICK

16. 22 April 1822. JAS. BABER and NANCY BOWMAN. Security:
G. BOWMAN. Officiant: EDWD. L. WARREN, 2 May.

SUSAN BABER--ELISHA WILLIAMS

FRS. BAILEY--JAS. W. HARLAN. I find FRS. in some items;
FRANCES, I am sure.

19. 26 July 1824. JNO. BAILEY and SUSAN CRITZER. Security:
GEO. CRITZER. Officiant: JAMES BOYD, same.

25. 20 March 1829. JNO. D. BAILEY and MARY DAWSON. Security:
NELSON DAWSON.

MARY D. BAILEY--JOS. MURRILL

NANCY A. BAILEY--GEO. W. NORVELL

SARAH R. BAILEY--SEATON R. HAMBLETT

SARAH T. BAILEY--THEOPHILUS SCRUGGS

23. 29 November 1827. WM. BAILEY and LYDIA SMITH. Security:
WESTLEY LANHAM. Officiant: EDWD. L. WARREN, same. Same means
same date as bond.

17. 3 April 1823. ALEX. BAKER and M. A. POLLARD. Security:
DANL. MOSBY. Officiant: JAMES BOYD, same.

MARY ANN BAKER--WM. HARDING

17. 13 February 1823. JONATHAN BALASLEY and NANCY GRAY. Security:
JNO. M. HAMNER. Officiant: JAMES BOYD, same.

22. 17 April 1827. JNO. M. BALL and ELMIRA M. HARLOW. Security:
WM. HARLOW. Officiant: CLEVELAND PORTER, 19th.

SARAH BALL--GENERAL M. JOHNSON

26. 16 December 1829. JNO. H. BALLARD and SELINA THOMAS.
Security: WM. SPENCER.

23. 5 December 1827. WM. BALLARD and ELIZ. KALER. Security:
CHAS. KALER. Officiant: WM. HAMERSLEY, 6th.

15. 15 November 1821. HUGH BARCLAY and MARY WOODS. Security:
NICHL. WOODS. Officiant: WM. H. FOSTER, same.

28. 7 November 1831. NATHAN I. BARNETT and SALINA HARRIS. Security:
JNO. E. ROBERTS. Note: clerks made what appears to be letter I,
but may be J.

12. 28 October 1820. ISAAC BEAL and POLLY WILLIAMS. Security: JNO. WILLIAMS. Officiant: ANTHONY GIANNIY, 29th.

POLLY BEAVER--HENRY CRITZER

30. 25 March 1833. RO. BEAZLEY and MARTHA A. CHRISTIAN. Security: HARROD B. SCOTT.

LUCY BECKNALL--JESSE THOMPSON

20. 30 July 1825. GREENBERRY V. BERNARD and ANN I. MITCHELL. Security: ANDREW WALLACE. Officiant: WM. WRIGHT, August 4th.

26. 8 December 1829. RICH. W. BERNARD and FRANCES HARLOW. Security: AUGUSTINE HARLOW.

22. 4 July 1827. WM. BEVERLEY and JUDITH SPARROW. Security: SIMPSON SPARROW.

BELINDA BIBB--RO. M. HALL

ELIZA A. BIBB--WALKER D. SPENCER

ELIZ. BIBB--JOS. RICKETS

JANE BIBB--AUSTIN SEAY

MARY JANE BIBB--WM. M. THURMOND

15. 26 November 1821. DANL. BLACK and ANN QUICK. Security: JNO. QUICK, JR.

15. 24 September 1821. SAML. BLAIN and JANE NALLEY. Security: WM. H. FOSTER--30th.

20. 28 March 1825. WM. H. BLAIR and GRISSEL C. SLAUGHTER. Security: FRS. SLAUGHTER and A. BLAIR. Officiant: WM. WRIGHT, April 56h.(?)

18. 4 March 1824. RICH. L. BOLTON and BETSY W. GRIFFIN. Security: H. GRIFFIN. Officiant: JNO. SHEPHERD, same.

34. 16 October 1835. WM. BOLTON and AMANDA I. SCRUGGS. Security: KINDALL SAVAGE.

REBECCA I. BOURNE--NATHL. MANTIPLY

ELIZ. BOUTWRIGHT--GEO. THOMPSON

MARY ANN BOWLER--PLEASANT D. MORRIS

28. 22 August 1831. DAVID BOWLES and JUDITH DENNIS.

23. 31 October 1827. NATHL. BOWLES and MARTHA GAY. Security: COSIN W. PARRISH. Officiant: JAMES BOYD, same.

MARY J. BOWLING--RO. MAYS

25. 6 July 1829. EPHM BOWMAN and ELIZ. E. W. CHANDLER. Security: C. and J. MOSES.

NANCY BOWMAN--JAS. BABER

SARAH J. BOWMAN--JNO. KIRBY

SARAH W. BOWMAN--WM. POWELL

SOPHIA J. BOWMAN--FRANCIS B. WEST

28. 24 October 1831. WM. H. BOWMAN and MALINDA M. MURRELL.
     Security: WM. MURRELL. Officiant: EDWD. L. WARREN,
November 3rd.

22. 11 September 1826. BENJ. BRADSHAW and RHODA A. GRIFFIN.
     Security: PRICE S. PERKINS. Officiant: J.S., 14th.

13. 11 August 1819. JNO. BRADSHAW and M. A. CAMP. Security:
     ARTHUR HOPKINS. Officiant: JAMES BOYD, same.

M. BRADSHAW--THOS. PARROCK

ELIZ. BRAMWELL--JNO. HOUSEWRIGHT

SARAH H. BREEDLOVE--NICHL. H. B. TALIAFERRO

29. 27 June 1832. JAS. BRIDGE and NANCY LEE. Security: WM. GRAY.

JANETTA BRIDGWATER--NICHL. HARLOW

MARY P. BRIDGWATER--HOLEMAN JOPLING

19. 23 October 1824. NATHAN BRIDWATER and SALLY PAGE. Security:
     JNO. PAGE.

P. W. BRIDGWATER--JAS. A. ROBERTS

34. 2 November 1835. WM. BRIDGWATER and JANE EWERS. Security:
     STEPHEN EWERS.

29. 15 February 1832. STEPHEN BRIGHT and CATH. GROAH. Security:
     ADAM BRIGHT.

S. BRITTAIN--RO. JOHNSON

13. 14 April 1819. ALEX. BROWN and LUCY L. RIVES. Security:
     JAS. S. (L) PENN. Officiant: JAMES BOYD, 27th.

31. 29 July 1833. GEO. I. BROWN and BETSY HUGHES. Security:
     AND. JOHNSON.

14. 25 December 1820. MARTIN BROWN and MATILDA SEAY. Security:
     JOS. SEAY.

18. 1 October 1823. WM. BROWN and MILLY DODD. Officiant:
     JAMES BOYD, 3rd.

13. -- April 1819. JAS. BRUCE and E. A. HENNY. Security: WM. J.
     CABELL. Officiant: SAML. DAY, 2nd.

17. 25 March 1823. AUSTIN BRYANT and SUSAN DRAKE. Security:
     WM. MASSIE.

ELIZ. BRYANT--LARKIN HARLOW

ELLENOR BRYANT--WM. CLASBY

ELVIRA BRYANT--WM. WOOD

JANE BRYANT--CHAS. THACKER

JUDITH BRYANT--NORVELL HUNTER

L. BRYANT--PARMENAS BRYANT

M. BRYANT--BURGESS WILLIAMS

MARY ANN BRYANT--JOS. KIDD

MARY E. BRYANT--RICH. R. WOOD

33. 16 February 1835. MENBELL BRYANT and MAHALA COFFEY. Security: GEO. MONROE.

P. BRYANT--WM. HARVEY

12. 22 February 1819. PARMENAS BRYANT and L. BRYANT. Security: WM. BRYANT. Officiant: S.D., 4 (?) March.

SOPHIA BRYANT--PEACHY SPENCER

33. 10 June 1835. WILSON BRYANT and SARAH J. WRIGHT. Security: BENJ. WRIGHT. Officiant: H. S. PAYTON, 12th.

16. 28 September 1822. WM. BRYANT and ISABELLA PHILLIPS. Security: BENJ. HATTER. Officiant: ANTHONY GIANNIY, 27th (sic).

33. 14 January 1835. WM. BRYANT and LURENA JOHNSON. Security: RO. JOHNSON.

27. 23 August 1830. JAS. BUNTER and ELIZ. MARTIN. Security: JNO. BETHEL.

M. BURCH--JAS. E. SMITH

N. G. BURCH--L. (S) POWELL

31. 22 October 1833. HOLEMAN BURFETT and FRANCES L. MC CARTER. Security: WM. ROBERTSON.

E. BURK--BENJ. MOORE

CELIA BURKS--THOS. GLASS

13. 8 November 1819. JESSE BURKS and BETSY PUGH. Security: S. F. PUGH. Officiant: JAMES BOYD, 9th.

BETSY BURNETT--WM. H. DAVIS

21. 15 November 1825. JNO. N. BURNETT and MALINDA WITT. Security: DENNITT WITT.

NANCY BURNETT--WM. PURVIS, JR.

18. 1 November 1823. RUBEN T. BURNETT and ELIZA C. PURVIS. Security: WM. PURVIS. Officiant: JAMES BOYD, 2nd.

27. 1 February 1831. SAML. H. BURNETT and JANE B. HARLOW. Security: A. HARLOW. Officiant: PORTER CLEVELAND, 3rd.

29. 17 March 1832. HOWELL P. BURTON and ROXANNA MOSS. Security: JACOB SMITH.

12. 17 December 1818. R. BURTON and S. (L) W. PENN. Security: THOS. PENN.

15. 16 June 1821. JNO. BUSH and ELIZ. D. MARTIN. Security: JNO. R. MARTIN. Officiant: WM. H. FOSTER, 21st.

17. 29 January 1823. HENRY BUSHNELL and PATSY M. MONTGOMERY. Security: WM. MONTGOMERY. Officiant: JAMES BOYD, 30th.

14. 2 April 1820. JESSE BUTLER and MARY HADEN. Security: F. GIANNIY. Officiant: ANTHONY GIANNIY, same.

MATILDA BUTLER--THOS. FORTUNE

MILDRED CABELL--JNO. HORSLEY

SARAH C. CABELL--THOS. MASSIE, JR.

RACHEL L. (S) CAMDEN--WM. WRIGHT

14. 21 December 1819. WM. W. CAMDEN and JANE HIGHT. Security: JNO. HIGHT. Officiant: JAMES BOYD, 22nd.

26. 9 November 1829. WYATT CAMDEN and RHODA GILL. Security: SAML. N. GILL.

ELIZ. CAMERON--JAS. RIPPETOE

M. A. CAMP--JNO. BRADSHAW

DICEY CAMPBELL--BENJ. WRIGHT

EADY CAMPBELL--JNO. CASH

ELIZ. CAMPBELL--JNO. SMITH

ELIZ. CAMPBELL--WILLIS JOHNSON

26. 23 February 1830. GEO. W. CAMPBELL and MARTHA ANN MASSIE. Security: THOS. MASSIE.

25. 5 January 1829. JAS. A. CAMPBELL and SUSANNA ALLEN. Security: C. CAMPBELL and J. ALLEN.

27. 14 June 1830. JAS. W. CAMPBELL and JANE MASSIE. Security: JAS. FITZGERALD.

14. 21 December 1820. JESSE CAMPBELL and POLLY SPEARS. Security: JOEL CAMPBELL. Officiant: ANTHONY GIANNIY, 28th.

MARY CAMPBELL--LEWIS TAYLOR

NANCY CAMPBELL--WM. DINSMORE

POLLY CAMPBELL--JOSHUA ALLEN

POLLY CAMPBELL--HENRY COFFEY

24. 4 March 1828. RO. S. CAMPBELL and ANNE MASINCUP. Security: JNO. MASINCUP. Officiant: W.H., 6th.

SALLY F. CAMPBELL--JNO. ALLEN

34. 27 April 1835. SAML. CAMPBELL and CATH. PAINTER. Security: SAML. FITZGERALD.

SARAH JANE CAMP--CHAS. H. SPENCER

SUSANNA CAMPBELL--WM. HIGHT

27. 14 February 1831. WASH. CAMPBELL and MARY THOMPSON. Security: JAS. THOMPSON.

23. 16 November 1827. WILLIS CAMPBELL and HANNAH PAINTER. Security: WM. BOWLING, CHAS. and DANL. PERROW.

WINIFRED CAMPBELL--ISAAC PAYNTER

MARGARET CAREY--WM. PANNELL

12. 16 September 1818. J. (I) F. CARR and M. H. MARTIN. Security: HENRY B. MARTIN. Officiant: --, 29th.

F. CARROLL--RICH. WOODY

16. 7 January 1822. CREED C. CARTER and MARY CLASBY. Security:
THOS. CLASBY.

ELIZ. R. CARTER--ALFRED WILLOUGHBY

GEMIMA C. CARTER--RICH. A. TILLER

JANE M. CARTER--JOS. W. FARRAR

SALLY CARTER--JNO. R. SCRUGGS

13. 10 July 1819. SHADRICK CARTER and SALLY PATTESON. Security:
S. GARLAND.

22. 27 (?) September 1826. SHADRICK CARTER, JR. and NANCY D.
SEAY. Security: CALM SEAY.

33. 22 January 1834. THOS. C. CARTER and MARTHA KIDD. Security:
WM. BURFORD.

27. 5 November 1830. WM. H. CARTER and JANE R. TURNER. Security:
WM. G. JOHNSON. Officiant: EDWD. L. WARREN, 17th.

ELIZ. CARY--WM. DEQUIER

ISABELLA CARY--SILAS ROGERS

12. 29 September 1818. HOWARD CASH and L. (S) PROFFITT. Security:
S. H. CASH.

28. 26 December 1831. JNO. CASH and EADY CAMPBELL. Security:
JAS. A. CAMPBELL. Officiant: MATTHEW P. STURDIVANT, 28th.

ROSY JANE CASH--JNO. E. JENKINS

17. 1 February 1823. ABRAM E. CHANDLER and ELIZ. DAMRON. Security:
SAML. SAMRON. Officiant: J.S., 3rd.

ELIZ. E. W. CHANDLER--EPHM BOWMAN

O. CHANDLER--J. FOX

30. 7 January 1833. ALBERT G. CHEWNING and NICEY H. DIGGES.
Security: P. EDMUNDS. Officiant: H. L. PEYTON, 28th.

ANN R. CHEWNING--WM. MAYS

AVY CHEWNING--JAS. MAYS

ELIZ. CHEWNING--RICE MORRIS

29. 26 July 1832. JAS. W. CHEWNING and POLLY MAYS. Security:
ANDREW W. WRIGHT.

28. 17 November 1831. JOEL CHEWNING and LOVENNA PAGE. Security:
RICH. FOX. Officiant: EDWD. L. WARREN, December 17th.

SARAH CHEWNING--ZACH FORTUNE

N. CHILDRESS--NATHAN TYREE

AMANDA D. CHRISTIAN--JNO. A. SCRUGGS

31. 28 October 1833. CHAS. W. CHRISTIAN and ELVIRA ANN WILLS.
Security: B. S. GARLAND.

ELIZ. F. CHRISTIAN--SILAS VAWTER

27. 30 October 1830. GEO. H. CHRISTIAN and ELVIRA M. LAYNE. Security: RO. T. MORRIS. Officiant: JNO. ALLCOCK, same.

MARTHA A. CHRISTIAN--RO. BEAZLEY

SARAH M. CHRISTIAN--HARROD B. SCOTT

MARTHA A. CLAIBORNE--JOS. K. IRVING

12. 26 January 1819. N. CLARKE and REBECCA SMALL. Security: N. B. WARWICK. Officiant: JAMES BOYD, 28th.

JARUSHA CLARKSON--JNO. F. P. HUGHES

32. 24 October 1834. JNO. N. CLARKSON and JUDITH DIGGS. Security: JNO. DIGGS.

S. C. CLARKSON--SYLVANUS MEEKS

SUSANNA CLARKSON--RO. C. JONES

MARY CLASBY--CREED C. CARTER

SUSAN CLASBY--THOS. HALES

22. 10 November 1826. WM. CLASBY and ELENOR BRYANT. Security: RO. C. CUTLER.

15. 7 April 1821. TYLER CLIFT and MATILDA WHEELER. Security: MICAJAH WHEELER.

MARIA CLINCH--RICH. H. MAUPIN

JANE H. G. COBBS and FRANKLIN THWING

34. 28 January 1836. BENJ. COFFEY and CANDIS W. COFFEY. Security: EDMD. F. COFFEY. Officiant: JNO. ALLCOCK, same.

32. 25 August 1834. EDMUND COFFEY and MARTHA COFFEY. Security: JNO. HALE. After EDMD.'s name is this: S. WM.--probably son of WM.

FRANCES COFFEY--WOODSON R. FITZGERALD

20. 14 March 1825. GARLAND COFFEY and NANCY COFFEY. Security: WM. BOWLING.

33. 22 December 1834. HENRY COFFEY and POLLY CAMPBELL. Security: FRANCIS CAMPBELL.

28. 11 August 1831. HOLLOWAY COFFEY and CATH. FITZGERALD. Security: WOODSON R. FITZGERALD.

JANE COFFEY--WM. W. COFFEY

JANE COFFEY--ANDERSON MEEKS

21. 15 October 1825. JNO. W. COFFEY and SUSANNA COFFEY.

21. 3 November 1825. JOS. COFFEY and ELIZ. PHILLIPS. Security: R. FITZGERALD.

MAHALA COFFEY--MENBELL BRYANT

MARTHA COFFEY--EDMUND COFFEY

MARY ANN COFFEY--JNO. DE MASTERS

MARY L. COFFEY--COSEN W. PARRISH

MILLY COFFEY--JNO. EVERETT

NANCY COFFEY--JORDAN L. QUINN

NANCY COFFEY--GARLAND COFFEY

22. 30 October 1826. OSBORNE COFFEY and MARY FITZGERALD.
Security: EDMD. FITZGERALD. Officiant: JAMES BOYD,
September 20th (sic).

22. 5 May 1827. PETER C. FOFFEY and NANCY MONROE. Security:
JAS. DEMASTERS.

POLLY COFFEY--ZDPH. FITZGERALD

POLLY COFFEY--JNO. STEEL

29. 14 January 1832. REUBEN P. COFFEY and POLLY C. DEMASTER.
Security: GEO. (? or THOS. E.) DEMASTER.

SOPHIA W. COFFEY--WM. CRISP

SUSANNA COFFEY--JNO. W. COFFEY

13 November 1824. WM. B. COFFEY and MARY F. (? blurred)
MARTIN. E. F. COFFEY and JNO. MARTIN.

29. 18 February 1832. WM. W. COFFEY and JANE COFFEY. Security:
REUBEN COFFEY. Officiant: M.P.S., March.

WINNEY COFFEY--SILAS M. RAMSEY

SARAH COFFMAN--ELIJAH PUGH

34. 4 April 1836. HAWES H. COLEMAN and MARY A. E. HARRIS.
Security: H. N. COLEMAN.

17. 15 May 1823. SPENCER COLEMAN and REBECCA DIGGS. Security:
H. N. COLEMAN. Officiant: JAMES BOYD, same.

20. 27 September 1825. JNO. B. COLES and FRANCES CRAWFORD.
Security: NELSON CRAWFORD. Officiant: JAMES BOYD, October 4th.

ADALINE CONNER--TIM SCRUGGS, JR.

SOPHIA W. T. CONNER--WM. SCRUGGS

33. 27 July 1835. LEVI COOK and SUSANNA D. WALLACE. Security:
AND. WALLACE.

MARIA COOK--RICH. QUISENBERRY

18. 26 November 1824. JAS. W. CRAIGE and ELIZ. KIDD. Security:
GEO. W. SUTLER. Officiant: JAMES BOYD, 28th.

FRANCES CRAWFORD--JNO. B. COLES

34. 23 November 1835. GEO. H. CRAWFORD and MARGARET W. MONTGOMERY.
Security: S. H. LOVING.

JUDITH A. CRAWFORD--JNO. W. DICKINSON

15. 14 June 1821. NELSON CRAWFORD and ELIZ. C. ANDERSON.
Security: N. C. ANDERSON. Officiant: WM. CRAWFORD, 18th.

23. 13 October 1827. JNO. CREWS and SARAH ANN TALIAFERRO.
Security: ROD. L. TALIAFERRO. Officiant: JAMES BOYD, 18th.

BETSY CRISP--THOS. HARRISON

24. 15 September 1828. SIMON CRISP and SUSANNA FLOYD. Security: CHAS. (?) FLOYD.

33. 23 March 1835. WM. CRISP and SOPHIA W. COFFEY. Security: PETER C. COFFEY.

ELIZ. CRITZER--THOS. J. GLENN

16. 7 January 1822. HENRY CRITZER and POLLY BEAVER. Security: JACOB ARISMAN.

SUSAN CRITZER--JNO. BAILEY

SUSANNA CRITZER--JESSE WILSON

24. 24 December 1827. JAS. CUNNINGHAM, JR. and MARTHA P. WILLS. Security: JNO. WILLS.

22. 15 March 1827. JESSE CUNNINGHAM and NANCY FORTUNE. Security: JNO. WILLS. Officiant: JAMES BOYD, same.

13. 22 October 1819. REESE CUNNINGHAM and JANE C. HYLTON. Security: JAS. D. WATTS.

29. 28 May 1832. ALBERT D. CURD and SARAH F. TURNER. Security: N. F. CABELL.

31. 8 January 1834. RO. C. CUTLER and MARY I. B. WHITHEAD. Security: JOHN WHITEHEAD. Officiant: EDWD. L. WARREN, 9th.

LUCY ANN DAFF--LEVI GROAH

NANCY DAFT--HENRY WOOD

22. 4 November 1826. DANL. B. DALY and NANCY C. HARRIS. Security: DANL. MOSBY. Officiant: JAMES BOYD, 5th.

LUCY T. DAMERON--WM. JOHNSON

19. 8 April 1824. DRURY C. DAMRON and CHARLOTTE D. MARTIN. Security: REUBEN MARTIN. Officiant: JNO. SHEPHERD, 8th.

ELIZ. DAMRON--ABRAM E. CHANDLER

ELIZ. DAMRON--PHILIP THURMOND

25. 24 November 1828. JAS. T. (?) DAMRON and MARTHA I. W. THURMOND. Security: WM. M. THURMOND.

34. 16 January 1836. LELAND DAMRON and SUSANNA POWELL. Security: LEOND. POWELL. Officiant: EDWD. L. WARREN, 21st.

21. 17 December 1825. WM. DAMRON and SARAH ANN HARDING. Security: RICH. HARDING. Officiant: J.S., 26th.

28. 20 October 1831. WM. DAMRON and HANNAH GRIFFIN. Security: JAS. E. SMITH. Officiant: EDWD. L. WARREN, same.

34. 27 April 1836. SAML. R. DANIEL and LUCINDA STEWART. Security: WM. L. LOVING.

ELIZ. DAVIS--WM. H. IRVIN

MARY DAVIS--SAML. IRVIN

NANCY DAVIS--WM. G. MARTIN

19. 6 April 1824. WM. DAVIS and MARGARET I. MILLS. Security: JAS. REID. Officiant: JAMES BOYD, 5th.

12. 14 January 1819. WM. W. DAVIS and BETSY BURNETT. Security: EDMD. DAVIS. Officiant: JAMES BOYD, same.

23. 30 October 1827. ALEX. B. DAWSON and BARBARY ALLEN. Security: WM. MURRILL. Officiant: EDWD. L. WARREN, November 1st.

MAHALEY DAWSON--PLEASANT L. DAWSON

MARY DAWSON--GUTHRIDGE THURMOND

MARY DAWSON--JNO. D. BAILEY

NANCY DAWSON--MATT. ROBERTS

17. 28 July 1823. PLEASANT L. DAWSON and MAHALEY DAWSON. Security: THOS. GILMORE. Officiant: JAMES BOYD, same.

20. 8 October 1825. JNO. DE MASTERS and MARY ANN COFFEY. Security: EDMOND F. COFFEY.

NANCY DEMASTERS--JNO. EMBLEY

POLLY C. DEMASTERS--REUBEN P. COFFEY

SARAH ANN DEMASTERS--JACOB J. THACKER

26. 26 October 1829. WM. H. DEMASTERS and CYNTHIA C. W. LILLY. Officiant: WM. WRIGHT.

ELIZ. C. DENNIS--LEWIS PROFFITT

JUDITH DENNIS--DAVID BOWLES

SALLY ANN DENNIS--JAS. PROFFITT

27. 23 August 1830. WM. DENNIS and SARAH MOSBY. Security: WM. ALLEN.

15. 26 November 1821. WM. DEQUISI and ELIZ. CARY. Security: JNO. M. SMITH.

ELIZ. L. DICKINSON--NICHL. L. (S) MARTIN

FRANCES E. DICKINSON--JNO. DUGGINS

24. 13 September 1828. HUDSON M. DICKINSON and BETSY ANN LANDCRAFT. Security: WM. L. LANDCRAFT. Officiant: JAMES BOYD, 23rd.

31. 27 May 1833. JNO. W. DICKINSON and JUDITHA A. CRAWFORD. Security: JNO. B. COLES.

LUCINDA DICKINSON--SAML. M. PAGE

MARY JANE DICKINSON--R. L. SUTHERLAND

MILDRED DICKINSON--THOS. Y. RODES

ELIZA T. DICKSON--DAVID N. MATTHEWS

SARAH A. DICKSON--ALBERT G. JOHNSON

JUDITH DIGGS--JNO. N. CLARKSON

NICEY H. DIGGS--ALBERT G. CHEWNING

REBECCA DIGGS--SPENCER COLEMAN

33. 30 (?) December 1834. WM. H. DIGGS, JR. and MILDRED GUTHREY. Security: CHAS. PERROW.

19.   14 June 1824. THOS. P. DILLARD and SOPHIA F. PERRY. Security:
      GEO. W. PERRY. Officiant: JAMES BOYD, 16th.

18.   8 September 1823. WM. DINSMORE and NANCY CAMPBELL. Security:
      GEO. PHILLIPS. Officiant: ANTHONY GIANNIY, 9th.

      MARGARET DIXON--HENRY W. MARTIN

      SARAH N. DIXON--ACTON N. MATTHEWS

30.   22 October 1832. JNO. T. DODD and ELIZ. MEEKS. Security:
      WM. DODD.

      LUCY DODD--JNO. GOWING

      MARY C. DODD--WM. MASSIE

      MILLY DODD--WM. BROWN

23.   21 November 1827. WM. C. DODD and MARTHA ANN FITZGERALD.
      Security: JOS. H. C. DODD. Officiant: JAMES BOYD, 22nd.

      SUSAN DRAKE--AUSTIN BRYANT

20.   26 September 1825. DAVID DRUMHELLER and FRANCES ANDERSON.
      Security: JOS. C. ROBERTS. Officiant: JAMES BOYD, 29th.

24.   16 June 1828. NICHL. DRUMHELLER and SALLY LOBBAN. Security:
      JAS. LOBBAN. Officiant: WM. HAMERSLEY, 26th.

18.   19 March 1824. JAS. DUDLEY and ELIZ. SPEARS. Security:
      JNO. SPEARS. Officiant: JAMES BOYD, 20th.

20.   18 January 1825. JNO. DUGGINS and FRANCES E. DICKINSON.
      Security: JNO. WOODS. Officiant: MOSES BROCK, 20th.

34.   21 December 1835. RICH. I. DUKE and VA. A. WILLIAMS.
      Security: GEO. WILLIAMS.

14.   12 February 1821. JAS. DURHAM, JR. and L. TAYLOR. Security:
      JAS. DURHAM, SR.

12.   28 September 1818. WM. L. DURRETT and E. ROBERTS. Security:
      FORREST ROBERTS.

17.   6 February 1823. WM. EAST and LOUISA FITZGERALD. Security:
      DAVID FITZGERALD. Officiant: ANTHONY GIANNIY, 13th.

      ELIZ. EDMUNDS--JNO. STRICKLAND

      MARY C. EDMUNDS--GEO. VAUGHAN, JR.

      N. EDMUNDS--RO. ANDERSON (Error: ANDREWS)

      SARAH EDMUNDS--AMOS A. GANDY

20.   1 January 1825. WM. ELSOM and ELIZA M. ROBERTSO. Security:
      GEN. JOHNSON. Officiant: EDWD. L. WARREN, same.

17.   4 January 1823. JNO. EMBLEY and NANCY DEMASTERS. Security:
      EDWD. DEMASTERS. Officiant: JAMES BOYD, 6th.

      SALLY EMBLEY--LEOND. HALE

      MARY ENOX--WM. GRIZZLE

23.   25 August 1827. THOS. EPES and ELEANOR FOSTER. Security:
      MATT. W. ALVIS. Officiant: W.H.

17. 22 January 1823. GEO. EUBANK and ELIZ. H. WINGFIELD.
     Security: DAVID W. TERRY.

19. 9 December 1824. GEO. EUBANK and MARY WILLS. Security:
     JNO. WILLS. Officiant: JAMES BOYD, same.

22. 13 November 1826. JNO. EUBANK and MARTHA GRIFFIN. Security:
     PRICE L. (S) PERKINS. Officiant: J.S., 15th.

13. 11 December 1819. WINGFIELD EUBANK and P. H. WINGFIELD.
     Security: JOS. B. WINGFIELD. Officiant: BENJ. BURGHER,
14th (?).

26. 7 April 1830. CHAS. EVANS and MILDRED SCRUGGS. Security:
     RO. C. CUTLER. Officiant: M. P. S., same.

     EVALINA I. EVANS--RICH. H. HARLOW (Error: see EWERS)

     LUCY M. A. EVANS--JNO. J. MADDOX

30. 16 January 1833. ELIAS EVERETT and LUCY L. STRATTON.
     Security: RO. C. CUTLER.

30. 24 December 1832. JNO. EVERETT and MILLY COFFEY. Security:
     JESSE A. CAMPBELL. Officiant: RO. I. CARSON, 27th.

     EVALINA I. EWERS--RICH. G. HARLOW

     JANE EWERS--WM. BRIDGWATER

19. 27 September 1824. CHRISTOPHER FABER and ELIZ. WHITE.
     Security: WM. FABER. Officiant: J.S., October 2nd.

12. 29 September 1818. J. P. FARRAR and R. TOMS. Security:
     CHAS. TOMS.

28. 15 November 1831. JOS. W. FARRAR and JANE M. CARTER.
     Security: JNO. ROBERTSON. Officiant: P. CLEVELAND, 16th.

     M. FARRAR--D. MARTIN

     MARY FARRAR--BENJ. MARTIN

14. 27 November 1820. SHELTON FARRAR and SARAH SUSAN THOMAS.
     Security: C. J. THOMAS.

26. 4 November 1829. JNO. FAULCONER and AGNES SPENCER. Security:
     GEO. VAUGHAN, JR.

     JULIA A. FAULCONDER--WM. F. SPENCER

26. 23 November 1829. EDWD. FEAGANS and MARY ANN HARVEY. Security:
     JNO. HARVEY.

     EVALINA M. FERGUSON--JAS. FULTON

26. 6 March 1830. JAS. FERGUSON and JANE J. WEST. Security:
     F. B. WEST. Officiant: EDWD. L. WARREN, 9th.

     L. FERGUSON--JOEL FORTUNE

     LOUISA ANN FERGUSON--JAS. PAINE

     SARAH C. FIELDS--MITCHELL WATTS. Error: see SARAH C. FULKS

25. 27 August 1829. HENRY W. FISHER and EVELINA A. WOODY.
     Security: THOS. WOODY. Officiant: JAMES BOYD, same.

26. 17 December 1829. ALBERT FITZGERALD and ELIZ. FITZGERALD.
     Security: JOS. H. C. DODD.

33. 15 June 1835. BENJ. FITZGERALD and MATILDA J. FITZGERALD.
     Security: RO. W. FITZGERALD. Officiant: CORNL. (?) GATES (?),
22nd.

     CATH. FITZGERALD--HOLLOWAY COFFEY

24. 27 April 1829. DAVID FITZGERALD and LUCINDA HARVIE. Security:
     JAS. FITZGERALD.

     E. FITZGERALD--JNO. C. HATTER

29. 26 March 1832. EDMUND FITZGERALD and JANE MEEKS. Security:
     EDMD. C. BRIDGE. Officiant: M.P.S., 29th.

     ELIS. FITZGERALD--ALBERT FITZGERALD

17. 19 February 1823. JAS. C. FITZGERALD and SARAH SNEED.
     Security: EDMD. CAMPBELL. Officiant: ANTHONY GIANNIY, 20th.

     JANE FITZGERALD--ANSIL GILES

25. 11 November 1828. JESSE W. FITZGERALD and MARIA W. HARVEY.
     Security: DAVID FITZGERALD. Officiant: JAMES BOYD, 26th.

     LOUISA FITZGERALD--WM. EAST

     MARTHA ANN FITZGERALD--WM. C. DODD

     MARY FITZGERALD--OSBORN COFFEY

     MATILDA A. J. FITZGERALD--BENJ. FITZGERALD

     NANCY FITZGERALD--HERBERT HINES

     SARAH A. FITZGERALD--WM. FITZGERALD

34. 23 November 1835. WM. FITZGERALD and SARAH A. FITZGERALD.
     Security: WOODSON R. FITZGERALD.

27. 23 August 1830. WOODSON R. FITZGERALD and FRANCES COFFEY.
     Security: REUBEN P. (?) COFFEY.

31. 27 August 1833. ZEPHANIAH FITZGERALD and POLLY COFFEY.
     Security: REUBEN COFFEY.

19. 2 December 1824. ALEX. FITZPATRICK and BETHELAND PENN.
     Secuirty: GEO. PENN. Officiant: JAMES BOYD.

30. 20 December 1832. JNO. FITZPATRICK and RHODA A. SMITH.
     Security: WM. G. SMITH. Officiant: JOS. A. BROWN, 21st.

22. 9 November 1826. NICHL. FITZPATRICK and MARY B. WOODSON.
     Security: RO. C. CUTLER. Officiant: JAMES BOYD, 15th.

     LYDIA FLOOD--SYLVANUS MEEKS

     SUSANNA FLOYD--SIMON CRISP

22. 26 February 1827. HENRY FOGUS and SUSAN HAYS. Security:
     JNO. B. SPICE. Officiant: WM. HAMERSLEY.

27. 20 December 1830. BENJ. L. FORTUNE and MARY I. THOMAS.
     Security: JNO. L. THOMAS. Officiant: EDWD. L. WARREN, 23rd.

     CYNTHIA L. FORTUNE and JAS. W. HARVIE

16. 24 December 1821. JOEL FORTUNE and L. FERGUSON. Security:
     JAS. J. BLAIR. Officiant: EDWD. L. WARREN, January 10th, 1822.

31. 25 November 1833. JOEL FORTUNE and MARY J. JOHNSON. Security: ABSALOM JOHNSON. Officiant: ALBERT G. BURTON, January 2, 1834.

30. 4 February 1833. JNO. P. FORTUNE and SALINA A. S. HARGROVE. Security: JNO. HARGROVE. Officiant: H. L. PAYTON, 6th.

NANCY FORTUNE--JESSE CUNNINGHAM

PATSY FORTUNE--CLEMEN LAVENDER

REBECCA FORTUNE--ZACH FORTUNE

REBECCA FORTUNE--THORNTON SPENCER

20. 23 May 1825. RICH. C. FORTUNE and MARY M. VAUGHAN. Security: GEO. VAUGHAN. Officiant: JAMES BOYD, 31st.

SALLY FORTUNE--JNO. MC ALEXANDER

15. 28 May 1821. THOS. FORTUNE and MATILDA BUTLER. Security: SPENCER FALCONER.

15. 19 April 1821. ZACH FORTUNE and REBECCA FORTUNE. Security: NICHL. FORTUNE. Officiant: JAMES BOYD, same.

28. 25 August 1831. ZACH FORTUNE and SARAH CHEWNING. Security: JNO. H. WINGFIELD.

ELEANOR FOSTER--THOS. EPES

FLORA B. FOSTER--BENJ. NORVELL

23. 10 December 1827. JNO. A. FOSTER and AMELIA C. MC ALEXANDER. Security: D. R. MC ALEXANDER.

15. 24 April 1821. RICH. FOSTER and ELIZ. TOMS. Security: CLIFTON TOMS.

12. 22 December 1818. J. FOX and O. CHANDLER. Security: J. C. JOHNSTON.

LUCY FOX--WM. RAINS

SALLY FOX--CHAS. TOMS

25. 14 (?10) August 1829. WOODSON B. FOX and POLLY ANDERSON. Security: WM. ANDERSON.

30. 5 November 1832. JAS. FULCHER, JR. and MAHALA W. HARVIE. Security: CURTIS GILL and THOS. HARVIE.

32. 23 August 1834. JOS. C. FULKS and ELIX. N. NABERS. Security: CARTER HARMEN.

MARY FULKS--CHAS. PETERS

SARAH C. FULKS--MITCHELL WATTS

27. 23 October 1830. JAS. FULTON and EVELINA M. FERGUSON. Security: G. V. BERNARD.

23. 22 October 1827. AMOS A. GANDY and SARAH EDMUNDS. Security: GEO. S. MAYS.

ELIZ. GARBER--JAS. SMITH

CATH. GARDNER--RICH. N. ANDERSON

CAROLINE M. GARLAND--MAURICE H. GARLAND

25. 10 October 1828. HUDSON M. GARLAND and LETITIA B. PENDLETON. JR. for groom. Officiant and security: JAS. BOYD, 14th.

26. 10 March 1830. MAURICE H. GARLAND and CAROLINE M. GARLAND. Security: WM. H. GARLAND. Officiant: JAMES BOYD, same.

26. 14 November 1829. MOSES GAULDIN and REBECCA RITTENHOUSE. Security: ISAAC RITTENHOUSE.

24. 28 April 1828. WM. GAULDIN and NANCY PUGH. Security: N. TOWNSEND. Officiant: JAMES BOYD, May 6th.

MARTHA GAY--NATHL. BOWLES

MARY I. GAY--THOS. R. GILES

20. 21 February 1825. DAVID GENTRY and JANE MC CUE. Security: CHAS. MC CUE. Officiant: W.H., 24th.

25. 19 December 1828. THOS. GIANNAY and POLLY TINNELL. Security: FRS. GIANNINAY.

18. 2 October 1823. ANSIL GILES and JANE FITZGERALD. Security: JNO. FITZGERALD. Officiant: ANTHONY GIANNIY, same.

MILDRED C. C. GILES and EDMD. J. (?) HARRIS

POLLY GILES--WM. PHILLIPS

32. 15 February 1834. THOS. R. GILES and MARY I. GAY. Security: SAML. GAY.

29. 11 January 1832. WM. GILES and ELIZA HIGHT. Security: JNO. HIGHT.

32. 7 March 1834. WM. GILES and POLLY B. WILLS. Security: JNO. I. LOVING.

RHODA GILL--WYATT CAMDEN

21. 28 November 1825. THOS. GLASS and CELIA BURKS. Security: TERISHA TURNER. Officiant: J.S., November.

17. 18 December 1822. MICHL. GLEESON and NANCY MARTIN. Security: JAS. N. MARTIN.

27. 25 September 1830. THOS. J. GLENN and ELIZ. CRITZER. Security: JACOB FRY. Officiant: ROSWELL TERRY.

12. 2 March 1819. WM. GLOVER and M. L. POOR. Security: JNO. GLOVER. Officiant: J.S., 3rd.

22. 12 July 1827. DABNEY P. GOOCH and EDNA PENDLETON. Security: CHAS. L. CHRISTIAN.

26. 9 September 1829. WM. O. GOODE and SARAH MASSIE. Security: M. ALEXANDER.

ANN M. GOODWIN--CHAS. P. RODES

20. 11 October 1825. JAS. D. GOODWIN and CATH. WATTS. Security: CHAS. WATTS. Officiant: JAMES BOYD, 13th.

14. 14 October 1820. THOS. C. GOODWIN and LUCINDA MONTGOMERY. Security: JNO. GOODWIN. Officiant: JAMES BOYD, 5th.

NANCY L. GOOLSBY and ARCHIBALD PAMPLIN

MARY JANE GORDON--OBADIAH GORDON

32. 15 October 1834. OBDIIH GORDON and MARY JANE GORDON. Security:
ARCH. B. PAMPLIN.

28. 28 July 1831. JNO. GOWING and LUCY DODD. Officiant:
M.P.S., 31st.

MARIAH GOWING--WM. WEBB

MARY ANN GOWING--JNO. PUGH

13. 20 December 1819. SAML. W. GRANT and M. HARRIS. Security:
ALEX. GRANT. Officiant: J.S., 22nd.

CATH. GRAVES--JAS. WEST

29. 30 January 1832. HAWES GRAVES and NANCY HARRIS. Security:
NATHAN J. BARNETT, J. H. WINGFIELD.

LOUISA GRAVES--JNO. W. N. PAGE

MALINDA GRAVES--THOS. JACKSON

PAULINA GRAVES--WM. JACKSON

NANCY GRAY--JONATHAN BALASLEY

14. 5 January 1821. WM. GRAY and PHEBE LEE. Security: JOS.
TRUSLER. Officiant: JAMES BOYD, 9th.

21. 19 December 1825. WM. GREGORY and SALLY L. WOOD. Security:
WM. WOOD. Officiant: JAMES BOYD, January 10th.

14. 24 August 1820. AUSTIN GRIFFIN and MATILDA WRIGHT. Security:
BENJ. WRIGHT. Officiant: JAMES BOYD, 30th.

BETSY W. GRIFFIN--RICH. L. BOLTON

HANNAH GRIFFIN--WM. DAMRON

JEMIMA GRIFFIN--ANDERSON PUCKET

MARTHA GRIFFIN--JNO. EUBANK

REBECCA GRIFFIN--HAZELWOOD MORRIS

RHODA A. GRIFFIN--BENJ. BRADSHAW

LUCY ANN DAFF--LEVI GROAH

18. 16 December 1823. CHESLEY GRIZLE and LUCY WESTBROOK.
Security: JNO. TYREE.

15. 17 July 1821. WM. GRIZZLE and MARY ENOX. Security:
JOS. HORSLEY.

CATH. GROAH--STEPHEN BRIGHT

32. 11 August 1834. JOS. GROAH and ELIZA C. MILLER. Security:
JOS. MILLER.

28. 17 May 1831. LEVI GROAH and LUCY ANN DAFF. Security:
JACOB DAFF.

MILDRED GUTHREY--WM. H. DIGGS, JR.

MARY HADEN--JNO. BUTLER

30. 8 October 1832. JAS. HAGER and ELIZ. MC BRIDE. Security:
EM. P. PAMPLIN.

MARY C. HAGER--AMBR. ROBERTS

15. 17 September 1821. LEONARD HALE and SALLY EMBLEY. Security:
    LUKE EMBLEY. Officiant: JAMES BOYD, 17th.

16. 28 May 1822. THOS. HALES and SUSAN CLASBY. Security:
    CREED C. CARTER.

BELINDA HALL--JACOB ARISMAN

33. 25 May 1835. HUGH N. HALL and ELIZA WALLACE. Security:
    ANDREW WALLACE. J. HARRISON, June 3rd.

MAHALY HALL--WM. MC QUERY

18. 27 November 1823. RO. M. HALL and BELINDA BIBB. Security:
    THOS. BIBB. Officiant: EDWD. L. WARREN, same.

32. 22 October 1834. DAVID HAMBLET and MARGARET PUCKET. Security:
    RO. COWPER.

31. 18 November 1833. HENRY W. HAMBLETT and MARY ANN WOOD.
    Security: JOEL N. WHEELER.

MARTHA A. HAMBLET and GEO. H. TURNER

MARY C. HAMBLETT and LORENZO D. TURNER

SALLY HAMBLETT--GEO. WOOD

25. 22 December 1828. SEATON R. HAMBLETT and SARAH R. BAILEY.
    Security: TERISHA BAILEY. JAMES BOYD, 25th.

22. 9 January 1827. WM. G. HAMBLETT and ELIZ. THURMOND. Security:
    ELIAS HAMBLETT. Officiant: JAMES BOYD, 11th.

19. 27 September 1824. BEVERLY HAMNER and LUCINDA SMALL.
    Security: JNO. M. HAMNER. Officiant: J.S., 30th.

ELIZ. HANSBROUGH--NELSON SMITH

30. 1 January 1833. ELIAS HARDING and SUSAN WIRGHT. Security:
    WM. DAWSON. Officiant: EDWD. L. WARREN, 4th.

LUCINDA L. HARDING--ALBERT M. JOHNSON

15. 18 May 1821. RICH. HARDING and SALLY PURVIS. Security:
    GEO. W. PURVIS.

SARAH ANN HARDING--WM. DAMRON

24. 12 August 1828. WM. HARDING and MARY ANN BAKER. Security:
    JACOB BAKER.

30. 15 October 1832. JOS. HARDY and JANE F. WOODS. Security:
    WM. N. WOODS.

POLLY HARE--PRICE PERKINS

26. 7 November 1829. BEVERLY HARGROVE and NANCY WHITE. Security:
    RO. C. CUTLER. Officiant: JAMES BOYD, 15th.

ELIZ. HARGROVE--EDMD. W. HILL

SALINA A. S. HARGROVE--JNO. P. FORTUNE

13. 3 November 1819. JAS. W. HARLAN and FRANCES BAILEY. Security:
    JNO. BAILEY, SR.

ELIZA HARLOW--LEEVIN HAWKINS

ELMIRA M. HARLOW--JNO. M. BALL

FRANCES HARLOW--RICH. W. BERNARD

JANE B. HARLOW--SAML. H. BURNETT

28. 6 October 1831. JOS. S. HARLOW and SARAH ANN HAWKINS.
Security: YOUNG HAWKINS.

29. 16 March 1832. LARKIN HARLOW and ELIZA BRYANT. Security:
WM. BRYANT.

MARY ANN HARLOW--SKILES H. ROBERTS

16. 23 September 1822. NICHL. HARLOW and JANETTA BRIDGWATER.
Security: N. HARLOW.

20. 21 March 1825. RUBIN HARLOW and ELEANOR THROP. Officiant:
JAMES BOYD, 22nd.

27. 24 July 1830. RICH. G. HARLOW and EVALINA I. EWERS.
Security: THOS. EWERS. Officiant: JAMES BOYD, 10th.

26. 9 September 1829. WILSON HARLOW and PATSY SPROUSE. Security:
JNO. C. ROBINSON.

26. 7 September 1829. CARTER HARMEN and MAHALA THACKER. Security:
WYATT THACKER.

14. 13 April 1820. BENJ. HARRIS and POLLY MONTGOMERY. Security:
S. GARLAND. Officiant: JAMES BOYD, same.

26. 30 September 1829. BENJ. D. HARRIS and CATH. T. WILLIAMS.
Security: RO. C. CUTLER.

18. 16 February 1824. CARTER B. HARRIS and MARY MARR. Security:
JNO. MARR. Officiant: JAMES BOYD, same.

21. 28 January 1826. EDMD. J.(?) HARRIS and MILDRED C. C. GILES.
Security: JAS. GILES. Officiant: JAMES BOYD, 14 February.

33. 10 March 1835. EDWD. J. HARRIS and NANCY TINNELL. Security:
JNO. TINNELL. Officiant: H. L. PEYTON, 13th.

ELIZ. HARRIS--JNO. NEESE

ELIZ. G. HARRIS--SCHYLER G. HARRIS

ELIZ. V. HARRIS--JAS. THOMPSON, JR.

ELVIRA HARRIS--J. W. SHELTON

18. 27 January 1824. JAS. HARRIS and MARGARET WOODS. Security:
HENRY T. HARRIS.

31. 7 December 1833. JAS. HARRIS and MARY PUGH. Security:
NELSON PUGH.

JANE W. HARRIS--JNO. S. STICKLEMAN

29. 28 March 1832. JNO. W. HARRIS and LUCINDA B. WILSON. Security:
JNO. H. CARROLL.

M. HARRIS--SAML. W. GRANT

MARTHA HARRIS--SAML. PUCKETT

MARY A. E. HARRIS--HAWES H. COLEMAN

NANCY HARRIS--HAWES GRAVES

NANCY C. HARRIS--DANL. B. DALY

SALINA HARRIS--NATHAN J. BARNETT

SALLY HARRIS--ARMISTEAD MAYS

31. 31 May 1833. SCHYLER G. HARRIS and ELIZ. G. HARRIS. Security:
LLOYD G. HARRIS.

16. 26 February 1822. THOS. HARRIS and LARCENIA LOVING. Security:
L. W. MC DOWELL.

22. 29 August 1826. WM. HARRIS and POLLY A. JOHNSON. Security:
WM. C. KIDD. Officiant: JAMES BOYD, same.

14. 10 April 1820. THOS. HARRISON and BETSY CRISP. Security:
LANDON S. GOWING. Officiant: JAMES BOYD, same.

28. 4 November 1831. WIATT HARRISON and FRANCES MOSS. Security:
JNO. STRATTON.

MARIA W. HARVEY--JESSE W. FITZGERALD

MARY ANN HARVEY--EDWD. FEAGANS

24. 8 April 1828. RICH. HARVEY and CATH. POWERS. Security:
MICHL. POWERS. Officiant: JAMES BOYD, 10th.

SOPHIA HARVEY--JNO. POWERS

13. 23 April 1819. WM. HARVEY and P. BRYANT. Security: JNO.
BRYANT. Officiant: SAML. DAY, 25th.

ELIZ. HARVIE--WM. J. MAYS

21. 21 November 1825. JAS. W. HARVIE and CYNTHIA L. FORTUNE.
Security: THOS. E. FORTUNE.

LUCINDA HARVIE--DAVID FITZGERALD

MAHALA W. HARVIE--JAS. FULCHER, JR.

SARAH ANN HARVIE--JNO. J. THOMPSON

SARAH S. HARVIE--LEROY MITCHELL

15. 20 March 1821. URIAH HATCHER and SUSANNA WITT. Security:
DENNITT WITT.

13. 6 April 1819. JNO. C. HATTER and E. FITZGERALD. Security:
SAML. FITZGERALD. Officiant: WALTER CHRISTIAN, 19th.

NANCY HATTER--HENRY PARROCK

POLLY HATTER--CARY SNEED

18. 29 December 1823. WM. HATTER and ELIZA MEEKS. Security:
JNO. MEEKS. Officiant: ANTHONY GIANNIY, January 13, 1824.

28. 5 August 1831. LEEVIN HAWKINS and ELIZA HARLOW. Security:
YOUNG HAWKINS. Officiant: PORTER CLEVELAND, 11th.

SARAH ANN HAWKINS--JOS. S. HARLOW

29. 6 August 1832. SAMUEL G. HAYES and CELIA P. TYREE.

191

14. 25 December 1819. GEO. HAYS and LUCINDA WILLIAMS. Security: JNO. WILLIAMS. Officiant: ANTHONY GIANNIY, 26th.

SUSAN HAYS--HENRY FOGUS

MARTHA HAYLETT--JAS. TAYLOR

32. 13 September 1834. RICH. HAZLETT and NANCY SAUNDERS. Security: JNO. SAUNDERS.

25. 20 September 1828. BENNETT HENDERSON and JANETTA S. JOHNSON. Security: WM. ELSOM. Officiant: EDWD. L. WARREN, same.

MARTHA J. HENDERSON--EDWD. JENNINGS

19. 21 September 1824. RO. HENDERSON and LUCINDA LOBBAN. Security: A. (?) H. LOBBAN. Officiant: MOSES BROCK, 28th.

25. 17 December 1828. JNO. HENDRIX and DELILA TYREE. Security: JNO. L. TYREE. Officiant: JNO. ALLCOCK.

ELIZ. HENDERSON--WM. F. HENDERSON

33. 2 March 1835. JAS. P. HENDERSON and MARGARET C. POLLARD. Security: RO. RIVES, JR. Officiant: WM. S. REID, 3rd.

29. 31 March 1832. WM. HENDERSON and PAULINA MORRIS. Security: GEO. MORRIS.

32. 9 April 1834. WM. F. HENDERSON and ELIZ. HENDERSON. Security: WM. BARNETT. Officiant: H.S.P., April 7 (sic).

LUCY T. HENLEY--WOOD RIPLEY

NANCY HERNDON--JAS. P. KIDD

POLLY HENNDON--GEO. PURVIS

E. A. HENRY--JAS. BRUCE

22. 28 September 1826. JNO. HENRY and ELVIRA H. MC CLELLAND. Security: E. (?) B. ESKRIDGE. Officiant: WM. REID.

NANCY HENRY--HENRY MANN

16. 26 September 1822. PATRICK H. HICKOK and ELIZA WATTS. Security: JAS. REID. Officiant: JAMES BOYD, same.

18. 27 October 1823. JAS. HIGGINBOTHAM and SARAH SHIELDS. Security: JAS. SHIELDS.

ELIZA HIGHT--WM. GILES

JANE HIGHT--WM. W. CAMDEN

POLLY HIGHT--SAML. ALLEN

18. 1 February 1824. WM. HIGHT and SUSANNA CAMPBELL. Security: JOEL HIGHT. Officiant: JAMES BOYD, March 2nd.

30. 16 November 1832. EDMD. W. HILL and ELIZ. HARGROVE. Security: RO. A. SMILEY. Officiant: RO. I. CARSON, 21st.

NANCY P. HILL--PHILLIP H. RYAN

12. 31 September 1818. T. D. HILL and B. ROBERTS. Security: BENJ. NORVELL. Officiant: JAMES BOYD, 1 October.

22. 24 November 1826. HERBERT HINES and NANCY FITZGERALD.
Security: BENJ. FITZGERALD. Officiant: JAMES BOYD,
December 4th.

POLLY HITE--CHRISTIAN SACK

SALLY HITE--WM. HITE

15. 17 September 1821. WM. HITE and SALLY HITE. Security:
JNO. HOUSEWRIGHT.

17. 17 March 1823. MEWLENBERG HOGG and MAHALA WHITE. Security:
V. W. THOMAS. Officiant: EDWD. L. WARREN, 18th.

12. 25 January 1819. JNO. HORSLEY and MILDRED CABELL. Security:
F. CABELL. Officiant: JAMES BOYD, February 4th.

17. 9 May 1823. JNO. HOUSEWRIGHT and ELIZ. BRAMWELL. Security:
JAS. Y. RODES.

27. 24 January 1831. BENJ. J. HUGHES and LORINDA R. PARRISH.
Security: SAML. PARRISH. Officiant: JAMES BOYD, February 3rd.

BETSY HUGHES--GEO. I. BROWN

ELIZ. HUGHES--PARKS H. PARRISH

ELIZ. B. (?) HUGHES--MOSES W. HUGHES

FRANCES E. HUGHES--JOS. MC COMB

32. 18 March 1834. JAS. B. HUGHES and ELIZ. C. PERRY. Security:
GEO. W. PERRY.

JANE F. HUGHES--GEO. T. NOEL

24. 28 January 1828. JNO. F. P. HUGHES and JARUSAH CLARKSON.
Security: D. R. CLARKSON. Officiant: JAMES BOYD, February 7th.

23. 27 August 1827. MOSES W. HUGHES and ELIZ. B. HUGHES. Security:
MOSES HUGHES. Officiant: JAMES BOYD, September 6th.

SALLY L. HUGHES--WM. MC COMB

18. 26 November 1823. WM. HUMPHREYS and C. A. ROBINSON. Security:
GEN. JOHNSON. Officiant: EDWD. L. WARREN, December 10th.

24. 1 March 1828. WM. HUMPHREY and BELINDA PANNELL. Security:
WM. PANNELL. Officiant: W. H., 6th.

27. 15 May 1830. VALENTINE HUNDLY and MARGARET C. WILLOUGHBY.
Security: JOSHUA WILLOUGHBY. Officiant: EDWD. L. WARREN, 16th.

29. 11 September 1832. DAVID HUNTER and SALLY N. WHITE. Security:
WALKER SPENCER.

JUDITH HUNTER--RO. PROFFITT

MARTHA HUNTER--JNO. N. MEEKS

JANE C. HYLTON--REESE CUNNINGHAM

26. 14 January 1830. NORVELL HUNTER and JUDITH BRYANT. Security:
DAVID P. BRYANT.

SALLY INNIS--CRAWFORD PUCKET

12. 20 February 1819. SAML. IRVIN and MARY DAVIS. Security:
DANL. NASH. Officiant: JNO. SHEPHERD, 24th.

14. 22 July 1820. WM. H. IRVIN and ELIZ. DAVIS. Security: JNO. P. APPLEBERRY. Officiant: J.S., 26th.

28. 17 September 1831. JOS. K. IRVING and MARTHA A. CLAIBORNE. Security: RO. J. KINCAID.

FRANCES JACKSON--DAVID MORRIS

33. 10 January 1835. JNO. P. JACKSON and SARAH ANN ROBERTS. Security: JOS. A. ROBERTS.

18. 3 October 1833. RICH. JACKSON and LUCINDA TOMS. Security: CLIFTON TOMS. Officiant: J.S., November 6th.

33. 9 February 1835. JNO. E. JENKINS and ROSY JANE CASH. Security: ELI A. JENKINS.

MARGARET JENKINS--ELIJAH ROSSEN

32. 28 January 1834. EDWD. JENNINGS and MARTHA J. HENDERSON. Security: G. HENDERSON.

27. 9 October 1830. ALBERT M. JOHNSON and LUCINDA L. HARDING. Security: WM. P. SHEPHERD. Officiant: EDWD. L. WARREN, 12th.

17. 6 November 1822. BENJ. JOHNSON and MARIAH MAYS. Security: MOSES J. MAYS.

CARRIA ANN C. M. JOHNSON--JACOB H. TILMAN

13. 5 October 1819. DAVID JOHNSON and NANCY SMALL. Security: WM. SMALL. Officiant: JAMES BOYD, 12th.

34. 23 November 1835. GENERAL M. JOHNSON and SARAH BELL. Security: JAS. JOHNSON. Officiant: EDWD. L. WARREN, 24th.

JANETTA S. JOHNSON--BENNETT HENDERSON

LURENA JOHNSON--WM. BRYANT

M. A. H. JOHNSON--MANSFIELD WHITEHEAD

MARGARET JOHNSON--THOS. KIDD

MARGARET S. JOHNSON--WM. P. SHEPHERD

MARY B. JOHNSON--GEO. W. QUICK

MARY J. JOHNSON--JOEL FORTUNE

NANCY JOHNSON--JAS. MARTIN

15. 28 July 1821. NORVELL JOHNSON and LUCINDA THURMOND. Security: JORDAN THURMOND.

POLLY A. JOHNSON--WM. HARRIS

12. 28 February 1819. RO. JOHNSON and S. BRITTAIN. Security: JNO. HARGROVE. Officiant: SAML. DAY, 4 March.

18. 25 November 1823. RO. JOHNSON and SALLY WILLOUGHBY. Security: JNO. BETHEL. Officiant: BENJ. BURGHER, same.

SALLY JOHNSON--DAVID ALLEN

23. 16 October 1827. THOS. H. JOHNSON and THANKFUL SHIELDS. Security: AMBR. R. MARR. Officiant: JAMES BOYD, November 6th.

16. -- July 1822. WM. JOHNSON and LUCY T. DAMERON. Security:
     WM. R. DAMERON. O.B., 17th.

20. 28 September 1825. WILLIS JOHNSON and ELIZ. CAMPBELL.
     Security: THOS. JONES.

     A. JONES--PLEASANT MITCHELL

     CLARISSA JONES--ZACH MITCHELL

27. 24 January 1831. COLEMAN JONES and SOPHIA MAYS. Security:
     ELIJAH MAYS. Officiant: JAMES BOYD, 26th.

     ELIZ. A. JONES--GEORGE V. HARLOW

13. 22 March 1819. ELLIS JONES and LUCINDA LAVANDER. Security:
     GEO. LAVENDER.

32. 31 March 1834. JESSE A. JONES and SARAH THURMOND. Security:
     BENJ. THURMOND.

     MARY ANN JONES--RICH. SAUNDERS

     PAULINA P. JONES--SHELTON WRIGHT

     POLLY JONES--AMBR. R. MC DANIEL

17. 9 May 1823. RO. C. JONES and SUSANNAH CLARKSON. Security:
     JAS. CLARKSON.

21. 31 (?) October 1825. WM. L. (S) JONES and ELIZ. AKERS.
     Security: WM. AKERS.

19. 17 November 1824. BENJ. JOPLING and BELINDA LOVING. Security:
     WM. LOVING. Officiant: JAMES BOYD, 18th.

28. 24 October 1831. HOLEMAN JOPLING and MARY P. BRIDGWATER.
     Security: NATHL. BRIDGWATER. Officiant: EDWD. L. WARREN, 31st.

     SALLY JOPLING--JESSE AUSTIN

     SARAH W. JORDAN--JAMES M. LOVING

12. 25 August 1818. T. P. JORDAN and L. LAVENDER. Security:
     WM. LAVENDER.

21. 15 May 1826. WM. JORDAN and JANE MAYS. Security:
     W. CUNNINGHAM.

     I am double-checking on cards and note three missing. I am
     saving room and , if not found, will go to Nelson and find
them. They are THOS. and WM. JACKSON and ALBERT G. JOHNSON. I
shall leave room at top of next page. I went back to Nelson and
recopied these missing cards:

28. 31 October 1831. THOS. JACKSON and MALINDA GRAVES. Security:
     SMITH TOMS.

28. 28 November 1831. WM. JACKSON and PAULINA GRAVES. Security:
     THOS. GRAVES.

30. 12 March 1833. ALBERT G. JOHNSON and SARAH A. DICKSON.
     Security: JNO. MATTHEWS. Officiant: EDWD. L. WARREN, 14th.

     ELIZ. KALER--WM. BALLARD

     POLLY KALER--WM. W. MAYS

31. 8 July 1833. JAS. KEITH and CARY ANN MAYS. Security:
     GEO. VAUGHAN, JR.

ANNE KELLY--JNO. ALLEN

ELIZ. KENNEDY--WM. L. TAYLOR

ELIZA KEY--RICH. VAUGHAN

O. KEY--R. PROFFITT

12. 26 October 1818. ALEX. KIDD and C. WILLOUGHBY. Security: J. WILLOUGHBY. Officiant: J.S., 29th.

34. 21 April 1836. ALEX. L. (S) KIDD and FRANS WILLOUGHBY. Security: RO. N. KIDD. Officiant: C. L. W., same.

ELIZ. KIDD--JAS. W. CRAIGE

J. KIDD--GEO. W. SUTLER

16. 28 January 1822. JAS. P. KIDD and NANCY HERNDON. Security: RICH. HERNDON. Officiant: JAMES BOYD, 31st.

33. 15 December 1834. JNO. KIDD and MARGARET MC CLURE. Security: ALEX. ROBERTS.

34. 25 November 1835. JOS. KIDD and MARY ANN BRYANT. Security: THOS. KIDD. Officiant: H. L. P., 25th.

MARTHA KIDD--THOS. C. CARTER

MARTHA KIDD--JOEL VEST

18. 26 March 1824. PLEASANT M. KIDD and MARGARET J. WRIGHT. Security: JSS. W. CRAIGE. Officiant: JAMES BOYD, 28th.

RHODA ANN KIDD--LEWIS E. PRICE

21. 3 June 1826. RO. J. KIDD and NANCY JANE PAMPLIN. Security: ARCH PAMPLIN.

SARAH A. KIDD--RO. WATKINS

29. 21 February 1832. THOS. KIDD and MARGARET JOHNSON.

FRANCES E. KINCAID--GEO. WILLIAMS

30. 20 October 1832. EDWIN M. KIRBY and PEGGY J. MARTIN. Security: JNO. KIRBY and H. MARTIN. Officiant: EDWD. L. WARREN, 23rd.

FRANCES E. KINCAID--GEO. WILLIAMS

30. 30 October 1832. EDWIN M. KIRBY and PEGGY J. MARTIN. Security: JNO. KIRBY and H. MARTIN. Officiant: EDWD. L. WARREN, 23rd.

24. 22 January 1828. ELIJAH KIRBY and JUDITH MATTHEWS. Security: R. LANNUM and C. KIRBY. Officiant: EDWD. L. WARREN, 24th.

29. 10 July 1832. JNO. KIRBY and SARAH J. BOWMAN. Security: WM. H. BOWMAN. Officiant: EDWD. L. WARREN, 15th.

23. 5 October 1827. WM. L. KNIGHT and ELIZ. RODES. Security: THOS. J. RODES. Officiant: RO. D. MERIWETHER, 16th.

29. 6 August 1832. WM. L. KNIGHT and MARTHA A. LOBBAN. Security: NICHL. DRUMHELLER.

A. B. LANDCRAFT--JNO. S. ROBERTS

BETSY ANN LANDCRAFT--HUDSON M. DICKINSON

WILLY LANE--WM. VIA

21. 4 February 1826. LOVING T. LANHAM and NANCY ALLEN. Security: RICH. SAUNDERS.

23. 17 December 1827. WM. LANHAM and NANCY SMITH. Security: JAS. E. SMITH. Officiant: J. S., 19th.

MARY A. LANKFORD--GUTRIDGE LYON

SALLY LANKFORD--HENRY MARTIN

15. 14 November 1821. CLEMEN LAVENDER and PATSY FORTUNE. Security: NICHL. FORTUNE. Officiant: JAMES BOYD, 15th.

ELIZ. LAVENDER--JNO. WILLIAMS

L. LAVENDER--T. P. JORDAN

LUCINDA LAVENDER--ELLIS JONES

ELVIRA M. LAYNE--GEO. H. CHRISTIAN

LUCY ANN LAYNE--ROWLAND M. RICHESON

27. 11 October 1830. WM. LAYNE and ELIZ. A. ARRINGTON. Security: JNO. HAGER and S. ARRINGTON. Officiant: JNO. ALLCOCK, same.

15. 8 August 1821. JOS. LAYTON and REBECCA PAINTER. Security: HENRY PAINTER.

JUDITH LEE--WASHINGTON LOWE

MILDRED LEE--WM. LOWE

NANCY LEE--JAS. BRIDGE

PHEBE LEE--WM. GRAY

L. (S) LEE--JOS. TRUSLER

PHEBE LEIGHTER--JNO. PAINTER

25. 22 September 1828. ADAM LEIGHTER and ELIZ. PAYNTER. Security: SALLY PAYNTER.

ELIZ. F. I. LIGON--GARLAND A. SHEPHERD

RUTH LIGGIN--WM. T. SUDDARTH

CYNTHIA C. W. LILLY--WM. H. DEMASTERS

26. 23 November 1829. JESSE LOBBAN and ELIZA PAGE. Security: JNO. M. SMITH.

LUCINDA LOBBAN--RO. HENDERSON

MARTHA LOBBAN--JAS. MC CUE

SALLY LOBBAN--NICHL. DRUMHELLER

MARTHA A. LOBBAN--WM. L. KNIGHT

27. 26 April 1830. THOS. LOBBAN and AMY D. RODES. Security: NICHL. DETTOR. Officiant: P. C., 28th.

28. 28 April 1831. WM. LOBBAN and SARAH A. MC CUE. Security: B. M. MC CUE. Officiant: P. C., May 17th.

12. 3 December 1818. N. LOFTUS and S. (L) WATTS. Security:
CHAS. PERROW. Officiant: JAMES BOYD, same.

ADELINE S. LOVING--CHAS. N. PATTESON

ALMIRA LOVING--JNO. H. WINGFIELD

BELINDA LOVING--BENJ. JOPLING

CARDELIA LOVING--BEVERLY B. NASH

DLVIRA LOVING--MARTIN D. PRICE

EMILY ANN LOVING--GEO. R. (?) WATTS

FRANCES E. LOVING--GEO. W. STRATTON

HARRIET E. LOVING--JORDAN M. HANSBROUGH

23. 14 November 1827. JAS. M. LOVING and SARAH W. JORDAN.
Security: F. L. WHITEHEAD. Officiant: JAMES BOYD, 21st.

29. 28 May 1832. JAS. M. LOVING and ELIZA HARLOW. Security:
LARKIN HARLOW.

24. 26 March 1828. JNO. I. LOVING and SARAH JANE WILLS. Security:
LAWRENCE WILLS. Officiant: JAMES BOYD, 10 April.

14. 7 December 1820. W. L. LOVING and POLLY PUCKET. Security:
JNO. PUCKET. Officiant: ANTHONY GIANNIY, 7th.

LARCENDA LOVING--JACOB ROBERTSON

LUCINDA LOVING--THOS. HARRIS

LUCY F. LOVING--RO. S. ADAMS

MARY LOVING--JNO. J. PERRY

MARY ANNE LOVING--DAVID R. MC ALEXANDER

MILDRED T. LOVING--WM. C. STEVENS

26. 5 September 1829. NICHL. M. LOVING and MARY ANN PATTESON.
Security: RO. C. CUTLER.

NOENY S. LOVING--CHAS. M. RYAN

SALLY LOVING--JACOB PUCKET

25. 14 October 1828. SEATON H. LOVING and LOUISA M. MONTGOMERY.
Security: SAML. LOVING. Officiant: JAMES BOYD, 22nd.

32. 16 April 1834. SPOTSWOOD G. LOVING and SARAH E. W. SPENCER.
Security: RICH. STEPHENS. Officiant: H. P., 17th.

33. 22 December 1834. WM. T. LOVING and SARAH W. THACKER.
Security: WYATT THACKER. Officiant: J. J. HICKS, 25th.

18. 20 January 1824. JNO. LOW and SARAH WOOD. Security:
JESSE WOOD. Officiant: JAMES BOYD, 22nd.

23. 15 August 1827. WM. LOW and POLLY WRIGHT. Security: LUKE
EMBLEY. Officiant: JAMES BOYD, 16th.

POLLY LOWE--THOS. O. STATON

33. 29 August 1835. WASH. LOWE and JUDITH LEE. Security:
REUBEN LOW.

198

33. 29 August 1835. WM. LOWE and MILDRED LEE. Security: REUBEN LOW.

12. 16 March 1819. JAS. LUCKEY and S. (L) PURVIS. Security: SAML. LOVING. Officiant: JAMES BOYD, 18th.

32. 29 May 1834. GUTRIDGE LYON and MARY A. LANKFORD. Security: RO. WATKINS. Officiant: EDWD. L. WARREN, same.

32. 24 October 1834. JAS. W. LYON and PAULINA LYON. Security: JAS. LYON.

29. 3 September 1832. JNO. I. MADDOX and LUCY M. A. EVANS. Security: TARLTON EVANS.

LUCINDA MAHA--RALEIGH PINN

17. 22 February 1823. HENRY MANN and NANCY HENRY. Security: WM. H. FARRAR. Officiant: J. S., 28th.

34. 18 January 1836. NATHL. MANTIPLY and REBECCA I. BOURNE. Security: DANL. H. COLEMAN.

23. 11 September 1827. GIDEON MARKS and ELEANOR MOSS. Security: AJAX MOSS and H. MARKS.

22. 6 October 1826. JAS. MARR and ELIZ. H. SHIELDS. Security: AMBR. R. MARR. Officiant: JAMES BOYD, 19th.

MARY MARR--CARTER B. HARRISS

26. 16 December 1829. BENJ. MARTIN and MARY FARRAR. Security: DAVID MARTIN.

CHARLOTTE D. MARTIN--DRURY C. DAWSON

13. 17 March 1819. D. MARTIN and M. FARRAR. Security: WM. CRISP.

ELIZ. MARTIN--JAS. WITT

ELIZ. MARTIN--JAS. BUNTER

ELIZ. D. MARTIN--JNO. BUSH

ELIZ. H. MARTIN--JAS. E. POWELL

20. 24 January 1825. HENRY MARTIN and SALLY LANKFORD. Security: HUDSON MARTIN (DC)--sic.

25. 26 November 1828. HENRY MARTIN and MAHALA PAGE. Security: W. B. LIVELY. Officiant: JAMES BOYD.

17. 23 December 1822. HENRY W. MARTIN and MARGARET DIXON. Security: JAS. JOHNSON.

20. 21 March 1825. HUDSON MARTIN and NANCY THROP. Security: WM. THROP. Officiant: JAMES BOYD, 22nd.

34. 24 December 1835. JAS. MARTIN and NANCY JOHNSON. Security: JAS. JOHNSON. Officiant: H. L. P., same.

29. 11 April 1832. JAS. N. MARTIN and CARY ANN C. M. TILMAN. Security: RO. C. CUTLER.

M. H. MARTIN--J. (I) F. CARR

MARY F. MARTIN--WM. B. COFFEY

NANCY MARTIN--MICHL. GLEESON

NANCY MARTIN--WM. MATTHEWS

19.   22 November 1824. NICHL. L. (S) MARTIN and ELIZ. L. DICKINSON. Security: JNO. DUGGING. Officiant: JAMES BOYD, 30th.

PEGGY J. MARTIN--EDWIN M. KIRBY

15.   28 July 1812. WM. G. MARTIN and NANCY DAVIS. Security: WM. H. IRVING.

ANNE MASINCUP--RO. S. CAMPBELL

ELIZ. MASINCOUP--JESSE MAYFIELD

JANE MASSIE--JAS. W. CAMPBELL

MARTHA ANN MASSIE--GEO. W. CAMPBELL

15.   27 August 1821. NATHL. MASSIE and SUSAN N. WOODS. Security: NICHL. WOODS. Officiant: WM. H. FOSTER, September 4th.

SARAH MASSIE--WM. O. GOODE

21.   29 July 1826. THOS. MASSIE, JR. and SARAH C. CABELL. Security: RO. C. CUTLER. Officiant: WM. REID.

16.   29 December 1821. WM. MASSIE and MARY C. DODD. Security: JNO. DODD.

ELIZ. W. MATCHETT--BAZALEEL M. MC CUE

15.   20 September 1821. ACTON N. (see original says note) MATTHEWS and SARAH N. DIXON. Security: JAS. JOHNSON.

31.   25 November 1833. DAVID N. MATTHEWS and ELIZA T. DICKSON. Security: JAS. JOHNSON.

ELIZ. MATTHEWS--DAVID WOOD

24.   24 December 1827. JNO. B. MATTHEWS and CATH. SIMPSON. Security: JNO. M. MC CUE. Officiant: W. H., same.

JUDITH MATTHEWS--ELIJAH KIRBY

SARAH MATTHEWS--HENRY E. SMITH

23.   8 November 1827. WM. MATTHEWS and NANCY MARTIN. Security: WM. MARTIN.

32.   4 December 1834. RICH. H. MAUPIN and MARIA CLINCH. Security: WM. RAYNES.

15.   26 February 1821. MOSES MAXWELL and P. MC CUE. Security: CHAS. MC CUE. Officiant: WM. H. FOOTE, 13 March.

16.   7 January 1822. HENRY MAYFIELD and CATH. ARISMAN. Security: JACOB ARISMAN.

21.   8 February 1826. JESSE MAYFIELD and ELIZ. MASINCOPE. Security: JACOB ARISMAN. Officiant: W. H.

28.   9 May 1831. JAS. C. MAYO and NANCY F. THOMAS. Security: JS. S. THOMAS. Officiant: EDWD. L. WARREN, 11th.

20.   No date, but in March, 1825 ARMISTEAD MAYS and SALLY HARRIS. Officiant: JAMES BOYD, 31st. This is evidently bond on page 21 for them on 30 March 1825. JOSHUA HARRIS and same officiant on 31st.

CARY ANN MAYS--JAS. KEITH

23. 19 November 1827. CHAS. MAYS and SARAH MAYS. Security:
ELIJAH MAYS. Officiant: JAMES BOYD, December 19th.

33. 13 October 1835. JAS. MAYS and AVY CHEWNING. Security:
WM. MAYS. Officiant: H. S. PEYTON, 15th.

26. 23 November 1829. JAS. L. MAYS and ROSANNA WRIGHT. Security:
WM. BIBB.

JANE MAYS--WM. JORDAN

31. 23 December 1833. JNO. R. MAYS and NANCY J. SMITH. Security:
JAS. W. SMITH.

25. 11 December 1828. JOS. MAYS, JR. and ELIZ. THOMPSON.
Security: RO. C. CUTLER. Officiant: JAMES BOYD, 14th.

MARIAH MAYS--BENJ. JOHNSON

25. 23 March 1829. MOSES I. MAYS and HARRIET ALLEN. Security:
CHAS. PERROW. Officiant: JNO. ALLCOCK.

PAULINA MAYS--SAML. SPENCER, JR.

POLLY MAYS--JAS. W. CHEWNING

21. 27 February 1826. RO. MAYS, JR. and LUCY SMITH. Security:
JNO. M. SMITH. Officiant: JAMES BOYD, March 2nd.

33. 15 August 1835. RO. MAYS and MARY J. BOWLING. Security:
JNO. MAYS.

SARAH MAYS--CHAS. MAYS

SARAH MAYS--JAS. SPENCER, JR.

SOPHIA MAYS--COLEMAN JONES

28. 18 November 1831. WM. MAYS and ANN R. CHEWNING. Security:
JOS. (?) CHEWNING, I. MAYS, SR.

33. 6 June 1835. WM. B. MAYS and LUCINDA WHITE. Security:
JAS. L. MAYS. Officiant: H. L. P., 12th.

16. 13 March 1822. WM. J. MAYS and ELIZ. HARVIE. Security:
JESSE CAMPBELL.

33. 22 August 1835. WM. W. MAYS and POLLY KALER. Security:
JNO. R. MAYS. Officiant: J. HARRIS, 27th.

AMELIA C. MC ALEXANDER--JNO. A. FOSTER

25. 21 October 1828. DAVID R. MC ALEXANDER and MARY ANNE LOVING.
Security: WINSTON L. LOVING.

14. 17 July 1820. JNO. MC ALEXANDER and SALLY FORTUNE. Security:
WM. LOVING.

PATSY MC ALEXANDER--JAS. ALEXANDER

ELIZ. MC BRIDE--JAS. HAGER

SARAH MC BRIDE--LEOND. SCRUGGS

FRANCES L. MC CARTER--HOLEMAN BURFETT

ELVIRA H. MC CLELLAND--JNO. HENRY

LAURA MC CLELLAND--GEO. M. Y. MILLER

LUCY MC CLURE--NELSON PUGH

MARGARET MC CLURE--JNO. KIDD

30. 3 December 1832. JOS. MC COMB and FRANCES E. HUGHES. Security: JAS. HUGHES. Officiant: JNO. S. WATT, 13th.

29. 28 May 1832. WM. MC COMB and SALLY L. HUGHES. Security: MOSES HUGHES.

31. 14 October 1833. ANDREW R. MC CREARY and SALLY WITT. Security: WM. FITZPATRICK.

26. 29 March 1830. BAZALEEL M. MC CUE and ELIZ. W. MATCHELL. Security: WM. LOBBAN, JR. Officiant: ROSEWELL TINNY, April 1st.

24. 4 February 1828. JAS. MC CUE and MARTHA LOBBAN. Security: WM. LOBBAN. Officiant: W. H., 7th.

JANE MC CUE--DAVID GENTRY

16. 1 April 1822. JNO. M. MC CUE and PEACHY SIMPSON. Security: THOS. MAXWELL.

P. MC CUE--MOSES MAXWELL

SARAH MC CUE--WM. LOBBAN

24. 24 March 1828. AMBR. MC DANIEL and POLLY JONES. Security: GEO. JONES.

ELIZ. MC FALL--JNO. WINGFIELD

MARY ANN MC FALL--JOSIAH L. D. WINGFIELD

18. 12 November 1823. WM. MC QUERY and MAHALY HALL. Security: SAML. S. FOX. Officiant: JAMES BOYD.

20. 25 September 1825. JAS. MC WANE and PAMELEA RYAN. Security: THOS. M. RYAN. Officiant: MOSES BROCK, October 11th.

13. 15 December 1819. ANDERSON MEEKS and JANE COFFEY. Security: GEO. HARRIS (?). Officiant: ANTHONY GIANNIY, 16th.

ELIZA MEEKS--WM. HATTER

ELIZ. MEEKS--JNO. T. DODD

16. 12 December 1821. FRANCIS MEEKS and MARIA WRIGHT. Security: RICH. MEEKS. Officiant: JAMES BOYD, 13th.

JANE MEEKS--EDMD. FITZGERALD

34. 2 January 1836. JNO. N. MEEKS and MARTHA HUNTER. Security: THOS. MEEKS.

25. 22 December 1828. LAWRENCE MEEKS and MARGARET HAMBLETON. Security: CARTER B. HARRIS.

12. 6 February 1819. SYLVANUS MEEKS and S. C. CLARKSON. Security: L. GIANNY. Officiant: JAMES BOYD, 7th.

20. 20 January 1825. SYLVANUS MEEKS and LYDIA FLOOD. Security: AUSTIN SEAY. Officiant: JAMES BOYD, 21st.

21. 7 December 1825. THOS. MEEKS and ELIZ. THOMAS. Security: FRANS. GIANNY. Officiant: JAMES BOYD, same.

19. 18 October 1824. ARCH. B. MIGGINSON and ANN R. WHITE.
Security: JAS. D. WHITE.

22. 7 November 1826. JOS. C. MIGGINSON and ALMIRE MONTGOMERY.
Security: RO. C. CUTLER. Officiant: JAMES BOYD, 9th.

27. 22 November 1830. DAVID MILLER and MARY TAYLOR. Security:
JOEL TAYLOR.

ELIZA C. MILLER--JOS. GROAH

31. 24 September 1833. GEO. M. Y. MILLER and LANRAR MC CLELLAND.
Security: T. S. MC CLELLAND, JR.

26. 27 October 1829. JESSE MILLS and FRANCES WOOD. Security:
JESSE WOOD.

MARGARET I. MILLS--WM. DAVIS

ANN I. MITCHELL--GREENBERRY V. BERNARD

21. 17 April 1825. LEROY MITCHELL and SARAH S. HARVIE. Security:
JAS. W. HARVIE.

13. 9 October 1819. PLEASANT MITCHELL and A. JONES. Security:
CHAS. PERROW. Officiant: JAMES BOYD, 14th.

19. 23 October 1824. ZACH MITCHELL and CLARISSA JONES. Security:
WILLIS JOHNSON.

NANCY MONROE and PETER C. COFFEY

ALMIRA MONTGOMERY--JOS. C. MIGGINSON

JANETTA W. MONTGOMERY--WILSON PETERS

LOUISA M. MONTGOMERY--SEATON H. LOVING

LUCINDA MONTGOMERY--THOS. C. GOODWIN

MARGARET W. MONTGOMERY--GEO. H. CRAWFORD

PATSY M. MONTGOMERY--HENRY BUSHNELL

PAULINA L. MONTGOMERY--SAML. H. SHELTON

POLLY MONTGOMERY--BENJ. D. HARRIS

12. 28 September 1818. BENJ. MOORE and E. BURK. Security:
JOSHUA HARRIS. Officiant: J. S.

29. 10 May 1832. JNO. S. MOORE and ELIZ. SAUNDERS. Security:
JAS. SAUNDERS.

CAROLINE MORGAN--WM. G. RAMSEY

24. 24 March 1828. JAS. M. MORGAN and ELIZ. F. PETERS. Security:
CHAS. PETERS.

28. 21 May 1831. DAVID MORRIS and FRANCES JACKSON. Security:
JNO. JACKSON. Officiant: M. P. S., same.

23. 6 December 1827. HAZELWOOD MORRIS and REBECCA GRIFFIN.
Security: NATHL. TOWNSEND. Officiant: J. S., 10 (18?).

32. 4 December 1834. HENRY MORRIS and FRANCES C. PUCKETT.
Security: JNO. PUCKETT.

PAULINA MORRIS and WM. HENDERSON

19.	22 November 1824. PLEASANT D. MORRIS and MARY ANN BOWLER.
Security: WM. MC CLAIN.

20.	28 November 1825. RICE MORRIS and ELIZ. CHEWNING. Security:
JAS. LANKFORD. Officiant: M. B., December 6th.

A. H. MOSBY--JNO. M. SHELTON

MARY MOSBY--FRANCIS WEST

SARAH MOSBY--WM. DENNIS

SARAH ANN MOSBY--HARDIN PERKINS

33.	6 April 1835. JONATHAN MOSES and ELIZ. PANNELL. Security:
E. BOWEN. Officiant: J. HARVIE, 8th.

ELEANOR MOSS--GIDEON MARKS

FRANCES MOSS--WIATT HARRISON

GENEVA ANN MOSS--JACOB SMITH

ROXANNA MOSS--HOWELL P. BURTON

28.	22 August 1831. JESSE MUNDY and LOUISA ANN NEVIL. Security:
JAS. L. NEVIL.

SUSANNA J. MURPHEYS--JNO. E. WITT

MALINDA M. MURRELL--WM. H. BOWMAN

14.	7 November 1820. JOS. MURRILL and MARY D. BAILEY. Security:
WM. BAILEY.

ELIZ. N. NABERS and JOS. C. FULKS

JANE NALLEY--SAML. BLAIN

25.	22 September 1828. SAML. NALLY and MARY C. ROBERTS. Security:
ALEX. ROBERTS. Officiant: JAMES BOYD, 24th.

20.	19 September 1825. WM. NALLEY and ELIZ. ROBERTS. Security:
ALEX. ROBERTS. Officiant: JAMES BOYD, 21st.

17.	28 May 1823. BEVERLY B. NASH and CARDELIA LOVING. Security:
DAVID WOOD. Officiant: JAMES BOYD, 29th.

23.	3 December 1827. GEO. NEESE and ANNIS SMITH. Security:
WILSON C. SMITH. Officiant: CLEVELAND PORTER, 6th.

27.	27 December 1830. JNO. NEESE and ELIZ. HARRIS. Security:
DANL. M. HARRIS.

LOUISA ANN NEVIL--JESSE MUNDY

SEMARIA L. NEVIL--ALMOND VAUGHAN

26.	22 February 1830. GEO. T. NOEL and JANE F. HUGHES. Security:
A. JOHNSON. Officiant: EDWD. L. WARREN, same.

34.	3 November 1835. JNO. NOEL and MARY H. PERRY. Security:
JAS. B. HUGHES.

28.	28 November 1831. BENJ. NORVELL and FLORA B. FOSTER. Security:
WM. C. ROBERTS.

34.	7 December 1835. GEO. W. NORVELL and NANCY A. BAILEY.
Security: JORDAN THURMOND.

23. 17 September 1827. GEO. OFFLIGHTER, JUNIOR, and ISABELLA WHITE. Security: SAML. MOSES. Officiant: WM. HAMERSLEY.

ELIZ. PAGE--JESSE LOBBAN

21. 7 November 1825. JAS. PAGE and MALINDA WEIR. Security: EDWD. WEIR. Officiant: JAMES BOYD, 15th.

22. 23 October 1826. JNO. PAGE and MILDRED WARE. Security: THOS. WARE. Officiant: JAMES BOYD, November 2nd.

18. 24 November 1823. JNO. N. PAGE and LOUISA GRAVES. Security: JNO. SPEARS. Officiant: J. S., same.

LOVENIA PAGE--JOEL CHEWNING

MAHALA PAGE--HENRY MARTIN

SALLY PAGE--NATHAN BRIDGWATER

32. 12 September 1834. SAML. M. PAGE and LUCINDA DICKINSON. Security: JNO. W. DICKINSON.

33. 28 August 1835. JAS. PAINE and LOIUSA ANN FERGUSON. Security: JAS. H. RODES.

24. 4 March 1828. ALBERT G. PAINTER and ELVIRA C. TOWNSEND. Security: CHAS. W. TOWNSEND. Officiant: JAMES BOYD, 6th.

CATH. PAINTER--SAML. CAMPBELL

HANNAH PAINTER--WILLIS CAMPBELL

23. 26 November 1827. JNO. PAINTER and PHEBE LEIGHTER. Security: ADAM LEIGHTER.

REBECCA PAINTER--JOS. LAYTON

31. 27 January 1833. ARCHIBALD PAMPLIN and NANCY L. GOOLSBY. Security: WM. H. PAGE (?).

LIGUS PAMPLIN--PETER RUTHERFORD

NANCY JANE PAMPLIN--RO. J. KIDD

28. 16 July 1831. RO. PAMPLIN and NANCY L. STRATTON. Security: WM. STRATTON.

BELINDA PANNELL--WM. HUMPHREY

ELIZ. PANNELL--JONATHAN MOSES

30. 2 February 1833. WM. PANNELL and MARGARET CAREY. Security: FRANK CAREY.

27. 21 December 1830. COSEN W. PARRISH and MARY L. COFFEY. Security: RUBEN P. COFFEY.

LORINDA R. PARRISH--BENJ. J. HUGHES

30. 5 November 1832. PARKS H. PARRISH and ELIZ. HUGHES. Security: BENJ. J. HUGHES.

20. 5 January 1825. HENRY PARROCK and NANCY HATTER. Security: WM. HATTER.

13. 11 August 1819. THOS. PARROCK and M. BRADSHAW. Security: THOS. WOODY. Officiant: JAMES BOYD, 11th.

26. 9 March 1830. DANL. W. PARSONS and ESTHER M. WRIGHT.
Security: HENRY DAWSON.

34. 9 March 1836. JNO. M. PATRICK and LUCY H. SMITH. Security:
WM. G. SMITH.

29. 17 January 1832. CHAS. N. PATTESON and ADELINE S. LOVING.
Security: SP. G. LOVING.

MARY ANN PATTESON--NICHL. M. LOVING

SALLY PATTESON--SHADRICK CARTER

23. 3 September 1827. ISAAC PAUL and HANNAH G. AUSTIN. Security:
RO. J. KINCAID. Officiant: WM. L. REID, same.

POLLY PAXTON--JAS. ANDERSON

ELIZ. PAYNTER--ADAM LEIGHTEN

22. 2 April 1827. ISAAC PAYNTER and WINIFRED CAMPBELL. Security:
JAS. CAMPBELL.

16. 7 June 1822. DAVID PEEBLES and JANE L. WATTS. Security:
JNO. A. KIDD.

EDNA PENDLETON--DABNEY P. GOOCH

LETITIA B. PENDLETON--HUDSON M. GARLAND

BETHELAND PENN--ALEX. FITZPATRICK

S. (L) W. PENN--R. BURTON

FANNY PERKINS--RICH. PERKINS

21. 7 November 1825. HARDIN PERKINS and SARAH ANN MOSBY. Security:
JNO. MOSBY. Officiant: JAMES BOYD, 10th (?).

19. 4 October 1824. POWHATAN PERKINS and SARAH PERKINS. Security:
SAML. PERKINS. Officiant: J. S., 12th.

12. 18 September 1818. PRICE PERKINS and POLLY HARE. Security:
RICH. HARE, JR. Officiant: J. S., October 4th.

13. 18 October 1819. RICH. PERKINS and FANNY PERKINS. Security:
PRICE S. PERKINS.

SARAH PERKINS--POWHATAN PERKINS

ELIZ. C. PERRY--JAS. B. HUGHES

33. 10 October 1835. JNO. J. PERRY and MARY LOVING. Security:
CHAS. PERRY. Officiant: H. S. PEYTON, 12th.

MARY H. PERRY--JNO. NOEL

SOPHIA F. PERRY--THOS. P. DILLARD

SUSANNA N. PERRY--WM. B. RIPPETOE

BELINDA PETERS--CATLETT WILLS

21. 11 March 1826. CHAS. PETERS and MARY FULKS. Security:
JNO. B. FULKS.

CYRENA B. PETERS--DAVID C. THOMAS

ELIZ. F. PETERS--JAS. M. MORGAN

ELIZ. H. PETERS--WILLIS H. WILLS

21. 2 August 1826. ESOM PETERS and MILLY WINTERS. Security:
THOS. WINTERS.

16. 16 April 1822. WILSON PETERS and JANETTA W. MONTGOMERY.
Security: S. GARLAND. Officiant: JAMES BOYD, 17th.

12. 21 December 1818. CHAS. PHILLIPS and E. ROBERTS. Security:
THOS. WHITEHEAD. Officiant: JAMES BOYD, 24th.

ELIZ. PHILLIPS--JOS. COFFEY

19. 13 September 1824. GEO. PHILLIPS and BETSY ROWSEY. Security:
WM. BRYANT.

ISABELLA PHILLIPS--WM. BRYANT

23. 27 November 1827. JAS. W. PHILLIPS and ELMIRA SCRUGGS.
Security: DANL. M. HARRIS.

27. 23 August 1830. JNO. PHILLIPS and POLLY SNEED. Security:
G. PHILLIPS and R. SNEED.

16. 26 August 1822. WM. PHILLIPS and POLLY GILES. Security:
BENJ. HATTER. Officiant: ANTHONY GIANNIY, 29th.

20. 14 May 1825. AMBROSE PIN and MARY WINTERS. Security:
S. GARLAND.

28. 30 April 1831. RALEIGH PINN and LUCINDA MAHA. Security:
SAML. COLEMAN. Officiant: EDWD. L. WARREN, May 12th.

M. A. POLLARD--ALEX. BABER

MARGARET C. POLLARD--JAS. P. HENDERSON

MARY H. POLLARD--JNO. WITT

SALLY POLLARD--TERISHA STEVENS

27. 4 December 1830. JEFF L. PONTON and MARTHA THOMPSON. Security:
BENJ. PONTON. Officiant: JAMES BOYD, 10th.

LUCY PONTON--JAS. B. THOMPSON

14. 21 June 1820. PLEASANT PONTON and MARGARET PUCKET. Security:
JACOB PUCKET. Officiant: JAMES BOYD, 22nd.

22. 1 March 1827. ABRAHAM POOR and JANE SIMPSON. Security:
CHAS. REKES (?).

M. L. POOR--WM. GLOVER

ELIZA R. PORTER--WYATT WRIGHT

ELIZ. POWELL--JNO. R. BOWLING

34. 21 October 1835. JAS. E. POWELL and ELIZ. H. MARTIN.
Security: ELIAS HARDING. Officiant: EDWD. L. WARREN, 22nd.

13. 14 April 1819. L. (S) POWELL and N. G. BURCH. Security:
RICH. BURCH. Officiant: JAMES BOYD, 15th.

SUSANNA POWELL--LELAND DAMRON

16. 30 September 1822. WM. POWELL and SARAH W. BOWMAN. Security:
LEOND. POWELL. Officiant: EDWD. L. WARREN, October 10th.

CARY ANN POWELL--WALKER L. WILLOUGHBY

CATH. POWERS--RICH HARVEY

25. 27 July 1829. JNO. POWERS and SOPHIA HARVEY. Security: RICH. HARLOW. Officiant: JAMES BOYD, 28th.

22. 26 February 1827. LEWIS E. PRICE and RHODA ANN KIDD. Security: JAS. W. CRAIG. Officiant: JAMES BOYD, 27th.

16. 27 December 1821. MARTIN D. PRICE and ELVIRA LOVING. Security and Officiant: WM. WRIGHT, 27th.

22. 31 March 1827. WILSON N. PRICE and SUSAN A. ROSE. Security: HENRY J. ROSE. Officiant: CHAS. H. PAGE, April 4th.

27. 29 April 1830. JAS. PROFFITT and SALLY ANN DENNIS. Security: FRANCIS WEST. Officiant: EDWD. L. WARREN, same.

JANE PROFFITT--JESSE WRIGHT

L. (S) PROFFITT--HOWARD CASH

15. 8 August 1821. LEWIS PROFFITT and ELIZ. C. DENNIS. Security: WM. DENNIS.

12. 4 November 1818. R. PROFFITT and O. KEY. Security: WALTER KEY. Officiant: SAML. DAY, 6th.

33. 7 February 1835. RO. PROFFITT and JUDITH HUNTER. Security: PEACHY SPENCER.

26. 23 November 1829. ANDERSON PUCKET and JEMIMA GRIFFIN. Security: ANDERSON ADCOCK. Officiant: JNO. ALLCOCK, same.

20. 12 March 1825. CRAWFORD PUCKET and SALLY INNIS. Security: JAS. INNIS. Officiant: W. H., 17th.

FRANCES PUCKET--NELSON WRIGHT

FRANCES C. PUCKET--HENRY MORRIS

14. 15 May 1820. JACOB PUCKET and SALLY LOVING. Security: LUCY LOVING. Officiant: JAMES BOYD, 17th.

MARGARET PUCKET--DAVID HAMBLET

MARGERET PUCKET--PLEASANT PONTON

MARTHA PUCKET--BENJ. TAYLOR

MILLY PUCKET--FRANCIS TINNELL

NANYC PUCKET--JESSE WOOD

POLLY PUCKET--L. LOVING

20. 4 August 1825. SAML. PUCKET and MARTHA HARRIS. Security: EDMD. T. HARRIS.

BETSY PUCH--JESSE BURKS

26. 26 September 1829. ELIJAH PUCH and SARAH COFFMAN. Security: ISAAC RITTENHOUSE.

16. 28 January 1822. JNO. PUGH and MARY ANN GOWING. Security: JAS. GOWING.

MARY PUGH--JAS. HARRIS

30. 23 January 1833. MORRIS PUGH and SARAH PUGH. Security:
N. TOWNSEND.

NANCY PUGH--WM. GAULDIN

28. 2 April 1831. NELSON PUGH and LUCY MC CLURE. Security:
ALEX. MC CLURE.

SARAH PUCH--MORRIS PUGH

22. 13 November 1826. CHAS. W. PURVIS and REBECCA WILLS.
Security: JNO. WILLS.

ELIZA C. PURVIS--REUBEN T. BURNETT

19. 4 December 1824. GEO. PURVIS and POLLY HERNDON. Security:
RICH. HERNDON.

18. 18 October 1823. GEO. W. PURVIS and MARTHA A. AKERS (changed
by clerk evidently from PURVIS). Security: WM. AKERS.

LUCINDA F. PURVIS--JOEL M. WHEELER

S. (L) PURVIS--JAS. LUCKEY

SALLY PURVIS--RICH. HARDING

SARAH L. PURVIS--JAS. WILLS

19. 27 December 1824. WM. PURVIS, JR. and NANCY BURNETT. Security:
WM. W. DAVIS. Officiant: JAMES BOYD, 28th.

ANN QUICK--DANL. BLACK

30. 2 March 1833. GEO. W. QUICK and MARY B. JOHNSON. Security:
JESSE P. FARRAR.

19. 30 November 1824. THOS. QUICK and ELIZ. BABER. Security:
JNO. BAILEY.

17. 11 June 1823. JORDAN L. QUINN and NANCY COFFEY. Security:
MOSES W. HUGHES. Officiant: ANTHONY GIANNIY, 15th.

31. 30 December 1833. RICH. QUISENBERRY and MARIA COOK. Security:
VAL. COOK.

12. 9 (?) March 1819. WM. RAINS and LUCY FOX. Security: RICH. FOX.

23. 17 September 1827. ELLIS RAMSEY and PAULINA M. R. RAMSEY.
Security: JAS. RAMSEY.

PAULINA M. R. RAMSEY--ELLIS RAMSEY

32. 3 May 1834. SILAS M. RAMSEY and WINNEY COFFEY. Security:
REUBIN C. COFFEY.

31. 18 July 1833. WM. G. RAMSEY and CAROLINE MORGAN. Security:
WM. MORGAN.

17. 23 December 1822. ALEX. REID and IRMA J. R. WATTS. Security:
JAS. L. WATTS.

16. 22 October 1822. JNO. A. REID and ELIZ. F. WATTS. Security:
JOEL CHRISTIAN.

30. 19 December 1832. ROWLAND M. RICHESON and LUCY ANN LAYNE.
Security: WM. R. CHRISTIAN. Officiant: EDWD. L. WARREN, 20th.

21. 12 November 1825. JOS. RICKETS and ELIZ. BIBB. Security: THOS. BIBB.

20. 24 October 1825. WOOD RIPLEY and LUCY T. HENLEY. Security: ABRAHAM POOR.

14. 17 December 1820. DAVID RIPPETOE and NANCY SPEARS. Security: NATHAN BRYANT. Officiant: WM. WRIGHT, 19th.

16. 30 March 1822. JAS. RIPPETOE and ELIZ. CAMERON. Security: D. CAMERON. Officiant: ANTHONY GIANNIY, April 3rd (?).

17. 24 April 1823. WM. B. RIPPETOE and SUSANNA M. PERRY. Security: WM. W. HUGHES.

32. 28 April 1834. WM. B. RIPPETOE and ANN L. (S) WITT. Security: WITT. DENNITT WITT. Officiant: I. J. HICKS, 12 May.

REBECCA RITTENHOUSE--MOSES GAULDIN

LUCY L. RIVES--ALEX. BROWN

27. 11 October 1830. AMBROSE ROBERTS and MARY C. HAGER. Security: JNO. HAGER and HARRIS and ROBERTS. Officiant: JNO. ALLCOCK,
same.

B. ROBERTS--T. D. HILL

E. ROBERTS--CHAS. PHILLIPS

E. ROBERTS--WM. L. DURRETT

ELIZ. ROBERTS--WM. NALLEY

ELIZA M. ROBERTSON--WM. ELSOM. Out of place.

13. 15 November 1819. JAS. A. ROBERTS and P. W. BRIDGWATER. Security: HENRY ROBERTS. Officiant: JAMES BOYD, 18th.

26. 6 September 1829. JNO. S. ROBERTS and A. B. LANDCRAFT. Security: W. S. LANDCRAFT.

MARY C. ROBERTS--SAML. NALLEY

13. 4 November 1819. MATT. ROBERTS and NANCY DAWSON. Security: NATHL. LOFFTUS. Officiant: JAMES BOYD, November 3 (sic).

SARAH ANN ROBERTS--JNO. P. JACKSON

SARAH N. H. ROBERTS--WM. TURNER

18. 28 February 1824. SKILER H. ROBERTS and MARY ANN HARLOW. Security: CALEB T. HARRIS. Officiant: JAMES BOYD, March 4th.

34. 31 October 1835. WM. ROBERTS and ELIZ. WARREN. Security: EDWD. L. WARREN. Officiant: H. L. PEYTON, November 2nd.

ELIZA M. ROBERTSON--WM. ELSOM

30. 29 November 1832. HUGH D. ROBERTSON and MARY SHIPMAN. Officiant: EDWD. L. WARREN, December 7th.

14. 16 September 1820. JACOB ROBERTSON and LARCENDA LOVING. Security: JNO. BRADSHAW. Officiant: JAMES BOYD, 17th.

C. A. ROBINSON--WM. HUMPHREY

AMY D. RODES--THOS. LOBBAN

20. 4 April 1825. CHAS. P. RODES and ANN N. GOODWIN. Security: JAS. D. GOODWIN. Officiant: JAMES BOYD, 5th.

ELIZ. RODES--JNO. RUDASILL

ELIZ. RODES--WM. L. KNIGHT

34. 18 February 1836. THOS. RODES and ELIZ. SPICE. Security: WM. SPICE.

22. 3 May 1827. THOS. Y. RODES and MILDRED DICKINSON. Security: JNO. DUGGINS. Officiant: illegible, 31st (?).

29. 26 March 1832. RYLAND RODEY and VA. WOODS. Security: WM. M. WOODS.

24. 11 September 1828. HENRY ROGERS and JANE TYREE. Security: JOS. TYREE.

29. 2 October 1832. SILAS ROGERS and ISABELLA CARY. Security: JNO. CAMPBELL. Officiant: M. P. S., 8th.

JANE ROSE--JAS. F. TALIAFERRO

SUSAN A. ROSE--WILSON N. PRICE

15. 1 October 1821. ELIJAH ROSSEN and MARGARET JENKINS. Security: JNO. JENKINS.

15. 9 May 1821. JNO. L. ROUSEUN and JANE A. WATT. Security: JNO. PHILLIPS. Officiant: JAMES BOYD, same.

BETSY ROWSEY--GEO. PHILLIPS

31. -- May 1833. BENJ. F. ROYALL and MARIA LOUISA SHELTON. Security: SAML. W. SHELTON.

23. 10 (11?) November 1827. NATHL. H. ROYAL and SALLY ANN WILLS. Security: JNO. WILLS. Officiant: JAMES BOYD, 13th.

19. 20 December 1824. JNO. RUDASILL and ELIZ. RODES. Security: JOEL Y. RODES.

18. 22 December 1823. PETER RUTHERFORD and LIGIS PAMPLIN. Security: WM. PAMPLIN.

23. 7 November 1827. CHAS. M. RYAN and NOENY S. LOVING. Security: RO. S. (L) ADAMS. Officiant: JAMES BOYD, 8th.

24. 5 January 1828. JAS. RYAN and LUCY SAUNDERS. Security: JAS. MC QUEEN. Officiant: JAMES BOYD, 18th.

14. 15 November 1820. JOS. RYAN and JANE TINNELL. Security: THOS. HICKS. Officiant: ANTHONY GIANNIY, 16th.

LOUISA ANN RYAN--JNO. P. (R) SCRUGGS

20. 25 April 1825. PAGE RYAN and LUCINDA WILLOUGHBY. Security: JOSHUA WILLOUGHBY.

PAMELA RYAN--JAS. MC WANE

23. 9 August 1827. PHILLIP H. RYAN and NANCY P. HILL. Security: WM. RYAN.

24. 15 April 1828. CHRISTIAN SACK and POLLY HITE. Security: GEO. ---. Officiant: P. C., 24th.

MARY SAUNDERS--JNO. W. WILLS

POLLY SAUNDERS--ELLISON H. WHITE

ELIZ. SAUNDERS--JNO. S. MOORE

LUCY SAUNDERS--JAS. RYAN

NANCY SAUNDERS--RICH. HAYLETT

PAULINA SAUNDERS--OBADIAH WOOD

32. 28 April 1834. RICH. SAUNDERS and MARY ANN JONES. Security: SHELTON C. JONES.

17. 15 February 1823. HARROD B. SCOTT and SARAH M. CHRISTIAN. Security: L. (?) CHRISTIAN.

AMANDA I. SCRUGGS--WM. BOLTON

ELMIRA SCRUGGS--JAS. W. PHILLIPS

34. 9 March 1836. JNO. A. SCRUGGS and AMANDA D. CHRISTIAN. Security: JOS. L. R. CLARK.

16. 10 September 1822. JNO. P. (R) SCRUGGS and LOIUSA ANN RYAN. Security: WM. RYAN. Officiant: JAMES BOYD, 12th.

30. 3 October 1832. JNO. R. SCRUGGS and SALLY CARTER. Security: WM. CLASBY.

25. 20 December 1828. LEOND. SCRUGGS and SARAH MC BRIDE. Security: GEO. GILBERT. Officiant: JNO. ALLCOCK.

MILDRED SCRUGGS--CHAS. EVANS

12. 17 November 1818. PATTESON SCRUGGS and M. THOMPSON. Security: JNO. THOMPSON. Officiant: HUGH A. MC CLAIN (blurred),
-- November.

14. 15 February 1821. THEOPHILUS SCRUGGS and SARAH T. BAILEY. Security: SAML. L. (S) SCRUGGS.

30. 27 February 1833. TIMOTHY SCRUGGS, JR. and ADALINE CONNER. Security: THOS. C. CONNER. Officiant: JNO. ALLCOCK, same.

31. 8 August 1833. WM. SCRUGGS and SOPHIA W. T. (?) CONNER. Security: JNO. L. TYREE.

14. 25 November 1821. AUSTIN SEAY and JANE BIBB. Security: S. GARLAND. Officiant: JAMES BOYD, 26th.

MATILDA SEAY--MARTIN BROWN

NANCY D. SEAY--SHADRICK CARTER, JR.

12. 23 December 1818. J. W. SHELTON and ELVIRA HARRIS. Security: BENJ. D. HARRIS. Officiant: JAMES BOYD, 24th.

13. 21 April 1819. JNO. M. SHELTON and A. H. MOSBY. Security: JNO. H. MOSBY and J. SHELTON. Officiant: JAMES BOYD, 23rd.

19. 3 April 1824. JOS. SHELTON, JR. and JUDITH W. SHELTON. Security: CLOUGH SHELTON. Officiant: JAMES BOYD, 5th.

JUDITH W. SHELTON--JOS. SHELTON, JR.

MARIA LOUISA SHELTON--BENJ. F. ROYALL

31. 10 June 1833. SAML. H. SHELTON and PAULINA L. MONTGOMERY. Security: JNO. DIGGS, JR.

30. -- May 1833. GARLAND A. SHEPHERD and ELIZ. F. I. LIGON.
Security: JNO. LIGON.

18. 24 November 1833. JAS. H. SHEPHERD and MARTHA WINGFIELD.
Security: JNO. WINGFIELD. Officiant: EDWD. L. WARREN, 27th.

27. 7 May 1830. WM. P. SHEPHERD and MARGARET S. JOHNSON. Security:
ABSALOM JOHNSON. Officiant: EDWD. L. WARREN, 12th.

ELIZ. H. SHIELDS--JAS. MARR

ELIZ. H. SHIELDS--error--see above

NANCY SHIELDS--WM. SMITH

PEGGY SHIELDS--JNO. E. SMITH

SARAH SHIELDS--JAS. HIGGINBOTHAM

THANKFUL SHIELDS--THOS. H. JOHNSON

MARY SHIPMAN--HUGH D. ROBERTSON

HARRIET SIMS--WM. H. STOCKTON

CATH. SIMPSON--JNO. B. MATTHEWS

JANE SIMPSON--ABRAHAM POOR

PEACHY SIMPSON--JNO. M. MC CUE

GRISSEL C. SLAIGHTER--WM. H. BLAIR

JANE M. SMALL--JESSE I. ALLEN

LUCINDA SMALL--BEVERLY HAMNER

NANCY SMALL--DAVID JOHNSON

REBECCA SMALL--N. CLARKE

MARTHA I. W. SMILEY--NATHAN C. ANDERSON

ANNIE SMITH--GEO. NEESE

ELIZ. SMITH--MICAJAH E. WHEELER

15. 3 November 1821. HENRY E. SMITH and SARAH MATTHEWS. Security:
JOS. MATTHEWS.

29. 17 March 1832. JACOB SMITH and GENEVA ANN MOSS. Security:
HOWELL P. BURTON.

23. 17 September 1827. JAS. SMITH and ELIZ. GARBER. Security:
N. W. ALVIS. Officiant: CLEVELAND PORTER, 18th.

13. 19 April 1819. JAS. E. SMITH and M. BURCH. Security:
JNO. BURCH. Officiant: J. S., 22nd.

19. 7 August 1824. JNO. SMITH and ELIZ. CAMPBELL. Security:
JAS. CAMPBELL.

17. 25 August 1823. JNO. E. SMITH and PEGGY SHIELDS. Security:
JAS. P. SMITH. Officiant: EDWD. L. WARREN, 28th.

13. 28 June 1819. JNO. G. SMITH and P. SMITH. Security: JAS. E.
SMITH. Officiant: J. S., July 31st.

LUCY SMITH--RO. MAYS, JR.

NANCY SMITH--WM. LANHAM

NANCY J. SMITH--JNO. R. MAYS

15. 15 September 1821. NELSON SMITH and ELIZ. HANSBROUGH.
Security: PETER HANSBROUGH. Officiant: JAMES BOYD, 20th.

P. SMITH--JNO. TAYLOR

P. SMITH--JNO. G. SMITH

RHODA A. SMITH--JNO. FITZPATRICK

18. 13 September 1823. WM. SMITH and NANCY SHIELDS. Security:
JNO. J. SHIELDS.

15. 5 November 1821. WM. D. SMITH and MARY ARISMAN. Security:
JACOB ARISMAN.

26. 28 December 1829. NOTLEY SMOOT and DEBORAH TYREE. Security:
RO. WATKINS.

12. 4 November 1818. CARY SNEED and POLLY HATTER. Security:
JNO. HATTER.

POLLY SNEED--JNO. PHILLIPS

SARAH SNEED--JAS. C. FITZGERALD

JUDITH SPARROW--WM. BEVERLY

ELIZ. SPEARS--JAS. DUDLEY

NANCY SPEARS--DAVID RIPPETOE

POLLY SPEARS--JESSE CAMPBELL

AGNES SPENCER--JNO. FAULCONER

27. 16 December 1830. CHAS. H. SPENCER and SARAH JANE CAMPBELL.
Security: GEO. P. FARRAR. Error: Bride is CAMP and not CAMPBELL.

25. 15 December 1828. JAS. SPENCER, JR. and SARAH MAYS. Security:
RO. MAYS. Officiant: JAMES BOYD, 18th.

MARY SPENCER--WILLIS ARRINGTON

25. 6 April 1829. PEACHY SPENCER and SOPHIA BRYANT. Security:
SYLVANUS BRYANT.

19. 26 April 1824. SAML. SPENCER, JR. and PAULINA MAYS. Security:
EDWD. CABELL. Officiant: JAMES BOYD, May 13th.

SARAH E. W. SPENCER--SPOTSWOOD G. LOVING

24. 21 April 1828. THORNTON SPENCER and REBECCA FORTUNE.
Security: Z. FORTUNE, JR. Officiant: EDWD. L. WARREN, 24th.

32. 20 October 1834. WALKER D. SPENCER and ELIZA A. BIBB.
Security: JNO. BIBB.

18. 22 September 1823. WM. SPENCER and CYNTHIA THOMAS. Security:
HENRY THOMAS. Officiant: WM. WRIGHT, 23rd.

27. 3 December 1830. WM. F. SPENCER and JULIA A. FAULCONER.
Security: SPENCER FAULCONER. Officiant: JNO. ALLCOCK, same.

ELIZ. SPICE--THOS. RODES

PATSY SPROUSE--WILSON HARLOW

25. 20 July 1829. THOS. O. STATON and POLLY LOWE. Security:
WM. LOWE. Officiant: JAMES BOYD, 28th.

13. 28 August 1819. JNO. STEEL and POLLY COFFEY. Security:
FRANCIS CAMPBELL.

21. 13 April 1826. TERISHA STEVENS and SALLY POLLARD. Security:
GEO. PENN. Officiant: JAMES BOYD, same.

25. 8 October 1828. WM. C. STEVENS and MILDRED T. LOVING.
Security: JAS. N. LOVING, JR. Officiant: JAMES BOYD, 9th.

LUCINDA STEWART--SAML. R. DANIEL

30. 26 November 1832. JNO. S. STICKLEMAN and JANE W. HARRIS.
Security: P. EDMUNDS. Officiant: ISAAC SOULE, 28th.

32. 23 August 1834. WM. H. STOCKTON and HARRIET SIMS. Security:
WM. L. LOVING. Officiant: H. L. P., same.

16. 18 December 1821. GEO. STONER and ELIZ. STRICKLAND. Security:
ABIEL STRICKLAND. Officiant: JAMES BOYD, 27th.

30. 29 January 1833. ASA STATON and ELIZ. M. WHITEHEAD. Security:
JNO. WHITEHEAD.

28. 23 November 1831. GEO. W. STRATTON and FRANCES E. LOVING.
Security: SP. G. LOVING and RO. C. CUTLER.

LUCY L. STRATTON--ELIAS EVERETT

NANCY L. STRATTON--RO. PAMPLIN

22. 30 July 1827. SAML. STRATTON and CATHERINE TRIBLE. Security:
RO. M. HALL.

ELIZ. STRICKLAND--GEO. STONER

32. 19 March 1834. ELLIS STRICKLAND and CATH. WITT. Security:
BRECK. FITZPATRICK.

30. 7 January 1833. ZEBULON M. STRICKLAND and NANCY WOODS.
Security: JESSE WOODS.

21. 1 August 1826. JNO. STRICKLAND and ELIZ. EDMUNDS. Security:
JAS. EDMUNDS. Officiant: JAMES BOYD, 10th.

16. 20 May 1822. WM. T. SUDDARTH and RUTH LIGGON. Security:
WILLIS LIGGIN.

24. 15 August 1828. R. L. SUTHERLAND and MARY JANE DICKINSON.
Security: WM. FABER.

13. 14 December 1819. GEO. W. SUTLER and J. KIDD. Security:
JNO. MARTIN. Officiant: JAMES BOYD, 15th.

13. 12 (?) May 1819. JAS. F. TALIAFERRO and JANE ROSE. Security:
HENRY ROSE. Officiant: JAMES BOYD, 20th.

15. 18 October 1821. NICHL. H. B. TALIAFERRO and SARAH H. BREEDLOVE.
Security: RICH. BREEDLOVE.

SARAH ANN TALIAFERRO--JNO. CREWS

34. 19 December 1835. BENJ. TAYLOR and MARTHA PUCKET. Security:
JNO. PUCKET. Officiant: H. L. P., same.

ISABELLA TAYLOR--WM. WOOD

34. 1 February 1836. JAS. TAYLOR and MARTHA HAYLETT. Security:
    I. SUDDARTH. Officiant: EDWD. L. WARREN, 4th.

19. 12 June 1824. JNO. TAYLOR and P. SMITH. Security: JNO.
    HORSLEY. Officiant: EDWD. L. WARREN, same.

    L. TAYLOR--JAS. DURHAM, JR.

22. 21 May 1827. LEWIS TAYLOR and MARY CAMPBELL. Security:
    GEO. HIGHT, JR.

    MARY TAYLOR--DAVID MILLER

34. 16 April 1835. WM. L. TAYLOR and ELIZ. KENNEDY. Security:
    JOS. COFFEY. Officiant: WM. B. RICE, 30th.

20. 22 June 1825. CHAS. THACKER and JANE BRYANT. Security:
    JNO. W. N. PAGE. Officiant: JAMES BOYD, same.

31. 30 December 1833. JACOB J. THACKER and SARAH ANN DE MASTERS.
    Security: EDWD. DEMASTERS.

    MAHALA THACKER--CARTER HARMAN

    SARAH W. THACKER--WM. T. LOVING

    CYNTHIA THOMAS--WM. SPENCER

20. 27 May 1825. DAVID C. THOMAS and CYRENA B. PETERS. Security:
    ELISHA PETERS. Officiant: JAMES BOYD, June 1st.

    ELIZ. THOMAS--THOS. MEEKS

28. 23 October 1831. JAS. THOMAS and JANE THOMAS. Security:
    JNO. THOMAS.

    JANE THOMAS--JAS. THOMAS

    LUCINDA THOMAS--GEO. TURNER

    MARY I. THOMAS--BENJ. L. FORTUNE

    NANCY F. THOMAS--JAS. C. MAYS

    SALLY THOMAS--THOS. J. ANDERSON

    SARAH SUSAN THOMAS--SHELTON FARRAR

    SELINA THOMAS--JNO. H. BALLARD

17. 12 January 1823. CHAS. THOMPSON and P. THOMPSON. Security:
    RO. COALES (?).

    ELIZ. THOMPSON--JOS. MAYS, JR.

16. 25 March 1822. GEO. THOMPSON and ELIZ. BOUTRIGHT. Security:
    T. W. F. TURNER. Officiant: EDWD. L. WARREN, 27th. (BOUTWRIGHT
for bride)

21. 19 July 1826. JAS. THOMPSON, JR. and ELIZ. V. HARVIE.
    Security: JNO. R. HARRIS. Officiant: JAMES BOYD, 20th.

27. 16 March 1831. JAS. B. THOMPSON and LUCY PONTON. Security:
    AUSTIN SEAY. Officiant: M. P. S., same.

14. 10 January 1820. JESSE THOMPSON and LUCY BECKNALL. Security:
    THOS. BECKNALL.

23. 27 August 1827. JOSHUA THOMPSON and MARIAH TINNELL. Security: JNO. TINNELL. Officiant: JAMES BOYD, 30th.

LUCINDA R. THOMPSON--WM. R. WOOD

M. THOMPSON--PATTESON SCRUGGS

MARTHA THOMPSON--JEFF. L. PONTON

MARY THOMPSON--WASH CAMPBELL

P. THOMPSON--CHAS. THOMPSON

ELEANOR THROP--REUBEN HARLOW

NANCY THROP--HUDSON MARTIN

ELIZ. THURMOND--WM. G. HAMBLET

17. 24 April 1823. GUTHRIDGE THURMOND and MARY DAWSON. Security: P. L. DAWSON. Officiant: JAMES BOYD, 28th.

LUCINDA THURMOND--NORVELL JOHNSON

MARTHA J. W. THURMOND--JAMES T. (?) DAMRON

22. 6 November 1826. PHILIP THURMOND and ELIZ. DAMRON. Security: LITTELPAGE DAMRON. Officiant: J. S., 9th.

SARAH THURMOND--JESSE A. JONES

33. 23 March 1835. WM. M. THURMOND and MARY JANE BIBB. Security: HENRY BIBB. Officiant: EDWD. L. WARREN, 26th.

30. 15 December 1832. FRANKLIN THWING and JANE H. G. COBBS. Security: CHAS. WILLIAMS.

21. 27 March 1826. RICH. A. TILLER and GEMIMA C. CARTER. Security: SHADRACK CARTER.

CARY ANN C. M. TILMAN--JAS. N. MARTIN

23. 11 August 1827. JACOB H. TILMAN and CARRIA ANN C. M. JOHNSON. Is JOHNSON. Security: T. TILMAN. Officiant: JAMES BOYD, 16th.

14. 12 October 1820. FRANCIS TINNELL and MILLY PUCKETT. Security: JACOB PUCKETT. Officiant: JAMES BOYD, same.

JANE TINNELL--JOS. RYAN

24. 3 September 1828. JOS. TINNELL and ELIZ. WILLS. Security: JNO. WILLS. Officiant: JAMES BOYD, September 4th.

MARIAH TINNELL--JOSHUA THOMPSON

NANCY TINNELL--EDWD. J. HARRIS

POLLY TINNELL--THOS. GIANNY

24. 5 January 1828. CHAS. TOMS and SALLY FOX. Security: WOODSON B. FOX. Officiant: W. H., 10th.

ELIZ. TOMS--RICH. FOSTER

LUCINDA TOMS--RICH. JACKSON

R. TOMS--J. P. FARRAR

ELVIRA C. TOWNSEND--ALBERT G. PAINTER

CATHARINE TRIBLE--SAML. STRATTON

12. 6 October 1818. JOS. TRUSLER and L. (S) LEE. Security:
JAS. EDMUNDS. Officiant: JAMES BOYD, 8th.

22. 22 January 1827. GEO. TURNER and LUCINDA THOMAS. Security:
SAML. TURNER.

34. 19 December 1835. GEO. H. TURNER and MARTHA A. HAMBLET.
Security: ELIAS HAMBLET. Officiant: H. L. P., 23rd.

JANE R. TURNER--WM. H. CARTER

26. 14 November 1829. LORENZO D. TURNER and MARY C. HAMBLETT.
Security: JORDAN THURMOND. Officiant: JAMES BOYD, 19th.

SARAH F. TURNER--ALBERT G. CURD

19. 30 December 1824. WM. TURNER and SARAH N. H. ROBERTS.
Officiant: JAMES BOYD, January 11th.

CELIA P. TYREE--SAML. G. HAYES

DELILA TYREE--JNO. HENDRIX

DEBORAH TYREE--NOTLEY SMOOT

JANE TYREE--HENRY ROGERS

31. 15 January 1834. JNO. L. TYREE and SARAH C. (?) TYREE.
Security: JNO. W. HAGER.

NANCY TYREE--MARTIN VIA

14. 27 December 1819. NATHAN TYREE and N. CHILDRESS. Security:
JAS. JOHNSON. Officiant: J. S., 30th.

SARAH C. TYREE--JNO. L. TYREE

14. 20 May 1820. ALMOND VAUGHAN and SEMARIA L. NEVIL. Security:
JAS. LOVING.

20. 17 October 1825. GEO. VAUGHAN, JR. and MARY C. EDMUNDS.
Security: JAS. N. EDMUNDS.

MARY M. VAUGHAN--RICH. C. FORTUNE

33. 14 March 1835. RICH. VAUGHAN and ELIZA KEY. Security:
JNO. KEY, JR. Officiant: WM. B. RICE, 17th.

18. 19 January 1824. SILAS VAWTER and ELIZ. F. CHRISTIAN.
Security: L. (W?) CHRISTIAN.

32. 26 May 1834. JOEL VEST and MARTHA KIDD. Security: JOS. KIDD.

19. 4 May 1824. MARTIN VIA and NANCY TYREE. Security: JESSE W.
TYREE. Officiant: WM. WRIGHT, 18th.

14. 24 November 1820. WM. VIA and WILLY LANE. Security: MARTIN
VIA.

NANCY WADE--RICH. WITT

ELIZA WALLACE--HUGH N. HALL

SUSANNA D. WALLACE--LEVI COOK

MILDRED WARE--JNO. PAGE

ELIZ. WARREN--WM. ROBERTS

CANDICE E. WARWICK--DAVID WITT

24.   31 January 1828. RO. WATKINS and SARAH A. KIDD. Security:
      JESSE N. KIDD. Officiant: JAMES BOYD, same.

CATH. WATTS--JAS. D. GOODWIN

ELIZA WATTS--PATRICK H. HICKOK

ELIZ. F. WATTS--JNO. A. REID

20.   19 September 1820. GEO. R. (?) WATTS and EMILY ANN LOVING.
      Security: WM. C. LOVING. Officiant: JAMES BOYD, 22nd.

IRMA J. R. WATTS--ALEX. REID

JANE A. WATTS--JNO. L. ROSEUR

JANE L. WATTS--DAVID PEEBLES

19.   24 May 1824. MITCHELL WATTS and SARAH C. FULKS. Security:
      THOS. A. MORRIS. Officiant: JAMES BOYD, June 17th. Note:
error made with SARAH--called FIELDS in F index; will change.

S. (L) WATTS--N. LOFFTUS

18.   27 January 1824. WM. WEBB and MARIAH GOWING. Security:
      JAS. GOWING.

MALINDA WEIR--JAS. PAGE

21.   22 November 1825. FRANCIS WEST and MARY MOSBY. Security:
      NICHL. B. WEST. Officiant: EDWD. L. WARREN, 23rd.

25.   23 March 1829. FRANCIS B. WEST and SOPHIA J. BOWMAN. Security:
      JAS. PAMPLIN, JR. Officiant: EDWD. L. WARREN, April 7th.

15.   26 November 1821. JAS. WEST and CATH. GRAVES (GRASS?).
      Security: JAS. BROOKS.

JANE J. WEST--JAS. FERGUSON

LUCY WESTBROOK--CHESLEY GRIZLE

28.   17 December 1831. JOEL M. WHEELER and LUCINDA F. PURVIS.
      Security: CHAS. PURVIS.

MATILDA WHEELER--TYLER CLIFT

MARY WHEELER--TARLTON WOODSON

24.   22 July 1828. MICAJAH E. WHEELER and ELIZ. SMITH. Security:
      MICAJAH WHEELER. Officiant: PORTER CLEVELAND, 29th.

ANN R. WHITE--ARCH. B. MIGGINSON

ELIZ. WHITE--CHRISTOPHER FABER

21.   2 August 1826. ELLISON H. WHITE and POLLY SAUNDERS. Security:
      JNO. SAUNDERS. Officiant: EDWD. L. WARREN, 3rd.

ISABELLA WHITE--GEO. OFFLIGHTER, JR.

LUCINDA WHITE--WM. B. MAYS

MAHALA WHITE--MEWLENBERG HOGG

NANCY WHITE--BEVERLY HARGROVE

SALLY M. WHITE--DAVID HUNTER

ELIZ. M. WHITEHEAD--ASA STRATTON

25. 27 November 1828. FLOYD L. WHITEHEAD and MARY E. ARMSTRONG. Security: SP. GARLAND.

17. 26 October 1822. MANSFIELD WHITEHEAD and M. A. H. JOHNSON. Security: ISHAM JOHNSON.

MARY I. B. WHITEHEAD--RO. C. CUTLER

13. 11 December 1819. BURGESS WILLIAMS and M. BRYANT. Security: WM. O. BRYANT; GEO. WILLIAMS. Officiant: JAMES BOYD, 12th.

CATH. T. WILLIAMS--BENJ. D. HARRIS

31. 13 July 1833. ELISHA WILLIAMS and SUSANNA BABER. Security: JNO. CRITZER. Officiant: ALBERT G. BURTON, August 13th.

22. 14 November 1826. GEO. WILLIAMS and FRANCES E. KINCAID. Security: SP. GARLAND.

24. 8 March 1828. JNO. WILLIAMS and ELIZ. LAVENDER. Security: D. G. DAVIDSON. Officiant: JNO. ALLCOCK.

LUCINDA WILLIAMS--GEO. HAYS

POLLY WILLIAMS--ISAAC BELL

VA. A. WILLIAMS--RICH. I. DUKE

28. 24 December 1831. ALFRED WILLOUGHBY and ELIZ. R. CARTER. Security: HENRY CARTER.

C. WILLOUGHBY--ALEX. KIDD

FRANS. WILLOUGHBY--ALEX. L. KIDD

LUCINDA WILLOUGHBY--PAGE RYAN

MARGARET C. WILLOUGHBY--VAL. HUNDLEY

SALLY WILLOUGHBY--RO. JOHNSON

30. 27 October 1832. WALKER L. WILLOUGHBY and CARY ANN POWELL. Security: JNO. POWELL. Officiant: EDWD. L. WARREN, 29th.

21. 27 March 1826. CATLETT WILLS and BELINDA PETERS. Security: ELISHA PETERS. Officiant: JAMES BOYD, 30th.

ELIZ. WILLS--JOS. TINNELL

ELVIRA ANN WILLS--CHAS. W. CHRISTIAN

34. 2 December 1835. JAS. WILLS and SARAH L. PURVIS. Security: CHAS. PURVIS. Officiant: H. L. P., 3rd.

24. 25 August 1828. JNO. WILLS and MARY SAUNDERS. Security: PETER SAUNDERS. Officiant: JAMES BOYD, September 2nd.
W. initial for groom.

MARTHA P. WILLS--JAS. CUNNINGHAM, JR.

MILDRED WILLS--WILLIS B. WILLS

MARY WILLS--GEO. EUBANK

POLLY B. WILLS--WM. GILES

REBECCA WILLS--CHAS. W. PURVIS

SALLY ANN WILLS--NATHL. H. ROYAL

SARAH JANE WILLS--JNO. I. LOVING

25. 27 July 1829. WILLIS B. WILLS and MILDRED WILLS. Security: LAWRENCE WILLS. Officiant: JAMES BOYD, 28th.

20. 17 September 1825. WILLIS H. WILLS and ELIZ. H. PETERS. Security: ELISHA PETERS. Officiant: JAMES BOYD, 21st.

13. 20 November 1819. JESSE WILSON and SUSANNA CRITZER. Security: LEE W. HARRIS.

LUCINDA B. WILSON--JNO. W. HARRIS

ELIZ. WINGFIELD--POWHATAN WINGFIELD

ELIZ. H. WINGFIELD--GEO. EUBANK

24. 16 February 1828. JAS. WINGFIELD and JANE WRIGHT. Security: REESE CUNNINGHAM.

32. 22 October 1834. JNO. WINGFIELD and ELIZ. MC FALL. Security: SAMMPSON MC FALL.

15. 18 June 1821. JNO. H. WINGFIELD and ALMIRA L. LOVING. Security: LUNSFORD LOVING. Officiant: JAMES BOYD, 19th.

33. 4 April 1834. JOSIAH L. D. WINGFIELD and MARY ANN MC FALL. Security: SAMPSON MC FALL.

MARTHA WINGFIELD--JAS. H. SHEPHERD

P. H. WINGFIELD--WINGFIELD EUBANK

18. 24 November 1823. POWHATAN WINGFIELD and ELIZ. WINGFIELD. Security: GENERAL JOHNSON. Officiant: EDWD. L. WARREN, 27th.

MARY WINTERS--AMBROSE PIN

MILLY WINTERS--ESOM PETERS

ANN L. (S) WITT--WM. B. RIPPETOE

CATH. WITT--ELLIS STRICKLAND

34. 18 January 1836. DAVID WITT and CANDICE E. WARWICK. Security: HUDSON MARTIN.

DICEY WITT--JNO. W. WITT

34. 30 November 1835. JAS. WITT and ELIZ. MARTIN. Security: HUDSON MARTIN. Officiant: EDWD. L. WARREN, December 2nd.

30. 8 February 1833. JNO. WITT and MARY H. POLLARD. Security: WM. P. PERKINS.

33. 20 January 1835. JNO. E. WITT and SUSANNA J. MURPHEYS. Security: F. MURPHEYS.

16. 28 January 1822. JNO. W. WITT and DICEY WITT. Security: DENNITT WITT. Officiant: JAMES BOYD, January 31st.

MALINDA WITT--JNO. N. BURNETT

13.   22 November 1819.   RICH. WITT and NANCY WADE.   Security: D. WADE.

SALLY WITT--ANDREW R. MC CREARY

SUSANNA WITT--URIAH HATCHER

12.   28 November 1818.   A. WOOD and G. ANDERSON.   Security: JNO. MC CLAIN.

17.   23 December 1822.   DAVID WOOD and ELIZ. MATTHEWS.   Security: JOS. MATTHEWS.   Officiant: EDWD. L. WARREN, 24th.

FRANCES WOOD--JESSE MILLS

27.   31 January 1831.   GEO. WOOD and SALLY HAMBLETT.   Security: WM. HAMBLETT.   Officiant: JAMES BOYD, February 2nd.

32.   24 March 1834.   HENRY WOOD and NANCY DAFT.   Security: JACOB DAFT.

13.   11 September 1819.   JESSE WOOD and NANCY PUCKET.   Security: JACOB PUCKET.   Officiant: JAMES BOYD, 14th or 16th.

MARY ANN WOOD--HENRY W. HAMBLETT

32.   13 September 1834.   OBADIAH WOOD and PAULINE SAUNDERS. Security: JNO. SAUNDERS.

31.   11 November 1833.   RICH. R. WOOD and MARY E. BRYANT.   Security: DABNEY P. BRYANT.

SALLY L. WOOD--WM. GREGORY

SARAH WOOD--JNO. LOW

29.   6 February 1832.   WM. WOOD and ELVIRA ANN BRYANT.   Security: DABNEY P. BRYANT.   This is a blurred item as to groom, but clerk and I examined it and finally found his name in the index.

31.   24 August 1833.   WM. WOOD and ISABELLA TAYLOR.   Security: LEWIS TAYLOR.

31.   4 November 1833.   WM. R. WOOD and LUCINDA R. THOMPSON. Security: JOS. MAYS, JR.

JANE F. WOODS--JOS. HARDY

MARGARET WOODS--JAS. HARRIS

MARY WOODS--HUGH BARCLAY

NANCY WOODS--ZEBULON M. STRICKLAND

SUSAN N. WOODS--NATHL. MASSIE

VA. WOODS--RYLAND RODEY

MARY B. WOODSON--NICHL. FITZPATRICK

17.   23 December 1822.   TARLTON WOODSON and MARY WHEELER.   Security: MICAJAH WHEELER.   Officiant: JAMES BOYD, 24th.

EVELINA A. WOODY--HENRY W. FISHER

13.   13 December 1819.   RICH. WOODY and F. CARROLL.   Security: OBADIAH THOMAS.

SARAH WOODY--LORENZO D. AISTROP

15. 19 March 1821. BENJ. WRIGHT and DICEY CAMPBELL. Security: JESSE WRIGHT.

ESTHER M. WRIGHT--DAN. W. PARSONS

JANE WRIGHT--JAS. WINGFIELD

12. 4 January 1819. JESSE WRIGHT and JANE PROFFITT. Security: HOWARD CASH.

MARGARET J. WRIGHT--PLEASANT M. KIDD

MARIA WRIGHT--FRANCIS MEEKS

MATILDA WRIGHT--AUSTIN GRIFFIN

16. 6 April 1822. NELSON WRIGHT and FRANCES PUCKET. Security: AUSTIN GRIFFIN. Officiant: JAMES BOYD, 7th.

POLLY WRIGHT--WM. LOW

ROSANNA WRIGHT--JAS. L. MAYS

SARAH J. WRIGHT--WILSON BRYANT

32. 21 April 1834. SHELTON WRIGHT and PAULINA P. JONES. Security: GEO. JONES.

SUSAN WRIGHT--ELIAS HARDING

31. 19 November 1833. WM. WRIGHT and RACHEL L. (S) CAMDEN. Security: DANL. L. WRIGHT.

27. 26 April 1830. WYATT WRIGHT and ELIZA R. PORTER. Security: JNO. PORTER.

I went back to Nelson to get the missing J cards and did a few more pages in the register. I did not finish the last page, but stopped at the end of the year. This card will be noted.

35. 9 November 1836. BENJ. ANDERSON and MARY M. KIRBY. Security: JNO. KIRBY. Officiant: EDWD. L. WARREN, 13th.

35. 24 October 1836. DAVID N. ANDERSON and SUSANNA BOWMAN. Security: JNO. KIRBY. Officiant: EDWD. L. WARREN, November 2nd.

ELIZ. ANDERSON--MOSES H. DODD

36. 18 August 1837. PETER A. BARHAM (index says "or BASHAW") and ANGELINA B. PERRY. Security: JNO. H. SNEAD.

35. 19 December 1836. DISON BLANKS and SARAH R. LAYNE. Security: JNO. S. GLOVER.

ELIZA BOHNES (index says "or BONES")--JOS. DUNNING

SUSANNA BOWMAN--DAVID N. ANDERSON

35. 22 September 1836. HENRY C. BOYD and JULIET A. MASSIE. Security: SP. GARLAND. Officiant: WM. S. REID, same.

JANE CAMPBELL--JAS. G. HENDERSON

FRANCES CARROLL--POWHATAN CARROLL

35. 17 December 1836. HENRY A. CARROLL and LUCY PUCH. Security: ELIJAH PUGH. Officiant: JOEL FORTUNE, 18th.

JULIAN CARROLL--GEO. OLES

37. 11 December 1837. POWHATAN CARROLL and FRANCES CARROLL.
     Security: JNO. C. HOWELL. Officiant: J. F., 14th.

ELIZ. A. CARTER--NICHS. HARDING

35. 10 December 1836. RO. H. CARTER and NANCY C. THURMOND.
     Security: JNO. H. THURMOND. Officiant: EDWD. L. WARREN, 22nd.

36. 2 October 1837. LLEWEN L. CASH and ARABELLA R. HARGROVE.
     Security: EDMD. W. HILL. Officiant: R. G. BASS, 11th.

35. 3 November 1836. POWHATAN CASH and NANCY JOHNSON. Security:
     WM. L. JOHNSON. Officiant: H. L. P., same.

LOCKY CHANDLER--LORENZO D. FULCHER

35. 15 November 1836. JNO. L. COLEMAN, JR. and MARTHA E. TALIAFERRO.
     Security: CHAS. N. PATTESON.

36. 23 October 1837. JNO. COLLINS and SARAH A. WITT. Security:
     BURGESS WITT.

MARY ANN CREWS--JNO. W. HARRIS

ELIZA A. CUNNINGHAM--REUBIN B. WARE

SUSAN F. DAFT--GEO. GROW

POLLY DAMRON--JSO. THOMAS

36. 24 July 1837. JNO. DAMRON and LUCY PEYTON. Security: SAML.
     SAWSON.

37. 11 December 1837. GEO. E. DEMASTER and LOUISA W. HARVEY.
     Security: JAS. W. HARRIS.

LUCRETIA DICKSON--RICE NEWMAN

35. 27 December 1836. MOSES H. DODD and ELIZ. ANDERSON. Security:
     WM. L. ANDERSON.

36. 27 November 1837. SAML. H. DUNCAN and ELVIRA W. SMITH.
     Security: WM. H. SMITH. Officiant: J. F., December 21st.

36. 5 August 1837. JOS. DUNNING and ELIZA BOHNES (index says or
     BONES). Security: JNO. HOHNES.

MARY EVANS--PATRICK MC LOCKLAN

JANE FARLEY--GEO. TRAVERS

36. 5 November 1837. SPENCER FAULCONER and SARAH SPENCER.
     Security: DAVID HUNTER.

36. 28 April 1837. JAS. FITZGERALD and RACHEL RAMSEY. Security:
     WM. RAMSEY. Officiant: JAS. PANIE, May 5th.

36. 26 September 1837. SAML. FITZGERALD and ELIZ. RYAN. Security:
     WM. FITZGERALD.

LYDIA FITZPATRICK--GEO. LITTLEFORD

36. 27 November 1837. GEO. W. FORTUNE and NANCY STEWART. Security:
     SAML. R. DANIEL. Officiant: H. S. P., 30th.

MARTHA I. FORTUNE--WM. H. WEBBER

ANNE W. FOX--CHAS. HANNAM

36. 25 September 1837. LORENZO D. FULCHER and LOCKY CHANDLER.
Security: PETER C. COFFEY.

37. 25 December 1837. DABNEY GAULDING and ELIZ. RITTENHOUSE.
Security: RO. C. COLEMAN.

36. 1 July 1837. WM. H. GAVING and MARY KIZER. Security: WM.
KIZER. Officiant: R. G. B., 5th. Index says "or GAINS".

36. 9 December (blurred?) 1837. WM. W. GIBBS and MARY JANE LOBBAN.
Security: JNO. LOBBAN. Officiant: T. FREEMAN, December 13,
1838 (sic).

35. 9 December 1836. JNO. T. GILES and MARTHA C. HENDERSON.
Security: JAS. CAMPBELL. Officiant: JOSHUA WIBB, 10th.

35. 19 December 1836. GEO. GROW and SUSAN F. DAFT. Security:
PHILIP GWOW. Officiant: JAS. PAYNE, 25th.

35. 26 December 1836. JAS. HAMBLETON and SUSAN HARLOW. Security:
A. HAMBLETON. Officiant: H. S. P., same.

MARY HAMNER--WM. HARRIS

36. 31 January 1837. CHAS. HAMMAM and ANNE W. FOX. Security:
JAS. HUGHES.

35. 8 November 1836. NICHS. HARDING and ELIZ. A. CARTER. Security:
JNO. I. CARTER.

ARABELLA R. HARGROVE--LLEWEN L. CASH

36. 25 January 1837. JNO. H. HARGVOVE (HARGROVE) and ANNE PENN.
Security: N. LOFFTUS.

SUSAN HARLOW--JAS. HAMBLETON

ELIZ. HARRIS--JNO. G. SMITH

37. 12 December 1837. JNO. W. HARRIS and MARY ANN CREWS.
Security: THOS. TILMAN. Officiant: J. F., 21st.

36. 20 February 1837. NELSON B. HARRIS and MARY WARE. Security:
EDWD. WARE.

35. 7 November 1836. WM. HARRIS and MARY HAMNER. Security:
NORBORN FOSTER.

LOUISA W. HARVEY--GEO. E. DEMASTER

ELENOR D. HARVIE--WM. D. HUDSON

37. 25 December 1837. JNO. R. HARVIE and ISABELLA S. HAWKINS.
Security: JNO. S. HARLOW. This is the last 1837 item on page 37
and I did not attempt to go into 1838.

ISABELLA S. HAWKINS--JNO. R. HARVIE

35. 9 December 1836. JAS. G. HENDERSON and JANE CAMPBELL.
Security: JAS. CAMPBELL. Officiant: JOSHUA WEBB or WIBB.

MARTHA C. HENDERSON--JNO. T. GILES

35. 22 August 1836. MADISON HIGHT and JEALES WILLS. Security:
WILLIS P. WILLS. Officiant: H. L. P., 23rd. I have heard
folk insist that Madison Heights in Amherst County is named for this
man, but I have no proof of this.

35. 24 October 1836. CHAS. B. HILL and MARTHA MELTON. Security:
     JNO. SHIPMAN. Officiant: H. L. P., 30th.

36. 15 April 1837. WM. D. HUDSON and ELENOR D. HARVIE. Security:
     ZEBULON P. ANGUS (?).

35. 25 September 1836. DAVID S. JOHNSON and LUCINDA L. WOODY.
     Security: E. P. STRATTON.

     NANCY JOHNSON--POWHATON CASH

     MARY M. KIRBY--BENJ. ANDERSON

     MARY KIZER--WM. H. GAVING (GAINS)

     SARAH R. LAYNE--DISON BLANKS

     MALINDA LEIGH--REUBEN LOWE

36. 25 November 1837. GEO. LITTLEFORD and LYDIA FITZPATRICK.
     Security: GUTRIDE LYON.

     MARY JANE LOBBAN--WM. W. GIBBS

36. 4 September 1837. WM. L. LOVING and ANN C. C. PERROW.
     Security: CHAS. PERROW.

35. 2 November 1836. REUBEN LOWE and MALINDA LEIGH. Security:
     WM. LOWE. Officiant: M. P. S., same.

36. 27 November 1837. GUTRIDGE L. LYON and NANCY M. WRIGHT.
     Security: WM. M. LYON. Officiant: EDWD. L. WARREN, 28th.

     MARY MARTIN--AUSTIN TYREE

     JULIET A. MASSIE--HENRY C. BOYD

36. 14 September 1837. EDWD. MC FADDEN and MARY PAMPLIN.
     Security: JNO. H. PAMPLIN.

36. 25 September 1837. PATRICK MC LOCKLAN and MARY EVANS.
     Security: JNO. KIRBY. Officiant: EDWD. L. WARREN, 28th.

     MARTHA MIELTON--CHAS. B. HILL

36. 2 August 1837. GEO. MURRER and LUCINDA C. TYREE. Security:
     JNO. F. TYREE.

36. 27 April 1837. RICE NEWMAN and LUCRETIA DICKSON. Security:
     MARTIN BRISTOW. Officiant: EDWD. L. WARREN, same.

35. 27 June 1836. GEO. OLES and JULIAN CARROLL. Security:
     P. CARROLL. Officiant: EDWARD L. WARREN, July 7th.

35. 13 September 1836. ALEX. PAMPLIN and MARTHA T. PHELPS.
     Security: SAML. I. PHELPS. Officiant: WM. CARTER, same.

     MARY PAMPLIN--EDWD. MC FADDEN

     ANNE PENN--JNO. H. HARGROVE

     ANN C. C. PERROW--WM. L. LOVING

     ANGELINA B. PERRY--PETER A. BARHAM (or BASHAW)

     LUCY PEYTON--JNO. DAMRON

     MARTHA T. PHELPS--ALEX. PAMPLIN

ELIZA ANN PNTTON--JAS. B. THOMPSON

LUCY PUGH--HENRY A. CARROLL

35. 26 July 1836. JAS. RANSEY and POLLY M. TAYLOR. Security:
     WM. S. TAYLOR. Officiant: JAS. PAINE, August 8th.

RACHEL RAMSEY--JAS. FITZGERALD

35. 24 October 1836. JAS. M. RICHARDSON and N. WILLS. Security:
     JNO. WILLS. Officiant: H. L. P., same.

ELIZ. RITTENHOUSE--DABNEY GAULDING

36. 28 July 1837. HENRY ROBERTS and MARY ANNE WARREN. Security:
     ED. L. WARREN.

ELIZ. RYAN--SAML. FITZGERALD

FRANCES E. SCOTT--RO. E. WILBOURNE

35. 7 November 1836. ANDREW I. SCRUGGS and SARAH I. SCRUGGS.
     Security: WM. P. SCRUGGS.

SARAH I. SCRUGGS--ANDREW I. SCRUGGS

ELVIRA W. SMITH--SAML. H. DUNCAN

35. 21 October 1836. JNO. G. SMITH and ELIZ. HARRIS. Security:
     WM. B. TURNER. Officiant: EDWD. L. WARREN, 30th.

SARAH SPENCER--SPENCER FAULCONER

NANCY STEWART--GEO. W. FORTUNE

MARTHA E. TALIAFERRO--JNO. L. COLEMAN, JR.

POLLY M. TAYLOR--JAS. RAMSEY

35. 14 November 1836. JOHN S. THOMAS and ELIZA A. WHITE.
     Security: THOS. H. WHITE. Officiant: J. F., 15th.

35. 16 December 1836. JOS. THOMAS and POLLY DAMRON. Security:
     D. DAMRON.

LUCY M. THOMAS--EDWIN I. WARWICK

36. 8 November 1837. JAS. B. THOMPSON and ELIZA ANN PNNTON.
     Security: PLEAST. PNNTON.

NANCY C. THURMOND--RO. H. CARTER

36. 9 September 1837. GEO. TRAVERS and JANE FARLEY. Security:
     HENRY SOUTHERN (?).

36. 25 September 1837. AUSTIN TYREE and MARY MARTIN. Security:
     JNO. MARTIN. Officiant: M. P. S., October 4th.

LUCINDA C. TYREE--GEO. MURRER

JANETTA WADE--DAVID WITT, JR.

MARY WARE--NELSON B. HARRIS

36. 25 January 1837. REUBEN B. WARE and ELIZA A. CUNNINGHAM.
     Security: REES CUNNINGHAM.

MARY ANNE WARREN--HENRY ROBERTS

36. 27 February 1837. EDWIN I. WARWICK and LUCY M. THOMAS.
     Security: N. M. THOMAS. Officiant: EDWD. L. WARREN,
March 2nd.

35. 5 September 1836. WM. H. WEBBER and MARTHA I. FORTUNE.
     Security: ALEX. FORTUNE.

     ELIZA A. WHITE--JNO. S. THOMAS

35. 10 October 1836. RO. E. WILBOURNE and FRANCES E. SCOTT.
     Security: FRED. G. PETERS.

37. 29 December 1837. JAS. B. WILLS and AMANDA E. WINGFIELD.
     Security: JAS. W. WINGFIELD. Officiant: EDWD. L. WARREN, 21st.

     JEALES WILLS--MADISON HIGHT

     N. WILLS--JAS. M. RICHARDSON

     AMANDA E. WINGFIELD--JAS. B. WILLS

35. 19 December 1836. DAVID WITT, JR. and JANETTA WADE.
     Security: F. GARLAND.

     SARAH A. WITT--JNO. COLLINS

     LUCINDA L. WOODY--DAVID S. JOHNSON

     NANCY M. WRIGHT--GUTRIDGE T. LYON

Eubank, Geo. 184,220,221;
Jno.112,117,119,122,123,
152,165,184,188;Jno.,Jr.
106; Thomas N. 109; Thos.
152,162; Wingfield 184,
221
Evans, Ailey 85; Aley 86;
Ann 19; Charles 85,86,96;
Chas. 184,212; Evalina I.
184; Jonathan 25,30;Lucy
M.A. 184,199;Mary 224,226;
Prissy 19,25;R. 152,160;
Tarlton 199;
Everett, Elias 184,215;Etta
105; Ithar(?) 133
Everitt, Illia 144
Everett, Jno. 180,184
Evileizer, Jacob 152,161
Ewers, ___ 184; Eliz. 142;
Evalina I. 184,190; Jane
175,184; Stephen 110,175;
Thomas 81,82;Thos. 142,
190
Faber, Christopher 184,219;
Wm. 141,152,160,184,215
Falconer, Spencer 186
Faris, Jas. 151,152; Jno. 76
108,124,133,143,156;Mary
143
Farley, Jane 224,227
Farmer, Ewell 50,53;Hubbard
53; Polley 51;Stephen 20,
46,48,51,52;Steven 53
Fransworth, Jonathan 25
Farrar, Elizabeth P. 85;
Geo. 152,166; Geo.P. 214;
George 85;J.P. 184,217;
Jesse P. 209;Jno. 76,85,
86,92,98,108,117,125; Jno.
M.152,170;Jno.S.85,86,87;
Jno.Jr.92,115;Jno.Sr.84,
140;John 85;Jos.86,87,89;
Jos.W.178,184; (L) 92,152,
160;Landon 86,117; M.199;
Mary 184,199;Perrin 123,
133; Peter 85,92,108,117,
168; Ro.L. 114;Ro.S. 85,
115,117;Rob S. 87; S.92,
152,160; Sally 115,117;
Shelton 85,86,108,184,216;
Thomas 85,86,87,92; Wil-
liam H. 98; Wm.H. 152,160,
161,199; Wm. 125
Faulconder, Julia A. 184;
Jno. 184,214; Julia A.
214; Spencer 108,214,224,
227; Spencer 89
Feagans, Edwd. 184,191
Feagle, Jacob 13
Fear, Ann 20,25
Feare, Ann 20; Elizabeth 20,
25;
Fears, ___ 3; Lee 38
Featherstone, William 26
Ferguson, Betsy 114; Danl.
114; David 106,116,117,
Edwd. 152,165; Evalina M.
184; Evelina M. 186; James
B. 76; JaS. 184,219; Jas.
B. 152,160; Jno. 76,152,
166; L. 184,185; Loiusa
Ann 205; Louisa Ann 184;
Thomas 20,26
Ferrill, ___ 56
Fidler, Jesse 78,108
Fields, Bitha 25
Field, Bithax 33
Fields, Sarah C. 184,219
Filder, Jesse 115
Finch, Jonathan 29; Nancy
25,29
Finney, Miles 25,27
Fishback, James C. 24,25,

26,63
Fisher, ___ 65; Elias 46,49;
Elizabeth 51,68; Henry W.
184,222; Sam 50; Samuel 51,
56,60,66,68
Fitzgerald, Albert 184,185;
Benj. 124,185,193;Benjamin
88; Cath.179,185; David
183,185,191; E. 185,191;
Edmd.180,202;Edmund 185;
Elis. 185; Eliz. 184; Jane
185,187; Jas. 153,162,177,
185,224,227; Jas. C. 185,
214; Jesse 143; Jesse W.
185,191; Jno. 149,153,161,
187; Jno. B. 120,153,155;
Louisa 183,185; Martha Ann
183,185, Matilda A.J. 185;
Matilda J. 185; Mary 180,
185; Nancy 185,193; R. 179;
Rachel 143; Ro.W. 149,153,
185; S.L.153,155; Saml.177,
191,224,227; Sarah A. 185;
Wm. 185,224; Woodson R.
179,185; Zdph 180; Zep-
haniah 185
Fitzhugh, Charles 108; Thomas
109; Thos. 119,120,121
Fitzpatrick, Alex. 95, 117,
119,134,185,206; Alexander
81,94; Br. 172; Breck 215;
Breckenridge 81; E. 153,
171; Fanny 118,128; Frances
81,94,95,144; Francis 96;
Frankey 81; G.B. 153;James
94,95,96; Jane 81,118,130,
153,170; Jas. 118,153; Jno.
81,96,100,112,117,118,119,
144,163,185,214; Jno.E.76,
80,81,83,94,85,105,109,113,
119,121,125,126,129,139;
John 94; L. 153; Lydia 224,
226; Moses 81,86,94,98,117,
123,144,153,157,170; Nichl.
185,222; P. 153; Peggy 81;
Polley 81; Rachel 117;
Rebecca 76,117,119,134,139;
S. 152,153; Salley 81; Sally
95; Saml. 134; Sarah 130;
Thomas 76,81,94,95,96,98,99;
Thos. 117,118,119,121,134
144,152,158,171; William
76,81,94,95,96; Wm.117,118,
119,128,130,134,170,202
Flack, Jas. 123,129
Flcak, Jas. 134
Fleming, Joseph 3
Fleshman, Allen S. 21; Mary
21,26; Simeon 20
Fletcher, Christopher 10; E.
13; Elijah 5,13,14,16,17;
Timothy 5
Flippen, ___ 124
Floed, Charles 105; Chas.
113,114
Flood, Charles 98,99,105;
Chas. 153,166; J. 139;Jas.
129; Lydia 185,202; Moses
143; Peggy 153,163
Flowers, L. 153,171
Floyd, Chas.(?) 181; Chris-
tian 124; M. 153,162;
Sarah 124; Susanna 181,185
Foe, Rebecca 26,42
Foffey, Peter C. 180
Foggs, A.N.P. 139
Fogus, A.G. 152,153; Andrew
111; Andrew N. 135;Henry
185,192
Foote, Wm.H. 200
Forbus, Jno. 150; Wm.125,144
Ford, Abner 84; Boaz 50; C.
140; Saml. 140; Waller 111,

140
Fore, Mary 26, 32
Forrill, William 56
Forsburg, Col. 49
Fortune, Alex. 228; B. 153,
166; Benj. L. 185, 216;
Cynthia L. 185, 191; Eddy
82,111,112,124,129,138,162;
Elisha 80,88,120,143,170;
Eliz. 114;Elizabeth 101;
Geo.W. 224,227; Jane 153,
163; Jesse 153,168; Jno.
92,105,113,115,163;Jno.P.
186,189;Joel 184,185,186,
194,223;Martha I. 224,228;
N. 151; Nancy 181,186;
Nichl. 166,186,197;P.153,
170; P.T. 153,160;Patsy
186,197; Rebecca 186,214;
Rich. C. 186,218; Sally
186,201; Thomas 80; Thomas
E. 77,88,91,92,94,97,99,
100,101,108,110; Thos.114,
153, 171, 176, 186; Z.,Jr.
214; Thos. E.113,115,125,
141,147,153,160,191;Zach.
77,108,114,124,137,160,178,
186; Zach Jr. 131
Foster, A.J.S.(?) 169; C.153,
169; Christian 83; Eleanor
183,186;Flora B. 186,204;
James 83; Jno.A 186,201;
Joshua 149,153;Lucy 141;
Norborn 225; Polly 141;
Rich. 141,186,217;S.J. 153,
169; Sus 153,162;William
83; Wm. 141,154; Wm.H. 173,
174,176,200
Fowler, Christopher 23; David
54; Eliza 26,37; Jane 23,
28,50; John 37; Jonathan
23,25,46,51,52;Jonathan,Jr.
52; Mahala 23,26;Sarah S.
26,28; Thomas G.17,25;
William 46,50,55,68; Elizabeth 92
Fowls, Jas. Jr. 135
Fox, Ann 75; Anne W. 224,225;
Bartlett 116,141,145,154,
159,166;J. 178,186; James
48,50; Jno. 75,116,129,141;
Jos. 75; Lucy 116,186,209;
Nancy 154,166;Rich. 178,
209; Richard 75; Sally 186,
217; Saml. 129,141; Saml.S.
202; Samuel 75,77; Sarah
50; Thomas 15; William 75;
Wm. 130; Woodson 172,186,
217.
Franklin, Abner 88; Henry
84; Jno. 91,99; Ro.78,99,
106,110,111,114,117,118,
120,121,124,126,127,128,
129,131,135,136,137,138,
139,140,142,143,144; Robt.
91; Saml. 116; Samuel 75,
81,83,105; Sarah W.19,26;
Susannah 19,;William C.26,
33
Frazel, Jacob 15
Frazer, James 4,8,9;Sarah 4.
Frazier, James 16
Freeland, James 109; Jas.
123,124,139; Mace 139;
William J. 111
Freeman, Frank 19,26; Holeman 127; T. 225
French, Mary 11; Mason 11;
Robert 26,32,43
Fry, Jacob 187
Fulcher, Jas. 140; Jas.,Jr.
186,191; Lorenzo D. 224,
225.

Perkins, L. 163,170; Letitia 24,36; Milley 132; Nancy 163,170; Nat. 138; Polly 5; Powhatan 206; Price 189,206; Price L. 184; Price S. 175,184,206; R. 163,171; Rich. 132,133, 206; Richard 3,13,24,36, 58,64,68,71; S. 163,170; Sally M. 36; Saml. 123, 125,131,133,171,206; Sarah 206; Thomas 58; William 5; William W. 36; Wm. P. 221

Perrice, Mary 16

Perrin, Robert 9

Perrow, Ann C. C. 226; Charles 23,36,87,88,101, 108; Charles G. 110; Chas. 112,113,118,121,125,128, 129,130,131,132,134,141, 142,163,167,172,177,182, 198,201,203,226; Daniel B. 27; Danl. 128,177; Eleanor 131,141;William 3

Perry, Angelina B. 223,226; B. 158,163; Chas. 206; Colen M. 29; Collin M.34, Eliz. C. 193,206; Geo.W. 183,193; J. 163,168; Jesse L. 13,15,23,26; Jno. J. 198,206; Maria M. 36; Mary H. 204,206; Reuben 71; Sophia F. 183,206; Susanna M. 210; Susanna N. 206; Wm. 128

Pervis, Charles 98; Chas. 119

Peters, Anderson 76; Belinda 206,220; Chas. 120,154, 163,186,203,206; Cintha 111; Cyrena B. 206,216; Elijah 76; Elisha 80,87, 91,105,107,108,111,112, 120,124,125,126,127,136, 138,139,143,216,220,221; Eliz. F. 203,206; Eliz.H. 207,221; Elizabeth 17; Elizha 77; Esom 207,221; Fred. G. 228; Key 120; Thos. 120; William 17; Wilson 203,207; Yancy 120

Petty, Jesse L.26

Pettyjohn, Mary Gayle 155; H. L. 178,190,210

Peyton, H. S. 201,206; Lucy 224,226

Phaup, William 22,36

Phelps, Martha T.226; Saml. I. 226

Phillip, F. 164

Phillips, Chas. 207,210; Dabney 163,170; E.163,167; Eliz. 179,207; Eliza 137; F. 163; Francis C. 96; G. 207; Geo. 96,183,207, 211; Isabella 176,207; Jas. W. 207,212;Jno. 163, 169,207,211,214; Jonathan 34,36; Jos. 125; Joshua 111; Leanna 137; Leonard 137; Leond. 137; Martha 127; Matt. 119,126; R.123; Rich. 120,127,137,139; Richard 79,81,83,84,92,97, 103,111; Thos. 112; Wm. 187,207

Pickett, Chas. B. 125

Pidgeaon, Isaac 62

Pidgeon,_____64; Isaac 41, 50,52,57,59,61,62,64,66, 67,70,71

Pierce, Cornelius 24,36;

Pierce, Danl. L. 160,163; Peter 111

Pigeon, Isaac 51

Pinn, Ambrose 207; 221; Raleigh 199,207

Pleasants, A., Jr.13; James 1; James, Jr. 1; Jno.144; Jonathan H. 16,36; Jonathan N. 29

Plummer, Asa 46,50,56,67;

Plunket, Jonathan R. 36,40; W. S. 163,166

Pnnton, Pleast. 227; Eliza Ann 227

Poe,_____17; Jonathan 36,40, 67

Poindexter, Peter 34

Pointer, John 58; Jonathan 47,56,58,59; Mary 58; Polly 56

Poll, Jno. 126

Pollard, A. M. 161,163; Arthur H. 143,145; E. C. 163,167; M. A. 173,207; Margaret C. 192,207; Mary H. 207,221; Rich. 163,164; Richard 8,111; Richard C. 105; Ro. 111; Robert 64; Sally 207,215; Thomas 45; Thos. 116; Wm. 116,125,126

Ponton, Benj. 153,163,207; Fleming. 163,170; Jeff L. 207,217; Jno. 153,163; Joel 92,130,132; Lucy 207,216; Pleasant 207, 208; S. 163,165; Thos. 165

Poor, Abraham 207,210,213; Emmanuel 163,166; M. L. 187,207

Pope, Nathl. 116

Porter, Cleveland 204,213; Eliza Ann 36,41; Eliza R. 207,223; Gleveland 173; Jno. 223; Jonathan H.41; Jos. 130

Powell, Abraham 128,132; Ambr. 114; Benj. 128,132, 163,164,168; Benj., Jr. 127, Benjamin 102; Cary Ann 208,220; Cornl. 141; Douglas 114; Edwd. 114; Elias 114; Eliz. 132,207; Elizabeth 83,102; George 46; Jas. 140; Jas. E. 199, 207; Jno. 220; L. 176,207; Leond. 181,207; Lucas 83, 84,102,128,132; M. 148, 164; Mrs._____13,16; Nathaniel 83,102; Nathl. 132; Norborn B. 83,131; Norborne B.132; R.151,164; Rich.113,140,143; Richard 60,69,107,110; S.151,176, 207; Seymour 102; Sophia 35,36; Susanna 181,207; Wilson 114; Wm.174,207

Powers, Cath. 191,208; Jno. 191,208; Michl. 191

Pratt, Eliz. 115; Thos.,Jr. 115; Thos.. Sr. 115

Presley, William 49

Preston, Moses H. 36,40; William 36; William R.22

Price,_____53; Benjamin 36, 38; Edward 13,15,30,32, 36,53,69; Fancis 161; Francis 96,164; Lewis E. 196,208; Martin D. 198, 208; Peter 95,96; Sally 17; Sarah 13,96; William

Price William 96; Wilson N. 208,211

Priddy, Henry 60

Proffitt, Jane 208,223; Jas. 182,208; Jesse 112, 136; Jesse S. 107,117, 120; L. 178,208; Lewis 182,208; Nancy 152,164; Obadiah 164,165; P. 164, 165; R. 196,208; Ro.193, 208; Rowland 129,157; S. 178,208

Profit, Randolph 124; Rowland 124

Pryor, Jonathan 38

Puch, Betsy 208; Elijah 208; Lucy 222; Sarah 209

Pucket, Anderson 188,208; Crawford 193,208; Frances 208,223; Jacob 113,122, 198,207,208,222; Jno.161, 164,198,215; Margaret 189,207,208; Margeret 208; Martha 208,215; Milly 208; Nancy 208,222; Polly 198,208; Saml. 208

Puckett, Crawford 91,92, 100; Eliz. 118; Frances C.203; Geo. B.119; Jacob 91,100,118,217; Jacob,Jr. 109,144; Jacob Sr. 109; Jno. 203; Milly 217; Saml. 190; Samuel 100

Pugh, A. 149,164; Betsy 176; Elijah 116,180,223; F. 163,164; James 85; Jno. 95,164,167,169,188, 208; Lucy 227; Mary 208; Morris 209; Nancy 187, 209; Nelson 190,202,209; P. 164,167; S. F. 176; Sarah 209; Thos. 162; Z. 157,164

Purvis, Chas. 129,142,166, 219,220; Chas W. 209,221; Eliza C. 176,209; Geo. 192,209; Geo. W. 172, 189,209; George 105; L. 199,209; Lucinda F. 209, 219; P. 148,164; S. 199, 209; Sally 189,209; Sarah L. 209,220; William 81; Wm. 164,167,176; Wm.Jr. 176,209

Puryear, Mahala 21,36

Quarles, David W. 11; G.N. 15; Garret M. 11; Wm.133

Quick, Ann 174,209; Geo.W. 194,209; Jno. 102; Jno., Jr. 174; Thos. 173,209

Quinn, Jordan L.180,209

Quisenberry, Rich. 180,209

Radford,_____54; W. 60; William 53,54,58,60,62, 63,64,69

Railey,_____94

Raines, Presley 110,120,135

Rains, Wm. 186,209

Ramsey, A. 161,164; Ellis 209; Jas. 209,227; Jno. 164; Mary 28,36; Nancy 154,164; Paulina M.R.209; Polly 34; Rachel 224,227; Richard 60; Richard D.61; Richard H. 56,58; Samuel P. 28; Silas M. 180,209; Wm. 154,224; Wm.G. 203,209

Rankin, Andrew C. 14; Frances Catherine Jane Cole 14; Richard 14; Thomas 14

Ransey, Jas. 227; Jno. 159; Polly 36

Ratcliff, Harrison 59

Raynes, Wm. 200
Rea, Elizabeth 36,40;
Lancelot 40
Read, E. 164; Henry 164;
Jonathan T.W. 6; Sally
161,164
Rees,____2; David 32,37;
Jonathan 31; Mary Ann
31,37
Reid,____122; A. 122; Alex
209,219; James 81; Jas.
181,192; Jno. A. 209,
219; Jno. N. 81; Jno.W.
99; Jonathan C.2; Saml.
W. D. 123; Thos. 138;
William S. 12,19,20,21,
22,23,24,25,26,27,28,29,
30,31,32,34,35,36,37,38,
41,42,43,58,63,64,66;
Wm. 192,200; Wm. L. 206;
Wm. S. 192,223
Reins, Lucy 102
Rekes (?), Chas. 207
Reynolds, Charles 22,37
Rhea, Arch. 122,128; Jane
122; Jno. 122,128; Ro.
122,128; Wm. 122,128
Rhor,____59
Ribpley, Wood 210
Rice, Jno. W.96; Jonathan
64; Wm. B. 216,218
Rich,____121
Richardson,____53; Alfred
15; David 83; Fanny 45;
George 11; Giles 163,164;
Jas. M.227,228; Jesse 15;
Jonathan 22,27,37,53,60;
Margaret 11; Mary Ann 37,
41; Nancy D. 125; Richard
109; Riles, Sr. 164; Wm.
W. 125
Richedson, Richard 93
Richerson, Jonathan 37
Richeson, Jesse 18; Row-
land M. 197,209; Varland
15
Rickets, Jos. 174,210
Rider, Elisha 157,164
Right, William 99
Ripley, Wood 192
Rippetoe, David 210,214;
Jas. 177,210; N. 154,164;
P. 162,164; Peter 113,
124,154; Peter, Jr. 124;
Sarah 124; Wm. B. 206,
210,221
Rishedson, Richard 93
Risque, Adaline E. 37;
Adeline E. 41
Rittenhouse, Eliz. 225,
227; Henry 137; Isaac
187,208; Patsey 137;
Rebecca 187,210
Rives, Henry 45,50; L. C.
114,163; Landon C. 117,
118; Landon E. 105; Lucy
160,164; Lucy L. 175,
210; Margaret 70,139;
Martha H. 37,41; Nathan-
iel 41,69; P. 163,164;
Ro. 78,91,93,95,102,105,
106,107,108,110,112,113,
116,117,119,120,124,127,
134,137,138,139,140,142,
144; Ro., Jr. 192; Robert
61,70; William E. 105;
William M. 6,41
Roberson, Elizabeth 93
Roberts, Mrs.____13;____71;
Alex. 98,103,106,117,196,
204, Alexander 80,85;
Ambr. 189; Ambrose 210;
Anthony 18; B.192,210;

Roberts, B.Sally C. 85;
Christopher 3,4,9,18;
E. 183,207,210; Eliz.
204,210; Elizabeth 3,6,9,
18; Elliot 151,164; Enoch
3,6,9,16,18,57; Enock 12;
F. B. 154; Fanny 78;
Flerry B. 85; Forrest
183; George 3,46,51,62,
63,64,66,68,70,71,85;
George E. 18; George Ed-
ward 4,6,9; George W.14,
15,27; Henry 78,85,99,
153,154,160,210,227;
Henry D. 158,165; Henry
G. 95; Isham 3; James 28,
29,37,85; Jas. A. 175,
210; Jno. 78,99,125,131,
145,152,155,165; Jno.Jr.
107, Jno.E. 173; Jno.S.
196,210; Johannah 71;
John 84,85; Jonathan 57;
Jonathan M. 10; Jos.80,
81,85,86,98,107,108,114,
115,127,140,156; Jos.,Sr.
112,113,116,117; Jos. A.
194; Jos. C. 95,131,183;
Joseph 85; Mary C. 204,
210; Matt. 95,182,210;
Mrs. M. 10; Matilda 3,9,
12,16,18,20,37; Morris
70; N. 152,165; Samuel 4,
9,10,13,16,18; Sarah 85;
Sarah Ann 95,194,210;
Sarah N. H. 210,218
Skiler H. 210; Skiles H.
190; Susanna 95; Susanna
B. 85; Thomas 85,86,107;
Thomas H. 15,18,20,71;
Thomas W. 14; Thos. 118,
154; William 9; William
Powell 4; Wm. 210,219;
Wm.C.204; Zach 84,87,89,
95,99,105,128,140,142,
143
Robertso, Eliza M. 183
Robertson, A. 1,14,15,54,
58,63,70; Arch. 11,46;
Archibald 59,62,72;
Eliza M. 210; Eliz.Meri-
wether 133; George 7;
Hugh D. 210,213; J. 90;
Jacob 198,210; James 96;
Jno. 133,135,165,170,184;
Jno. C. 172; Jno. F. 90,
135; Thos. 129,130; W.I.
90; William 86,90; William
C. 28; Wm. 176; Wm. J.
127,135,143,172; William
J. 97
Robinson, Arthur 126; C.A.
193,210; James 75; Jno.
108; Jno. C. 190; John
59; Jonathan 8,47,50,54,
58; Nicholas 11; Peter
150,165; Robert 28,37;
Simeon 22,37; Thomas 46;
William 37,26,68
Rodes, Amy D. 197,210;
Chas. 145; Chas. P. 187,
211; Charles 92; D. 11,29,
165,170; Daniel 13,15,39;
David 6,92; Eliz. 196,
211; Janes Y.(?) 165;
Jas. H. 205; Jas. Y 162,
193; Jas. Z.(?) 170; Jno.
H. 165,166; Joel Y. 211;
Polly 151,165; Thomas 92;
Thos. 165,211,214; Thos.
J. 196; Thos. Y. 182,211
Rodey, Ryland 211,222
Rogers, Henry 211,218; Par-
menas 135; Silas 178,211;

Rogers, Wm. 154
Rohr,____66,71; Ann Maria
20,37; Jacob 17,48;
Lucinda Ann 27,37; Mary
2,17,49,59; Mrs. Mary 54,
63; Michael 49,59; Philip
17,20,56,63; Phillip 57,
62,71; Salley 56, Sarah
17
Ronald, George W. 23,57,64
Rorh, Ann 17; Philip 17;
William 17
Rose, Alex. 119; Alex. B.
106,108,109,110,113,115,
120,121,122,123,132,137,
140; Alex. F. 122,127,
129,144; Ann W. 129; Caroline Matilda 1,51,56;
Cath. 152,165; Charles
108; Chas. 134,137; Chas.
R. 122,144; G. A. 12,55,
66,108; Gustavus A. 1,56,
57,139; Henry 108,109,118,
119,120,121,144,215; Henry,
Dr. 122,129; Henry J. 208;
Hugh 1,56,134,135,137,141,
Hugh, Col. 136,139 141;
James 6,37,39; Jane 211,
215; Jno. 108,109,119,134,
140; Jno., Col. 119,120,
122,129,144; Jno. N. 84,
88,108,117,122,124,144;
Jno. Nichl. 122; Jno.
Nicholas 110; John Nichl.
127; L. 165,167; Littleton
141; Mary 122,127; Mary S.H.
119; Mildred 122,129; Pat.
119,120,137; Patrick 108,
124,134,135,137,139; Paul-
ina 135,137,139,141; Ro.
119,120,122; Ro. H. 120;
Robert M. 55; Saml. 134,
135; Samuel 1; Susan A.
208,211; Will 53
Roseur, Jno. L. 219
Ross, David 123
Rossen, Elijah 194,211;
James 95
Rothon,____50
Rouse, Elizabeth 8; Lucy 8;
William 8
Roussun, Jno. L. 211
Rowan, Francis T. 8
Rowsey, Betsy 211
Rowland,____89
Royal, Eliza 37,39; Nathl.
H. 211,221
Royall, Benj. F. 211,212;
Benjamin Franklin 2;
James L. 27; James Townes
2; Jo E. 16; Jonathan James
2; Joseph Archer 2; Joseph
E.2,27,37; Joseph Edwin 2;
Judith Archer 2; Mary
Eliza 2; Thomas Edwin 2;
William 2,64,70; William
Richard 2
Rucker,____106; Elizabeth
28,37; Isaac 96; Isaac M.
28,37; Jane E. 28; Jno.
106; Joshua 37; Reuben 28,
37; Susan 37
Rudacill, Jacob 151
Rudasi, Eliz. 165
Rudasil, Eliz. 165; Jacob
145
Rudasill, Jno. 211;
Ruffin, James 63
Ruley, Geo. 125
Russell, Andrew 141
Ruston, Charles 54
Rutherford, Peter 205,211;
Robert 61

www.ingramcontent.com/pod-product-compliance
Lightning Source LLC
Chambersburg PA
CBHW021858020426
42334CB00013B/388